The **Rough Guide** to

# Barcelona

written and researched by

**Jules Brown**

ROUGH
GUIDES

NEW YORK · LONDON · DELHI

www.roughguides.com

# Contents

**Antoni Gaudí and modernisme** colour section following p.80

**Festive Barcelona** colour section following p.208

**Colour maps** following p.320

3

◀◀ Parc Güell ◀ Casa Batlló at night

# Introduction to

# Barcelona

**It's tempting to say that there's nowhere like Barcelona – there's certainly not another city in Spain to touch it for sheer style, looks or energy. The glossy mags and travel press dwell enthusiastically on its outrageous architecture, designer shopping, hip bars and vibrant cultural scene, but Barcelona is more than just this year's fad. It's a confident, progressive city, one that is tirelessly self-renewing while preserving all that's best about its past. As neighbourhoods are rebuilt with panache, and locals and visitors alike pursue the latest, most fashionable sensation, there's also an enduring embrace of the things that make life worth living – the daily market visit, strolling down the famous Ramblas, a lazy harbourside lunch, frenetic festival nights, a Sunday by the beach or a ticket for FC Barcelona's next big game.**

It's no accident that Barcelona is the least Spanish city in the country. With the return to democracy following the death of Franco, the various regions were allowed to consolidate their cultural identities through varying degrees of political autonomy. **Catalunya** (Catalonia in English), of which Barcelona is the capital, has a historical identity going back as far as the ninth century, when the first independent County of Barcelona was established, and through the long period of domination by Castile, and even during the Franco dictatorship when a policy of cultural suppression was pursued, it proved impossible to stifle Catalan identity. Barcelona itself has long had the reputation of being at the forefront of Spanish political activism, and of radical design and architecture, but these cultural distinctions are rapidly becoming secondary to the city's position as one of the most dynamic commercial centres in the country.

Gaining the **1992 Olympics** was an important initial boost. Along with a construction programme that touched every corner of the city went the indisputable knowledge that these had been Barcelona's Games, and not Spain's – an important distinction to the Catalan people. Since then the economic and physical transformation of Barcelona has been extraordinary, with some remarkable new buildings and public spaces sharing the limelight with renovated historic quarters, revamped museums and a sparkling city beachfront.

If there's a pattern emerging in how Barcelona presents itself to the outside world, it's the emphasis on a remarkable fusion of economic energy and cultural expression. This is seen most perfectly in the glorious *modernista*

## Talking the talk

**Catalan** (Català) is a Romance language, stemming directly from Latin, and closely resembling Occitan. It's spoken by over ten million people in total, in Barcelona and Catalunya, part of Aragón, much of Valencia, the Balearic islands, Andorra, and parts of the French Pyrenees – and is thus much more widely spoken than Danish, Finnish and Norwegian. Other Spaniards tend to belittle it by saying that to get a Catalan word you just cut a Castilian one in half but, in fact, the grammar is more complicated and it has eight vowel sounds compared to Castilian's five. During Franco's time in power, Catalan was banned from the radio, TV, daily press and schools, which is why many older people cannot read or write it (even if they speak it all the time) – the region's best-selling Catalan-language newspaper sells far fewer copies than the most popular Castilian-language daily paper. Virtually every Catalan is bilingual, but most regard Catalan as their mother tongue and it's estimated that it is the dominant language in over half of Catalunya's households – a figure that's likely to grow given the amazing revival of the language in recent times.

(Art Nouveau) buildings that stud the city's streets and avenues. Antoni Gaudí is the most famous of those who have left their mark on Barcelona in this way: his Sagrada Família church is rightly revered, but just as fascinating are the (literally) fantastic houses, apartment buildings and parks that he and his contemporaries designed. The city also boasts a stupendous artistic legacy, from national (ie Catalan) collections of Romanesque, Gothic and contemporary art to major galleries containing the life's work of the Catalan artists Joan Miró and Antoni Tàpies (not to mention a celebrated showcase of the work of Pablo Picasso). Add

> **Much of what you'll want to see in the city centre – Gothic cathedral, Picasso museum, Gaudí buildings and art galleries – can be reached on foot from the central Plaça Catalunya.**

a medieval old town – full of pivotal buildings from an earlier age of expansion – a welter of churches and markets, and an encircling belt of parks and green spaces, and Barcelona demands as much time as you can spare.

For all its go-ahead feel, though, Barcelona does have its problems, not least a high petty crime rate. However, there's no need to be unduly paranoid and it would be a shame to stick solely to the main tourist sights, since you'll miss so much. Tapas bars hidden down alleys little changed for a century or two, designer boutiques in gentrified old town quarters, street opera singers belting out an aria, bargain lunches in workers' taverns, neighbourhood funicular rides, unmarked gourmet restaurants, craft outlets and workshops, *fin-de-siècle* cafés, restored medieval palaces, suburban walks and specialist galleries – all are just as much Barcelona as the Ramblas or Gaudí's Sagrada Família.

▶ Parc de la Ciutadella

# What to see

Most sights of historic interest are in the old town, with the modern city beyond a late nineteenth-century addition, part of a vast project conceived to link the small core of the old town with the villages around it. Barcelona itself has a **population** of 1.6 million (metropolitan population 4.8 million, Catalunya 7.1 million) but remains, in effect, a series of self-contained neighbourhoods stretching out from the harbour, flanked by a brace of parks and girdled by the wooded Collserola mountains. Much of what you'll want to see in the city centre – Gothic cathedral, Picasso museum, markets, Gaudí buildings, history museums and

▲ Volleyball on the beach

art galleries – can be reached on foot in under twenty minutes from the central Plaça de Catalunya, while a fast metro system takes you directly to the more peripheral attractions and suburbs.

The **Ramblas** – a kilometre-long tree-lined avenue mostly given over to pedestrians, pavement cafés and performance artists – splits the *ciutat vella*, or old town, in two. On the eastern side of the avenue is the **Barri Gòtic** (Gothic Quarter), the medieval nucleus of the city – a labyrinth of twisting streets and historic buildings, including La Seu (the cathedral) and the palaces and museums around Plaça del Rei. Further east lies the **Sant Pere** neighbourhood, set around its terrific market, which adjoins the fashionable boutique-and-bar *barri* of **La Ribera** to the south, home to the Picasso museum. Over on the western side of the Ramblas is the edgier, artier neighbourhood of **El Raval**, containing both the flagship museum of contemporary art (MACBA) and the pick of the latest designer shops, bars and restaurants.

At the bottom of the Ramblas is **the waterfront**, whose spruced-up harbour area is known as **Port Vell** (Old Port). Walking east from here takes you past the aquarium and marina, through the old fishing and restaurant

▲ La Seu

quarter of **Barceloneta**, past the **Parc de la Ciutadella** and out along the promenade to the cafés and restaurants of the **Port Olímpic**. This whole area is where Barcelona is most like a resort, with city beaches right along the waterfront from Barceloneta as far as the conference and leisure zone of **Parc del Fòrum**

**Antoni Gaudí is the most famous of those who left their mark on Barcelona.**

at **Diagonal Mar**. Art- and garden-lovers, meanwhile, aim for the fortress-topped hill of **Montjuïc** to the southwest, where Catalunya's national art gallery (MNAC), the Miró museum, botanic garden and main Olympic stadium are sited, among a host of other cultural attractions.

At the top of the Ramblas, **Plaça de Catalunya** marks the start of the gridded nineteenth-century extension of the city, known as the **Eixample**, a symbol of the thrusting expansionism of Barcelona's early industrial age. This is where some of Europe's most extraordinary architecture – including Gaudí's **Sagrada Família** – is located. Beyond the Eixample lie the northern suburbs, notably **Gràcia**, with its small squares and lively bars, and the nearby **Parc Güell**, while you'll also come out this way to see the famous **Camp Nou** FC Barcelona stadium or the city's applied art museums at the **Palau Reial**. It's worth making for the hills, too, where you can join the crowds at Barcelona's famous **Tibidabo** amusement park – or escape them with a walk through the woods in the peaceful **Parc de Collserola**.

The good public transport links also make it easy to head further out of the city. The mountain-top monastery of **Montserrat** is the most obvious day-trip to make, not least for the extraordinary ride up to the monastic eyrie by cable car or mountain railway. **Sitges** is the local beach town *par excellence*, while with more time you can follow various trails around the local **wine country**, head south to the Roman town of **Tarragona** or Gaudí's birthplace of **Reus**, or north to medieval **Girona** or the Dalí museum in **Figueres**.

# When to go

The best times to go to Barcelona are late **spring** and early **autumn**, when the weather is still comfortably warm (around 21–25°C) and walking the streets isn't a chore. In **summer**, the city can be unbearably hot and humid, with temperatures averaging 28°C (but often a lot more). August, especially, is a month to be avoided, since the climate is at its most unwelcoming and many shops, bars and restaurants close as local inhabitants head out of the city in droves. It's worth considering a **winter** break in the city, as long as you don't mind the prospect of occasional rain. It's generally still warm enough to sit out at a café, even in December, when the temperature hovers around 13°C.

Out of the city, the weather varies enormously from region to region. On the coast either side of Barcelona it's best – naturally enough – in summer, though from June to September tourist resorts like **Sitges** are packed. **Tarragona**, too, can be extremely hot and busy in summer, though it's worth knowing that **Girona** is considered to have a much more equable summer climate, and escaping from the coast for a few cool days is easy.

## Temperature chart

|  | Jan | Feb | Mar | Apr | May | Jun | Jul | Aug | Sep | Oct | Nov | Dec |
|---|---|---|---|---|---|---|---|---|---|---|---|---|
| **Average maximum temperatures** | | | | | | | | | | | | |
| degrees C | 13 | 14 | 16 | 18 | 21 | 25 | 28 | 28 | 25 | 21 | 16 | 13 |

# 21

## things not to miss

*It's not possible to see everything that Barcelona has to offer on a short trip – and we don't suggest you try. What follows is therefore a selective taste of the city's highlights, from modernista masterpieces and laid-back café life as well as tranquil parks – all arranged in five colour-coded categories to help you find the very best things to see, do and experience. All entries have a page reference to take you straight into the Guide, where you can find out more.*

**01 Museu Nacional d'Art de Catalunya (MNAC)** Page **99** • The National Museum of Art celebrates the grandeur of Romanesque and Gothic art, two periods in which Catalunya artists were pre-eminent in Spain.

**02 Bike tour** Page **29** • Touring the city by bike is a great way to get off the city's beaten track.

**03 La Seu** Page **53** • One of the greatest Gothic cathedrals in Spain.

**04 The Ramblas** Page **45** • A stroll down Barcelona's famous thoroughfare is a must for both tourists and locals alike.

**05 Els Encants** Page **126** • Haggle hard and pick up a bargain in the city's largest flea market.

**06** **Designer shopping** Page **245** • Some of the hottest European designers display their wares in the city's classy shops and hip boutiques.

**07** **Museu Picasso** Page **76** • Trace the genesis of the artist's genius in the city that Picasso liked to call home.

**08** **Gran Teatre del Liceu** Page **50** • Take a tour or enjoy a night at the opera at the renowned Liceu opera house.

**09** **La Boqueria** Page **49** • The city's best known market presents an extraordinary range of fresh produce.

**10** **Cross-harbour cable car** Page **90** • Wait for a clear day for a ride on the iconic cross-harbour cable car.

**11** **La Pedrera** Page **117** • Apartment building or work of art? Both, when designed by Antoni Gaudí.

**13 Tibidabo** Page **145** • Scale the heights of Mount Tibidabo for fantastic views and a wonderful amusement park.

**12 Castell de Montjuïc** Page **107** • The ramparts of the hill-top Bourbon fortress offer an eagle-eye view of the city.

**14 A tapas tour** Pages **192–196** • Hop from bar to bar, tasting some of Barcelona's finest food.

**15 Sagrada Família** Page **121** •
The temple dedicated to the Sacred Family is the essential pilgrimage for Gaudí fans.

**16 City beaches** Page **90** •
Barcelona has 5km of sand-fringed ocean stretching from Barceloneta to Diagonal Mar.

**17 Fundació Joan Miró** Page **106** • The adventurous Fundació Joan Miró celebrates the work of one of the greatest Catalan artists.

**18 Camp Nou** Page **138** • Home of FC Barcelona, one of Europe's premier sides, with a cabinet full of trophies to prove it.

**19** **Parc Güell** Page **135** • The city's most extraordinary park is a fantasy land born of Antoni Gaudí's fertile imagination.

**21** **Museu Frederic Marès** Page **59** • Dont miss Marès' extraordinary range of religious sculpture, household utensils, toys and ephemera.

**20** **Montserrat** Page **154** • For centuries this mountain and monastery have been a place of pilgrimage – and now make a great day-trip from the city.

# Basics

# Basics

# Getting there

It's never been easier to reach Barcelona by air, with a variety of budget airlines from regional UK and European airports competing with the Spanish national carrier Iberia to get you directly to the city, quickly and cheaply. There's also a fair amount of choice from North America, though you may have to fly there via Madrid or another European city to get the best fare.

**Air fares** vary wildly, depending on how far in advance you book and on the season. To get the very cheapest fares advertised by the budget airlines you'll need to book weeks, if not months, in advance. Flights with Iberia and other major airlines tend to be more expensive and seasonal, with the highest fares from June to September, at Christmas, New Year and Easter, and at weekends all year.

Most airlines prefer you to book tickets online these days and you can turn up some great deals, but always check the small print as most budget airline tickets are non-changeable and non-refundable. Another option is to contact a general flight or travel agent – these have similar deals on flights and services, and some are particularly geared towards youth, student and independent travel. Other specialist tour operators can book you onto a variety of city breaks or themed tours in Barcelona and Catalunya.

Travelling to Barcelona from elsewhere in Europe by **train** or **bus** inevitably takes much longer than flying and usually works out more expensive given the travelling time involved. However, if Barcelona and Spain are part of a longer European trip it can be an interesting proposition, and is an increasingly popular "green" alternative to flying. Driving to Barcelona is also something of an undertaking and, with motorway tolls in France and Spain, fuel costs, cross-Channel ferry and Eurotunnel fares, it's certainly not a cheap option.

## Booking flights and services online

ⓦ**www.cheapflights.com** Price comparison on flights, short breaks, packages and other deals.

ⓦ**www.ebookers.com** Flights, hotels, cars and holiday packages.
ⓦ**www.expedia.com** Discount air fares, all-airline search engine, and daily deals on hotels, cars and packages.
ⓦ**www.lastminute.com** Good last-minute flights, holiday packages, hotel bookings and car rental deals.
ⓦ**www.travelocity.com**, ⓦ**www.zuji.com.au** Destination guides, hot fares and good deals on car rental, rail passes and accommodation.

## Flights and tours from the UK, Ireland and Europe

**Flying time** to Barcelona from the UK or Ireland is between two and two and a half hours, depending on your departure airport.

A whole host of budget **no-frills airlines** compete on the Barcelona route from the UK and Ireland, notably easyJet (ⓦwww.easyjet.com), Monarch (ⓦwww.flymonarch.com), Jet2 (ⓦwww.jet2.com), bmibaby (ⓦwww.bmibaby.com) and Aer Lingus (ⓦwww.aerlingus.com), with daily departures throughout the year from more than a dozen regional airports, including all the London airports, plus Belfast, Birmingham, Bristol, Cardiff, Dublin, East Midlands, Leeds, Bradford, Liverpool, Manchester and Newcastle. The earlier you book, the cheaper your flight will be – and special offers can even mean the seats are free, or virtually free, with just the taxes to pay (from £20 each way). Even Iberia (ⓦwww.iberia.com) is forced to compete, with good-value promotional fares – however, their more flexible tickets (allowing cancellation and/or date changes) are considerably more expensive and can rise to £200 (€260) return or more in peak season.

There's a second gateway to the city at **Girona**, 90km north of Barcelona, which is used almost exclusively by no-frills airline Ryanair (ⓦwww.ryanair.com), which flies there from around fifty British, Irish and European airports, including smaller UK airports like Bournemouth, Durham Tees Valley and Doncaster. The other regional airport is at **Reus**, 110km south of Barcelona, near Tarragona, served by Ryanair from half a dozen UK airports and from Dublin. You've over an hour's journey from either airport to the centre of Barcelona, but there are reliable connecting bus services.

Other **European budget airlines** fly into Barcelona airport from across the continent, including Air Berlin (ⓦwww.airberlin.com from Germany and Austria), Spanair (ⓦwww.spanair.com from Scandinavia, Germany and Spain), Vueling (ⓦwww.vueling.com from Spain, the Balearics, Italy, Paris, Brussels and Amsterdam) and Transvia (ⓦwww.transvia.com from Amsterdam, Berlin, Brussels and elsewhere).

Three-night **city breaks** to Barcelona start from as little as £200 (€260) per person flying from London, Manchester or Dublin.

For this price, accommodation is most likely in a two-star hotel, and sometimes on a room-only basis. For three nights bed-and-breakfast in a three- or four-star hotel you can usually expect to pay more like £300–400 (€390–520). A few operators offer rather more **specialist holidays** in and around Barcelona, concentrating on things like art and architecture, cooking classes, wine tours or rural Catalunya.

## General flight and travel agents

**North South Travel** ☎01245/608 291, ⓦwww.northsouthtravel.co.uk. Competitive travel agency, offering discounted fares worldwide – profits are used to support projects in the developing world, especially the promotion of sustainable tourism.

**STA Travel** Australia ☎134 782, ⓦwww.statravel.com.au; US ☎800/781 4040, ⓦwww.statravel.com; UK ☎0871/230 0040, ⓦwww.statravel.co.uk. Worldwide specialists in low-cost flights and tours for students and under-26s, though other customers welcome. Also student IDs, travel insurance, car rental and rail passes etc.

**Trailfinders** Australia ☎1300/780 212, ⓦwww.trailfinders.com.au; Republic of Ireland

☎01/677 7888, ⓦwww.trailfinders.ie; UK ☎0845/058 5858, ⓦwww.trailfinders.com. One of the best-informed and most efficient agents for independent travellers.

## Specialist tour operators and agencies

**Martin Randall Travel** ☎0208/742 3355, ⓦwww.martinrandall.com. Experts lead small groups on annual, all-inclusive quality tours to Spain, concentrating on "Gastronomic Catalonia" (six nights, £1980) – though tours and themes change each year.

**Mundi Color** ☎0207/828 6021. Spanish specialists for flights, accommodation, tours and city breaks.

**Ramblers Holidays** ☎01707/331133, ⓦwww.ramblersholidays.co.uk. The walking specialists offer a one-week Barcelona holiday with guided walks, sightseeing and trips out of the city; flights and most meals included, from around £700.

**Secret Destinations** ☎0845/612 9000, ⓦwww.secretdestinations.com. Tailor-made holidays and city breaks can combine Barcelona with Sitges or the Costa Brava, or cycling in the wine region.

**A Taste of Spain** ☎856 079 626 or 934 170 716, ⓦwww.atasteofspain.com. Interesting food-based tours from a company with offices in Barcelona and Madrid – from lunch and olive-oil tasting in Barcelona (€220) to a five-day culinary Catalan tour (land-only, €2550).

## Flights and tours from the USA and Canada

Most **direct scheduled services** to Spain from North America are to Madrid, but the Spanish national airline Iberia (ⓦwww.iberia.com), and Continental (ⓦwww.continental.com) and American Airlines (ⓦwww.aa.com), have year-round nonstop Barcelona services, daily from New York; meanwhile Delta (ⓦwww.delta.com) flies direct from both New York and Atlanta. European-based airlines (like Air France, British Airways, Lufthansa, KLM and TAP) can also get you to Barcelona, though you'll be routed through their respective European hubs. Flying time from New York is around seven hours to Madrid, eight to Barcelona direct, though with an onward connection it can take up to eleven hours to reach Barcelona.

Return **fares** are as much as US$1000 in summer, though outside peak periods you should be able to fly for under US$600. Special promotional deals sometimes undercut these prices, or it might even pay you to buy a cheap flight to the UK and travel on to Barcelona from there with a budget airline (see "Flights and tours from the UK, Ireland and Europe").

**Tour companies** tend to include a couple of days in Barcelona as part of a whirlwind escorted itinerary around Spain, costing from US$1500 to US$2000 for a standard two-week tour, or up to US$4000 for something more luxurious. However, for a more in-depth Barcelona experience, consider a **city break** – a typical three-night stay in a central Barcelona three-star hotel starts at around US$1000, rising to around US$2000 and these are the city breaks prices "from US" etc for a week, including flights, breakfast and transfers.

### Specialist tour operators and agencies

**Food & Wine Trails** ☎ 1-800/367-5348, ⊛ www .foodandwinetrails.com. Their "Catalan Food and Wine" tour spends two nights in Barcelona and four on the Costa Brava, visiting markets and tapas bars, taking cooking classes, touring and eating. From US$2155, land only.

**Olé Spain** ☎ 1-888/869-7156, ⊛ www.olespain .com. Eight-day cultural walking tours in Catalunya, beginning and ending in Barcelona, with time to explore the city. US$3795.

**Petrabax** ☎ 1-800/634-1188, ⊛ www.petrabax .com. City breaks, escorted Catalunya tours or self-drive Spanish holidays, plus independent travel services – such as accommodation bookings and car rental.

**Saranjan Tours** ☎ 1-800/858-9594, ⊛ www .saranjan.com. Upscale, fully guided, customized tours concentrating on unusual combinations, like Barcelona and its nearby wine country or a two-centre Barcelona and Bilbao holiday.

## Flights from Australia and New Zealand

There are no direct flights to Spain from Australia or New Zealand. However, a number of airlines do fly to Barcelona with a stopover elsewhere in Europe or Asia (flights via Asia are generally the cheaper option). Another possibility is to fly to Madrid, from where you can pick up a connecting flight or train. It's best to discuss your route and preferences with a flight and travel agent like Flight Centre (⊛ www.flightcentre.com.au /co.nz) or STA Travel (⊛ www.statravel.com .au/co.nz), especially if your visit to Barcelona is part of a wider Spanish trip – in which case, you might be better off buying a Round-The-World (RTW) ticket. If you'd

rather someone else made all the arrangements, talk to a specialist tour operator, like Ibertours (⊛www.ibertours.com.au), who can arrange an organized visit to Barcelona, sorting out your accommodation, guided tours and car rental.

## By rail

Travelling by **train** to Barcelona can't compete in price with the cheapest budget-airlines' fares – but it can be a real adventure. First stop should be ⊛www.seat61.com, an amazingly useful website that provides route, ticket, timetable and contact information for all European train services.

The quickest and most straightforward option from the UK is to take the **Eurostar** service (☎08705/186 186, ⊛www.eurostar .com; from £59 return) from London St Pancras International via the Channel Tunnel to Paris, and then the overnight **Paris–Barcelona "train-hotel"**, which arrives in Barcelona at around 8.30am (total journey time 17hr). This is a sleeper service (with restaurant and café), with various levels of comfort available – the cheapest ticket is in a four-berth compartment, currently from £108 return, depending on availability; you

have to book well in advance to get the lowest prices.

There are other alternatives, but they take longer, can be more complicated to arrange and sometimes work out more expensively. For example, you can use the cross-Channel ferries and Seacats and local trains to Paris instead of Eurostar, and instead of the overnight "train-hotel" there are regular daytime services through France and Spain.

You can book the whole journey online with **Rail Europe** (☎0870/584 8848, ⊛www .raileurope.co.uk) or call a specialist rail agent like Ffestiniog Travel (☎01766/772050, ⊛www.ffestiniogtravel.co.uk) or the Spanish Rail Service (☎020/7725 7063, ⊛www .spanish-rail.co.uk). If you live outside the UK, you can book Eurostar and "train-hotel" tickets through the websites ⊛www.raileurope.com, ⊛www.raileurope.ca and ⊛www.raileurope .com.au.

If you plan to travel extensively in Europe by train, a **rail pass** might prove a good investment. However, if you're just headed for Barcelona, InterRail (⊛www.raileurope .co.uk/inter-rail) and Eurail (⊛www.eurail .com) aren't a good deal, and even if you intend to travel around Catalunya by train,

---

## Fly less – stay longer! Travel and climate change

Climate change is perhaps the single biggest issue facing our planet. It is caused by a build-up in the atmosphere of carbon dioxide and other greenhouse gases, which are emitted by many sources – including planes. Already, **flights** account for three to four percent of human-induced global warming: that figure may sound small, but it is rising year on year and threatens to counteract the progress made by reducing greenhouse emissions in other areas.

Rough Guides regard travel as a **global benefit**, and feel strongly that the advantages to developing economies are important, as are the opportunities for greater contact and awareness among peoples. But we also believe in travelling responsibly, which includes giving thought to how often we fly and what we can do to redress any harm that our trips may create.

We can travel less or simply reduce the amount we travel by air (taking fewer trips and staying longer, or taking the train if there is one); we can avoid night flights (which are more damaging); and we can make the trips we do take "climate neutral" via a carbon offset scheme. **Offset schemes** run by climatecare.org, carbonneutral .com and others allow you to "neutralize" the greenhouse gases that you are responsible for releasing. Their websites have simple calculators that let you work out the impact of any flight – as does our own. Once that's done, you can pay to fund projects that will reduce future emissions by an equivalent amount. Please take the time to visit our website and make your trip climate neutral, or get a copy of the Rough Guide to Climate Change for more detail on the subject.

rail travel in that part of Spain is fairly limited (and quite cheap), so you probably won't get your money's worth.

## By bus

**Eurolines** (www.eurolines.co.uk) operates a year-round bus service to Barcelona from London which takes up to 28 hours. It usually costs around £100 return, though there are advance deals and special offers – it's always cheapest to book online. Eurolines also sells Barcelona tickets and transport to London at all UK National Express bus terminals.

## Driving to Barcelona

It's about 1600km from London to Barcelona, which, with stops, takes almost two full days to drive. To plan your route, try motoring organizations such as AA, (www.theaa.com) and the RAC (www .rac.co.uk) which also provide advice on insurance requirements, documentation matters and how to avoid toll roads. If you're bringing your own car, carry your licence, vehicle registration and insurance documents with you; you should also have two warning triangles and a fluorescent vest in case of breakdown. For more details about driving conditions in the city, see p.28.

Many people use the conventional **cross-Channel** ferry links, principally Dover–Calais, though services to Brittany or Normandy might be more convenient. However, the quickest way of crossing the Channel is to go via the **Eurotunnel** service (℡08705/353535, www.eurotunnel.com), which operates drive-on-drive-off shuttle trains between Folkestone and Calais/Coquelles. The twenty-four-hour service runs every twenty minutes throughout the day and, though you can just turn up, booking is advised, especially at weekends.

Alternatively, Brittany Ferries operates a car and passenger ferry from **Plymouth to Santander** (twice weekly; 20hr). From Santander, it's about nine hours' drive to Barcelona, via Bilbao and Zaragoza. Or there's the P&O service from **Portsmouth to Bilbao** (twice weekly; 34hr), east of Santander in the Basque country. Both services are very expensive, especially in summer, when return fares can cost as much as £800.

Any ferry company or travel agent can supply up-to-date schedules and ticket information, or you can consult the encyclopedic www.directferries.com, which has information and links to every European ferry service.

# Arrival and departure

There are three main, adjacent terminals (A, B and C) at Barcelona's airport and a fourth on the way, with taxis and airport buses found immediately outside each terminal and the airport train station a short distance away. The city's main Barcelona Sants train station and the Barcelona Nord bus station are both more central, with convenient metro stations for onward travel. In most cases, you can be off the plane, train or bus and in your hotel room within the hour.

## By air

**Barcelona airport** (℡902 404 704, www .aena.es) is 18km southwest of the city centre at El Prat de Llobregat. There are tourist offices in terminals A and B, handling

hotel bookings; there are also ATMs, exchange facilities and car-rental offices.

The **airport train service** (daily 6am–11.44pm; journey time 20min; €2.60; info on ℡902 240 202) runs every thirty minutes to

Barcelona Sants (the main train station), and continues on to Passeig de Gràcia (best stop for Eixample, Plaça de Catalunya and the Ramblas) and Estació de França (for La Ribera). **Trains back to the airport** run from Barcelona Sants on a similar half-hourly schedule (daily 5.33am–10.55pm). City travel passes (*targetes*) and the Barcelona Card are valid on the airport train service.

Alternatively, the **Aerobús** service (Mon–Sat 6am–1am; €3.90; departures every 6–15min; ☎934 156 020) runs from each terminal, stopping in the city at Plaça d'Espanya, Gran Via de les Corts Catalanes (at c/Comte d'Urgell), Plaça Universitat, Plaça de Catalunya and Passeig de Gràcia (at c/la Diputació). It takes around thirty minutes to reach Plaça de Catalunya, though allow longer in the rush hour. Aerobús departures to the airport from Plaça de Catalunya leave from in front of El Corte Inglés department store (Mon–Sat 5.30am–12.15am).

A metered **taxi** from the airport to the city centre costs roughly €20–25, including the airport surcharge. You will, however, be charged more after 9pm and at weekends, and there's a surcharge for any luggage that goes in the boot.

Ryanair arrivals at **Girona airport**, 90km north of Barcelona, can take the connecting Barcelona Bus service (☎902 361 550, ⊕www.barcelonabus.com), which runs to Girona train station (for hourly trains to Barcelona Sants; 1hr 15min–1hr 30min) or direct to Barcelona Nord bus station (€12 one-way, €21 return; journey time 1hr 10min). From **Reus airport**, 110km south of Barcelona, there's a connecting Hispano Igualadina bus (☎902 447 726, ⊕www .igualadina.com) to Barcelona Sants (€12 one-way, €20 return; 1hr 20min).

The return buses to Girona or Reus all connect with the relevant Ryanair and other airline departures. Note that there are also direct buses linking Barcelona airport with Sitges, Reus, Tarragona and Girona.

## Airlines

**Air Berlin** ☎902 320 737, ⊕www.airberlin.com.
**Aer Lingus** ☎902 502 737, ⊕www.aerlingus.com.
**Air Europa** ☎902 401 501, ⊕www.aireuropa .com.
**bmibaby** ☎902 100 737, ⊕www.bmibaby.com.
**British Airways** ☎902 111 333, ⊕www .britishairways.com.

Delta ☎901 116 946, ⓦ www.delta.com.
easyJet ☎807 260 026, ⓦ www.easyjet.com.
Iberia ☎902 400 550, ⓦ www.iberia.com.
Jet2 ☎902 881 269, ⓦ www.jet2.com.
Monarch ☎800 099 260, ⓦ www.flymonarch.com.
Ryanair ☎807 220 032, ⓦ www.ryanair.com.
Spanair ☎902 131 415, ⓦ www.spanair.com.
Transvia ☎902 114 478, ⓦ www.transvia.com.
Vueling ☎902 333 933, ⓦ www.vueling.com.

## By train

The main station for domestic and international arrivals is **Barcelona Sants**, 3km west of the city centre. There is a tourist office here (with an accommodation booking service), as well as ATMs, an exchange office, car-rental outlets, a police station and left-luggage facilities. The metro station (accessed from inside Barcelona Sants) is called ⓂSants Estació – line 3 from here runs direct to Liceu (for the Ramblas), Catalunya (for Plaça de Catalunya) and Passeig de Gràcia, while line 5 runs to Diagonal.

Some Spanish intercity services and international trains also stop at **Estació de França**, 1km east of the Ramblas and close to ⓂBarceloneta. Other possible arrival points by train are **Plaça de Catalunya**, at the top of the Ramblas (for trains from coastal towns north of the city, and towns on the Puigcerdà–Vic line), and **Passeig de Gràcia** (Catalunya provincial destinations).

The high-speed **AVE line** (Alta Velocidad Española) between Barcelona and Madrid (via Tarragona and Zaragoza) started operation in 2008, cutting journey times in half between the two cities (2hr 45min to 3hr 25min, depending on the service). Arrivals and departures are at Barcelona Sants, though a second high-speed station is planned at La Sagrera, east of the centre beyond Glòries (though probably not until 2013).

For information about the local rail network in and around the city, see "City transport".

### Train information

**RENFE** ☎902 240 202, ⓦ www.renfe.es. For all national rail enquiries, sales and reservations. At Barcelona Sants station (Pl. dels Paisos Catalans, Sants; ⓂSants Estació) there are train information desks and advance ticket booking counters, some with English speakers.

## By bus

The main bus terminal, used by international, long-distance and provincial buses, is **Barcelona Nord** on c/Ali-Bei (☎902 260 606, ⓦ www.barcelonanord.com; ⓂArc de Triomf), three blocks north of Parc de la Ciutadella. There's a bus information desk on the ground floor (daily 7am–9pm), plus a tourist office (Mon–Sat 9am–2pm), accommodation agency, ATMs, shops and luggage lockers. Various companies operate services across Catalunya, Spain and Europe – it's a good idea to reserve a ticket in advance on long-distance routes (a day before at the station is usually fine, or buy online).

Some intercity and international Eurolines services also make a stop at the bus terminal behind Barcelona Sants station on c/de Viriat (ⓂSants Estació). Either way, you're only a short metro ride from the city centre.

## By ferry

Ferries from the Balearics dock at the **Estació Marítima**, Moll de Barcelona, Port Vell (☎900 760 760; ⓂDrassanes), at the bottom of Avinguda Paral.lel. There are ticket offices inside the terminal, and taxis nearby, though no other services, but you're only a short walk from Drassanes metro station at the bottom of the Ramblas. Ferries from Genoa (Italy) dock at the **Moll de Sant Bertran**, just along from the Moll de Barcelona, while **cruise ships** tie up at several points in the inner harbour – the Port-Bus shuttle-bus runs cruise passengers to and from the Ramblas.

## By car

Driving into Barcelona is reasonably straightforward, with traffic only slow in the morning and evening rush hours. Parking, however, is a different matter altogether – rarely easy and not cheap. If your trip is just to the city and its surroundings, our advice is not to bother with a car at all, but you'll find some useful pointers in any case in the "City transport" section.

Coming into Barcelona along any one of the motorways (*autopistes*), head for the Ronda Litoral, the southern half of the city's ring road. Following signs for "Port Vell" will take you towards the main exit for the old town, though there are also exits for Gran Via de les Corts Catalanes and Avinguda Diagonal if uptown Barcelona is your destination.

# City transport

Barcelona's excellent integrated transport system comprises the metro, buses, trams and local trains, plus a network of funiculars and cable cars. The local transport authority is Transports Metropolitans de Barcelona (ⓦ www.tmb.net), whose useful website (English-language version available) has full timetable and ticket information. There are also TMB customer service centres at Barcelona Sants station, and at Universitat, Diagonal and Sagrada Família metro stations, where you'll be able to pick up a free public transport map. The map and ticket information is also posted at major bus stops and all metro and tram stations. Our public transport map is in the colour pages at the back of the book.

## Tickets and travel passes

A transit plan divides the province into six zones, but as the entire metropolitan area of Barcelona (including the airport) falls within Zone 1, that's the only one you'll need to worry about on a day-to-day basis.

On all the city's public transport (including night buses and funiculars) you can buy a single ticket every time you ride (€1.30), but if you're staying for a few days it's much cheaper to buy a *targeta* – a **discount ticket** strip which you pass through the box on top of the metro or train barrier, or slot in the machine on the bus, tram or funicular. The *targetes* are available at metro, train and tram stations, but not on the buses.

The best general deal is the **T-10** ("tay day-oo" in Catalan) *targeta* (€7.20), valid for ten separate journeys, with changes between methods of transport allowed within 75 minutes. The ticket can also be used by more than one person at a time – just make sure you punch it the same number of times as there are people travelling. It's also available at newsstands and tobacconists.

Other useful (single-person) *targetes* for Zone 1 include the **T-Dia** ("tay dee-ah"; one day's unlimited travel; €5.50), plus combinations up to the 5-Dies (five days; €21.70); the **T-50/30** (fifty trips within a thirty day period, €29.80); or the **T-Mes** (one month; €46.25) – for the latter, the station ticket office will need to see some form of ID (driving licence or passport). The Barcelona Card (see p.31) also offers free city transport between two and five days.

Heading for Sitges, Montserrat or further out of town, you'll need to buy a specific ticket or relevant-zoned *targeta* as the Zone 1 *targetes* outlined above don't run that far. Anyone caught without a valid ticket anywhere on the system is liable to an on-the-spot fine of €40.

## The metro

The quickest way of getting around Barcelona is by metro, which runs on six lines though two more are currently under construction. Metro entrances are marked with a red diamond sign with an "M". Its **hours of operation** are Monday until Thursday, plus Sunday and public holidays, 5am to midnight; Friday, 5am to 2am; Saturday and the day before a public holiday, 24hr service. There's a colour **metro map** at the back of this book, or you can pick up a little fold-out one at metro stations (ask for *una guia del metro*).

The system is perfectly safe, though many of the train carriages are heavily graffitied. Buskers and beggars are common, moving from one carriage to the next at stations.

## Buses

Most buses operate daily, roughly from 4 or 5am until 10.30pm, though some lines stop earlier and some run until after midnight. Night bus (*Nit bus*) services fill in the gaps on all the main routes, with services every twenty to sixty minutes from around 10pm to 4am. Many bus routes (including all night buses) stop in or near Plaça de Catalunya, but the full route is marked at each bus stop,

## Funiculars and cable cars

Several **funicular railways** still operate in the city to Montjuïc, Tibidabo and Vallvidrera. Summer and year-round weekend visits to Tibidabo also combine a funicular trip with a ride on the antique tram, the **Tramvia Blau**. There are two **cable car** (*telefèric*) rides: from Barceloneta across the harbour to Montjuïc, and then from the top station of the Montjuïc funicular right the way up to the castle. Both aerial rides are pretty good experiences, worth doing just for the views alone. Ticket and service details for all funiculars and cable cars are given in the relevant sections of the text.

along with a timetable – useful bus routes are detailed in the text.

### Trams

The tram system (ⓦwww.trambcn.com) runs on four lines, with departures every eight to twenty minutes throughout the day from 5am to midnight. **Lines T1, T2 and T3** depart from Plaça Francesc Macià and run along the uptown part of Avinguda Diagonal to suburban destinations in the northwest – useful tourist stops are at L'Illa shopping and the Maria Cristina and Palau Reial metro stations. Line **T4** operates from Ciutadella-Vila Olímpica (where there's also a metro station) and runs up past the zoo and TNC (the National Theatre) to Glòries before running down the lower part of Avinguda Diagonal to Diagonal Mar and the Fòrum site.

### Trains

The city has a cheap and efficient commuter train line, the **Ferrocarrils de la Generalitat de Catalunya** (FGC; ☏932 051 515, ⓦwww.fgc.cat), with its main stations at Plaça de Catalunya and Plaça d'Espanya. These go to Sarrià, Vallvidrera, Tibidabo, Sant Cugat, Terrassa and Montserrat, and details are given in the text where appropriate. The Zone 1 *targeta* is valid as far as the city limits, which in practice is everywhere you're likely to want to go except for Montserrat, Sant Cugat and Terrassa.

The national rail service, operated by **RENFE** (☏902 240 202, ⓦwww.renfe.es), runs all the other services out of Barcelona, with local lines – north to the Costa Mareseme and south to Sitges – designated as Rodiales/Cercanías. The hub is Barcelona Sants station, with services also passing

through Plaça de Catalunya (heading north) and Passeig de Gràcia (south). Arrive in plenty of time to buy a ticket, as queues are often horrendous, though for most regional destinations you can use the automatic vending machines instead.

### Taxis

Black-and-yellow taxis (with a green roof-light on when available for hire) are inexpensive, plentiful and well worth using, especially late at night. There's a minimum charge of €1.80 (€1.90 after 8pm Sat, Sun & hols) and after that it's €0.82/1.04 per kilometre, with small surcharges for baggage and picking up from Barcelona Sants station and the airport, However, the taxis have meters so charges are transparent – if not, asking for a receipt (*rebut* in Catalan, *recibo* in Spanish) should ensure that the price is fair. Most short journeys across town run to around €7.

There are taxi ranks outside major train and metro stations, in main squares, near large hotels and along the main avenues. You can call a taxi in advance, but few of the cab company operators speak English – you'll also be charged an extra €3–4 on top of the fare for calling a cab.

### Taxi companies

**Barna Taxis** ☏933 577 755.
**Fono-Taxi** ☏933 001 100.
**Radio Taxi** ☏933 033 033.
**Servi-Taxi** ☏933 300 300.
**Taxi Amic** ☏934 208 088.

### Driving and vehicle rental

You don't need a car to get around Barcelona, but you may want to rent one if

## Follow that trixi

A fun way to get around the old town, port area and beaches is by **trixi** (Ⓦwww .trixi.com), a kind of love-bug-style bicycle-rickshaw. They tout for business between 11am and 8pm near the Columbus statue at the bottom of the Ramblas, and outside La Seu (cathedral) in the Barri Gòtic, though you can also flag them down if one cruises by. Fares are fixed (€6 for 15min, €10 for 30min, €18 for 60min) and the *trixistas* are an amiable, multilingual bunch for the most part.

you plan to see anything else of the region. However, in summer the coastal roads in particular are a nightmare, so if all you aim to do is zip to the beach or wine region for the day, it's far better to stick to the local trains. Driving in the city itself is not for the faint-hearted either, parking is notoriously difficult, and vehicle crime is rampant – never leave anything visible in the car.

Most foreign **driving licences** are honoured in Spain – including all EU, US and Canadian ones. Remember that you drive on the right in Spain, and away from main roads you yield to vehicles approaching from the right. Speed limits are posted – maximum on urban roads is 60kph, other roads 90kph, motorways 120kph. Wearing seatbelts is compulsory.

### Parking

Indoor **car parks** in the city centre are linked to display boards that indicate where there are free spaces. Central locations include Plaça de Catalunya, Plaça Urquinaona, Arc de Triomf, Passeig de Gràcia, Plaça dels Angels/MACBA and Avinguda Paral.lel, and though parking in one of these is convenient it's also fairly expensive (60min from €2.60, 24hr up to €25).

There's a cheaper park-and-ride facility called **Metropark** for day visitors at Plaça de les Glòries in the eastern Eixample (junction of Avgda. Diagonal and Gran Via de les Corts Catalanes; ⓂGlòries). The €7 fee includes up to 18 hours parking and a ticket for unlimited travel on the city's public transport.

**Street parking** is permitted in most areas, but it can be tough to find spaces, especially in the old town and Gràcia, where it's nearly all either restricted access or residents' parking only. The ubiquitous residents' **Àrea Verda meter-zones** (Ⓦwww.bcn.es/areaverda) throughout the city allow pay-and-display

parking for visitors, for €2.80 per hour, with either a one- or two-hour maximum stay. Elsewhere, don't be tempted to double-park, leave your car in loading zones or otherwise park illegally – the cost of being towed can exceed €150, and no mercy is shown to foreign-plated vehicles.

### Vehicle rental

**Car rental** is cheapest arranged in advance through one of the large multinational chains (Avis, Budget, EasyCar, Europcar, Hertz, Holiday Autos, National or Thrifty, for example). In Barcelona, the major chains have outlets at the airport and at, or near, Barcelona Sants station. Inclusive rates start from around €40 per day for an economy car (less by the week, and often with good rates for a three-day weekend rental, around €150). Drivers need to be at least 21 (23 with some companies) and to have been driving for at least a year. It's essential to take out fully comprehensive insurance and pay for Collision Damage Waiver, otherwise you'll be liable for every scratch.

Some of the local Barcelona rental outlets – like Motissimo (☎934 908 401, Ⓦwww .motissimo.es) and Vanguard (☎934 393 880, Ⓦwww.vanguardrent.com) – have **mopeds** and **motorcycles** available, though given the traffic conditions (and the good public transport system) it's not really recommended as a means of getting around the city. Note that mopeds and motorcycles are often rented out with insurance that doesn't include theft – always check with the company. You will generally be asked to produce a driving licence as a deposit.

### Cycling

The city council has embraced cycling as a means of transport, and is investing heavily in cycle lanes and bike schemes, notably the **Bicing** pick-up and drop-off scheme (ⓦwww.bicing.com), which is touted as Barcelona's new public transport system. You'll see the red bikes and bike stations all over the city, but Bicing is aimed at locals rather than tourists (you need to register as a user, either online or at the office at Pl. Carles Pi i Sunyer 8–10, Barri Gòtic, between c/Canuda and c/Duran i Bas).

In any case, there are plenty of **bike-rental** outfits more geared to tourist requirements. Rental costs around €15–20 a day with one of the companies listed below, and many bike tour companies (see "City tours") can also fix you up with a rental bike. For more on bike paths and cycling, see Chapter 16, "Sports and outdoor activities".

## Bike rental

**Barnabike** Pg. Sota la Murralla 3 ⓜBarceloneta ☎932 690 204, ⓦwww.barnabike.com.
**Biciclot** Pg. Marítim 33–35, Port Olímpic, ⓜCiutadella-Vila Olímpica ☎932 219 778, ⓦwww.biciclot.net.
**Un Coxte Menys/Bicicleta Barcelona** c/Esparteria 3, La Ribera ⓜBarceloneta ☎932 682 105, ⓦwww.bicicletabarcelona.com.

# City tours

The number of available tours grows at a bewildering pace, and you can now see the city on anything from a Segway to a hot-air balloon. Bike tours in particular are hugely popular — at times it seems as if every tourist in the city is playing follow-my-leader down the same old-town alley — while other operators offer tapas-bar crawls, party nights and out-of-town excursions. Highest profile are the open-top sightseeing bus tours, whose board-at-will services can drop you outside every attraction in the city. Otherwise, Barcelona has some particularly good walking tours, showing you parts of the old town you might not find otherwise, while sightseeing boats offer a different view of the city.

## Bike tours

**Bike Tours Barcelona** ☎932 682 105, ⓦwww .biketoursbarcelona.com. Find the red-T-shirted guides in Plaça de Sant Jaume in the Barri Gòtic, outside the tourist office (top of c/de la Ciutat) – tours last three hours (daily 11am, plus April–Sept Fri–Mon 4.30pm; €22), no reservations required.
**Fat Tire Bike Tours** ☎933 013 612, ⓦwww .fattirebiketoursbarcelona.com. Four-hour bike tours (€22) with genial guides to the old town, Sagrada Família, port area and beach – where there's time for a swim and a drink. Tours meet at the c/de Ferran side of Plaça de Sant Jaume, Barri Gòtic (twice daily mid-April to mid-Sept, once daily rest of the year; no tours mid-Dec to end of Feb). Reservations not required, but you can check details at the rental shop at c/Escudellers 48. No credit cards.

## Bus tours

**Barcelona Tours** ⓦwww.barcelonatours.es. The orange-coloured rival to Bus Turístic; buses make twenty stops on a circular three-hour sweep through the city from Plaça. de Catalunya (daily: 9am–8pm, May–Sept 9am–9pm; departures every 10–20min). Tickets available on board and online: one-day €21, two-day €25 (under-14s €13/16 respectively). No credit cards.
**Bus Turístic** ⓦwww.tmb.net, ⓦwww .barcelonaturisme.com. Sightseeing service (departures every 5–25min) with over forty stops on three combined routes, linking all the main tourist sights. Northern (red) and southern (blue) routes depart from Plaça de Catalunya (daily 9am–7pm, April–Sept 9am–8pm), and a full circuit on either route takes two hours. The green Forùm route (daily

April–Sept 9.30am–8pm) runs from Port Olímpic to the Forùm site at Diagonal Mar and back, via the beaches. Tickets (valid for all routes) cost €20 for one day, €26 for two days (children aged 4–12 €12/16 respectively). The ticket also gives discounts at various sights, attractions, shops and restaurants. Buy online, or on board the bus, at any tourist office, Sants station and TMB customer centres.

## Walking tours

**Barcelona Walks** ☎ 932 853 832, ⓦ www .barcelonaturisme.com. The Pl. de Catalunya tourist office coordinates a popular series of walks and tours, including a 90min historical walking tour of the Barri Gòtic (daily 10am; €11). There are also 90min Picasso walking tours (Tues–Sun 10.30am; €13.50, includes entry to Picasso Museum), a two-hour Modernisme tour (Fri & Sat 4pm; €11) and two-hour Gourmet and Cuisine tour (Fri & Sat 11am; €15, includes tastings). Times given are for the current English-language tours, advance booking essential (discount for online bookings).

**Follow the Baldie** ⓦ www.followthebaldie.com. Follow erudite, self-professed baldie tour guide and longtime Barcelona resident, Trevor, on walks around anarchist Barcelona or over the hills to Tibidabo, tracking tarantulas near Sitges, or staggering from bar to bar in rural Catalunya. These are not your normal tours, as a perusal of the website soon shows. Trips from €35 per person.

**My Favourite Things** ☎ 637 265 405, ⓦ www .myft.net. Highly individual tours which reveal the city in a new light – whether it's bohemian Barcelona, where and what the locals eat, or the signature tour, My Favourite Fusion, which gives an insider's view of the city. Tours (in English) cost €26 per person and last around four hours, and there's always time for anecdotes, diversions, workshop visits and café visits. Tour numbers are limited to ten, and departures are flexible, so call or email for latest information or tailor-made requests.

## Water tours

**Catamaran Orsom** ☎ 934 410 537, ⓦ www .barcelona-orsom.com. Afternoon catamaran trips around the port in season (Easter week & June–Sept daily, May & Oct daily except Tues & Thurs; €12.50) and summer evening jazz cruises (daily June–Aug; €14.90). There's a ticket kiosk at the quayside opposite the Columbus statue, at the bottom of the Ramblas (ⓂDrassanes), but you should call in advance to be certain of departures.

**Las Golondrinas** ☎ 934 423 106, ⓦ www .lasgolondrinas.com. Daily sightseeing boats depart from Pl. Portal de la Pau, behind the Columbus monument (ⓂDrassanes) – trips are either around the port (35min; €5.50), or port and coast including the Port Olímpic and Diagonal Mar (90min; €11.50). Departures are at least hourly June–Sept; less frequently Oct–May but still daily.

# Information

The city tourist board, Turisme de Barcelona (ⓦ www.barcelonaturisme.com), is the best first stop for information about Barcelona, with a really useful English-language website and offices at the airport, Barcelona Sants station, Plaça de Catalunya and Plaça de Sant Jaume.

There are also staffed kiosks in main tourist areas, such as outside the Sagrada Família and on the Ramblas, which should be able to point you in the right direction. For information about the wider province of Catalunya, you need the Generalitat's information centre (Centre d'Informació de Catalunya) at **Palau Robert**, while events, concerts, exhibitions, festivals and other cultural diversions are covered in full at the Institut de Cultura in the **Palau de la Virreina** on the Ramblas.

For anything else you might need to know, you can try the city's ☎010 **telephone enquiries service** (Mon–Sat 8am–10pm). They'll be able to help with questions about transport, public services and other matters, and there are English-speaking staff

## Discount cards and packages

If you're going to do a lot of sightseeing, you can save yourself money by buying one of the widely available discount cards.

- **Barcelona Card** (2 days €25, 3 days €30, 4 days €34 or 5 days €40, full details on Ⓦ www.barcelonaturisme.com). Free public transport, plus big discounts at museums, venues, shops, theatres and restaurants. It's available at tourist offices, points of arrival and other outlets, though there's a ten percent discount if you buy online.

- **Articket** (€20, valid six months, Ⓦ www.articketbcn.org). Free admission into seven major art centres and galleries (MNAC, MACBA, CCCB, Museu Picasso, Fundació Antoni Tàpies, Fundació Joan Miró, and Centre Cultural Caixa Catalunya at La Pedrera). Buy at participating galleries, or at Plaça de Catalunya and Barcelona Sants tourist offices.

- **Arqueoticket** (€17, valid calendar year). In the same vein as Articket, offers free entry into five historical museums (Museu d'Arqueologia de Catalunya, Barbier-Mueller, Egipci, Historia de la Ciutat and Maritim), available at participating museums and tourist offices.

- **Ruta del Modernisme** (€12, valid one year, Ⓦ www.rutadelmodernisme.com). An excellent English-language guidebook, map and discount-voucher package that covers 115 *modernista* buildings in Barcelona and other Catalan towns, offering discounts of up to fifty percent on admission fees, tours and purchases. It's also packaged with *Let's Go Out*, a guide to *modernista* bars and restaurants (total package €18), with both available from the Centre del Modernisme desk at the main Plaça de Catalunya tourist office.

---

available. The city hall (Ajuntament, Ⓦ www .bcn.cat) and regional government (General-itat, Ⓦ www.gencat.cat) websites are also absolute mines of information about every aspect of cultural, social and working life in Barcelona, from museum opening hours and festival dates to local politics and council office locations; they both have English-language versions. For arts and events listings, the websites of the local newspapers and magazines (see next section, "The media") are also pretty useful.

### Information offices

Barcelona Informació (Oficina d'Atenció als Ciutadans) Pl. de Sant Miquel, Barri Gòtic, Ⓜ Jaume I ☎ 010, Ⓦ www.bcn.cat (June–Sept Mon–Fri 8.15am–2.15pm, Sat 9am–2pm, Oct–May Mon–Fri 8.30am–5.30pm, Sat 9am–2pm). Citizens' information office, around the back of the Ajuntament in the new building. It's not really for tourists, but invariably helpful (though you can't count on English being spoken).
Centre d'Informació de Catalunya Palau Robert, Pg. de Gràcia 107, Eixample, Ⓜ Diagonal ☎ 932 388 091, Ⓦ www.gencat.cat/palaurobert (Mon–Sat 10am–7pm, Sun & hols 10am–2.30pm). It has

information about travel in Catalunya and provides maps, guides, details of how to get around and lists of places to stay. Also exhibitions and events relating to all matters Catalan.
Centre del Modernisme ☎ 933 177 652, Ⓦ www.rutadelmodernisme.com. Offices inside the Turisme de Barcelona tourist office at Pl. de Catalunya, Ⓜ Catalunya (Mon–Sat 10am–7pm, Sun & hols 10am–2pm); at Hospital de la Santa Creu i Sant Pau, c/Sant Antoni M. Claret 167, Eixample, Ⓜ Hospital de Sant Pau (daily 10am–2pm); and Pavellons Güell, Avgda. de Pedralbes 7, Pedralbes, Ⓜ Palau Reial (Mon & Fri–Sun 10am–2pm). The staffed information desks provide details of visits to the city's *modernista* buildings and monuments, and sell the Ruta del Modernisme package.
Institut de Cultura Palau de la Virreina, Ramblas 99, Ⓜ Liceu ☎ 933 161 000, Ⓦ www.bcn.cat /cultura (Mon–Sat 10am–8pm, Sun 11am–3pm). Cultural information office, with advance information on everything that's happening in the city, from events and concerts to exhibitions and festivals; you can also buy tickets here. The website portal has daily updated cultural news and web TV previews, or pick up the free "Cultural Agenda" (in English), a useful free monthly what's on listings guide.
Turisme de Barcelona ☎ 807 117 222 if calling from within Spain, ☎ 932 853 834 if calling from

abroad, ⓦwww.barcelonaturisme.com. Main office, Pl. de Catalunya 17, ⓂCatalunya (daily 9am–9pm); also at Pl. de Sant Jaume, entrance at c/Ciutat 2, Barri Gòtic, ⓂJaume I (Mon–Fri 9am–8pm, Sat 10am–8pm, Sun & hols 10am–2pm); Airport Terminals A & B (daily 9am–9pm); and Barcelona Sants, Pl. dels Països Catalans, ⓂSants Estació (Mon–Fri 8am–8pm, Sat, Sun & hols 8am–2pm; April–Sept daily 8am–8pm). The main Pl. de Catalunya office is down the steps in the southeast corner of the square, opposite El Corte Inglés. It's always busy and can be frustrating if you just want a quick answer to a question. There's also a money exchange service, separate accommodation desk, tour and ticket sales, and a gift shop.

## Useful websites

### Art, architecture and design

ⓦwww.fundaciomiro-bcn.org The Joan Miró Foundation's official website is the main source for the artist – a complete biography, plus clickable art and a round-up of his works in the city and elsewhere, and exhibition news.

ⓦwww.gaudiclub.com The best first stop for Antoni Gaudí, his life and works, with plenty of links to other sites, plus Gaudí-related gifts, games, news, books and tours.

ⓦwww.qdq.com Every building in the city has been photographed – to view, click on "Callejeros

Fotografiicos", then click on the map or type in the street name.

ⓦwww.rutadisseny.com The "design route" is a guide (in English) to the city's most cutting-edge shops, bars, restaurants and buildings, with maps, reviews and walking itineraries.

### General

ⓦwww.barcelona-online.com Packed with information in English on Barcelona, with punchy reviews and links to scores of other websites.

ⓦwww.enciclopedia.cat. English-language online encyclopaedia, for everything you ever wanted to know about Catalan people, history, buildings, economy, climate and geography. It also has links to a Catalan dictionary.

### News and views

ⓦwww.barcelonareporter.com Barcelona Reporter offers daily updated news and views from the city in English, pulling in very useful reports from newspapers and other sources.

ⓦwww.diaridebarcelona.com Up-to-the-minute city news, comment, reviews, weather and listings (in Catalan), with a daily city news video slot.

ⓦwww.lecool.com Hip cultural agenda and city guide, available online or as a weekly graphic email.

ⓦwww.vilaweb.cat Online newspaper, directory and portal, updated daily, with excellent links to Catalan sites, many in English. Also links to a huge variety of Barcelona webcams.

# The media

You can buy foreign newspapers at the stalls down the Ramblas, and around Plaça de Catalunya, on Passeig de Gràcia, on Rambla de Catalunya and at Barcelona Sants station. The same stalls often sell international magazines and trade papers too, but if you can't find what you're looking for, try FNAC at El Triangle on Plaça. de Catalunya, which has an excellent ground-floor magazine section.

## Newspapers and magazines

Best of the **local newspapers** is the Barcelona edition of the liberal *El País* (ⓦwww.elpais.es), which has a daily Catalunya supplement and is good on entertainment and

the arts. The conservative Barcelona paper *La Vanguardia* (ⓦwww.lavanguardia.es) also has a good arts and culture listings section on Friday, while *El Periódico* (ⓦwww.elperiodico.com) is more tabloid in style; it also comes in a Catalan edition. *Avui* (ⓦwww.avui.cat) is the chief nationalist paper, printed in Catalan.

Metro (W www.diariometro.es) and *20 Minutos* (W www.20minutos.es), both with useful local listings, are given away free in the city on weekday mornings. For wall-to-wall coverage of sport (for which, in Barcelona, read FC Barcelona), buy the specialist dailies *Mundo Deportivo* (W www.elmundodeportivo.es /fcbarcelona) or *Sport* (W www.sport.es).

The two most useful weekly **city listings publications** are *Guia del Ocio* (W www .guiadelociobcn.es), a small paperback-book-sized magazine (in Spanish), and the newer, magazine-format *Time Out Barcelona* (W www.timeout.cat; in Catalan), both available at kiosks all over the city.

### English-language publications

English-language publications include *Catalonia Today* (W www.cataloniatoday .cat), a weekly newspaper about the city and region. *Barcelona Metropolitan* (W www .barcelona-metropolitan.com) is a free monthly magazine for English-speakers living in Barcelona, available from hotels, bars and other outlets; or there's *b-guided* (W www .b-guided.com), a painfully cool quarterly style magazine on sale at newsagents. There's also the free monthly *Barcelona Connect* (W www.barcelonaconnect.com), containing an idiosyncratic mixture of news, views, reviews and classified ads.

### Television

In Catalunya you can pick up **two national TV channels,** TVE1 and TVE2 (La 2), a couple of **Catalan-language channels**, TV3 and Canal 33, and the private Antena 3, Cuatro (ie, Four), Tele 5 and La Sexta (The Sixth) channels. In Barcelona you can also get the city-run **Barcelona TV** (W www .barcelonatv.com), which is useful for information about local events, and news programmes on the otherwise subscriber-only Digital Plus channel. TVs in most pensions and small hotels tend to offer these stations, with cable and satellite channels available in higher-rated hotels.

# Travel essentials

### Addresses

Addresses are written as: c/Picasso 2, 4° – which means Picasso street (*carrer*) number two, fourth floor. You may also see *esquerra*, meaning "left-hand" (apartment or office); *dreta* is right; *centro* centre. C/Picasso s/n means the building has no number (*sense numero*). In the gridded streets of the Eixample, building numbers run from south to north (ie lower numbers at the Plaça de Catalunya end) and from west to east (lower numbers at Plaça d'Espanya).

The main address abbreviations used in Barcelona (and this book) are: Avgda. (for Avinguda, avenue); c/ (for Carrer, street); Pg. (for Passeig, more a boulevard than a street); Bxda. (for Baixada, alley); Ptge. (for Passatge, passage); and Pl. (for Plaça, square).

### Admission charges

Admission charges for all attractions vary between €3 and €12, though most museums and galleries cost around €5 or €6. Many offer free admission on the first Sunday of every month, and most museums are free on the saints' days of February 12, April 23 and September 24. There's usually a reduction or free entrance if you show a student, youth or senior citizen card. Several discount cards are also available (see p.31), that give heavily reduced admission to Barcelona's museums and galleries – worth considering if you're planning to see everything that the city has to offer.

## Churches

Apart from the cathedral (La Seu) and the Sagrada Família – the two churches you're most likely to visit, which have tourist-friendly opening hours – other churches are usually kept locked, opening only for worship in the early morning (around 7–8am) and the evening (around 6–9pm). For all churches, "decorous" dress is required, with no shorts or bare shoulders.

## Costs

Barcelona is not a particularly cheap place to visit and it's more expensive on the whole than other major cities in Spain. However, it still rates as pretty good value when compared with the cost of visiting cities in Britain, France or Germany, especially when it comes to dining out or getting around on public transport. Hotel prices are the main drain on the budget, and they have increased considerably over the last few years. Realistically, you'll be paying from €70 a night for a room in a simple pension, and from €100 for a three-star hotel. Still, once you're there, a one-day public transport pass gives you the freedom of the city for €5.50, and most museums and galleries cost €3–6 (though a few of the showpiece attractions have higher entry fees). A set three-course lunch goes for around €9–15, and dinner from around €20, though of course the Michelin-starrred destination restaurants are much pricier – even

so, at up to €100 a head, they're still a far better deal than the equivalent places in London or Paris.

## Electricity

The electricity supply is 220v and plugs come with two round pins – bring an adaptor (and transformer) to use UK and US cellphone chargers, etc.

## Embassies and consulates

Most countries have their embassies in Madrid and maintain a consulate in Barcelona. You'll need to contact them if you lose your passport or need other assistance. Most consulates are open to the public for enquiries Mon–Fri, usually 9am–1pm & 3–5pm, though the morning shift is the most reliable.

### Foreign consulates in Barcelona

**Australia** Pl. Gala Placidia 1–3, Gràcia, Ⓜ Diagonal/FGC Gràcia ☎ 934 909 013, ⓦ www.embaustralia.es.
**Britain** Avgda. Diagonal 477, Eixample, Ⓜ Hospital Clinic ☎ 933 666 200, ⓦ www.ukinspain.com.
**Canada** c/Elisenda de Pinós 10, Sarrià, FGC Reina Elisenda ☎ 932 042 700, ⓦ www.canada-es.org.
**Republic of Ireland** Gran Via Carles III 94, Les Corts, Ⓜ Maria Cristina/Les Corts ☎ 934 915 021.
**New Zealand** Trav. de Gràcia 64, Gràcia, FGC Gràcia ☎ 932 090 399, ⓦ www.nzembassy.com.
**USA** Pg. de la Reina Elisenda 23, Sàrria, FGC Reina Elisenda ☎ 932 802 227, ⓦ www.embusa.es.

### Budget Barcelona

Here's how to keep costs to a minimum in Barcelona.
• Eat your main meal of the day at lunchtime, when the *menú del dia* offers fantastic value.
• Buy a public transport travel pass, which will save you around forty percent on every ride.
• Purchase one of the useful city discount cards or packages.
• Visit museums and galleries on the first Sunday of the month, when admission is usually free.
• Drink and eat *inside* cafés – there's usually a surcharge for terrace service.
• Bring along any student, youth or senior citizen card you're entitled to carry, as they often attract discounts on museum, gallery and attraction charges.
• Take advantage of the discount nights at the cinema (Mon & sometimes Wed), and at the theatre (Tues).
• Go to the Ramblas, La Seu, Santa María del Mar, Parc de la Ciutadella, Parc de la Collserola, Port Vell, Port Olímpic, city beaches, Els Encants flea market, Diagonal Mar/Fòrum, Olympic stadium, Caixa Fórum and Parc Güell – all free.

## Catalan names

Traditionally, a person gets two surnames, one from dad and one from mum. They are not always used, but it explains why many of the names given in this book may be longer than those you are used to seeing. Thus, Antoni Gaudí i Cornet took Gaudí from his father and Cornet from his mother (the "i" simply means "and").

### Emergency services

In an emergency, dial: ☏112 for ambulance, police and fire services; ☏061 for ambulance; ☏080 for fire service; ☏091 for national police. For local police numbers see "Police and crime", below.

### Entry and residence requirements

EU citizens need only a **valid national identity card or passport** to enter Spain. Other Europeans, and citizens of the United States, Canada, Australia and New Zealand, require a passport but no visa and can stay as a tourist for up to ninety days. Other nationalities may need to get a visa from a Spanish embassy or consulate before departure. Visa requirements do change and it's always advisable to check the current situation before leaving home.

Most EU citizens who want to stay in Spain for longer than three months, rather than just visit as a tourist, need to register at the Oficina de Extranjeros (foreigners' office), where they'll be issued with a residence certificate. You don't need the certificate if you're an EU citizen living and working legally in Barcelona, or if you're legally self-employed or a student. US citizens can apply for one ninety-day extension, showing proof of funds, but this must be done from outside Spain. Other nationalities wishing to extend their stay will need to get a special visa from a Spanish embassy or consulate before departure.

The office in Barcelona dealing with residency matters for foreigners is the **Oficina de Extranjeros**, Avgda. Marqués de l'Argentera 4, La Ribera, ⓂBarceloneta ☏935 201 410 (Mon–Fri 9am–2pm), though this is scheduled to be replaced by new offices at c/Murcia 42, Sant Marti, ⓂNavas/Clot. There's also a telephone helpline on ☏012 (Mon–Fri 9am–5pm) that deals with all aspects of **residency and immigration**, and you'll find more information at ⓦwww.gencat.cat.

Anyone planning to stay in Barcelona for more than just a few weeks will need a *Numero de Identidade de Extranjeros* (NIE), an ID number that's essential if you're to open a bank account, sign a utilities, job or accommodation contract, or for many other financial transactions. Applications are dealt with at Pg. de Joan Borbó 32, Barceloneta, ⓂBarceloneta ☏932 440 610, ⓦwww.mir.es.

### Health

The **European Health Insurance Card** gives EU citizens access to Spanish state public health services under reciprocal agreement. While this will provide free or reduced-cost medical care in the event of minor injuries and emergencies, it won't cover every eventuality – and it only applies to EU citizens in possession of the card – so travel insurance (see next section) is essential.

For minor health complaints look for the green cross of a **pharmacy** (*farmàcia*), where highly trained staff can give advice (often in English), and are able to dispense many drugs (including some antibiotics) available only on prescription in other countries. Usual hours are weekdays 9am–1pm & 4–8pm. At least one in each neighbourhood is open daily 24hr (and marked as such), or phone ☏010 for information on those open out of hours – Farmacia Clapies, Ramblas 98, ⓂLiceu (☏933 012 843) is a convenient 24hr pharmacy. A list of out-of-hours pharmacies can also be found in the window of each pharmacy store.

Any local **health-care centre** (Centre d'Atenció Primària, CAP) can provide non-emergency assistance. In the old town, there's one at Ptge. Pau 1, Barri Gòtic, ⓂDrassanes ☏933 425 549, and another at c/del Rec Comtal 24, Sant Pere, ⓂArc de Triomf ☏933 101 421 (both Mon–Fri 9am–8pm, Sat 9am–5pm). Or call ☏010 or consult ⓦwww.bcn.cat for a full list.

For emergency hospital treatment, call ℡061 or go to one of the following **central hospitals**, which have 24hr accident and emergency services: Centre Perecamps, Avgda. Drassanes 13–15, El Raval, ⓂDrassanes ℡934 410 600; Hospital Clinic i Provincial, c/Villaroel 170, Eixample, ⓂHospital Clinic ℡932 275 400; Hospital del Mar, Pg. Marítim 25–29, Vila Olímpica, ⓂCiutadella-Vila Olímpica ℡932 483 000; Hospital de la Santa Creu i Sant Pau, c/Sant Antoni Maria Claret, Eixample, ⓂHospital de Sant Pau ℡932 919 000.

## Insurance

You should take out a comprehensive **insurance policy** before travelling to Barcelona, to cover against loss, theft, illness or injury. A typical policy will provide cover for loss of baggage, tickets and – up to a certain limit – cash or travellers' cheques, as well as cancellation or curtailment of your journey. With medical coverage you should ascertain whether benefits will be paid as treatment proceeds or only after you return home, and whether there is a twenty-four-hour medical emergency number. When securing baggage cover, make sure that the per-article limit will cover your most valuable possession. Most policies exclude so-called dangerous sports unless an extra premium is paid: in Spain this can mean most water sports are excluded, though probably not things like bike tours or hiking.

If you need to make a claim, you should keep receipts for medicines and medical treatment, and in the event you have anything stolen you must obtain an official statement from the police – see the section on "Police and crime" for where to go in Barcelona to make a report.

## Internet access

There are Internet shops and cybercafés all over Barcelona, and competition has driven prices down to around €1 an hour. A stroll down the Ramblas, or through the Barri Gòtic, La Ribera, El Raval and Gràcia will reveal a host of possibilities. Most youth hostels and many small pensions provide cheap or free Internet access for their guests, but hotel business centres or hotel bedrooms wired for access tend to be far more expensive than going out on the street to an internet place. Wireless access is widespread in bars, hotels and other public "hotspots", though if the networks are password-protected you'll have to check first with your host to get online. If you take your own laptop make sure you've got insurance cover and all the relevant plugs and adaptors for recharging.

## Language schools

The **Generalitat** (the government of Catalonia) offers low-cost **Catalan classes** for non-Spanish speakers through the Consorci per a la Normalització Lingüística (ⓌWww.cpnl.cat; call ℡010 for information). Otherwise, the cheapest Spanish or Catalan classes in Barcelona are at the Escola Oficial d'Idiomes, Avgda. Drassanes s/n, El Raval,

---

### Rough Guides travel insurance

Rough Guides has teamed up with Columbus Direct to offer you travel insurance that can be tailored to suit your needs.

Readers can choose from many different travel products, including a low-cost backpacker option for long stays; a short-break option for **city getaways**; a typical **holiday package** option and many others. There are also annual **multi-trip policies** for those who travel regularly, with variable levels of cover available. Different sports and activities (trekking, skiing, etc) can be included, if required.

Rough Guides travel insurance is availabe to the residents of 36 different countries with different language options to choose from via our website – ⓌWww.roughroughguidesinsurance.com – where you can purchase the insurance.

Alternatively, UK residents can call ℡0800/083 9507; US citizens ℡1800/749-4922; and Australians ℡1300/669 999. All other nationalities should call ℡+44 870/890 2843.

ⓂDrassanes ☎933 249 330, ⓦwww.eoibd
.es – expect queues when you sign on.
Language courses for beginners are also
offered at Barcelona University, Gran Via de
les Corts Catalanes 585, Eixample,
ⓂUniversitat ☎934 035 519, ⓦwww.ub.es.
There's a basic Spanish and Catalan primer
in our "Language" section, p.289.

## Laundry services

There are inexpensive laundry services in
most of the youth hostels and some
pensions; hotels will charge considerably
more. **Self-service laundries** include
Lavomatic, at Pl. Joaquim Xirau 1, Barri
Gòtic, ⓂDrassanes ☎933 425 119, and
c/Consolat del Mar 43–45, Pl. del Palau, La
Ribera, ⓂBarceloneta ☎932 684 768 (both
open Mon–Sat 9am–9pm); and LavaExpress,
at six city locations, including c/Ferlandina
34, El Raval, ⓂUniversitat, ☎933 183 018,
ⓦwww.lavaxpres,com (daily 8am–11pm). At
La Lavanderia de Ana, c/Carme 63, El Raval,
ⓂLiceu, ☎934 437 280 (Mon–Sat 9am–
8pm) you can leave your laundry for a
standard wash-and-dry (from around €7–8).

## Left luggage

At Barcelona Sants the left-luggage office
(consigna) is open daily 7am–11pm and
costs €3–4.50 a day. There are lockers at
Estació de França, Passeig de Gràcia
station and Barcelona Nord bus station (all
6am–11.30pm; €3–4.50).

## Libraries

The **British Council**, c/Amigó 83, Sant
Gervasi, FGC Muntaner ☎932 419 977,
ⓦwww.britishcouncil.es, has the only English-
language lending library in Barcelona. There's
also a full arts and events programme here.

The Catalan national library, the **Biblioteca
de Catalunya**, is at c/de l'Hospital 56, El
Raval, ⓂLiceu ☎932 702 300, ⓦwww.bnc
.cat (Mon–Fri 9am–8pm, Sat 9am–2pm) – a
letter of academic reference is required,
though there is the **Biblioteca Sant Pau-
Santa Creu** (public library) in the same
building (Tues, Thurs & Sat 10am–2pm,
Mon, Wed & Fri 3.30–8pm).

The **Mediateca** library at the Caixa Fórum
arts centre, Avgda. Marquès de Comillas

6–8, Montjuïc ⓂEspanya (☎934 768 651,
ⓦwww.mediatecaonline.net), is an open-
access library for arts and culture books,
music, magazines and reference material.

## Lost property

Anything recovered by the police, or left on
public transport, is sent to the **Oficina de
Troballes** (municipal lost property office), at Pl.
Carles Pi i Sunyer 8–10, Barri Gòtic, ⓂJaume
I/Catalunya (Mon–Fri 9am–2pm; phone
enquiries Mon–Sat 8am–2pm, ☎010). Most
items are kept for three months. You could
also try the TMB (public transport) customer
service centre at Universitat metro station.

## Mail

The main post office in Barcelona, is near the
harbour in the old town, while each city
neighbourhood also has a post office,
though these have far less comprehensive
opening hours and services. However, if all
you need are stamps it's usually quicker to
visit a tobacconist (look for the brown-and-
yellow *tabac* sign), found on virtually every
street. These can also weigh letters and
small parcels, advise about postal rates, and
send express mail (*urgente*). Use the yellow
on-street postboxes and put your mail in the
flap marked *províncies i estranger* or *altres
destins*. Letters or cards take around three
to four days to European countries, five days
to a week to North America.

### Postal services

**Main post office** (*Correus*) Pl. d'Antoni López, at
the eastern end of Pg. de Colom, Barri Gòtic,
ⓂBarceloneta/Jaume I ☎934 868 050, ⓦwww
.correos.es (Mon–Fri 8.30am–9.30pm, Sat
8.30am–2pm). There's a poste restante/general
delivery service here (*llista de correus*), plus express
post, fax service, mobile phone top-ups, phonecard
sales and bill payments.
**Postal Transfer** Pl. Urquinaona at c/Roger
de Lluria, Eixample, ⓂUrquinaonoa (Mon–Fri
10am–11pm, Sat 11am–midnight, Sun noon–
11pm). Offers after-hours postal services plus money
exchange, fax, photocopying and phonecard sales.

## Maps

The city tourist offices charge a euro for their
maps – you can pick up a good free one

instead from the information desk on the ground floor of El Corte Inglés department store, right outside the main tourist office. With that, and the maps in this book, you'll easily find your way around. You can also check the location of any building or address on the city council's extremely useful **interactive street plan** at ⓦwww.bcn.cat (click on "Plànol BCN", or "BCN map" in the English-language version).

For an excellent **fold-out street plan** on durable waterproof paper, look no further than *Barcelona: The Rough Guide Map* which also includes practical information and dining, lodging and shopping listings. Map and travel shops in your home country should be able to supply a copy of this and, if you need one, a road map of Catalunya or northern Spain (by Michelin, Firestone or Rand McNally). Alternatively, try mail order from ⓦwww.amazon.com or a map specialist like ⓦwww.stanfords.co.uk or ⓦwww.randmcnally.com. In Barcelona, you'll find a good selection of maps in most bookshops and at street newspaper kiosks or petrol stations.

## Money

Spain's **currency** is the euro (€), with notes issued in denominations of 5, 10, 20, 50, 100, 200 and 500 euros, and coins in denominations of 1, 2, 5, 10, 20 and 50 cents, and 1 and 2 euros.

By far the easiest way to get money is to use your bank debit card to withdraw cash from an **ATM**, found all over the city, including the airport and major train stations. You can usually withdraw up to €200 a day and instructions are offered in English once you insert your card. Make sure you have a personal identification number (PIN) that's designed to work overseas, and take a note of your bank's emergency contact number in case the machine swallows the card. Some European debit cards can also be used directly in shops to pay for purchases; you'll need to check first with your bank.

All major **credit cards** are accepted in hotels, restaurants and shops, and for tours, tickets and transport, though don't count on being able to use them in every small hotel or backstreet café. You can also use your credit card in an ATM to withdraw cash.

Spanish **banks** (*bancos*) and savings banks (*caixas*) have branches throughout Barcelona, with concentrations down the Ramblas and around Plaça de Catalunya. Normal banking hours are Monday to Friday from 8.30am to 2pm, although from October until May most institutions also open Thursday 4pm to 6.30pm (savings banks) or Saturday 9am to 1pm (banks).

For out-of-hours banking you can use *bureaux de change* or a **foreign-exchange office** (*canvi, cambio*), found down the Ramblas (often open until midnight), at Barcelona Sants (daily 8am–8pm), El Corte Inglés department store, Pl. de Catalunya (Mon–Sat 10am–9.30pm), or the Turisme de Catalunya tourist office, Pl. de Catalunya 17 (Mon–Sat 9am–9pm, Sun 9am–2pm). Exchange offices don't always charge commission, though their rates aren't usually as good as the banks. Other exchange options are the automatic currency exchange machines (available at the airport, Barcelona Sants and outside some banks) or one of the larger hotels or travel agents, though again rates can be variable.

## Opening hours and public holidays

Basic **working hours** are Monday to Saturday 9.30 or 10am to 1.30pm and 4.30 to 8 or 9pm, though many offices and shops don't open on Saturday afternoons. However, local cafés, bars and markets open earlier, usually from around 7am, while shopping centres, major stores and large supermarkets tend to remain open all day from 10am to 9pm, with some even opening on Sunday. In the lazy days of summer everything becomes a bit more relaxed, with offices working until around 3pm and many shops and restaurants closing for part or the whole of August.

Most of the showpiece **museums and galleries** in Barcelona open all day, from 10am to 8pm, though some of the smaller collections and attractions close over lunchtime between 1 and 4pm. On Sundays most open in the morning only and on Mondays most are closed all day. On public holidays, most museums and galleries have Sunday opening hours, while pretty much everything is closed on Christmas Day and New Year's Day.

Not all **public and bank holidays** in Spain are observed in Catalunya, and vice versa. On the days listed below, and during the many local festivals (see Chapter 15), you'll find most shops closed, though bars and restaurants tend to stay open.

## Barcelona's public holidays

**January 1** Cap d'Any, New Year's Day
**January 6** Epifanía, Epiphany
**Variable** Good Friday & Easter Monday
**May 1** Día del Treball, May Day/Labour Day
**June 24** Día de Sant Joan, St John's Day
**August 15** L'Assumpció, Assumption of the Virgin
**September 11** Diada Nacional, Catalan National Day
**September 24** Festa de la Mercè, Our Lady of Mercy, Barcelona's patron saint
**October 12** Día de la Hispanidad, Spanish National Day
**November 1** Tots Sants, All Saints' Day
**December 6** Día de la Constitució, Constitution Day
**December 8** La Imaculada, Immaculate Conception
**December 25** Nadal, Christmas Day
**December 26** Sant Esteve, St Stephen's Day

## Police and crime

Catalunya has its own autonomous police force, the **Mossos d'Esquadra** (@www .gencat.net/mossos), in navy-blue uniforms with red trim. They have gradually taken over most of the local duties traditionally carried out by the other police services in Spain, namely the **Policía Nacional** (@www.policia.es) – the national police, in uniforms resembling blue combat gear – and the **Guàrdia Urbana** (@www.bcn.es/guardiaurbana), municipal police in blue shirts and navy jackets. There's also the **Guàrdia Civil**, a national paramilitary force in green uniforms, seen guarding some public buildings, and at airports and border crossings.

In theory you're supposed to carry some kind of **identification** at all times, and the police can stop you in the street and demand to see it. In practice they're rarely bothered if you're clearly a tourist – and a photocopy of your passport, or photo-driving licence should suffice. The police tend to be little worried about personal use of cannabis, though public possession or consumption of drugs is illegal. Larger quantities (and any other drugs) are a very different matter, and if you're arrested or detained for a drugs offence, don't expect any sympathy or help from your consulate.

If you're robbed, you need to go to the police to report it, not least because your insurance company will require a police report. Don't expect a great deal of concern if your loss is relatively small – but do expect the process of completing forms and formalities to take ages.

The easiest place to report a crime is at the **Guàrdia Urbana station** at Ramblas 43, opposite Pl. Reial, @Liceu @932 562 430 (24hr; English spoken), though there's a Guàrdia Urbana office in each city district (shown on their website).

However, to get a police report for your insurance you need to go to the **Mossos d'Esquadra station** at c/Nou de la Rambla 76–80, El Raval, @Paral.lel @933 062 300. You can fill in a report online (under "Serveis", then "Denúncies per internet" on the website, English option available), but you'll still have to go to the office within 72hr to sign the document.

## Staying safe

Barcelona has a reputation as a city plagued by petty crime, but you don't need to be unduly paranoid. Take all reasonable precautions, and your trip should be a safe one. Sling bags across your body, not off one shoulder; don't carry wallets in back pockets; and don't hang bags on the back of a café chair. Make photocopies of your passport, leaving the original and any tickets in the hotel safe. Be on your guard when on public transport, or on the crowded Ramblas and the medieval streets to either side – at night, avoid unlit streets and dark alleys. While you can take many beggars at face value (deciding whether or not you give them money), you should beware of people directly accosting you or who in any other manner try to distract you – like the "helpful" person pointing out bird shit (shaving cream or something similar) on your jacket while someone relieves you of your money.

In an **emergency**, contact the police on the following numbers: Mossos d'Esquadra ☎088, Policía Nacional ☎091, Guàrdia Urbana ☎092.

## Smoking laws

Since January 1, 2006, smoking in public places has been regulated by law. You can't smoke in public buildings, while bars, restaurants, clubs and cafés smaller than 100 square metres can choose to be entirely smoking or non-smoking – signs on the door tell you which it is. Premises bigger than 100 square metres can have separate smoking areas. Compared to other countries with smoking restrictions in force, you'll find there's still an awful lot of puffing going on, though the ban is generally observed on public transport and in public buildings.

## Taxes

Local sales tax, **IVA**, is seven percent in hotels and restaurants, and sixteen percent in shops. It's usually included in the price though not always, so some hotel or restaurant bills can come as a bit of a surprise – though quoted prices should always make it clear whether or not tax is included.

## Telephones

Spanish **telephone numbers** have 9 digits, and in Barcelona the first two digits of all landline phone numbers are 93 (the regional prefix), which you dial even when calling from within the city. Spanish mobile numbers begin with a 6, freephone numbers begin 900, while other 90-plus- and 80-plus-digit numbers are nationwide standard-rate or special-rate services. To call Barcelona from abroad, dial your international access number + 34 (Spain country code) + 9-digit number.

**Public telephones** in Barcelona have instructions in English, and accept coins, credit cards and phonecards. Phonecards (*targetes/tarjetas*) with discounted rates for calls are available in tobacconists, newsagents and post offices, issued in various denominations either by Telefónica (the dominant operator) or one of its rivals. Credit cards are not recommended for local and national calls, since most have a minimum charge which is far more than a normal call is likely to cost. It's also best to avoid making calls from the phone

in your hotel room, as even local calls will be slapped with a heavy surcharge.

You can make **international calls** from any public pay-phone, but it's cheaper to go to one of the ubiquitous **phone centres**, or *locutorios*, which specialize in discounted overseas connections – you'll find them scattered through the old city, particularly in the Raval. If the rates to the country that you want to call are not posted, just ask. You'll then be assigned a cabin to make your calls, and afterwards you pay in cash. For reverse-charge calls, dial the **international operator** (☎1008 Europe, ☎1005 rest of the world).

Most European **mobile phones** will work in Barcelona, though it's worth checking with your provider whether you need to get international access switched on and whether there are any extra charges involved. Even though prices are coming down, it's still expensive to use your own mobile extensively while abroad, and you will pay for receiving incoming calls for example. Provided your own phone isn't blocked you could simply buy a local **SIM card** instead for your mobile, from operators like Vodafone (ⓦwww.vodafone.es) or Movistar (ⓦwww.movistar.es). Or if you plan to spend some time in the city it's almost certainly better to buy a **Spanish mobile**, as the cheapest non-contract, pay-as-you-go phones cost from around €29. You can buy top-up cards, or have them recharged for you, in phone shops and post offices and from ATMs.

### Useful telephone numbers

**Calling home** ☎00 (Spain international access code) + your country code + city/area code minus initial zero + number
**Barcelona general information** ☎010
**National directory enquiries** ☎11818
**The time** ☎093
**Alarm call** ☎096
ⓦwww.paginasamarillas.es Yellow Pages finds any business in Barcelona and has links to the Paginas Blancas (White Pages), to find a person.

## Ticket agencies

You can buy concert, sporting and exhibition tickets with a credit card using the **Servi-Caixa** (ⓦwww.servicaixa.com) automatic dispensing machines in branches of La Caixa savings bank. It's also possible to order tickets online through ServiCaixa or **TelEn-trada** (☎902 101 212, ⓦwww.telentrada .com). Both websites have English-language versions. In addition, there's a concert ticket desk in the FNAC store, El Triangle, Plaça de Catalunya, while for advance tickets for all Ajuntament-sponsored concerts and events visit the Palau de la Virreina, Ramblas 99.

## Time

Barcelona is 1hr ahead of the UK, 6hr ahead of New York and Toronto, 9hr ahead of Los Angeles, 9hr behind Sydney and 11hr behind Auckland. This applies except for brief periods during the changeovers to and from daylight saving (in Spain the clocks go forward in the last week of March, back again in the last week of Oct).

## Tipping

In most restaurants and bars service is considered to be included in the price of meals and drinks (hence the premium you pay for sitting at a terrace). Tipping is more a recognition that service was good or exceptional than an expected part of the server's wage. Locals actually tip very little, leaving a few cents or rounding up the change for a coffee or a drink, and a euro or two for most meals. However, fancier restaurants may specifically indicate that service is not included, in which case you will be expected to leave ten to fifteen percent. Taxi drivers usually get around five percent, more if they have helped you with bags or been similarly useful, while hotel porters should be tipped a euro or two for their assistance.

## Toilets

Public toilets are few and far between, and only averagely clean. Bars and restaurants are more likely to have proper (and cleaner) toilets, though you can't guarantee it – even in the poshest of places. Ask for *toaleta* or *serveis* (*lavabo* or *servicios* in Spanish). Dones or Damas (Ladies) and Homes/Hombres or Caballeros (Gentlemen) are the usual signs.

## Travellers with disabilities

There's no better single resource for city information for disabled travellers than the

**AccessibleBarcelona** website (ⓦwww .accessiblebarcelona.com). The city informa-tion line (☎010, English spoken) also has accessibility information for sights and services, while the Ajuntament information office in Plaça Sant Miquel (see "Informa-tion") can provide a map showing accessible routes for tourists.

Barcelona's **airport** and **Aerobús** are fully accessible to travellers in wheelchairs, though the bus gets very busy and can be difficult if you have lots of luggage. At **Barcelona Sants** there are no access ramps for the trains themselves, and the steps and escalators are fairly steep, but there are access ramps at Estació de França and a lift to the platforms at Plaça de Catalunya's FGC station. Using the **metro** is more problematic, though improve-ments are ongoing – at present, only lines 1, 2 and 11 are fully accessible, with elevators at major stations (including Plaça de Catalunya, Universitat, Paral.lel, Passeig de Gràcia and Sagrada Família) from the street to the platforms. However, all **city buses** have been adapted for wheelchair use, with automatic ramps/steps and a designated wheelchair space inside; simply ring the bell on the bus door. All trams and night buses are also wheelchair-accessible, as is the sightseeing Bus Turístic. The Transports Metropolitans de Barcelona (TMB) website (ⓦwww.tmb.net, English version available) lets you view all adapted metro stations and bus routes (look under "Transport for everyone"). If you need a **wheelchair-accessible taxi** call Taxi Amic (☎934 208 088, ⓦwww.taxi-amic-adaptat .com, English rarely spoken).

Out on the streets, the number of acoustic traffic-light signals is slowly growing, while dropped kerbs are being put in place across the city. However, most old-town attractions, including the Museu Picasso, have steps, cobbles or other impediments to access. Fully accessible **sights and attractions** include MNAC, Fundacío Antoni Tàpies, Fundacío Joan Miró, La Pedrera (though not the roof terrace), Caixa Forum, CosmoCaixa, Museu d'Història de Catalunya and the Palau de la Música.

### Useful contacts

**AccessibleBarcelona** ☎934 285 227, ⓦwww .accessiblebarcelona.com. An invaluable website that lists and reviews accessible city tourist sights, hotels, bars and restaurants. You can also book accommodation – all inspected for suitability – and arrange airport transfers and wheelchair-friendly guided tours. **Institut Municipal de Persones amb Discapacitat** Avgda. Diagonal 233, 1°, Eixample, ⓜGlòries ☎934 132 775, ⓦwww.bcn.cat/accessible. Has information (some in English) on most aspects of life and travel in the city for disabled residents and visitors.

## Water

Water from the tap is safe to drink, but it doesn't taste very nice. You'll always be given bottled mineral water in a bar or restaurant.

## Women's Barcelona

**Ca la Dona**, c/de Casp 38, Eixample, ⓜUrquinaona ☎934 127 161, ⓦwww.caladona.org, is a women's centre hosting meetings for women's groups, and with a library and bar. The Ajuntament's official women's resource centre, the **Centre Municipal d'Informació i Recursos per a les Dones (CIRD)**, c/Camèlies 36–38, Gràcia, ⓜAlfons X ☎932 850 357, ⓦwww.cird.bcn.cat (Mon–Thurs 9am–2pm & 4–7pm, Fri 9am–2pm), publishes a monthly calendar of events and news (see the website). **Llibreria Pròleg**, c/Dagueria 13, Barri Gòtic, ⓜJaume I ☎933 192 425, ⓦwww.llibreriaproleg.com, is a bookshop specializing in women's issues. The **Barcelona Women's Network** (ⓦwww.bcnwomensnetwork.com) is a social, business and networking club for English-speaking women living and working in the city.

# The City

# The City

# The Ramblas

I t is a telling comment on Barcelona's character that one can recommend a single street – the **Ramblas** – as a highlight. No day in the city seems complete without a stroll down at least part of what, for Spanish poet Federico García Lorca, was "the only street in the world which I wish would never end". Lined with cafés, shops, restaurants and newspaper kiosks, and thronged by tourists, locals, buskers and performance artists, it's at the heart of Barcelona's life and self-image. There are important buildings and sights along the way, not least the Liceu Opera House and the famous **Boqueria** food market, but undoubtedly it's the street life which is the greatest attraction – and that you're a part of it every time you set foot on Spain's most famous thoroughfare.

The name, derived from the Arabic *ramla* (sand), refers to the bed of the seasonal stream that once flowed here. In the dry season, the channel was used as a road, and by the fourteenth century this had been paved over in recognition of its use as a link between the harbour and the old town. In the nineteenth century, benches and decorative trees were added, overlooked by stately balconied buildings, and today – in a city choked with traffic – this wide tree-lined swath is still given over to pedestrians, with cars forced up the narrow strips of road on either side. There are **metro stops** at Catalunya (top of the Ramblas), Liceu (middle) and Drassanes (bottom), or you can walk the entire length in about twenty minutes.

The Ramblas splits the old town areas of Barcelona in half, with the Barri Gòtic on the east flank of the avenue and El Raval on the west. It also actually comprises **five separate sections** strung head to tail – from north to south, Rambla Canaletes, Estudis, Sant Josep, Caputxins and Santa Mònica – though it's rare to hear them referred to as such. However, you will notice changes as you walk down the Ramblas, primarily that the streets on either side become a little less polished – even seedy – as you get closer to the harbour. The shops, meanwhile, reflect the mixed clientele, from patisseries to pizza takeaways, and stores selling handcrafted jewellery to shops full of sombreros, bullfight posters ("your name here"), football shirts and imitation Gaudí ashtrays. On the central avenue under the plane trees you'll find pet canaries, rabbits, tropical fish, flowers, plants, postcards and books. You can buy sunglasses from a blanket stretched out on the ground, cigarettes from itinerant salespeople, have your palm read and your portrait painted, or just listen to the buskers and watch the pavement artists. Human statues are much in evidence and will take any coins you can spare; card and dice sharps, operating from foldaway tables and cardboard boxes, will skin you for much more if you let them. Drag yourself home with the dawn, and you'll rub shoulders with the street cleaners, watchful policemen and bleary-eyed stallholders. It's a never-ending show, of which visitors and locals alike rarely tire.

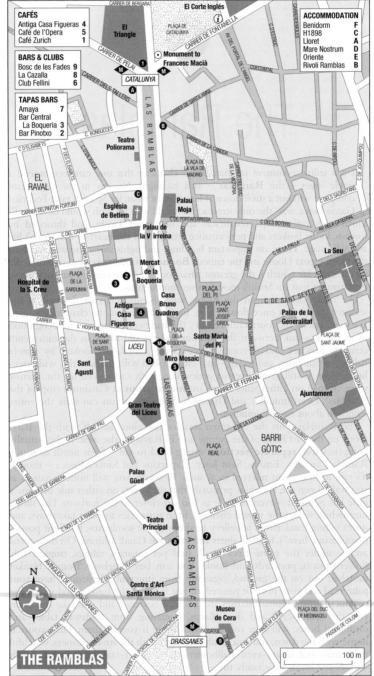

**CAFÉS**

Antiga Casa Figueras **4**
Café de l'Opera **5**
Café Zurich **1**

**BARS & CLUBS**

Bosc de les Fades **9**
La Cazalla **8**
Club Fellini **6**

**TAPAS BARS**

Amaya **7**
Bar Central
La Boqueria **3**
Bar Pinotxo **2**

**ACCOMMODATION**

Benidorm **F**
H1898 **C**
Lloret **A**
Mare Nostrum **D**
Oriente **E**
Rivoli Ramblas **B**

CARRER DE BERGARA

El Corte Inglés

PLAÇA DE CATALUNYA

CARRER DE FONTANELLA

El Triangle

CARRER DE PELAI

Monument to Francesc Macià

M CATALUNYA M

A

LAS RAMBLAS

CARRER DELS TALLERS

CARRER DE SANTA ANNA

B

AV DEL PORTAL DE L'ANGEL

C DE COMTAL

C. BONSUCCES

Teatre Poliorama

CARRER DE LA CANUDA

PLAÇA DE LA VILA DE MADRID

DE LA MÚTOTA

CATEDRAL

C DE RIPOLL

C DELS SAGRISTANS

C DE JOAQUIM PONS

EL RAVAL

C D'ELISABETS

P DES ELISABETS

C DE XUCLÀ

Església de Betlem

CARRER DEL PINTOR FORTUNY

C

Palau Moja

CARRER DEL DUC

C DE PORTAFERRISSA

C DELS BOTERS

AV DE LA CATEDRAL

La Seu

C DEL CARME

Palau de la V irreina

CARRER DE PETRITXOL

C DE LA PALLA

C DELS COMTES

C DE LES ÒRRESTES SE

PLAÇA DE LA GARDUNYA

Mercat de la Boqueria

CARRER BANYS NOUS

C DE SANT SEVER

C DEL PI

PLAÇA DEL PI

PLAÇA SANT JOSEP ORIOL

C DEL CALL

C DE L'ARC DE SANT RAMON DEL CALL

Palau de la Generalitat

Hospital de la S. Creu

3 2

Casa Bruno Quadros

Santa Maria del Pi

PLAÇA DE SANT JAUME

CARRER DE L'HOSPITAL

Antiga Casa Figueras 4

PLAÇA DE SANT AGUSTI

PLAÇA DE LA BOQUERIA

C DE LA BOQUERIA

PLAÇA DE SANT JAUME

CARRER D'EN ROBADOR

Sant Agusti

LICEU M

D

Miro Mosaic 5

CUDALLERS

Ajuntament

CARRER DE FERRAN

CARRER DE LA JUNTA DE COMERÇ

LAS RAMBLAS

Gran Teatre del Liceu

CARRER DE SANT PAU

CARRER DE LA UNIÓ

E

PLAÇA REAL

CARRER DE LA LLEONA

CARRER D'AVINYÓ

BARRI GÒTIC

C DE CARABASSA

C DE LA CIUTAT

PLAÇA DE SANT JAUME

CDEL MARQUÈS DE BARBERÀ

Palau Güell

CARRER NOU DE LA RAMBLA

F

6

Teatre Principal

8

CNOU DE SANT FRANCESC

C DELS ESCUDELLERS

7

C JOSEP PIJOAN

PIGFDA PAU

Centre d'Art Santa Mònica

N

AVINGUDA DE LES DRASSANES

C DEL ARC DEL TEATRE

Museu de Cera

PLAÇA DEL DUC DE MEDINACELI

PASSEIG DE COLOM

LAS RAMBLAS

M DRASSANES

PASSATGE

C DE JOSEP ANSELM CLAVÉ

9

0                    100 m

**THE RAMBLAS**

*Drassanes (Museu Marítim) & Mirador de Colón*

# Plaça de Catalunya

The huge **Plaça de Catalunya** square at the top of the Ramblas stands right at the heart of the city, with the old town and port below it, and the planned Eixample district above and beyond. It was laid out in its present form in the 1920s, centred on a formal arrangement of statues, circular fountains and trees, and is the focal point for local events and demonstrations – notably the mass gathering here on New Year's Eve. The most prominent monument is the towering angular slab and bust dedicated to **Francesc Macià**, leader of the Republican Left, parliamentary deputy for Barcelona and first president of the Generalitat, who died in office in 1933. It was commissioned from the pioneer of Catalan avant-garde sculpture, Josep María Subirachs, perhaps best known for his continuing work on the Sagrada Família cathedral.

For visitors, an initial orientation point is the white-faced **El Corte Inglés** department store on the eastern side of the square, whose ninth-floor cafeteria has some stupendous views. The main tourist office is just across from here, while on the southwest side, over the road from the top of the Ramblas, **El Triangle** shopping centre makes another landmark. Incorporated in its ground floor is the **Café Zurich**, a traditional Barcelona meeting place, whose ranks of outdoor tables – patrolled by supercilious waiters – are a day-long draw for beggars, buskers and pan-pipe bands.

# Rambla Canaletes and Estudis

Heading down from Plaça de Catalunya, the first two stretches of the Ramblas are **Rambla Canaletes**, with its iron fountain (a drink from which supposedly means you'll never leave Barcelona), and **Rambla Estudis**, named after the university (L'Estudi General) that was sited here until the beginning of the eighteenth century. This part is also known locally as Rambla dels Ocells, as it contains a **bird market**, the little captives squawking away from a line of cages on either side of the street.

It seems hard to believe, but this part of the Ramblas became a combat zone during the Spanish Civil War as the city erupted into factionalism. George Orwell (see box, p.48) was caught in the crossfire between the *Café Moka* – the current café of the same name is a modern replacement – and the Poliorama cinema, now the **Teatro Poliorama**. This was built in 1863 as the Royal Academy of Science and Arts, and restored as a theatre in 1985. Further down

---

## The Ramblas statues

You can't move for human statues on the Ramblas, standing on their little home-made plinths. Classical figures and movie characters have always formed part of the parade, most daring you to catch them out in a blink, but there are also plenty of statues prepared to join in the fun, like "Fruit Lady", a one-woman mobile market stall, or "Matador" swirling a cape for the camera. Many are actors (or at least waiters who say they're actors), and others make a claim to art – how else to begin to explain "Tree Sprite", clinging chameleon-like to one of the Ramblas plane trees, or the twin "Bicycling Skeletons"? Then there's the plain weird, like "Lady Under Rock", crushed under a boulder, issuing plaintive shrieks at passers-by, or the kennel-dwelling "Human Dog". They all put in long hours on the Ramblas, gratefully receiving small change, though tourists or no tourists, many of them would probably just turn up anyway, lock the bicycle, put down the battered suitcase and strike the pose. What else is a statue going to do?

## George Orwell in Barcelona

Barcelona is a town with a long history of street-fighting.

*Homage to Catalonia*, 1938

When he first arrived in Barcelona in December 1936, **George Orwell** was much taken with the egalitarian spirit he encountered, as loudspeakers on the Ramblas bellowed revolutionary songs, café waiters refused tips, brothels were collectivized and buildings draped in anarchist flags. After serving as a militiaman on the Aragonese front, Orwell returned on leave to Barcelona in April 1937 to find that everything had changed. Not only had the city lost its revolutionary zeal, but the various leftist parties fighting for the Republican cause had descended into a "miserable internecine scrap". From the **Hotel Continental** (Ramblas 138), where Orwell and his wife Eileen stayed, he observed the deteriorating situation with mounting despair, and when street-fighting broke out in May, Orwell was directly caught up in it. As a member of the Workers Party of Marxist Unification (POUM), Orwell became a target when pro-Communist Assault Guards seized the city telephone exchange near Plaça de Catalunya and began to try to break up the workers' militias. Orwell left the hotel for the **POUM headquarters** (Ramblas 128) just down the street, sited in the building that's now the *Rivoli Ramblas* hotel – a plaque here by the "Banco Popular" sign honours murdered POUM leader Andrés Nin ("victim of Stalinism"). With the trams on the Ramblas abandoned by their drivers as the shooting started, and Assault Guards occupying the adjacent **Café Moka** (Ramblas 126), Orwell holed up with a rifle for three days in the rotunda of the **Teatro Poliorama** (Ramblas 115) opposite, in order to defend the POUM HQ if necessary. Breakfasting sparsely on goat's cheese bought from the Boqueria market (its stalls largely empty), concerned about Eileen and caught up in rumour and counter-rumour, Orwell considered it one of the most unbearable periods of his life.

When the fighting subsided, Orwell returned to the front, where he was shot through the throat by a fascist sniper. Yet that was only the start of his troubles. Recuperating in a sanatorium near Tibidabo, he learned that the POUM had been declared illegal, its members rounded up and imprisoned. He avoided arrest by sleeping out in gutted churches and derelict buildings and playing the part of a tourist by day, looking "as bourgeois as possible", while scrawling POUM graffiti in defiance on the walls of fancy restaurants. Eventually, with passports and papers arranged by the British consul, Orwell and Eileen escaped Barcelona by train – back to the "deep, deep sleep of England" and the writing of his passionate war memoir, *Homage to Catalonia*.

on the right, the **Església de Betlem** (daily 8am–6pm), built in 1681 in Baroque style for the Jesuits, was completely gutted during the Civil War as anarchists sacked the city's churches at will – an activity of which Orwell quietly approved. Consequently, the interior is plain in the extreme, though the main facade on c/del Carme sports a fine sculpted portal and relief.

Opposite the church, the arcaded **Palau Moja** at no. 188 dates from the late eighteenth century and still retains an exterior staircase and elegant great hall. The ground floor of the building is now a cultural bookshop, while the palace's gallery, the **Sala Palau Moja**, is open for art and other exhibitions relating to all things Catalan (Tues–Sat 11am–8pm, Sun 11am–3pm; usually free; ☎933 162 740) – the gallery entrance is around the corner in c/Portaferrissa. Take a look, too, at the illustrated tiles above the **fountain** at the start of c/Portaferrissa, which show the medieval gate (the Porta Ferriça) and market that were once sited here. The streets to the west, towards Avinguda del Portal del Àngel, are good for shopping, especially for clothes.

# Palau de la Virreina

The graceful eighteenth-century **Palau de la Virreina** (Virreina Palace) stands at no. 99 (Ⓜ Liceu), on the corner of c/del Carme, set back slightly from the Ramblas. Commissioned by a Peruvian viceroy, Manuel Amat, and named after the wife who survived him, its five Ramblas-facing bays are adorned with pilasters and Rococo windows. Today the palace is used by the city council's culture department, with a ground-floor shop (Tues–Sat 10am–8.30pm) featuring locally produced arts and crafts and souvenirs and a walk-in **information centre** and ticket office for cultural events. Two galleries are used for changing **exhibitions** of contemporary art and photography (Tues–Fri 11am–2pm & 4–8.30pm, Sat 11am–8.30pm, Sun 11am–3pm; admission usually charged; ☎933 161 000, ⓦ www.bcn.cat/virreinacentredelaimatge), while in the courtyard are usually displayed the city's two official **Carnival giants** (*gegants vells*), representing the celebrated thirteenth-century Catalan king, Jaume I, and his wife Violant. The origin of Catalunya's outsized (five-metre-high) wood-and-plaster Carnival figures is unclear, though they probably once formed part of the entertainment at medieval travelling fairs. The first record of specific city giants is in 1601 – they were later used to entertain the city's orphans but are now an integral part of Barcelona's festival parades.

# Mercat de la Boqueria

Beyond the Palau de la Virreina starts **Rambla Sant Josep**, the switch in names marked by the sudden profusion of flower stalls – it's sometimes known as Rambla de les Flors. The city's glorious main food market is over to the right, officially the Mercat Sant Josep though referred to locally as **La Boqueria** (Mon–Sat 8am–8pm; ☎933 182 584, ⓦ www.boqueria.info). While others might protest, the market really can claim to be the best in Spain. Built on the site of a former convent between 1836 and 1840, the cavernous hall stretches

▲ Newspaper stall, the Ramblas

high wrought-iron entrance arch facing the Ramblas. It's a riot
olour, as popular with locals who come here to shop daily as with
urists. Everything radiates out from the central banks of fish and
– glistening piles of fruit and vegetables, bunches of herbs and pots
skets of wild mushrooms, mounds of cheese and sausage, racks of
ing hams, and overloaded meat counters. Many get waylaid at the
y the eye-candy seasonal fruit cartons and squeezed juices, but the
flagship fruit and veg stalls here are pricey. It's usually better value right inside,
and even more so in the small outdoor square just beyond the north side of the
market where the local allotment-holders and market-gardeners gather.
Everyone has a favourite market stall, but don't miss seeing *Petras*, the wild
mushroom and dried insect stall (it's at the back, by the market restaurant, the
*Garduña*). If you really don't fancy chilli worms, ant candy and crunchy beetles,
there are some excellent stand-up **tapas bars** in the market as well, open from
dawn onwards for the traders – the *Pinotxo* is the most famous.

## Plaça de la Boqueria

Just past the market, the halfway point of the Ramblas is marked by **Plaça de
la Boqueria**, which sports a large round **mosaic by Joan Miró** in the middle
of the pavement. It's become something of a symbol for the city and is one of
a number of public works in Barcelona by the artist, who was born just a couple
of minutes' walk off the Ramblas in the Barri Gòtic (there's a plaque to mark
the building on Passatge del Credit, off c/de Ferran). Close by, at Ramblas 82,
Josep Vilaseca's **Casa Bruno Quadros** – the lower floor is now the Caixa
Sabadell – was built in the 1890s to house an umbrella store. Its unusual facade
is decorated with a green dragon and Oriental designs, and scattered with
parasols. On the other side of the Ramblas at no. 83 there are more *modernista*
flourishes on the **Antiga Casa Figueras** (1902), which overdoses on stained
glass and mosaics, and sports a corner relief of a female reaper. It's now a
renowned bakery-café.

## Gran Teatre del Liceu

Facing the Ramblas at c/de Sant Pau is the restored **Gran Teatre del Liceu**
(Ⓜ Liceu), Barcelona's celebrated opera house, which was founded as a private
theatre in 1847. It was rebuilt after a fire in 1861 to become Spain's grandest
theatre, regarded as a bastion of the city's late nineteenth-century commercial and
intellectual classes – it still has no royal box in a nod to its bourgeois antecedents.
The Liceu was devastated again in 1893, when an anarchist threw two bombs into
the stalls during a production of *William Tell*. He was acting in revenge for the
recent execution of a fellow anarchist assassin – twenty people died in the
bombing. It then burned down for the third time in 1994, when a worker's
blowtorch set fire to the scenery during last-minute alterations to an opera set.

The latest restoration of the lavishly decorated interior took five years, and the
opera house opened again in 1999. **Tours** depart from the modern extension,
the **Espai Liceu** (tours daily 10am, 11.30am noon, 12.30pm & 1pm; €4/8.50
Ⓣ 934 859 011, Ⓦ www.liceubarcelona.com), which also houses a music and gift
shop and café. You'll learn most on the more expensive hour-long 10am guided
tour; the other, cheaper tours are self-guided and last only twenty minutes.
Highlights include the classically inspired Salon of Mirrors, unaffected by any
of the fires and thus largely original in decor, and the impressive gilded auditorium containing almost 2300 seats – making it one of the world's largest opera

houses. Offered as an option only on the 10am tour is the chance to visit the private rooms of the **Cercle del Liceu** (€3 extra), the opera house's members' club. The highly decorative rooms are certainly worth seeing, inlaid with burnished wood, and featuring tiled floors and painted ceilings, and culminating in an extraordinary *modernista* games room, illuminated by a celebrated series of paintings by Ramon Casas representing Catalan music and dance. For most of its 160-year history the Cercle membership was restricted to men, until challenged by **Montserrat Caballé**, who won a court battle to become one of the first women to join. They could hardly refuse. Caballé was born in Barcelona (1933), studied at the Liceu conservatory and made her Liceu debut in 1962, later becoming widely acknowledged as Spain's greatest soprano with a string of extraordinary performances in the 1960s and 1970s.

Meanwhile, the traditional meeting place for post-performance refreshments for audience and performers alike is the famous **Café de l'Opera**, just across the Ramblas.

# Rambla de Santa Mònica

After the Liceu, attractions just off the Ramblas include the Palau Güell down c/Nou de la Rambla (El Raval) and, on the opposite side, the lovely Plaça Reial (Barri Gòtic). Below here, the last named stretch is the **Rambla de Santa Mònica** (Ⓜ Drassanes), historically a theatre and red-light district that still has a rough edge or two. Across from the Teatre Principal stands the lavish **monument to Frederic Soler** (1839–95), better known as Serafí Pitarra, the playwright, impresario and founder of modern Catalan theatre. But for an earthier memorial to the old days, walk down the Ramblas a little further to the entrances to nos. 22 and 24 (by the *Amaya* restaurant), where the deep depressions in the marble stoops were worn away by the heels of decades of loitering prostitutes – the doorways now have protected city monument status. Back across the Ramblas, street-walkers and theatre-goers alike drank stand-up shots and coffee at **La Cazalla** (Ramblas 25), under the arch at the start of c/de l'Arc del Teatre, a famous hole-in-the-wall bar (really just a street counter), recently restored, that's straight out of sleaze-era central casting.

On the same side, at no. 7, the Augustinian convent of Santa Mònica dates originally from 1626, making it the oldest building on the Ramblas. It was entirely remodelled in the 1980s and now houses the **Centre d'Art Santa Mònica** (Tues–Sat 11am–8pm, Sun 11am–3pm; free; ☎ 933 162 810, Ⓦ www .centredartsantamonica.net), which displays temporary exhibitions of

## Under the arch and into the shadows

One early summer morning in 1945, ten-year-old Daniel Sempere and his father walk under the arch of c/de l'Arc del Teatre, "entering a vault of blue haze ... until the glimmer of the Ramblas faded behind us". And behind a large, carved wooden door, Daniel is shown for the first time the "Cemetery of Forgotten Books", where he picks out an obscure book that will change his life. It is, of course, the beginning of the mega-successful novel *Shadow of the Wind*, by Carlos Ruiz Zafón (2002), a gripping mystery set in postwar Barcelona that uses the city's old town in particular to atmospheric effect. With copy in hand you can trace Daniel's early progress, from the street where he lives (c/Santa Anna) to the house of the beautiful, blind Clara Barceló on Plaça Reial, not to mention a score of other easily identifiable locations across the city, from the cathedral to Tibidabo – always keeping a wary eye out for a pursuing stranger with "a mask of black scarred skin, consumed by fire".

contemporary art in grand, echoing galleries – the current programme is detailed outside the building and on the website. There's also a city events information office at the centre, and a café-bar upstairs with a finely sited *terrassa* above the Ramblas. Pavement artists, caricaturists and palm readers set up stalls outside here on the Ramblas, augmented on weekend afternoons by a street market selling jewellery, beads, bags and ornaments.

Final stop on the Ramblas is the city's wax museum, the **Museu de Cera** (July–Sept daily 10am–10pm; Oct–June Mon–Fri 10am–1.30pm & 4–7.30pm, Sat & Sun 11am–2pm & 4.30–8.30pm; €6.65; ☎933 172 649, ⓦwww .museocerabcn.com), located at nos. 4–6, in an impressive nineteenth-century bank building; the entrance is along Passatge. de Banca. This presents an ever more ludicrous series of tableaux in the building's cavernous salons and gloomy corridors, depicting recitals, meetings and parlour gatherings attended by an anachronistic – not to say perverse – collection of personalities, film characters, public figures, heroes, villains, artists and musicians. Thus Yasser Arafat lectures Churchill, Hitler and Bill Clinton, while a concert by Catalan cellist Pau Casals numbers Princess Diana and Mother Theresa among the audience. Needless to say, it's extremely ropey and enormously amusing, culminating in cheesy underwater tunnels and space capsules and an unpleasant "Terror" room. You also won't want to miss the museum's extraordinary grotto-bar, the *Bosc de les Fades*.

By now, you've almost reached the foot of the Ramblas, passing Drassanes metro station to be confronted by the column at the very bottom of the avenue that's topped by a statue of Columbus. For this, the neighbouring maritime museum and the rest of the harbour area, see Chapter 5.

# Barri Gòtic

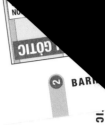

T he **Barri Gòtic**, or Gothic Quarter ((M)Jaume I), forms the very heart of the old town, spreading out from the east side of the Ramblas. Within lies a remarkable concentration of beautiful medieval buildings dating principally from the fourteenth and fifteenth centuries, when Barcelona reached the height of her commercial prosperity before being absorbed into the burgeoning kingdom of Castile. It will take the best part of a day to see everything here, with the cathedral – **La Seu** – a particular highlight, and you certainly won't want to miss the archeological remains at the **Museu d'Història de la Ciutat** or the unclassifiable collections of the **Museu Frederic Marès**. There are also plenty of other quirks and diversions, from exploring the old Jewish quarter to touring the grand salons of City Hall. That said, sauntering through the medieval alleys, shopping for antiques or gifts, following the remains of the Roman walls, or simply sitting at a café table in one of the lovely squares is just as much an attraction.

The picture-postcard images of the Barri Gòtic are largely based on the streets north of c/de Ferran and c/de Jaume I, where tourists throng the boutiques, bars, restaurants, museums and galleries. South of here – from Plaça Reial and c/d'Avinyo to the harbour – the Barri Gòtic is rather less gentrified (or sometimes just plain run-down). There are no specific sights or museums in this section, though there are plenty of great shops, cafés, tapas bars and restaurants – just take care at night in the poorly lit streets.

## La Seu

Barcelona's cathedral, **La Seu** (daily 8am–12.45pm & 5.15–7.30pm, cathedral and cloister free; otherwise 1–5pm, (€5), includes entrance to all sections; Ⓦwww.catedralbcn.org), is one of the great Gothic buildings of Spain. Located on a site previously occupied by a Roman temple and then an early Christian basilica, it was begun in 1298 and finished in 1448, save for the neo-Gothic principal facade, which was completed in the 1880s (and is currently obscured by scaffolding). The cathedral is dedicated to the city's second patroness, **Santa Eulàlia** (known as Laia in Barcelona), a young girl brutally martyred by the Romans in 304 AD for daring to prefer Christianity. Her remains were first placed in the original portside church of Santa María del Mar in La Ribera, which explains why she's also patron saint of local sailors and seafarers. In 874 Laia was re-interred in the cathedral and her ornate alabaster tomb rests in a crypt beneath the high altar. Among the finest of the carved and painted tombs of the 29 **side-chapels** are those reputedly belonging to Ramon Berenguer I (Count of Barcelona from 1035 to 1076) and his wife Almodis; however, the tombs actually hold the remains of an earlier count and Petronila, the Aragonese princess whose betrothal to Ramon Berenguer IV united Aragon and Barcelona.

BARRI GÒTIC

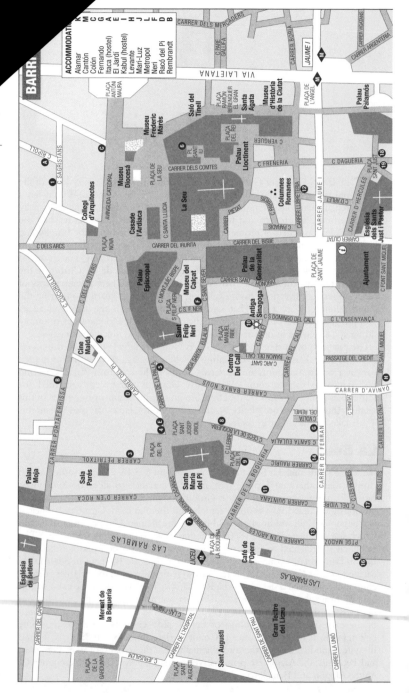

ACCOMMODATION
| Alamar | K |
| Cantón | M |
| Colón | C |
| Fernando | G |
| Itaca (hostel) | A |
| El Jardi | E |
| Kabul (hostel) | I |
| Levante | H |
| Mari-Luz | J |
| Metropol | L |
| Neri | F |
| Racó del Pi | D |
| Rembrandt | B |

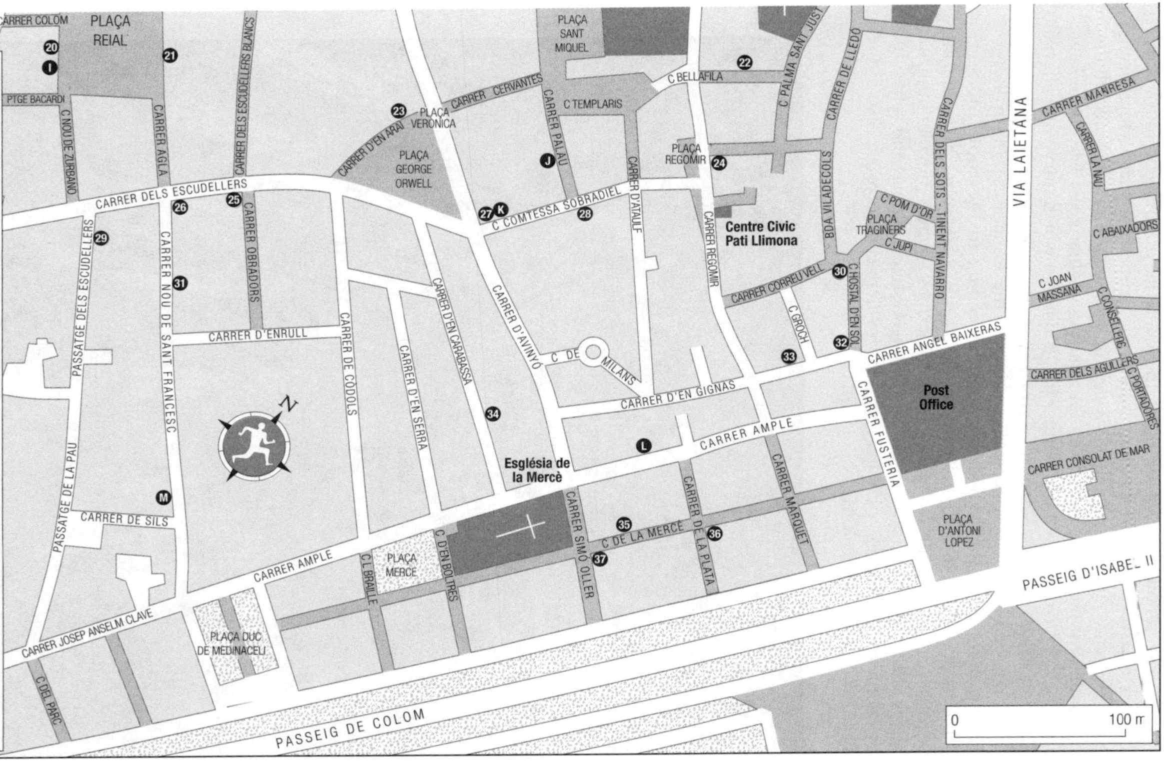

**RESTAURANTS**

| | |
|---|---|
| Arc Café | 34 |
| Café de l'Academia | 18 |
| Los Caracoles | 26 |
| Can Culleretes | 11 |
| Juicy Jones | 7 |
| Limbo | 35 |
| Matsuri | 24 |
| El Salón | 30 |
| Shunka | 1 |
| Venus Delicatesse | 27 |

**TAPAS BARS**

| | |
|---|---|
| Bar Celta Pulperia | 37 |
| Bodega La Plata | 36 |
| Ginger | 19 |
| La Pineda | 2 |
| Taller de Tapas | 8 |
| La Vinateria del Call | 10 |

**CAFÉS**

| | |
|---|---|
| Caelum | 5 |
| Café d'Estiu | 6 |
| Dulcinea | 3 |
| Mesón del Cafe | 12 |

**BARS AND CLUBS**

| | |
|---|---|
| L'Ascensor | 22 |
| Bar del Pi | 4 |
| La Cerveteca | 32 |
| Fantástico | 29 |
| Fonfone | 25 |
| Glaciar | 15 |
| Harlem Jazz Club (jazz) | 28 |
| Jamboree (jazz) | 20 |
| Karma | 21 |
| La Macarena | 31 |
| Milk | 33 |
| Molly's Fair City | 13 |
| Oviso | 23 |
| Pipa Club | 16 |
| Schilling | 14 |
| Sidecar (live music) | 17 |
| Tarantos (flamenco) | 20 |
| Travel Bar | 9 |

The most renowned part of the cathedral is its magnificent fourteenth-century **cloister**, which looks over a lush tropical garden complete with soaring palm trees and – more unusually – a gaggle of honking geese. If they disturb the tranquillity of the scene, they do so for a purpose: white geese have been kept here for over five hundred years, either (depending on which story you believe) to reflect the virginity of Santa Eulàlia, or as a reminder of the erstwhile Roman splendour of Barcelona, as geese were kept on the Capitoline Hill in Rome. Finally, don't leave the cathedral without ascending to the **roof** (Mon–Fri 10.30am–12.30pm & 5.15–6.30pm, Sat 10.30am–12.30pm; €2.20) – the lift (*ascensor als terrats*) is just to the left of the crypt steps – which provides intimate views of the cathedral towers and surrounding Gothic buildings and spires. It's by no means the highest view in town, but nowhere else do you feel so at the heart of medieval Barcelona.

▲ La Seu

There's not much to see in the shopping zone north of the cathedral, but a century or so ago a tavern called **Els Quatre Gats** (The Four Cats, c/Montsió 3, ⓦwww.4gats .com) burned brightly and briefly as the epicentre of Barcelona's bohemian in-crowd. It was opened by Pere Romeu and other *modernista* artists in 1897 as a gathering place for their contemporaries, and the building itself is gloriously decorated inside and out in exuberant Catalan Art Nouveau style – it was the classy architect Josep Puig i Cadafalch's first commission. *Els Quatre Gats* soon thrived as the birthplace of *modernista* magazines, the scene of poetry readings and shadow-puppet theatre and the venue for cultural debate. A young Picasso designed the menu and, in 1901, the café was the setting for his first public exhibition. *Els Quatre Gats* has always traded on its reputation – a place where "accountants, dreamers and would-be geniuses shared tables with the spectres of Pablo Picasso, Isaac Albéniz, Federico García Lorca and Salvador Dalí" (*The Shadow of the Wind*, Carlos Ruiz Zafón). Today, a modern restoration displays something of its former glory, with the bar-restaurant (see p.208) overseen by a copy of Ramon Casas' famous wall-painting of himself and Pere Romeu on a tandem bicycle (the original is in MNAC).

# Plaça de la Seu and Plaça Nova

The cathedral square, **Plaça de la Seu**, is a regular weekly venue for the dancing of the *sardana*, the Catalan national dance (every Sat at 6pm, Easter to Nov). Anyone can join in, though you'd best read the feature on p.223 first. Meanwhile, in front of the cathedral, the wide, pedestrianized Avinguda de la Catedral hosts an **antiques market** every Thursday, and a **Christmas craft fair** every December.

Stand back to look at the cathedral buildings and it's easy to see the line of fortified Roman towers that stood originally on this spot, before being incorporated into the later medieval buildings. One such tower formed part of the cathedral almshouse (La Pia Almoina), now the **Museu Diocesà** (Tues–Sat 10am–2pm & 5–8pm, Sun & holidays 11am–2pm; €6; ☎933 152 213), with exhibition space spread across four floors, and with views over the cathedral square from the top. The impressive permanent collection is of religious art, artefacts and church treasures from around Barcelona, notably a series of frescoes of the Apocalypse (1122 AD) from Sant Salvador in Polinyà and a series of graphic retables, including one of St Bartholomew being skinned alive.

On the other flank of the cathedral are two more late-medieval buildings closely associated with it. The **Casa de l'Ardiaca** (once the archdeacon's residence, now the city archives) encloses a tiny cloistered and tiled courtyard with a small fountain. To the right of the badly worn Renaissance gateway on c/de Santa Llúcia look for the curious carved swallow-and-tortoise postbox. The **Palau Episcopal**, just beyond at the western end of c/de Santa Llúcia, was the bishop's palace and built on a grander scale altogether. Though you're not allowed inside, you can go as far as the courtyard to see the fine outdoor stairway; there's a patio at the top with Romanesque wall paintings.

The large **Plaça Nova**, facing the cathedral, marks one of the medieval entrances to the old town – north of it, you're fast entering the wider streets and more regular contours of the modern city. Even if you're sticking with the Barri Gòtic for now, walk over to study the frieze surmounting the modern College of Architects, the **Collegi d'Arquitectes**, on the other side of the square. Designed in 1960 from sketches supplied by Picasso, it has a crude, almost graffiti-like quality, at odds with the more stately buildings to the side.

Picasso himself refused to come to Spain to oversee the work, unwilling to return to his home country while Franco was still in power.

## ② Plaça del Rei and around

The most concentrated batch of historic monuments in the Barri Gòtic is the grouping around **Plaça del Rei** (Perfect Squares), behind the cathedral apse. The square was once the palace courtyard of Barcelona's counts, and also houses a stone staircase leading to the great fourteenth-century **Saló del Tinell**, the palace's main hall. It was on the steps leading from the Saló del Tinell into the Plaça del Rei that Ferdinand and Isabel stood to receive Christopher Columbus on his triumphant return from his famous voyage of 1492. With the old town streets packed, Columbus advanced in procession with the monarchs to the palace, where he presented the queen with booty from the trip – exotic birds, sweet potatoes and six Indians (actually Haitians, taken on board during Columbus' return). The hall itself is a fine example of secular Gothic architecture, with interior arches spanning 17m. At one time the Spanish Inquisition met here, taking full advantage of the popular belief that the walls would move if a lie was spoken. Nowadays it hosts temporary exhibitions, while concerts are occasionally held in the hall or outside in the square. The palace buildings also include the beautiful fourteenth-century **Capella de Santa Àgata**, with its tall

---

### A walk around the Roman walls

The Barri Gòtic was once entirely enclosed by **Roman walls and towers**, dating from the fourth century AD, though they were largely pulled down in the nineteenth century to create more space for the expanding city. Parts of Roman Barcelona still exist, however, easily seen on an hour-long stroll – the city council has posted brown information boards showing the route at various points.

Outside the cathedral, in Plaça Nova, block metal letters a metre high spell out the word "Barcino" (the name of the Roman city), underneath a restored tower and a reconstructed part of the Roman **aqueduct**. There's more of the aqueduct on display north of here on c/Duran i Bas (set into the facade of a building), while over on **Plaça Vila de Madrid** is a line of sunken Roman tombs. The line of the wall itself runs past the cathedral and Museu Diocesà, with the next surviving section visible at **Plaça Ramon Berenguer El Gran** (at Via Laietana). Some of the walls and towers here are over 13m high, and back onto the chapel of Santa Àgata on Plaça del Rei. There's more wall to see down **c/Sots-Tinent Navarro**, while the most romantic section is the truncated Roman tower in the sunken **Plaça dels Traginers**, planted with palms and a solitary olive tree. Along nearby **c/Correu Vell** part of the wall and defence towers were incorporated into a medieval palace – you can see this section in the courtyard of a civic centre (through a gate, opposite c/Groch).

A right turn after here, up c/Regomir, leads to the **Centre Cívic Pati Llimona** (usually Mon–Fri 9am–2pm & 4.30–8pm, Sat 10am–2pm & 4–8pm), where lie the remains of one of the original gates through the Roman wall into inner Barcino. This and other remains are visible through a glass window from c/Regomir, and if the centre is open you'll be able to go inside for a closer look. Then head up c/Ciutat and cross Plaça de Sant Jaume for c/Paradis, where four impressive **Roman columns** ("columnes Romanes") and the architrave of a temple are preserved in the interior courtyard of the Centre Excursionista de Catalunya (c/Paradis 10; usually open Tues–Sat 10am–2pm & 4–8pm, Sun 10am–3pm, though may vary). From here you're just a short walk from the cathedral again, though no Roman enthusiast should miss the nearby Museu d'Història de la Ciutat, which features the underground excavations of Barcino itself.

single nave and fine Gothic retable, and the romantic Renaissance **Torre del Rei Martí**, which rises above one corner of the square. There's currently no public access to the tower, but the interiors of the hall and chapel can be seen during a visit to the Museu d'Història de la Ciutat.

## Museu d'Història de la Ciutat

The building that closes off the rest of Plaça del Rei houses the splendid city history museum, the **Museu d'Història de la Ciutat de Barcelona** (MHCB; April–Sept Tues–Sat 10am–8pm, Sun & holidays 10am–3pm; Oct–March Tues–Sat 10am–2pm & 4–8pm, Sun & holidays 10am–3pm; €6, includes entry to other MHCB sites; ☎933 151 111, ⓦwww.museuhistoria.bcn.cat), whose crucial draw is its underground archeological section – nothing less than the extensive remains of the Roman city of Barcino. Descending in the lift (the floor indicator shows "12 BC"), you are deposited onto walkways running through excavations that extend for 4000 square metres, stretching under Plaça del Rei and the surrounding streets as far as the cathedral. The remains date from the first century BC to the sixth century AD and reflect the transition from Roman to Visigothic rule – at the end of the sixth century, a church was erected on top of the old Roman salt-fish factory, the foundations of which are preserved down here almost in its entirety. Not much survives above chest height, but explanatory diagrams show the extent of the streets, walls and buildings – from lookout towers to laundries – while models, mosaics, murals and displays of excavated goods help flesh out the reality of daily life in Barcino. Note that your ticket is also valid for the monastery at Pedralbes and the interpretation centre at Parc Güell.

## Museu Frederic Marès

Another extraordinary display greets visitors in the **Museu Frederic Marès** (Tues–Sat 10am–7pm, Sun 10am–3pm; €4.20, Wed afternoon & first Sun of month free; ☎932 563 500, ⓦwww.museumares.bcn.es), which occupies a further wing of the old royal palace, behind Plaça del Rei; the entrance is through Plaça de Sant Iu, off c/dels Comtes. The large arcaded courtyard, studded with orange trees, is one of the most romantic in the old town, and the **summer café** here (*Cafè d'Estiu*, open April–Sept; closed Mon) makes a perfect place to take a break from sightseeing.

Frederic Marès (1893–1991) was a sculptor, painter and restorer who more or less single-handedly restored, often not entirely accurately, Catalunya's decaying medieval treasures in the early twentieth century. The **ground** and **basement floors** of the museum consist of his personal collection of medieval sculpture – an important body of work that includes a comprehensive collection of wooden crucifixes showing the stylistic development of this form from the twelfth to the fifteenth century. There are also antiquities, from Roman busts to Hellenistic terracotta lamps, while the craftsmanship of medieval masons is displayed in a series of rooms focusing on carved doorways, cloister fragments, sculpted capitals and alabaster tombs. However, it's the **upper two floors**, housing Marès' personal collectibles, that tend to make jaws drop. These present an incredible retrospective jumble gathered during fifty years of travel, with entire rooms devoted to keys and locks, pipes, cigarette cards and snuffboxes, fans, gloves and brooches, playing cards, draughtsmen's tools, walking sticks, dolls' houses, toy theatres, old gramophones and archaic bicycles, to list just a sample of what's on show. In the artist's library on the second floor, some of Marès' own reclining nudes, penitent saints and bridling stags give an insight into his more orthodox work.

# Església de Santa María del Pi and around

With the cathedral area and Plaça del Rei sucking in every visitor at some point during the day, the third focus of attraction in the Barri Gòtic is to the west, around the church of Santa María del Pi – five minutes' walk from the cathedral or just two minutes from the Ramblas (ⓂLiceu).

The fourteenth-century **Església de Santa María del Pi** (Mon–Sat 8.30am–1pm & 4.30–9pm, Sun 9am–2pm & 5–9pm, Ⓦwww.parroquiadelpi. com) stands at the heart of three delightful little squares. Burned out in 1936, and restored in the 1960s, the church boasts a Romanesque door but is mainly Catalan-Gothic in style, with just a single nave with chapels between the buttresses. The rather plain interior only serves to set off some marvellous stained glass, the most impressive of which is contained within a ten-metre-wide rose window, often claimed (rather boldly) as the largest in the world. The church flanks **Plaça Sant Josep Oriol**, the prettiest of the three adjacent squares, an ideal place to take an outdoor coffee, listen to the buskers or browse the weekend **artists' market** (Sat 11am–8pm, Sun 11am–2pm). The statue here is of Àngel Guimerà, nineteenth-century Catalan playwright and poet, who had a house on the square.

The church is named – like the squares on either side, Plaça del Pi and Placeta del Pi – after the pine trees that once stood here (there's a solitary example still in Plaça del Pi). A **farmers' market** spills across Plaça del Pi on the first and third Friday and Saturday of the month, selling honey, cheese, cakes and other produce, while the cafés of **Carrer de Petritxol** (off Plaça del Pi) are the place to come for a hot chocolate – *Dulcinea* at no. 2 is the traditional choice – and a browse around the street's commercial art galleries. The most famous is at c/de Petritxol 5, where the **Sala Pares** was already well established when Picasso and Miró were young. Meanwhile, off Plaça Sant Josep Oriol, the old town's **antiques trade** is concentrated in glittering galleries and stores along c/de la Palla and c/Banys Nous.

# Plaça Sant Felip Neri

Head east from Plaça Sant Josep Oriol, back towards the cathedral, and behind the Palau Episcopal you'll stumble upon **Plaça Sant Felip Neri**, scarred by a bomb dropped during the Civil War and now used as a playground by the children at the square's school. Antoni Gaudí walked here every evening after work at the Sagrada Família to hear Mass at the eighteenth-century church of Sant Felip Neri. Many of the other buildings that now hedge in the small square come from other points in the city and have been reassembled here over the last fifty years. One of these, the former headquarters of the city's shoemakers' guild (founded in 1202), houses a one-room footwear museum, the **Museu del Calçat** (Tues–Sun 11am–2pm; €2.50; ℡933 014 533), whose collection of reproductions (models dating back as far as the first century), originals (from as early as the 1600s) and oddities is of some interest, not least the world's biggest shoe, made for the Columbus statue.

# El Call Major and the Antiga Sinagoga

South of Plaça Sant Felip Neri you enter what was once the medieval Jewish quarter of Barcelona, centred on c/Sant Domènec del Call. After decades of neglect, the city authorities have signposted some of the surrounding streets and points of interest in what's known as **El Call Major** (*Call* is the Catalan word for a narrow passage), most notably the site of the main synagogue, the

There were Jews living in Barcelona as early as the ninth century, and a Jewish district was documented in the city by the eleventh. Later, as elsewhere in Spain, Barcelona's **medieval Jewish quarter** lay nestled in the shadow of the cathedral – under the Church's careful scrutiny. In the thirteenth and early fourteenth centuries some of the realm's greatest and most powerful administrators, tax collectors and ambassadors hailed from here, but reactionary trends sparked persecution and led to the closing off of the community in these narrow, dark alleys. Nevertheless a prosperous settlement persisted until the pogrom and forced conversion of 1391 and exile of 1492. Today little, except the street name and the rediscovered synagogue survives as a reminder of the Jewish presence – after their expulsion, most of the buildings used by the Jews were torn down and used for construction elsewhere in the city. With the demise of the Franco regime, a small community was again established in Barcelona, and in recent years there has been a revival in interest in Barcelona's Jewish heritage. As well as the synagogue, the sites of the butchers', bakers', fishmongers' and Jewish baths have all been identified, while over on the eastern side of Montjuïc (Jewish Mountain) was the Jewish cemetery – the castle at Montjuïc displays around thirty tombstones recovered from the cemetery in the early twentieth century.

**Antiga Sinagoga** (Mon–Fri 11am–6pm, Sat & Sun 11am–3pm, sometimes closed Sat for ceremonies; €2; ☎933 170 790, ⓦwww.calldebarcelona.org) – it's at c/Marlet 5, on the corner with c/Sant Domènec del Call. A small synagogue existed here, on the edge of the Roman forum, from the third century AD until the pogrom of 1391, but even after that date the building survived in various guises – the sunken dye vats from a family business of fifteenth-century New Christian (forcibly converted Jews) dyers are still visible, alongside some original Roman walling. Not many people stop by the synagogue – if you do, you'll get a personalized tour of the small room by a member of the local Jewish community.

Most other local Jewish buildings were destroyed, though a plaque further down c/Marlet (junction with c/Arc Sant Ramon del Call) marks the site of the former rabbi's house, while up in Plaçeta Manuel Ribé another house originally belonging to a veil-maker now serves as a small museum, the **Centre d'Interpretació del Call** (Wed–Fri 10am–2pm, Sat 11am–6pm, Sun & holidays 11am–3pm; free; ☎932 562 122, ⓦwww.museuhistoria.bcn.cat). You can ask here about guided tours, open days and activities that aim to shed more light on Barcelona's Jewish heritage.

# Plaça de Sant Jaume

**Plaça de Sant Jaume** marks the very centre of the Barri Gòtic. A spacious square at the end of c/de Ferran, which runs east from the Ramblas, this was once the site of Barcelona's Roman forum and marketplace; now it's at the heart of city and regional government business, containing two of the city's most significant buildings. Whistle-happy local police try to keep things moving in the *plaça*, while taxis and bike-tour groups weave between the pedestrians. The square is also the traditional site of demonstrations, gatherings and local festivals.

**Ajuntament de Barcelona**

On the south side of the square stands the City Hall, the **Ajuntament**, parts of which date from as early as 1373, though the Neoclassical facade is nineteenth-century, added when the square was laid out. You get a much better idea of the grandeur of the original structure by nipping around the corner, down c/de la Ciutat, for a view of the former main entrance. It's a typically exuberant Catalan-Gothic facade, but was badly damaged during renovations in the nineteenth century. On Sundays (10am–2pm; free; entrance on c/Font de Sant Miquel; English-language leaflet provided; ☎934 027 000) you're allowed into the building for a self-guided tour around the rather splendid marble halls, galleries and staircases. The highlights are the magnificent restored fourteenth-century council chamber, known as the **Saló de Cent**, and the dramatic historical murals by Josep Maria Sert in the **Saló de les Cròniques** (Hall of Chronicles), while the ground-floor courtyard features sculpted works by some of the most famous Catalan artists.

### Palau de la Generalitat

Right across the square rises the **Palau de la Generalitat**, traditional home of the Catalan government, from where the short-lived Catalan Republic was proclaimed in April 1931. Begun in 1418, this presents its best – or at least its oldest – aspect around the side on c/del Bisbe, where the early fifteenth-century facade by Marc Safont contains a spirited medallion portraying St George and the Dragon. (Incidentally, the enclosed Gothic bridge across the narrow street – the so-called Bridge of Sighs – is an anachronism, added in 1928, though it's at one with its surroundings and features on many a postcard of the "Gothic" quarter. It connects the Generalitat with the former canons' houses across c/del Bispe, now used as the official residence of the president.) There's a beautiful cloister on the first floor with superb coffered ceilings, while opening off this are the intricately worked chapel and salon of Sant Jordi (St George, patron saint of Catalunya as well as England), and an upper courtyard planted with orange trees, overhung by gargoyles and peppered with presidential busts.

You can visit the interior on a **guided tour** on the second and fourth Sunday of each month (10am–2pm, every 30–60min; free; entrance on c/Sant Honorat, passport or ID required; ☎934 024 600). These last about an hour, and include an introductory video about the Catalan state and its history, though only one or two of the tours each day are conducted in English. The Generalitat is also open to the public on the **Dia de Sant Jordi**, or Saint George's Day (April 23; expect a two-hour wait), which has been conflated with a Catalan version of St Valentine's Day – it's traditional to exchange books and roses, available from stalls on Plaça de Sant Jaume and the Ramblas. It's also usually open for visits on two other public holidays, September 11 and September 24.

# Plaça de Sant Just

Behind the Ajuntament, off c/de la Ciutat, **Plaça de Sant Just** is a medieval gem, sporting a restored fourteenth-century fountain and flanked by unassuming palaces. Apart from the excellent *Café de l'Acadèmia*, which puts out dining tables on the square, the highlight here is the **Església dels Sants Just i Pastor** (open for Mass Mon–Sat 7.30pm, Sun at noon, and occasional other times), whose very plain stone facade belies the rich stained glass and elaborate chapel decoration inside (enter from the back, at c/de la Ciutat; the main doors on Pl. de Sant Just are open less often). The name commemorates the city's earliest Christian martyrs, and it's claimed (though there's no real evidence) that this is the oldest parish church site in Barcelo[...] first supported a foundation at the beginning of the ninth century; [...] interior, though, dates from the mid-fourteenth century. In the late [...] Ages it was the only place where Jews could swear legal oaths in deals w[...] Christians, and even today a last will and testament declared verbally here has the full force of a written document.

## Plaça Reial and around

Of all the old-town squares, the most popular with visitors is the elegant nineteenth-century **Plaça Reial** – hidden behind an archway, just off the Ramblas (to the left, walking down; Ⓜ Liceu). Laid out in around 1850 by Francesc Daniel Molina, the Italianate square is studded with tall palm trees and decorated iron lamps (made by the young Antoni Gaudí), bordered by high, pastel-coloured arcaded buildings, and centred on a fountain depicting the Three Graces. Taking in the sun at one of the benches puts you in very mixed company – punks, bikers, buskers, Catalan eccentrics, tramps and bemused tourists drinking a coffee at one of the pavement cafés. It used to be a bit dodgy in Plaça Reial, but most of the truly unsavoury characters have been driven off over the years as tourists have staked an increasing claim to the square. There's an almost permanent police presence, and the surrounding bars, clubs and restaurants are becoming increasingly more upmarket.

If you pass through Plaça Reial on a Sunday morning, look in on the **coin and stamp market** (10am–2pm). Otherwise, the arcaded passageways connecting the square with the surrounding streets throw up a few interesting sights. Tucked away on the north side on c/del Vidre is the quirky **Herborista del Rey** (closed Mon), an early nineteenth-century herbalist's shop, which stocks more than 250 medicinal herbs designed to combat all complaints. Walk down the opposing alley on the south side of the square and you'll emerge on c/dels Escudellers, right opposite the turning spits of **Los Caracoles** restaurant, whose ranks of grilled chickens make a good photograph. **Carrer dels**

▲ Plaça Reial

...nce a thriving red–light street, and still has a late-night
...t teeters on the edge of respectability. Bars and restau-
...ract a youthful clientele, nowhere more so than those
...**ge Orwell**, at the eastern end of c/dels Escudellers. The
...e was created by levelling an old-town block – a favoured
...to let in a bit of light – and it has quickly become a hangout
...wd.

## Avinyo and La Mercè

**Carrer d...nyo**, running south from c/de Ferran towards the harbour, cuts
through the most atmospheric part of the southern Barri Gòtic. It used to be a
red-light district of some renown, littered with brothels and bars, and frequented
by the young Picasso, whose family moved into the area in 1895. It still looks
the part – a narrow thoroughfare lined with dark overhanging buildings – but
the funky cafés, streetwear shops and boutiques tell the story of its recent
gentrification. The locals aren't overly enamoured of the influx of bar-crawling
fun-seekers – banners and notices along the length of this and neighbouring
streets plead with visitors to keep the noise down.

Carrer d'Avinyo ends at the junction with **Carrer Ample**, the latter an aristocratic address in the eighteenth century. Here, in the neighbourhood known as
**La Mercè** – just a block from the harbour – lived nobles and merchants
enriched by Barcelona's maritime trade. Most fashionable families took the
opportunity to move north to the Eixample later in the nineteenth century, and
the streets of La Mercè took on an earthier hue. Since then, Carrer de la Mercè
and the surrounding streets (particularly Ample, d'en Gignas and Regomir) have
been home to a series of characteristic old-style **taverns** known as *tascas* or
*bodegas* – a glass of wine from the barrel in *Bodega la Plata*, or a similar joint, is
one of the old town's more authentic experiences.

At Plaça de la Mercè, the eighteenth-century **Església de la Mercè** is the
focus of the city's biggest annual celebration, the Festes de la Mercè every
September, dedicated to the co-patroness of Barcelona, whose image is paraded
from here. The church was burned in 1936 but the gilt side-chapels, stained-
glass medallions and apse murals have been authentically restored. The square
outside was remodelled in the twentieth century around its statue of Neptune,
though the more pleasing local square is the older **Plaça Duc de Medinaceli**,
a block to the west, with its palms and commemorative cast-iron column
saluting a Catalan admiral.

**3**

# El Raval

The old-town area west of the Ramblas is known as **El Raval** (from the Arabic word for "suburb"). Standing outside the medieval city walls, this has always formed a world apart from the power and nobility of the Barri Gòtic. In medieval times it was the site of hospitals, churches and monasteries and, later, of noxious trades and industries that had no place in the Gothic quarter. Many of the street names still tell the story, like c/de l'Hospital or c/dels Tallers (named for the district's slaughterhouses). By the twentieth century the area south of c/de l'Hospital had acquired a reputation as the city's main red-light area, known to all (for obscure reasons) as the Barrio Chino, or **Barri Xinès** in Catalan – China Town. According to the Barcelona chronicler Manuel Vázquez Montalbán, in the days when the French writer Jean Genet crawled its streets – an experience he recounted in his *Thief's Journal* – the district housed "theatrical homosexuals and anarcho-syndicalist, revolutionary meeting places; women's prisons . . . condom shops and brothels which smelled of liquor and groins". George Orwell later related how, after the 1936 Workers' Uprising, "in the streets were coloured posters appealing to prostitutes to stop being prostitutes". Even today in the backstreets between c/de Sant Pau and c/Nou de la Rambla visitors may run the gauntlet of cat-calling prostitutes and petty drug dealers, while a handful of atmospheric old bars – the *Bar Pastis*, *London Bar*, *Marsella* and *Almirall* – trade on their former reputations as bohemian hangouts.

However, El Raval is changing rapidly. The 1992 Olympics and then European Union funding achieved what Franco never could, and cleaned up large parts of the neighbourhood almost overnight. North of c/de l'Hospital, in the "upper Raval", the main engine of change was the building of the contemporary art museum, **MACBA**, and the adjacent culture centre, the **CCCB**, around which entire city blocks were demolished, open spaces created and old buildings cleaned up. To the south, in the "lower Raval" between c/de l'Hospital and c/de Sant Pau, a new boulevard – the **Rambla de Raval** – has been gouged through the former tenements and alleys, providing a huge new pedestrianized area. This part of the Raval is also home to the neighbourhood's two other outstanding buildings, namely Gaudí's **Palau Güell** and the church of **Sant Pau del Camp**, one of the city's oldest churches.

The local character of El Raval is changing perceptibly, too, with the years. The area's older, traditional residents are gradually being supplanted by a younger, more affluent and arty population, especially following the opening of new university faculty buildings near MACBA. There's also a growing influx of immigrants from the Indian subcontinent and North Africa, so alongside the surviving spit-and-sawdust bars you'll find new restaurants, galleries and boutiques, not to mention a burgeoning number of specialist grocery stores,

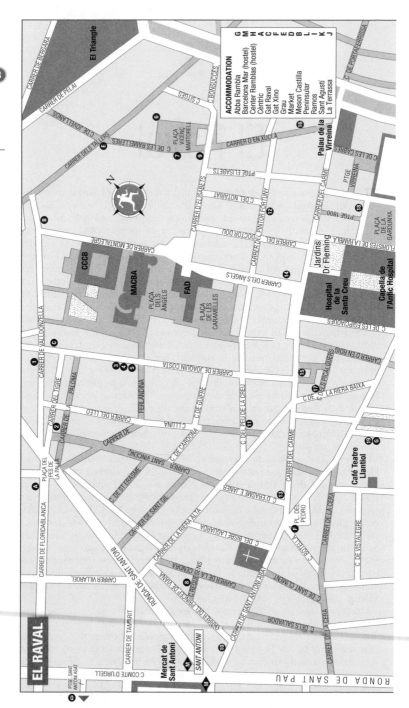

EL RAVAL

ACCOMMODATION
Abba Rambla — G
Barcelona Mar (hostel) — M
Center Ramblas (hostel) — H
Cèntric — A
Gat Raval — C
Gat Xino — F
Grau — E
Market — D
Meson Castilla — B
Peninsular — L
Ramos — I
Sant Agustí — K
La Terrassa — J

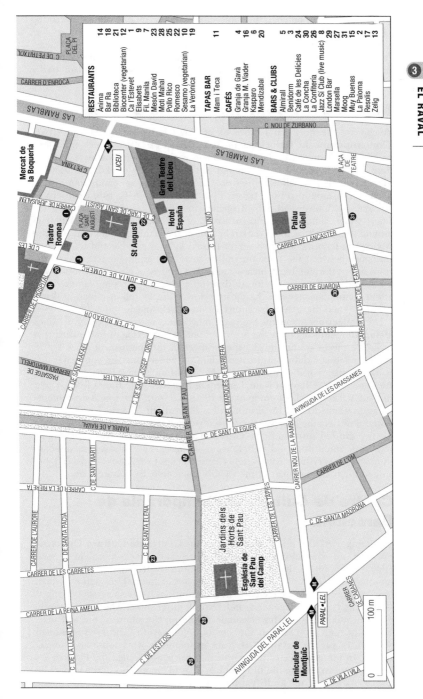

**RESTAURANTS**

| | |
|---|---|
| Anima | 14 |
| Bar Ra | 18 |
| Biblioteca | 21 |
| Biocenter (vegetarian) | 12 |
| Ca l'Estevet | 1 |
| Elisabets | 9 |
| Fil. Manila | 7 |
| Mesón David | 23 |
| Moti Mahal | 28 |
| Pollo Rico | 25 |
| Romesco | 22 |
| Sesamo (vegetarian) | 10 |
| La Veronica | 19 |

**TAPAS BAR**

| | |
|---|---|
| Mam i Teca | 11 |

**CAFÉS**

| | |
|---|---|
| Granja de Gavà | 4 |
| Granja M. Viader | 16 |
| Kasparo | 6 |
| Mendizabal | 20 |

**BARS & CLUBS**

| | |
|---|---|
| Almirall | 5 |
| Benidorm | 3 |
| Café de les Delícies | 24 |
| La Concha | 30 |
| La Confitería | 26 |
| Jazz Sí Club (live music) | 8 |
| London Bar | 29 |
| Marsella | 27 |
| Moog | 31 |
| Muy Buenas | 15 |
| La Paloma | 2 |
| Resolis | 17 |
| Zelig | 13 |

curry houses, *halal* butchers and hole-in-the-wall telephone offices advertising cheap international calls.

You'd hesitate to call El Raval gentrified, as it clearly still has its rough edges. You needn't be unduly concerned during the day as you make your way around, but it's as well to keep your wits about you at night, particularly in the southernmost streets.

## Museu d'Art Contemporani de Barcelona

Anchoring the northern reaches of El Raval is the iconic **Museu d'Art Contemporani de Barcelona**, or **MACBA**, in Plaça dels Angels (mid-June to mid-Sept Mon & Wed 11am–8pm, Thurs & Fri 11am–midnight, Sat 10am–8pm, Sun & holidays 10am–3pm; rest of the year closes weekdays at 7.30pm; closed Tues all year; admission €4 or €7.50, depending on exhibitions visited, Wed €3, 3-month season ticket €10; ☎934 120 810, ⓦwww.macba.es; ⓜCatalunya/Universitat), which opened in 1995. The contrast between the huge, white, almost luminous, structure of the museum and the buildings around it couldn't be more stark. The aim of the architect, American Richard Meier, was to make as much use of natural light as possible and to "create a dialogue" between the museum and its surroundings; this is reflected in the front side of the building, which is contructed entirely of glass. Once inside, you go from the ground to the fourth floor up a series of swooping ramps which afford continuous views of the square below – usually full of careering skateboarders – and the sixteenth-century Convent dels Àngels.

The **collection** represents the main movements in contemporary art since 1945, mainly in Catalunya and Spain but with a smattering of foreign artists as well. The pieces are not usually shown together in a permanent space but in smaller rotating exhibitions, so, depending on when you visit, you may catch works by major names such as Joan Miró, Antoni Tàpies, Eduardo Chillida, Alexander Calder, Robert Rauschenberg or Paul Klee. Joan Brossa, leading light of the Catalan Dau al Set group of the 1950s, has work here too, as do contemporary multimedia and installation artists like Antoni Muntadas and Francesc Torres. Probably the best way to acquaint yourself with the collection is to take the free **guided tour** (in English on Mon at 6pm, otherwise Mon–Sat at 6pm, plus Sat & Sun at 1pm, and night tours in summer). There's also a good museum shop selling everything from designer espresso cups to art books, and a café-bar around the back that's part of the CCCB (contemporary culture centre).

## Centre de Cultura Contemporània de Barcelona

Adjoining MACBA, up c/Montalegre, is the **Centre de Cultura Contemporània de Barcelona**, or **CCCB** (Tues–Sun 11am–8pm, Thurs until 10pm; €4.50 or €6 depending on exhibitions visited, free on 1st Wed of month; ☎933 064 100, ⓦwww.cccb.org; ⓜCatalunya/Universitat), which hosts temporary art and city-related exhibitions as well as supporting a cinema and a varied concert and festival programme. The imaginatively restored building is a prime example of the juxtaposition of old and new; originally built in 1714 on the site of a fourteenth-century Augustinian convent, it was for hundreds of years an infamous workhouse and lunatic asylum. In the entrance to the centre, in what is now called the Plaça de les Dones, you can see the old tile panels and facade in a patio presided over by a small statue of Sant Jordi (patron saint of Catalunya). At the back of the building, the *C3* café-bar has a sunny *terrassa* on the modern square joining the CCCB to the MACBA, while a relaxed meal can also be had just up the street in the the arcaded and tiled **Pati Manning** (c/Montalegre 7), where a daytime café serves a good-value al fresco lunch.

# FAD and around

Across the open expanse from MACBA, part of the former Convent dels Àngels now houses the headquarters of the **Foment de les Artes Décoratives** (**FAD**; Tues–Fri 11am–8pm, Sun 11am–4pm; free; ☏934 437 520, Ⓦwww.fadweb.org), a decorative art and design organization founded in 1903. Their exhibition spaces (including the former convent chapel) are dedicated to industrial and graphic design, arts, crafts, architecture, contemporary jewellery and fashion. Drop by to see the latest temporary exhibitions, or call in for the spiffy bar and restaurant.

While you're in the vicinity, it's worth looking around the other small private galleries and boutiques or having a drink or meal in one of the new bars and restaurants that have sprung up in the wake of MACBA, especially on c/del Pintor Fortuny, c/de Ferlandina, c/dels Angels and c/del Dr Joaquim Dou. For a sit-down in one of Barcelona's nicest traffic-free squares, head back along c/d'Elisabets to the arcaded **Plaça de Vicenç Martorell**, where *Kasparo's* tables overlook a popular children's playground. Meanwhile, around the corner, the narrow Carrer del Bonsuccés, Carrer Sitges and Carrer dels Tallers house a concentrated selection of the city's best independent **music stores** and urban and streetwear shops.

# Hospital de la Santa Creu and around

The district's most substantial historic relic is the **Hospital de la Santa Creu** (ⓂLiceu), which occupies a large site between c/del Carme and c/de l'Hospital. The attractive complex of Gothic buildings was founded as the city's main hospital in 1402, a role that it assumed for over 500 years – Antoni Gaudí, knocked down by a tram in 1926, was brought here for treatment but died three days later. The hospital shifted site to Domènech i Montaner's new creation in the Eixample in 1930 and the spacious fifteenth-century hospital wards were subsequently converted for cultural and educational use, and now hold the Academy of Medicine, and two libraries, including the Catalan national library, the Biblioteca de Catalunya. Visitors can wander freely through the pleasant medieval cloistered **garden** (daily 10am–dusk; access from either street), and inside the c/del Carme entrance (on the right) are some superb seventeenth-century *azulejos* (painted tiles) of various religious scenes and a tiled Renaissance courtyard. There's also a rather nice café-*terrassa* in the garden at the c/de l'Hospital side.

Walking west along c/de l'Hospital, it's 100m or so to the bottom of **c/de la Riera Baixa**, a narrow street that's at the centre of the city's secondhand and vintage clothing scene. Walking the other way down c/de l'Hospital, back towards the Ramblas, one of the Raval's prettiest squares reveals itself: **Plaça de Sant Agustí**, backed by the Catalan Baroque bulk of the Església de Sant Agusti, an Augustinian foundation from 1728. Turning north, up c/de Jerusalem, you soon find yourself at the back of the Boqueria market, another area in which hip bars have proliferated recently. A couple overlook the **Jardins Dr Fleming**, a children's playground tucked into an exterior corner of the Hospital de la Santa Creu on c/del Carme.

# Rambla de Raval and around

The most obvious manifestation of the changing character of El Raval is the **Rambla de Raval**, an urban boulevard driven right through the centre of the district (between c/de l'Hospital and c/de Sant Pau). In many ways it's still finding its feet – the ongoing Illa Robabdor construction site halfway down will eventually house a hotel, film institute, offices and social housing, while the juvenile trees are yet to throw much shade on the *rambla*'s benches. But the local inhabitants – many of Asian origin – have been quick to appreciate the open space of the *rambla*, while an increasing number of fashionable bars are interspersed amongst the video stores, kebab shops, *halal* butchers, phone offices and grocery stores. A Saturday **street market** (selling anything from *samosas* to hammocks) adds a bit more character, while children find it hard to resist a clamber on the massive, bulbous cat sculpture.

The two extremes of the *rambla* offer a snapshot of the changing neighbourhood. At the bottom end, off **c/de Sant Pau**, the *barri*'s remaining prostitutes accost passers-by as they head back towards the Liceu and the Ramblas. The top end, meanwhile, leads you straight into the streets of the upper Raval, flush with boutiques, bars and galleries. Pause at least in **Plaça del Pedro** (junction of c/del Carme and c/de l'Hospital), where a cherished statue of Santa Eulàlia (co-patron of the city) stands on the site of her supposed crucifixion, facing the surviving apse of a Romanesque chapel. Carrer de Botella, just off the square, is unremarkable, save for the plaque at no. 11 which records the **birthplace of Manuel Vasquez Montalban**, probably the city's most famous writer, whose likes and prejudices found expression in his favourite character, detective Pepe Carvalho.

## Palau Güell

El Raval's outstanding building is the **Palau Güell**, at c/Nou de la Rambla 3 (Tues–Sat 10am–2.30pm; free; ☎933 173 974, ⓂDrassanes/Liceu), an extraordinary townhouse designed by the young Antoni Gaudí for wealthy shipowner

▲ Cat sculpture on Rambla de Raval

## High society at the Hotel España

There's a hidden gem tucked around the back of the Liceu opera house, on the otherwise fairly shabby c/de Sant Pau. Here, in the lower reaches of the Raval, some of the most influential names in Catalan architecture and design came together at the beginning of the twentieth century to transform the dowdy **Hotel España** (c/de Sant Pau 9–11, ⓦwww.hotelespanya.com) – originally built in 1860 – into one of the city's most lavish addresses. With a tiled dining room designed by Lluís Domènech i Montaner, a bar with an amazing marble fireplace by Eusebi Arnau, and a ballroom with a glass ceiling whose marine murals were executed by Ramon Casas, the hotel was the fashionable sensation of its day. It's been well looked after ever since, and you can soak up the atmosphere and the decor for the price of lunch (there's a reasonably priced *menú del día*) or even stay the night – though it has to be said that the rooms are nowhere near as impressive as the public areas.

and industrialist Eusebi Güell i Bacigalupi. It was commissioned in 1885 as an extension of the Güell family's house located on the Ramblas, and was later the first modern building to be declared a World Heritage Site by UNESCO. While restoration continues the house is only partially open (and there's no access at present to the famous roof terrace), but even the dramatic facade is worth walking past to see – there's usually a gaggle of visitors trying to take a decent snap from the confines of the narrow street.

At a time when architects sought to conceal the iron supports within buildings, Gaudí turned them to his advantage, displaying them as decorative features in the grand rooms on the main floor, which are lined with dark marble hewn from the Güell family quarries. Columns, arches and ceilings are all shaped, carved and twisted in an elaborate style that was to become the hallmark of Gaudí's later works. Even the basement stables bear Gaudí's distinct touch, a forest of brick capitals and arches that with a touch of imagination become mushrooms and palms. Meanwhile the roof terrace culminates in a fantastical series of chimneys decorated with swirling patterns made from fragments of glazed tile, glass and earthenware. The family rarely ventured up here – it was the servants instead who were exposed to the fullest flight of Gaudí's fantasy as they hung the washing out on lines hung from chimney to chimney.

The building is under long-term restoration, which isn't expected to be completed until 2010. At the time of writing, there was free access to view the facade, ground floor and part of the basement, but with limited hours and limited numbers allowed in at any one time, expect to queue or be given a specific time-slot.

## Església de Sant Pau del Camp

Carrer de Sant Pau cuts west through the Raval to the church of **Sant Pau del Camp** (Mon 5–8pm, Tues–Fri 10am–1.30pm & 5–8pm, Sat 10am–1.30pm; admission to cloister €2; ⓂParal.lel), its name – St Paul of the Field – a graphic reminder that it once stood in open fields beyond the city walls. One of the most interesting churches in Barcelona, Sant Pau was a Benedictine foundation of the tenth century, built after its predecessor was destroyed in a Muslim raid of 985 AD and constructed on a Greek cross plan. It was renovated again at the end of the thirteenth century; above the main entrance are curious, primitive carvings from that period of fish, birds and faces, while other animal forms adorn the twin capitals of the charming twelfth-century cloister. Inside, the church is dark and rather plain, enlivened only by tiny arrow-slit windows and small stained-glass circles high up in the central dome.

## Mercat de Sant Antoni

The Raval's western edge is defined by the Ronda de Sant Pau and the Ronda de Sant Antoni, and where the two meet stands the handsome **Mercat de Sant Antoni** (Mon–Thurs & Sat 7am–2.30pm & 5.30–8.30pm, Fri 7am–8.30pm; ⓂSant Antoni), the neighbourhood's major produce market, dating from 1876. It makes a pointed contrast to the Boqueria – there are not nearly so many tourists, for a start – and unlike the other city markets, it's surrounded by enclosed aisles packed with stalls selling cheap shoes, underwear, T-shirts, children's clothes, bed linen, towels and other household goods. Come on Sunday and there's a **book and coin market** (9am–2pm) here instead, with collectors and enthusiasts arriving early to pick through the best bargains.

Most of Barcelona's old markets are being revamped, as the nineteenth-century engineering starts to fail, and Sant Antoni is no exception: it is to be remodelled entirely by 2012, though its external character will be retained and a temporary market installed on Ronda de Sant Antoni while works continue. The book and coin market will continue in the vicinity too. Meanwhile, the traditional place to take a break from shopping is *Els Tres Tombs,* the restaurant-bar across the road on the corner of Ronda de Sant Antoni, open from 6am until late for a good-natured mix of market traders, locals, students and tourists.

# Sant Pere, La Ribera and Ciutadella

The Barri Gòtic is bordered on its eastern side by Via Laietana, which was cut through the old town from north to south at the beginning of the twentieth century. Across it lie the two easternmost old-town neighbourhoods of Sant Pere and La Ribera, often thought of as one, but each with a very distinct character, while flanking La Ribera is the green lung of Parc de la Ciutadella.

The medieval *barri* of **Sant Pere** is perhaps the least visited part of the old town, but it has two remarkable buildings, the *modernista* concert hall known as the **Palau de la Música Catalana** and the stylishly designed neighbourhood market, the **Mercat Santa Caterina**. The area around the market has seen a fair amount of regeneration in recent years, as new boulevards and squares are opened up, and a slew of cool bars and restaurants has emerged, some of them destinations in their own right.

By way of contrast, the old artisans' quarter of **La Ribera**, to the south – lying across c/de la Princesa – has always been a big draw, by virtue of the presence of the graceful church of **Santa María del Mar**, the city's most perfect expression of the Catalan-Gothic style, and the **Museu Picasso**, Barcelona's biggest single tourist attraction. The *barri's* cramped, narrow streets were at the heart of medieval industry and commerce, and the neighbourhood is still a centre of creativity, the location of choice for many contemporary designers, craftspeople and artists. Meanwhile La Ribera is at its most hip in the area around the **Passeig del Born**, whose cafés, restaurants and bars make it one of the city's premier nightlife centres.

For time out from the old town's historic intrigues and labyrinthine alleys, retreat to the city's favourite park, the **Parc de la Ciutadella**, on the eastern edge of La Ribera. It holds a full set of attractions, from greenhouses to museums, but on lazy summer days there's little incentive to do any more than stroll the shady garden paths and pilot rowboats across the placid ornamental lake.

## Palau de la Música Catalana

Stumble upon *modernista* architect Lluís Domènech i Montaner's stupendous **Palau de la Música Catalana** (ⓂUrquinaona) from narrow c/Sant Pere Més Alt and it barely seems to have enough space to breathe. The concert hall was

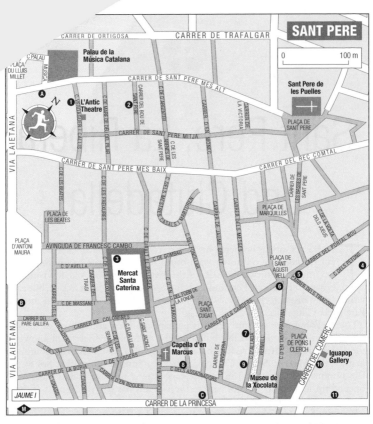

| ACCOMMODATION | | RESTAURANTS | | | TAPAS BARS | | BARS | |
|---|---|---|---|---|---|---|---|---|
| Ciutat | C | Comerç 24 | 4 | Espai Sucre | 11 | El Bitxo | 1 | Black Horse | 9 |
| Grand Hotel Central | B | Cuines Santa Caterina | 3 | Lar O'Marulo | 2 | Mosquito | 6 | Casa Paco | 7 |
| Pensió 2000 | A | L'Econòmic | 5 | Pla de la Garsa | 8 | Santa Maria | 10 | | |

built in 1908 for the Orfeo Català choral group (it's still privately owned) and made an immediate statement of nationalistic intent. Its bare brick structure is smothered in tiles and mosaics, typical of *modernisme*, with the highly elaborate facade resting on three great columns, like elephant's legs. The corner sculpture, by Miquel Blay, represents Catalan popular song, its allegorical figures protected by a strident Sant Jordi. There's little restraint inside either, as Domènech i Montaner strove to make his concert hall a veritable "box of light", achieved by a mighty bulbous stained-glass skylight capping the second-storey auditorium – contemporary critics claimed it to be an engineering impossibility. Sculptures of the Muses ring the main stage, peering down on the performers, while allegorical decoration is everywhere, from the sculpted red and white roses in the colours of the Catalan flag to the representations of music and nature in the glistening stained glass.

Successive extensions and interior remodelling have opened up the original site – the **Petit Palau** offers a smaller auditorium space, while to the side an enveloping glass facade provides the main public access to the box office, terrace restaurant and foyer bar. This is where you come to buy tickets for the very popular fifty-minute-long **guided tours** of the original interior (daily 10am–3.30pm, plus Easter week & Aug 10am–6pm, in English on the hour; €10; ☎902 475 485, ⓦwww.palaumusica.org) – you can also reserve tickets by phone or online, but as visitor numbers are limited you'll almost certainly have to book a day or two in advance. The tours start with a short video extolling the virtues of the building, followed by a close-up look at the decorated facade columns and a brief visit to the two floors of the main concert hall. Or, of course, you can always come to see a performance – the **concert season** here runs from October until June (see p.221 for details).

## Mercat Santa Caterina and around

At the very heart of Sant Pere is the **Mercat Santa Caterina** (Mon 8am–2pm, Tues, Wed & Sat 8am–3.30pm, Thurs & Fri 8am–8.30pm; ☎933 195 740, ⓦwww.mercatsantacaterina.net; ⓜJaume I), whose splendid restoration has retained its original nineteenth-century balustraded market walls and added slatted wooden doors and windows and a dramatic multicoloured wave roof. During the renovation work, the foundations of a major medieval convent were discovered on the site – parts of the medieval walls are visible behind glass at the rear of the market. Santa Caterina is one of the best places in the city to come and shop for food, and its market restaurant and bar are definitely worth a special visit in any case.

Just to the north, the three old main streets, carrers de Sant Pere Més Baix (lower), Mitja (middle) and Alt (upper), contain the bulk of the district's finest medieval buildings and the nicest shops. They converge to the east at Plaça de Sant Pere, site of the much-restored church of **Sant Pere de les Puelles**, one of the oldest in the city, rebuilt in 1147 on tenth-century foundations. It's been destroyed and burned too many times since to retain any interior interest, and the high-walled facade – although it looks medieval – is a twentieth-century renovation.

▲ Mercat Santa Caterina

East of the market, the pretty, tree-shaded **Plaça de Sant Agustí Vell** and its amiable neighbourhood restaurants make a great target for lunch. It sits right in the middle of Sant Pere's most ambitious regeneration project, which has opened up a couple of city blocks to the north as a landscaped boulevard. The southern extension, across c/dels Carders, was completed in the 1990s and has had time to settle in. Now, **Carrer d'Allada Vermell** is one of the most agreeable old-town *ramblas*, its overarching trees and small children's playground complemented by outdoor cafés and bars. Meanwhile, running down from Plaça de Sant Agustí Vell, **c/dels Carders** is now a funky retail quarter mixing grocery stores and cafés with shops selling streetwear, African and Asian arts and crafts and contemporary jewellery. The little Romanesque chapel at the end of the street is the **Capella d'en Marcus** (usually locked), dating back to the twelfth century, though otherwise stripped of interest during the Civil War.

## Museu de la Xocolata

The only other tourist sight in Sant Pere is the city's **Museu de la Xocolata,** c/del Comerç 36 (Mon & Wed–Sat 10am–7pm, Sun 10am–3pm; €3.90; ☎932 687 878, ⓦwww.pastisseria.com; ⓜJaume I) housed in the former Convent de Sant Agustí. The thirteenth-century cloister, rediscovered when the building was renovated, can still be viewed through the building's main doors. Plodding audiovisual displays in the museum recount the history of chocolate, from its origins as a sacred and medicinal product of prehistoric Central America through to its introduction to Europe as a confection in the sixteenth century. It's a topic with some local relevance. The Bourbon army, which was once quartered in this building, demanded the provision of chocolate for its sweet-toothed troops. However, whether you go in or not probably depends on how keen you are to see models of Gaudí buildings or religious icons sculpted from chocolate. Nonetheless, the museum café serves a fine cup of hot chocolate – and the *choccie* counter is something to behold – while at the adjacent Escola de Pastisseria, glass windows allow you to look onto the students learning their craft in the kitchens. There are also chocolate workshops, tastings and children's days organized on a regular basis – enquire at the museum.

## Museu Picasso

The celebrated **Museu Picasso**, c/Montcada 15–23 (Tues–Sun & holidays 10am–8pm; general admission €9, exhibitions €5.80, first Sun of month free; ☎932 563 000, ⓦwww.museupicasso.bcn.cat; ⓜJaume I) is one of the most important collections of Picasso's work in the world, but even so some visitors are disappointed since the museum contains none of his best-known works, and few in the Cubist style. But there are almost 4000 works in the permanent collection, which provide a fascinating opportunity to trace Picasso's development from his early paintings as a young boy to the major works of later years. It might often seem as if every visitor to Barcelona is trying to get into the place at the same time, but you can hardly come to the city and not make the effort. The museum is actually much larger than it first appears, occupying five adjoining medieval palaces converted specifically to house the artist's works. Arriving when it opens is a good way to beat the worst of the crowds. There are free **guided tours** in English (currently on Thurs at 6pm and Sat at noon), but you'll need to book in advance (by phone or by email through the

## Picasso in Barcelona

Although born in Málaga, **Pablo Picasso** (1881–1973) spent much of his youth – from the age of 14 to 23 – in Barcelona. He maintained close links with Barcelona and his Catalan friends even when he left for Paris in 1904, and is said to have always thought of himself as Catalan rather than *andaluz*. The time Picasso spent in Barcelona encompassed the whole of his Blue Period (1901–04) and provided many of the formative influences on his art.

Apart from the Museu Picasso, there are echoes of the great artist at various sites throughout the old town. Not too far from the museum, you can still see many of the buildings in which Picasso lived and worked, notably the **Escola de Belles Arts de Llotja** (c/Consolat del Mar, near Estació de França), where his father taught drawing and where Picasso himself absorbed an academic training. The **apartments** where the family lived when they first arrived in Barcelona – Pg. d'Isabel II 4 and c/Reina Cristina 3, both near the Escola – can also be seen, though only from the outside, while Picasso's first real **studio** (in 1896) was located over on c/de la Plata at no. 4. A few years later, many of his Blue Period works were finished at a studio at c/del Comerç 28. His first **public exhibition** was in 1901 at *Els Quatre Gats* tavern (c/Montsió 3, Barri Gòtic); you can still have a meal there today. The other place to retain a link with Picasso is **c/d'Avinyó** in the Barri Gòtic, which cuts south from c/Ferran to c/Ample. Large houses along here were converted into brothels at the end of the nineteenth century, and Picasso used to haunt the street sketching what he saw. Some accounts of his life – based on Picasso's own testimony, it has to be said – claim that he had his first sexual experience here at the age of 14, but certainly the women at one of the brothels inspired his seminal Cubist work, *Les Demoiselles d'Avignon*.

website). A **café** with a *terrassa* in one of the palace courtyards offers refreshments, and there is of course a **shop**, stuffed full of Picasso-related gifts. Incidentally, works are due to start soon on a new main entrance to the museum (from c/dels Flassaders, to the rear), which will reduce congestion in the narrow c/Montcada.

### The collection

The museum opened in 1963 with a collection based largely on the donations of Jaime Sabartes, longtime friend and former secretary to the artist. On Sabartes' death in 1968, Picasso himself added a large number of works – above all, the works of the Meninas series – and in 1970 he donated a further vast number of watercolours, drawings, prints and paintings.

The works on show are extremely well laid out, as they follow the artist's development chronologically, with the early periods by far the best represented. The **early drawings**, particularly, are fascinating, in which Picasso – still signing with his full name, Pablo Ruiz Picasso – attempted to copy the nature paintings in which his father specialized. Paintings from his art school days in **Barcelona** (1895–97) show tantalizing glimpses of the city that the young Picasso was beginning to know well – the Gothic old town, the cloisters of Sant Paul del Camp, Barceloneta beach – and even at the ages of 15 and 16 he was producing serious works, including knowing self-portraits and a closely observed study of his mother from 1896. Works in the style of Toulouse-Lautrec, like the menu Picasso did for *Els Quatre Gats* tavern in 1900, reflect his burgeoning interest in Parisian art at the turn of the century, while other sketches, drawings and illustrations (many undertaken for competitions and magazines) clearly show Picasso's development of his own unique personal style. His paintings from the

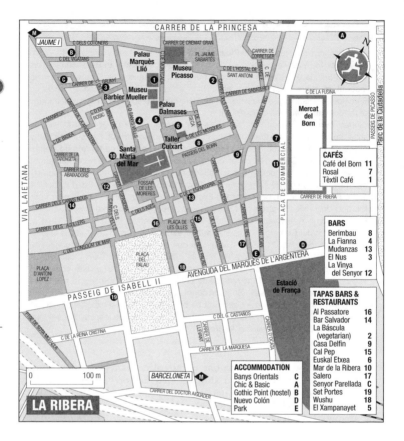

famous **Blue Period** (1901–04) burst upon you – whether its moody Barcelona rooftops or the cold face of *La Dona Morta* – and subsequent galleries trace the Pink Period (1905–06), though with the barest nod to his Cubist (1907–20) and Neoclassical (1920–25) stages.

The large gaps in the main collection (for example, nothing from 1905 until the celebrated *Harlequin* of 1917) only underline Picasso's extraordinary changes of style and mood. This is best illustrated by the large jump to 1957, a year represented by his 44 interpretations of Velázquez's masterpiece, **Las Meninas**, completed in just four months between August and December. In these, Picasso brilliantly deconstructed the individual portraits and compositions that make up Velázquez's work; in addition, and neatly juxtaposed, are displayed nine more donated works by Picasso, gorgeous light-filled Mediterranean scenes inspired by the pigeons and dovecotes of his Cannes studio.

The museum also addresses Picasso as **ceramicist**, highlighting the vibrantly decorated dishes and jugs given to the museum by his wife, Jacqueline. There are various portraits of Jacqueline here, too, though it's the deep friendship Picasso shared with Jaime Sabartes for almost seventy years that provokes the clearest expression of endearment, in a separate room of mature portraits, character studies and jokey sketches by one friend of another. Finally, separate rooms, opened in 2008, display annually changing exhibitions of **Picasso's**

**prints**, culled from the 1500 or so engravings and lithographs that the museum possesses.

## Along Carrer de Montcada

The street on which the Museu Picasso stands – **Carrer de Montcada** – is one of the best looking in the city. It was laid out in the fourteenth century and, until the Eixample was planned almost five hundred years later, was home to most of the city's leading citizens. They occupied spacious mansions built around central courtyards, from which external staircases climbed to the living rooms on the first floor; the facades facing the street were all endowed with huge gated doors that could be swung open to allow coaches access to the interior. Today, almost all the mansions and palaces along La Ribera's showpiece street serve instead as museums, private galleries and craft and gift shops, sucking up the trade from Picasso-bound visitors.

Almost opposite the Museu Picasso, at no. 12, the fourteenth-century **Palau del Marquès de Lió** used to contain the collections of the Textile and Clothing Museum, though these have now moved up to the Palau Reial at Pedralbes. The Carrer Montcada palace will serve as a design archive and activity centre until the city's new Design Centre opens in 2011, and the courtyard *Textil Café* here remains open to the public.

The sixteenth-century Palau Nadal at c/de Montcada 14 houses the **Museu Barbier-Mueller** (Tues–Fri 11am–7pm, Sat 10am–7pm, Sun 10am–3pm; €3, first Sun of month free; T 933 104 516), a terrific collection of pre-Columbian art. Temporary exhibitions – all beautifully presented – highlight wide-ranging themes, and draw on a peerless collection of sculpture, pottery, jewellery, textiles and everyday items, with some pieces dating back as far as the third century BC. Depending on the exhibition, you're as likely to see decorated Mongolian belt-buckles as carved African furniture – there's nothing restrictive about the term "pre-Columbian" – and the shop is also worth a browse, with a wide range of ethnic artefacts for sale.

At the end of the street, in the little Placeta Montcada, **Taller Cuixart BCN** (Tues 5–8pm, Wed–Fri 11am–2pm & 5–8pm, Sat 11am–2pm; €2, free on Tues; T 933 191 947, W www.cuixart.org) is a collection of the works of Catalan artist Modest Cuixart, co-creator of the influential magazine and art movement Dau al Set. Four rooms trace the development of his work, from early Surrealism in the 1940s and 1950s to the sober, abstract landscapes of the 1990s.

### Drinking in the atmosphere

Carrer de Montcada features no fewer than three of the city's most atmospheric café-bars, all found within a 100m stretch and each with its own distinct character. In the **Textil Café** (c/de Montcada 12, W www.textilcafe.com) there are seats in the parasol-shaded courtyard of a medieval mansion, or inside under the impressive stone vaults. Another old mansion, the **Palau Dalmases** (c/de Montcada 20), shows off its seventeenth-century Baroque remodelling every evening, when it's open as a rather grand and very pricey candlelit bar – come on Thursday evenings and singers belt out arias as you sip fine wines under the chandeliers. Finally, there's a change of style at the rather more traditional **El Xampanyet** (c/de Montcada 22), a lavishly tiled, family-run tapas bar near the foot of the street whose speciality is a decidedly non-vintage "champagne" served with anchovies. All, incidentally, take their lead from the neighbourhood's lodestone up the street, the Museu Picasso, and close on Mondays.

# Església de Santa María del Mar

La Ribera's flagship church of **Santa María del Mar** (daily 9am–1.30pm & 4.30–8pm; Sun choral Mass at 1pm; Ⓜ Jaume I/Barceloneta) was begun on the order of King Jaume II in 1324, and finished in only five years. Built on what was the seashore in the fourteenth century, the church was at the heart of the medieval city's maritime and trading district, and it came to embody the supremacy of the Crown of Aragon (of which Barcelona was capital) in Mediterranean commerce. Built quickly, and therefore consistent in style, it's an exquisite example of Catalan-Gothic architecture, with a wide nave and high, narrow aisles, and for all its restrained exterior decoration is still much dearer to the heart of the average local than the cathedral, the only other church in the city with which it compares. The Baroque trappings were destroyed during the Civil War, which is probably all to the good, since the long-term restoration work has concentrated on showing off the simple spaces of the interior; the stained glass, especially, is beautiful.

To the south of the church is the modern brick-lined square known as **Fossar de les Moreres**, which was formally opened in 1989 to mark the spot where, following the defeat of Barcelona on September 11, 1714, Catalan martyrs fighting for independence against the king of Spain, Felipe V, were executed. A red steel scimitar with an eternal flame commemorates the fallen.

# Passeig del Born

Fronting the eastern side of Santa María is the fashionable **Passeig del Born**, once the site of medieval fairs and tournaments ("born" means tournament) and now an avenue lined with a parade of plane trees shading a host of classy bars, delis and shops. Cafés at the eastern end put out tables in front of the old **Mercat del Born**, which was built in 1876 and served as the city's main wholesale fruit and veg market until 1971. It was due to be demolished but was saved by local protests, with the idea of turning it into a library. However, during initial works it became apparent that the market stood directly on top of the partial remains of the eighteenth-century city, dating from before the huge works associated with the building of the nearby Ciutadella fortress and the Barceloneta district. The massive rectangular cast-iron frame of the market is still in place, now protecting the surviving metre-high walls of eighteenth-century shops, factories, houses and taverns. Work is still ongoing, but the current plan is to retain the extensive archeological remains within a cultural and interpretation centre.

Boutiques and **craft workshops** hide in the narrow vaulted medieval alleys on either side of the *passeig* – carrers Flassaders, Vidreria and Rec in particular are noted for clothes, shoes, jewellery and design galleries. At night the Born becomes one of Barcelona's biggest bar zones as spirited locals frequent a panoply of drinking haunts, from old-style cocktail lounges to thumping music bars.

# Parc de la Ciutadella and around

The Bourbons took no chances after the War of the Spanish Succession. Barcelona had put up a spirited resistance, and to quell any further dissent Felipe V ordered the building of a star-shaped citadel close to the water, on the edge of the old town. A great part of La Ribera was destroyed, and a garrison, parade ground and defensive walls were constructed over a twenty-year period

# Antoni Gaudí and modernisme

Antoni Gaudí i Cornet is the most famous proponent of Barcelona's *modernisme* (Art Nouveau style) and, together with his contemporaries Lluís Domènech i Montaner and Josep Puig i Cadafalch, created the weird and wonderful buildings that are a major draw for visitors to Barcelona today. The Catalan offshoot of Art Nouveau was the expression of a renewed upsurge in Catalan nationalism. The early nineteenth-century economic recovery in Catalunya had provided the initial impetus, and the subsequent cultural renaissance – the Renaixença – led to the fresh stirrings of a new Catalan awareness and identity.

# Gaudí's work and style

Born in Reus, near Tarragona, to a family of artisans, the work of **Antoni Gaudí i Cornet** (1852–1926) was never strictly *modernista* in style, but the imaginative impetus he provided was incalculable. His buildings are the most daring creations of all Art Nouveau, yet whether an apartment building (La Pedrera), private housing estate (Parc Güell), or church (Sagrada Família), Gaudí's apparently lunatic flights of fantasy are always rooted in functionality. Spiritual symbolism and Catalan pride are evident in every building too, while his architectural influences were Moorish and Gothic, embellished with elements from the natural world. Gaudí rarely wrote a word about the theory of his art, preferring the buildings to demand reaction – no one stands mute in front of an Antoni Gaudí masterpiece.

Parc Güell ▲
La Pedrera ▼

# The Gaudí trail

There's a constant stream of visitors to the major sites, notably the **Sagrada Família** – probably the most famous church in the world – the roof terrace of **La Pedrera, Casa Batlló** and the glorious **Parc Güell**, but even in this most Gaudí-obsessed city there are a few places where you can meet the master without the crowds. While he was rebuilding his **Palau Güell** townhouse, the architect's longtime patron, industrialist Eusebi Güell, commissioned the young Gaudí to revamp his summer house in the northern suburbs, and at the **Pavellons Güell** Gaudí's celebrated dragon gate and innovative stables await. Meanwhile, on the city's western outskirts, Gaudí was also designing his patron's utopian industrial town, the **Colònia Güell**, with an uplifting chapel whose design foreshadowed that of the Sagrada Família.

# The other modernistas

With Gaudí in a class of his own, it was **Lluís Domènech i Montaner** (1850–1923) who was perhaps the greatest pure *modernista* architect. Drawing on the rich Catalan Romanesque and Gothic traditions, his work combined traditional craft methods with modern technological experiments, seen to triumphant effect in his masterpiece, the **Palau de la Música Catalana**. This exciting marriage of techniques first inspired **Josep Puig i Cadafalch** (1867–1957) to become an architect, and his work too contains a wildly inventive use of ceramic tiles, ironwork, stained glass and stone carving. His first commission, the Casa Martí, housed the *Quatre Gats* tavern for the city's *modernista* artists and avant-garde hangers-on, while mansions like Casa Macaya and Casa de les Punxes display distinct Gothic and medieval influences.

▲ Casa Batlló

▼ Sagrada Família

# Crafts and collaborators

*Modernisme* was a collaborative effort between the architects and their craftsmen and artisans. Domènech i Montaner in particular recognized the importance of ensemble working, establishing a workshop in the building he designed initially as a restaurant for Barcelona's Universal Exhibition of 1888 (now the Museu de Zoologia). Gaudí's longtime collaborator was **Josep Maria Jujol i Gilbert**, a master of mosaic decoration, responsible for most of the startling ceramic work in Parc Güell, while **Eusebi Arnau** provided meticulous carvings for all the main *modernista* architects – much loved are his quirky figures adorning

▼ Palau Güell

Casa Macaya ▲

Almirall bar ▼

Puig i Cadafalch's Casa Macaya. Some projects brought together the cream of *modernista* craft talent, so at Domènech i Montaner's Palau de la Música Catalana, for example, the glorious stained glass by **Antoni Rigalt** and facade sculpture by **Miquel Blay** are an integral part of the whole.

# Eat, drink, sleep, shop – the modernista way

**Almirall** The city's oldest bar is also a fine example of period decor, notably the main entrance, marble counter and display cabinet. See p.213.

**Antiga Casa Figueras** Bakeries and confectioners often got the *modernista* treatment – this Ramblas pastry shop is a famous example. See p.189.

**Camiserá Pons** Hot Spanish fashion on show in a classy old shop. See p.245.

**Casa Calvet** A private townhouse built by Gaudí is the setting for an upscale Catalan restaurant. See p.208.

**Casa Fuster** This hugely stylish hotel takes a landmark *modernista* building and adds state-of-the-art comforts. See p.185.

**Hotel Espanya** Have lunch in one of the city's most splendidly decorated dining rooms. See p.71.

**El Indio** If you're in town for the week-end and need some linen or a new pillowcase, there's only one place to go. See p.247.

**London Bar** The bar, and its eye-catching decor, has been a city fixture since 1910. See p.213.

**Muy Buenas** Behind the *modernista* facade is one of the Raval's best bars. See p.213.

**Els Quatre Gats** Mingle with the ghost of the young Picasso in Barcelona's original style bar. See p.57.

in the mid-eighteenth century. This Bourbon symbol of authority survived uneasily until 1869, when the military moved base. Many of the buildings were subsequently demolished and the surrounding area made into a park, the **Parc de la Ciutadella** (daily 8am–dusk). In 1888, the park was chosen as the site of the **Universal Exhibition** and the city's *modernista* architects, including the young Gaudí, left their mark here in a series of eye-catching buildings and monuments.

The Parc de la Ciutadella is still the biggest green space in the city centre, home to a splendid fountain, large lake, plant houses, two museums and the city zoo. It's a very popular place for a stroll, and Sundays especially see couples and families taking time out here, while a younger crowd assembles for a bit of vigorous didgeridooing or bongo-work. The only surviving portion of the citadel, the much-altered Arsenal in the southeastern reaches of the park, has since 1980 housed Catalunya's legislative assembly, the **Parlament** (no public access – see p.271, for more on the institution). Near the park, within short walking distance, are a couple of other attractions, including one of the city's most peculiar museums, devoted to funeral carriages.

The park's **main gates** are on Passeig de Picasso (Ⓜ Barceloneta, or a short walk from La Ribera), and there's also an entrance on Passeig de Pujades (Ⓜ Arc de Triomf); only use Ⓜ Ciutadella-Vila Olímpica if you're going directly to the zoo, as there's no access to the park itself from that side. The whole Ciutadella area is shown on colour map 6 at the back of the book.

## Inside the park

The first of the major projects undertaken inside the park was the **Cascada**, the monumental fountain in the northeast corner. It was designed by Josep Fontseré i Mestrès, the architect chosen to oversee the conversion of the former citadel grounds into a park, and his assistant in the work was the young Antoni Gaudí, then a student. The Baroque extravagance of the Cascada is suggestive of the flamboyant decoration that was later to become Gaudí's trademark. The best place to contemplate the fountain's tiers and swirls is from the small **open-air café** just to the south. Here you'll also find a lake, where for a few euros you can **rent a rowboat** and paddle about among the ducks. Incidentally, Gaudí is also thought to have had a hand in the design of the Ciutadella's iron park gates.

Just inside the northern entrance to the park, architect Lluís Domènech i Montaner designed a castle-like building intended for use as the exhibition's café-restaurant. Dubbed the *Castell dels Tres Dragons*, it became a centre for *modernista* arts and crafts, and many of Domènech's contemporaries spent time here experimenting with new materials and refining their techniques. It's now used by the zoological section of the city's Natural Science Museum, but it's fair to say that the decorated red-brick exterior of the **Museu de Zoologia** (Tues–Sun 10am–2.30pm, Thurs & Sat until 6.30pm; combined ticket with Geology Museum €3.70, first Sun of month free, separate charge for special exhibitions; ℡ 933 196 912, Ⓦ www.bcn.es/museuciencies) knocks spots off the rather dry displays of stuffed birds, insects and animals. However, temporary popular-science exhibitions tend to be of more interest, while you can liven up a visit for under-12s by asking for the free educational activities kit. The sister museum is the nearby **Museu de Geologia** (same hours, price and website as Museu de Zoologia, ℡ 933 196 895), which opened in 1882 and was actually the first public museum in the city. Based on the geological bequest of Francesc Martorell i Peña, who gave his name to the original museum, it's another restored period piece, with nineteenth-century cases of exhibits housed in a classical, pedimented building. There are rocks and minerals on one side, and fossils on the other, with many of the exhibits found in Catalunya, from fluorescent rocks to mammoth bones.

However, the two real unsung glories of Ciutadella are its plant houses, arranged either side of the Geological Museum (both open daily 8am–dusk; free). The imposing **Umbracle** (palmhouse) is a handsome structure with a barrelled wood-slat roof supported by cast-iron pillars, which allows shafts of light to play across the palms and ferns. Both materials and concept are echoed in the larger **Hivernacle** (conservatory), whose enclosed greenhouses are separated by a soaring glass-roofed terrace. A refined **café-bar** at the Hivernacle (open from 10am) is the best stop in the park for drinks or a meal, with tables set amongst the palm trees under the glass roof.

## Parc Zoològic

Ciutadella's most popular attraction by far is the city's zoo, the **Parc Zoològic** (daily: June–Sept 10am–7pm; March–May & Oct 10am–6pm; Jan, Feb, Nov & Dec 10am–5pm; €16; ☎932 256 780, ⓦwww.zoobarcelona.com), taking up most of the southeastern part of the park. The main entrance is on c/Wellington, and is signposted from ⓜCiutadella-Vila Olímpica, or tram T4 stops outside. It boasts 7000 animals from 400 different species – which is simply too many for a zoo that is still essentially nineteenth-century in character, confined to the formal grounds of a public park and devoted to entertainment rather than education. Brown bears beg for food, dolphins perform antics daily, while elephants, giraffes and tigers pace their minimal concrete enclosures. Although there's a nod to conservation issues it's difficult to see beyond the unimaginative presentation, fast-food concessions, picnic areas and mini-train rides.

However, the zoo's days here in its current form are numbered – the powers that be, perhaps having finally appreciated the irony of its juxtaposition next to the parliament building, have grown weary of explaining to visiting dignitaries the source of the strong smell pervading the area. There are advanced plans to move the marine animals to a new coastal zoo and wetlands area (possibly by 2010) at the Diagonal Mar seashore, though the mammals are likely to stay at Ciutadella.

## Arc de Triomf and around

From the northern entrance of the Parc de la Ciutadella, the wide Passeig Lluís Companys runs up to the giant brick **Arc de Triomf** (ⓜArc de Triomf). Roman in scale, yet reinterpreted by its *modernista* architect, Josep Vilaseca i Casanoves, as a bold statement of Catalan intent, it's studded with ceramic figures and motifs, and topped by two pairs of bulbous domes. The reliefs on the main facade show the city of Barcelona welcoming visitors to the 1888 Universal Exhibition.

To the east lies the **Barcelona Nord** bus station, behind which stretches the undistinguished **Parc de l'Estacío del Nord**, which cuts across several city blocks as far as Avinguda Meridiana, ten minutes from the arch. The only reason to walk or ride out this way would be to present yourself at the front desk of the Serveis Funeraris (funerary services) de Barcelona, a few metres along c/Sancho de Ávila from the avenue (by the blue "Banc Sabadell" sign). You'll be escorted into the bowels of the building and the lights will be thrown on in the **Museu de Carrosses Fúnebres** (Mon–Fri 10am–1pm & 4–6pm, Sat & Sun 10am–1pm; free; ☎934 871 700; ⓜMarina) to reveal a staggering set of twenty-two funerary carriages, each parked on its own cobbled stage, complete with ghostly attendants, horses and riders suspended in frozen animation. Used for city funeral processions from the end of the nineteenth century onwards, most of the carriages and hearses are extravagantly decorated in gilt, black or white – the service was mechanized in the 1950s, when the silver Buick, also on display, came into use. Old photographs show some of the carriages in use in the city's streets, while showcases highlight antique uniforms, mourning wear and formal riding gear.

# The waterfront: from Port Vell to Diagonal Mar

Perhaps the greatest recent transformation in the city has been along the **waterfront**, where harbour and Mediterranean have once again been placed at the heart of Barcelona. Dramatic changes here over the last two decades have shifted the cargo and container trade away to the south, opened up the old docksides as promenades and entertainment areas, and landscaped the city's beaches to the north – it's as if a theatre curtain has been lifted to reveal that, all along, Barcelona had an urban waterfront of which it could be proud.

Reaching the bottom of the Ramblas puts you within strolling distance of some heavyweight tourist attractions, including the **Mirador de Colón** (Columbus statue), **Museu Marítim**, the sightseeing harbour **boat trips**, and the boardwalks and promenades of the inner harbour, known as **Port Vell**. The old wharves and warehouses have been replaced by an entertainment zone that encompasses the Maremàgnum shopping and nightlife centre, the city's high-profile aquarium and IMAX screens and, across the marina, the impressive **Museu d'Història de Catalunya**. The wedge of land backing the marina is **Barceloneta**, an eighteenth-century fishing quarter that's the most popular place to come and sample the fish and seafood dishes of which Barcelona is most proud.

From Barceloneta, six interlinked **beaches** stretch up the coast, backed by an attractive promenade. The city's inhabitants have taken to these in a big way, strolling, jogging and skating their length and descending in force at the weekend for a leisurely lunch at a nearby restaurant. The main development is around the **Port Olímpic**, filled with places to eat, drink and shop, and although fewer tourists keep on as far as the old working-class neighbourhood of **Poble Nou**, its beaches, historic cemetery and pretty *rambla* make for an interesting diversion. The coastal redevelopment extends as far as **Diagonal Mar**, where the Avinguda Diagonal meets the sea. This conference and exhibition district expands upon the buildings and infrastructure of the Universal Forum of Cultures, the diversity and sustainability exposition held here in 2004.

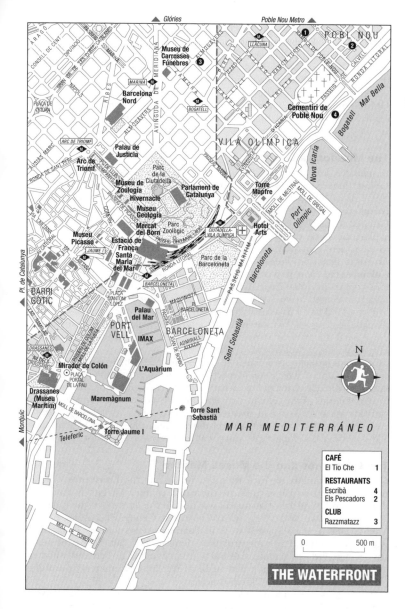

Map key:

**CAFÉ**
El Tio Che   **1**

**RESTAURANTS**
Escribà   **4**
Els Pescadors   **2**

**CLUB**
Razzmatazz   **3**

0     500 m

**THE WATERFRONT**

## Plaça Portal de la Pau and around

The Ramblas ends at **Plaça Portal de la Pau** (ⓂDrassanes), coming up hard against the teeming traffic that runs along the harbourside road. The maritime museum is over to the right, and the Columbus monument is straight ahead in the middle of the traffic circle, with the quayside square beyond flanked by the **Port de Barcelona** (Port Authority) and **Duana** (Customs House) buildings.

Away to the south is the Moll de Barcelona, a landscaped wharf leading to the Torre de Jaume I **cable-car station** and the **Estació Marítima**, where ferries leave for the Balearics. The large, bulbous building perched in the centre of the wharf is the city's **World Trade Centre**, where a luxury hotel complements the complex of offices, convention halls, shops and restaurants.

From the quayside just beyond the foot of the Columbus monument, **Las Golondrinas** sightseeing boats and the **Catamaran Orsom** depart on regular trips throughout the year around the inner harbour – all the details are on p.30.

## The Mirador de Colón

Inaugurated just before the Universal Exhibition of 1888, the **Mirador de Colón** (June–Sept daily 9am–8.30pm; Oct–May daily 10am–6.30pm; €2.50; ☎933 025 224) commemorates the visit made by Christopher Columbus to Barcelona in June 1493. The Italian-born navigator was received in style by the Catholic monarchs Ferdinand and Isabella, who had supported his voyage of exploration a year earlier, when Columbus had set out to chart a passage west to the Orient. Famously, he failed in this, as he failed also to reach the North American mainland (instead "discovering" the Bahamas, Cuba and Haiti), but Columbus did enough to enhance his reputation and made three more exploratory voyages by 1504. Later, nineteenth-century Catalan nationalists took the navigator to their hearts – if he wasn't exactly Catalan, he was the closest they had to a local Vasco da Gama, and so they put him on the pedestal that they thought he deserved. Awkwardly for the locals, the statue is actually pointing in the general direction of Libya, not North America, but, as historian Robert Hughes puts it, at least "the sea is Catalan".

Columbus himself tops a grandiose, iron column, 52m high, guarded by lions at the base, around which unfold reliefs telling the story of his life and travels – here, if nowhere else, the old mercenary is still the "discoverer of America". On the harbour side of the column, steps lead down to a ticket office and lift, which you ride up to the enclosed *mirador* at Columbus' feet. The 360-degree views are terrific but the narrow viewing platform, which tilts perceptibly outwards and downwards, is emphatically not for anyone without a head for heights.

## The Drassanes and the Museu Marítim

Opposite Columbus, set back from the avenue, are the **Drassanes**, unique medieval shipyards dating from the thirteenth century. Originally used as a dry dock to fit and arm Catalunya's war fleet in the days when the Catalan-Aragonese crown was vying with Venice and Genoa for control of the Mediterranean, the shipyards were in continuous use until well into the eighteenth century. The basic structure – long parallel halls facing the sea – has changed little; its singular size and position couldn't be bettered, whether the shipbuilders were fitting out medieval warships or eighteenth-century trading vessels destined for South America.

The huge, stone-vaulted buildings make a fitting home for the **Museu Marítim** (daily 10am–8pm; €6.50, free on afternoon of 1st Sat of month; ☎933 429 920, ⓦwww.museumaritimbarcelona.com; ⓂDrassanes). The centrepiece is a copy of the sixteenth-century Royal Galley (*Galera Roial*), a soaring red-and-gold barge which was originally constructed here and was present at the great naval victory over the Ottoman Turks at Lepanto in 1571. This aside, it's really the building that's the main attraction, since the rest of the exhibits – fishing skiffs, sailing boats, figureheads, old maps and charts, ship portraits, navigation instruments – fail to spark much casual interest. You'll get the most out of a visit if you pick up the free audio-guide and hone in on some of the more illuminating digressions, for example on steam navigation, fishing methods, life at sea or the growth of the port of Barcelona. Combination tickets available at the desk are more worthwhile, offering discounted trips on the harbour sightseeing boats or up the Columbus monument, while **children's activities** at weekends and school holidays are well regarded. There's also a good **café-restaurant** at the museum (open Mon–Sat lunch, plus Thurs–Sat dinner), which puts out tables in the pleasant courtyard – on summer evenings, this becomes a popular patio lounge-bar.

Moored over on the Moll de la Fusta (beyond the harbour's swing bridge), the **Santa Eulàlia** (May–Oct Tues–Fri noon–7.30pm, Sat & Sun 10am–7pm; rest of the year closes 5.30pm; €2.40, free with Museu Marítim ticket) is another of the museum's showpiece exhibits. Dating from 1908, and previously named the *Carmen Flores*, the three-masted ocean schooner once made the run between Barcelona and Cuba. It's been fully restored since being acquired by the museum, and a short tour lets you walk the deck and view the interior.

## Port Vell

Barcelona's inner harbour has been rebranded as **Port Vell** (Old Port; Ⓜ Drassanes/Barceloneta), an area that encompasses the Moll d'Espanya wharf, the adjacent marina and the Palau de Mar development at the northwestern head of the Barceloneta district. It has its local critics – it's undoubtedly tourist-oriented, showy and expensive – but there's no denying the improvement made to what was formerly a decaying port area. The city's old timber wharf was among the first to be prettified. Backed by sedate nineteenth-century buildings along the Passeig de Colom, the **Moll de la Fusta** is a landscaped promenade with a note of humour injected by the addition of a giant fibreglass crayfish by Catalan designer Xavier Mariscal and, further on, the Roy Lichtenstein totem-pole sculpture known as "Barcelona Head". From the Columbus statue end of

▲ Waterside café

the wharf, the wooden **Rambla de Mar** swing bridge strides across the harbour to the **Moll d'Espanya**, whose main features are the leisure complex known as Maremàgnum – jammed with fast-food joints, shops, restaurants and bars – plus the aquarium and IMAX cinema. The eastern arm of the Moll d'Espanya connects back to the Moll de la Fusta, providing pedestrian access to the **Palau de Mar** at the northern end of Barceloneta's Passeig Joan de Borbó. This old warehouse has been beautifully restored, with a series of restaurants in the lower arcade overlooking the marina and the regional history museum occupying the upper floors.

## Maremàgnum and the Moll d'Espanya

**Maremàgnum** (daily 10am–10pm; ⓦwww.maremagnum.es; ⓂDrassanes) is a typically bold piece of Catalan design, the soaring glass lines of the complex tempered by the surrounding undulating wooden walkways. Inside are two floors of gift shops and boutiques, plus a range of bars and restaurants with harbourside seating and high prices. It's a fun place to come at night, though no self-respecting local would rate the food as anything but ordinary. Outside, benches and park areas provide fantastic views back across the harbour to the city.

Anchoring Moll d'Espanya, **L'Aquàrium** (daily: July & Aug 9.30am–11pm; Sept–June 9.30am–9pm, until 9.30pm at weekends; €16; ☎932 217 474, ⓦwww.aquariumbcn.com; ⓂDrassanes) drags in families and school parties throughout the year to see "a magical world, full of mystery". Or, to be more precise, to see 11,000 fish and sea creatures in 35 themed tanks representing underwater caves, tidal areas, tropical reefs and the planet's oceans. It's vastly overpriced and despite the claims of excellence it offers few new experiences, save perhaps the eighty-metre-long walk-through underwater tunnel which brings you face to face with gliding rays and cruising sharks. Some child-centred displays and activities, and a nod towards ecology and conservation matters, pad out the attractions before you're tipped out in the aquarium shop so they can part you from even more of your money.

**IMAX Port Vell** (☎932 251 111, ⓦwww.imaxportvell.com) stands next to the aquarium, with three screens showing films hourly from 11am in 3D or giant screen format. The themes are familiar – the mysteries of the human body, forces of nature, heroic exploration, alien adventure etc – and tickets are fairly reasonably priced (€8 or €12, depending on the film), but you'll find that the films are in Spanish or Catalan only. Instead, you might saunter down to the sloping lawn nearby, where there's usually a school party examining the replica of the strange fish-shaped submarine, the **Ictineo**, a genuine Catalan curiosity (see opposite). From here, it's only a ten-minute walk down the *moll*, past the towering Roy Lichtenstein sculpture, and around the marina to the Palau de Mar and Barceloneta.

## Museu d'Història de Catalunya

The only surviving warehouse on the Port Vell harbourside is known as the Palau de Mar, home to the **Museu d'Història de Catalunya** (Tues & Thurs–Sat 10am–7pm, Wed 10am–8pm, Sun & holidays 10am–2.30pm; €4, first Sun of month & public holidays free; ☎932 254 700, ⓦwww.mhcat.net; ⓂBarceloneta), which traces the history of Catalunya from the Stone Age to the twentieth century. It's a spacious exhibition area wrapped around a wide atrium, with temporary shows on the ground floor and a lift to take you to the permanent displays on the upper floors: second floor for year dot to the

## Monturiol and the Catalan submarine

**Narcís Monturiol i Estarriol** (1819–1885) was born in Figueres in northeastern Catalunya but studied in Barcelona, soon falling in with radicals and revolutionaries. Although a law graduate, he never practised, turning his energetic talents instead to writing and publishing. He set up his first publishing company in 1846, the same year he married Emilia; they later had eight children. A series of journals and pamphlets followed, all espousing Monturiol's radical beliefs – in feminism, pacifism and utopian communism – and it was no surprise when one of his publications was suppressed by the government in the heady revolutionary days of 1848. Monturiol was forced briefly into exile and on his return to Barcelona, with the government now curtailing his publishing activities, he turned his hand instead to self-taught science and engineering.

It was a period in which scientific progress and social justice appeared as two sides of the same coin to utopians like Monturiol – indeed, his friend, the civil engineer Ildefons Cerdà, would later mastermind the building of Barcelona's Eixample on socially useful grounds. Monturiol's mind turned to more immediately practical matters and, inspired by the harsh conditions in which the coral fishermen of Cadaques worked, he conceived the idea of a man-powered submarine. It would improve their lot, he had no doubt, though Monturiol's grander vision was of an underwater machine to explore the oceans and expand human knowledge.

The **Ictineo** – the "fish-boat" – made its maiden voyage in Barcelona harbour on June 28, 1859. At 7m long, it could carry four or five men, and eventually made more than fifty dives at depths of up to 20m. An improved design was started in 1862 – *Ictineo II* – a seventeen-metre-long vessel designed to be propelled by up to sixteen men. Trials in 1865 soon showed that human power wasn't sufficient for the job, so Monturiol installed a steam engine near the stern. This, the world's first steam-powered submarine, was launched on October 22, 1867 and dived to depths of up to 30m on thirteen separate runs (the longest lasting for over seven hours). However, Monturiol's financial backers had finally run out of patience with a machine that, though technically brilliant, couldn't yet pay its way. They withdrew their support and the submarine was seized by creditors and sold for scrap – the engine ended up in a paper mill.

Monturiol spent the rest of his life in a variety of jobs, but continued to come up with new inventions. With the *Ictineo*, he had pioneered the use of the double hull, a technique still used today, while Monturiol also made advances in the manufacture of glues and gums, copying documents, commercial cigarette production and steam engine efficiency. He died in relative obscurity in 1885 and was buried in Barcelona, though his remains were later transferred to his home town. There's a memorial there, while others to Monturiol's pioneering invention, the *Ictineo*, are scattered throughout Barcelona. Monturiol himself is remembered in the city by a simple plaque at the Cementiri de Poble Nou.

Industrial Revolution, and third for periods and events up to 1980 (though later coverage is planned). You can pick up full English notes at the desk, and there's plenty to get your teeth into, whether it's poking around the interior of a Roman grain ship or comparing the rival nineteenth-century architectural plans for the Eixample. There's a dramatic Civil War section, while other fascinating asides shed light on matters as diverse as housing in the 1960s or the origins of the design of the Catalan flag. On the fourth floor, *La Miranda* café boasts a glorious view from its huge terrace of the harbour, Tibidabo, Montjuïc and the city skyline – you don't need a museum ticket to visit this and it's open as a café during museum hours, with a set lunch, as well as for à la carte dinners.

## The cross-harbour cable car

The most thrilling ride in the city centre is across the inner harbour on the cable car, the **Trasbordador Aeri** (☎932 252 718), which sweeps right across the water from the **Torre de Sant Sebastiá**, at the foot of Barceloneta, to Montjuïc, with a stop in the middle at **Torre de Jaume I**, in front of the World Trade Centre on the Moll de Barcelona. The views are stunning, and you can pick out with ease the familiar towers of La Seu (the cathedral) and Sagrada Família, while the trees lining the Ramblas look like the forked tongue of a serpent.

**Departures** are every fifteen minutes (daily 10.30am–7pm, June–Sept until 8pm), though in summer and at weekends you may have to wait for a while at the top of the towers as the cars only carry about twenty people at a time. **Tickets** cost €9 one way or €12.50 return.

The fish and seafood **restaurants** in the Palau de Mar arcade are some of the most popular in the city, especially at weekends. Here you overlook the packed **marina**, where Catalans park their yachts like they park their cars – impossibly tightly – fronted in summer by hawkers spreading blankets on the ground to sell jewellery and sunglasses. A boat near the Palau de Mar in the marina has been converted into a floating bar, the *Luz de Gas*.

# Barceloneta

There's no finer place for lunch on a sunny day than the **Barceloneta** neighbourhood (ⓂBarceloneta), bound by the harbour on one side and the Mediterranean on the other. It was laid out in 1755 in a classic eighteenth-century grid, where previously there had been only mud flats, and replaced part of the Ribera district that was destroyed to make way for the Ciutadella fortress to the north. The long, narrow streets are still very much as they were planned, broken at intervals by small squares and lined with abundantly windowed houses designed to give the sailors and fishing folk who originally lived here plenty of sun and fresh air. Some original houses feature a decorative flourish, a sculpted balcony or a carved lintel, while in Plaça de la Barceloneta survives an eighteenth-century fountain and the Neoclassical church of **Sant Miquel del Port**. A block over in Plaça de la Font is the stylish neighbourhood market, **Mercat de la Barceloneta** (Mon 7am–3pm, Tues–Thurs 7am–3pm & 4.30–8.30pm, Fri 7am–8.30pm, Sat 7am–4pm), beautifully refurbished in 2007 and boasting a couple of classy restaurants (one, the *Lluçanès*, now Michelin-starred). Barceloneta's many other seafood restaurants are found scattered right across the tight grid of streets but most characteristically lined along the harbourside **Passeig Joan de Borbó**, where for most of the year you can sit outside and enjoy your meal.

On the seaward side of Barceloneta, what was once a scrappy fishermen's strand is now furnished with boardwalks, outdoor cafés, showers, benches, climbing frames, water fountains and public art. **Platja de Sant Sebastià** is the first in a series of landscaped **city beaches** that stretches north from here along the coast to the River Besòs. On the spit at the harbour end, work is well underway on a marina, office and leisure development by Catalan architect Ricardo Bofill whose signature building will be a sail-shaped hotel providing a "balcony over the sea". In the other direction, a double row of palms backs the **Passeig Marítim**, a sweeping stone esplanade that runs as far as the Port Olímpic, a fifteen-minute walk away. On the way, you'll pass the **Parc de la Barceloneta**, a rather plain expanse enlivened only by its whimsical *modernista* water tower (1905), rising like a minaret above the palms.

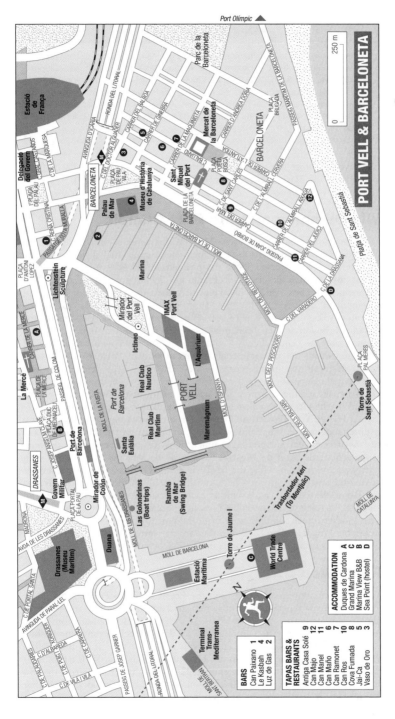

PORT VELL & BARCELONETA

Port Olímpic ▲

0        250 m

**BARS**
Can Paixano        1
Le Kasbah          4
Luz de Gas         2

**TAPAS BARS &
RESTAURANTS**
Antiga Casa Solé   9
Can Majó           12
Can Manel          11
Can Maño           6
Can Ramonet        7
Can Ros            10
Cova Fumada        8
Jai-Ca             5
Vaso de Oro        3

**ACCOMMODATION**
Duques de Cardona  A
Grand Marina       C
Marina View B&B    B
Sea Point (hostel) D

> ## Beach business
>
> On the boardwalk arcade, in front of the Hospital del Mar, the city council has opened a beach visitor centre, the **Centre de la Platja** (March–May Sat 11am–1.30pm & 4–6.30pm, Sun & holidays 11am–1.30pm, June–Sept daily 10am–7pm; ☎932 247 571, ⓦwww.bcn.cat/platges), as a kind of one-stop-shop for information and activities along the seafront. There's a programme of walks, talks and sports, a small summer lending library for beach reading, and volleyball gear available for pick-up games on the sand.

Just beyond, before the port, rises the dramatic latticed funnel of wood and steel that is the **Parc Recerca Biomèdica Barcelona** (PRBB), the city's biomedical research centre.

# Vila Olímpica and the Port Olímpic

From any point along the Passeig Marítim, the soaring twin towers of the Olympic village and port impose themselves upon the skyline, while a shimmering golden mirage above the promenade slowly reveals itself to be a **huge copper fish** (courtesy of Frank O. Gehry, architect of the Bilbao Guggenheim). These are the showpiece manifestations of the huge seafront development constructed for the 1992 Olympics. The **Vila Olímpica** (Olympic Village) housed the 15,000 competitors and support staff, with the apartment buildings and residential complexes converted into permanent housing after the Games. It was a controversial plan, not least because the local population from the old industrial neighbourhood of Poble Nou – part of which was destroyed in the process – were excluded as property prices here later soared. Generally agreed to have been more beneficial is the **Port Olímpic**, site of the Olympic marina and many of the watersports events. Backed by the city's two tallest buildings – the **Torre Mapfre** and the steel-framed **Hotel Arts Barcelona**, both 154m high – the port area has filled up with restaurants, bars, shops and nightspots, and is a major target for visitors and city dwellers at weekends and on summer nights. Two wharves contain the bulk of the action: the **Moll de Mestral** has a lower deck by the marina lined with cafés, bars and *terrassas*, while the **Moll de Gregal** sports a double-decker tier of seafood restaurants. Beyond here, on the far side of the port, **Nova Icària** and **Bogatell** beaches – each with a beachside café, play facilities, showers and loungers – stretch up to the Poble Nou neighbourhood.

It's another fifteen minutes' walk from the port to the end of Bogatell beach and Poble Nou. Heading back into the city, the entrance to ⓂCiutadella-Vila Olímpica lies over the main Ronda del Litoral, behind the port.

# Poble Nou

The next neighbourhood along from the Port Olímpic is **Poble Nou** (New Village), a largely nineteenth-century industrial area that has been in the throes of redevelopment since the early 1990s. As with the Vila Olímpica before it, the redevelopment has its critics amongst the locals, who feel they're being pushed out as the money floods in – "Poble Nou is not for sale" reads the graffiti, though it's an increasingly forlorn cry. The authorities have given the regeneration area a suitably contemporary epithet, **22@** (ⓦwww.22barcelona.com), and are currently overseeing the transformation of almost 120 city blocks, straddling 200 hectares of land, into "the innovation district".

The redevelopment of old factories and the like has already had a significant effect, as some of the city's hottest clubs, galleries and art spaces are now found in Poble Nou. Meanwhile, the few local attractions are easily seen by anyone with a couple of hours to spare. The spruced-up **beaches** – Bogatell, Mar Bella and Nova Mar Bella – are reached along the promenade from the Port Olímpic, while crossing the main highway backing Bogatell beach puts you at the bottom of the pretty tree-lined **Rambla Poble Nou**. This runs inland through the most attractive part of nineteenth-century Poble Nou and is entirely local in character – no cardsharps or human statues here. Stop off for an *orxata* (a sweet drink made from ground nuts) or a crushed ice lemon drink at *El Tío Ché* or lunch at *Els Pescadors* – Ⓜ Poble Nou (line 4) is at the top of the *rambla* and a block over to the right, and will take you back to Ciutadella, Barceloneta or the city centre.

Back near the beach, it's also worth taking the time to walk around the long walls to the entrance of the **Cementiri de Poble Nou** (daily 8am–6pm), at the northern end of Avinguda d'Icaria. This vast nineteenth-century mausoleum has its tombs set in walls 7m high, tended by families who have to climb great stepladders to reach the uppermost tiers. With traffic noise muted by the high walls, and birdsong accompanying a stroll around the flower-lined pavements, quiet courtyards, sculpted angels and tiny chapels, this village of the dead is a rare haven in contemporary Barcelona.

## Diagonal Mar and the Fòrum

The waterfront north of Poble Nou has seen the latest city transformation, in the wake of the Universal Forum of Cultures Expo, held here in 2004. The district is promoted as **Diagonal Mar** (Ⓜ El Maresme Fòrum, or tram T4), anchored by the Diagonal Mar shopping mall, and with several four- and five-star hotels, plus convention centres and exhibition halls grouped nearby. The

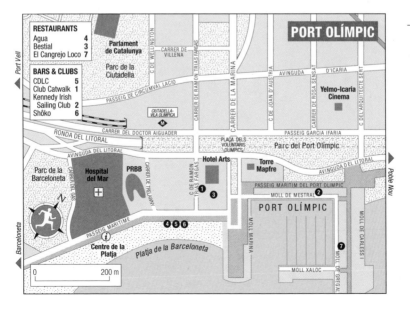

dazzling **Edifici Fòrum** building, a giant blue biscuit tin hovering – seemingly unsupported – above the ground is the work of Jacques Herzog, architect of London's Tate Modern. Everything here is on a grand scale: the main convention centre is the biggest in southern Europe, while the boast about the main open space is that it's the second largest square in the world (150,000 square metres) after Beijing's Tiananmen Square. This immense, undulating expanse spreads towards the sea, culminating in a giant solar-panelled canopy that overlooks the marina, and landscaped beach, park and performance areas. In summer, temporary bars, dance floors, open-air cinema and chill-out zones are established at the **Parc del Fòrum** (Ⓦ www.bcn.cat/parcdelforum), and the city authorities have shifted many of the bigger annual music festivals and events down here to inject a bit of life outside conventions. It can still seem a bit soulless at times – hot as Hades in summer, buffeted by biting winter winds – but it's worth the metro ride if you're interested in heroic-scale public projects. The tram comes down here too, so you could always glide there or back via Avinguda Diagonal and Glòries to see more of Barcelona in transformation.

# 6

# Montjuïc

You'll need to reserve at least a day to see **Montjuïc**, the steep hill and park rising over the city to the southwest. It takes its name from the Jewish community that once settled on its slopes, and there's been a castle on the heights since the mid-seventeenth century. But it's as a cultural leisure park that contemporary Montjuïc is positioned, anchored around the heavyweight art collections in the **Museu Nacional d'Art de Catalunya** (**MNAC**). This unsurpassed national collection of Catalan art is supplemented by works in two other superb galleries, namely international contemporary art in the **Caixa Forum** and that of the famous Catalan artist Joan Miró in the **Fundació Joan Miró**. In addition, there are separate archeological, ethnological, military and theatrical **museums**, quite apart from the buildings and stadiums associated with the 1992 **Olympics**, which was centred on the heights of Montjuïc.

As late as the 1890s, the hill was nothing more than a collection of private farms and woodland on the edge of the old town, though some landscaping had already taken place by the time Montjuïc was chosen as the site of the **International Exhibition** of 1929. The slopes were then laid with gardens, terraces and fountains, while monumental Neoclassical buildings were added to the north side, many of them later adapted as museums. The famous **Poble Espanyol** (Spanish Village) – a hybrid park of collected Spanish buildings – is the most extraordinary relic of the Exhibition, while the various lush **gardens** still provide enjoyment and respite from the crowds. Above all, perhaps, there are the city and ocean views to savour from this most favoured of Barcelona's hills: from the steps in front of the Museu Nacional, from the castle ramparts, from the Olympic terraces, or from the cable cars that zigzag up the steepest slopes of Montjuïc.

The hill covers a wide area, so it's vital to plan your visit carefully around the various opening times. If you're intent on covering everything, it might be better to see Montjuïc in two separate visits – MNAC, Poble Espanyol and Olympic area on one day, and Fundació Joan Miró, cable car and castle on the other. There are several approaches to Montjuïc, depending on where you want to start, and various means of **transport** around the hill: the box on p.97 has all the details. The **Barcelona Card**, **Articket** and **Bus Turístic pass** provide discounted entry into Montjuïc's museums, galleries and attractions. Places to eat are thin on the ground, though there are good **cafés** in Caixa Forum and the Fundació Joan Miró, outdoor snack bars at the castle and on the slopes below MNAC, and a **restaurant** with outdoor terrace at the Font del Gat in the Jardins Laribal, below the Fundació Joan Miró. There are also plenty of decent restaurants and bars in the neighbouring *barri* of **Poble Sec**.

# Plaça d'Espanya and around

Gateway to the 1929 International Exhibition was the vast **Plaça d'Espanya**, based on plans by noted architect Josep Puig i Cadafalch. Arranged around a huge Neoclassical fountain, the square is unlike any other in Barcelona, a radical departure from the *modernisme* so in vogue elsewhere in the contemporary city. Striking twin towers, 47m high, stand at the foot of the imposing **Avinguda de la Reina Maria Cristina**, which heads up towards Montjuïc, the avenue lined by huge exhibition halls used for trade fairs. At the end of the avenue is Plaça de Carles Buïgas, from where monumental steps (and modern escalators) ascend the hill to the Palau Nacional, past water cascades and under the flanking walls, busts and roofline "kiosks" of two grand Viennese-style pavilions. It's an overtly showy approach to Montjuïc, with little whimsy in evidence, save for the **Font Màgica** (Magic Fountain) at the foot of the steps. On selected evenings (May–Sept Thurs–Sun 8–11.30pm, music starts 9.30pm; Oct–April Fri & Sat only at 7pm, 7.30pm, 8pm & 8.30pm; free) the fountain becomes the centrepiece of an impressive if slightly kitsch sound-and-light show – the brightly coloured water appears to dance to the strains of Holst and Abba.

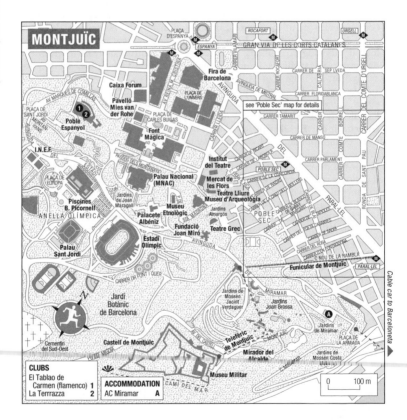

## Montjuïc transport

**Getting there**

- **Metro** Ⓜ Espanya deposits you at the foot of Avinguda de la Reina Maria Cristina, for easy access to Caixa Forum, Poble Espanyol and the Museu Nacional d'Art de Catalunya (MNAC). The Olympic area can then be reached by escalators behind MNAC.

- **Funicular** The Funicular de Montjuïc (April–Sept Mon–Fri 7.30am–10pm, Sat, Sun & holidays from 9am, Oct–March until 8pm; services every 10min; normal city transport tickets and passes valid) departs from inside the station at Ⓜ Paral.lel and takes a couple of minutes to ascend the hill. At the upper station on Avinguda de Miramar you can switch to the Montjuïc cable car or bus services (see "Getting around" below), or you're only a few minutes' walk from the Fundació Joan Miró.

- **Cable car** The Transbordador Aeri, or cross-harbour cable car (see p.90), from Barceloneta drops you outside the Jardins de Miramar, on the far southeastern slopes. From here, it's a ten-minute walk to the Montjuïc cable car and funicular stations and another five to the Fundació Joan Miró.

**Getting around**

- **Walking** It takes a good hour to walk on the road around the hill from Avinguda de la Reina Maria Cristina, past the Poble Espanyol, Olympic area and Fundació Joan Miró to the cross-harbour cable-car station at the far end of Montjuïc. Escalators up the hill between MNAC and the Olympic area cut out the worst of the slog. Walking up the steep hill all the way to the castle is not advised in hot weather (though there are steps through the gardens and between the roads) – use the cable car.

- **Bus Montjuïc Turístic** Montjuïc's open-top bus service (daily Easter week, and last week June to 1st week Sept, otherwise weekends and holidays only; departures every 40min, 10am–9.20pm; €3; ☎934 414 982) runs on two routes, one starting at Pl. d'Espanya (Ⓜ Espanya), the other at the foot of the Ramblas at Pl. Portal de la Pau (Ⓜ Drassanes). The service covers every major sight on the hill, including out-of-the-way attractions like the castle and botanic gardens. There are several connecting stops, so you can switch routes, and the all-day ticket lets you get on and off at will. The other bus service is the city bus designated "PM" (ie, Parc de Montjuïc; city transport tickets and passes valid), covering much the same route, while the sight-seeing Bus Turístic also serves the main Montjuïc attractions. There are stops for all these services right outside the upper station of the Funicular de Montjuïc.

- **Telefèric de Montjuïc** The Montjuïc cable car (daily June–Sept 10am–9pm, April, May & Oct 10am–7pm, Nov–March 10am–6pm; €5.70 one way, €7.90 return; ⓦ www.tmb.net), from Avinguda de Miramar, whisks you up to the castle and back in automated eight-seater gondolas.

# Caixa Forum

To the right of the fountain (before climbing the steps/escalators), and hidden from view until you turn the corner around Avinguda del Marquès de Comillas, is **Caixa Forum** (Mon–Fri & Sun 10am–8pm, Sat 10am–10pm; free; ☎934 768 600, ⓦ www.fundacio.lacaixa.es), a terrific arts and cultural centre set within the old Casamarona textile factory. Constructed in 1911 in the modernist style of Josep Puig i Cadafalch, the factory shut down in 1920 and lay abandoned until pressed into service as a police building after the Civil War. The subsequent renovation and expansion under the auspices of the Fundació La Caixa has produced a remarkable building, entered beneath twin iron-and-glass canopies representing spreading trees. You descend into a palatial white marble foyer (with a vibrant mural and a good arts bookshop), beyond which are the exhibition halls, fashioned within the former factory buildings. The external structure has been left untouched, so original girders, pillars and stanchions, factory brickwork and crenellated walls appear at every turn – look for the sign to the "terrats" where you can ascend to the undulating roof for unique views. The Casamarona tower, etched in blue and yellow tiling, rises high above the walls, as readily recognizable as the huge Miró starfish logos emblazoned across the building.

The centre houses the foundation's celebrated **contemporary art collection**, focusing on the period from the 1980s to the present, with hundreds of artists represented, from Antoni Abad to Rachel Whiteread. Works are shown in partial rotation, along with an excellent free programme of changing **exhibitions** across all aspects of the arts – recent exhibitions have highlighted subjects as diverse as Etruscan funerary sculpture and the films of Charlie Chaplin. There's also a library and resource centre, the Mediateca multimedia space, regular children's activities and a 400-seat auditorium with a full calendar of music, art, poetry and literary events. The **café** is worth knowing about, too – an airy converted space within the old factory walls, serving breakfast, sandwiches, snacks and lunch.

## Pavelló Mies van der Rohe

Immediately across Avinguda del Marquès de Comillas from Caixa Forum, set back from the road, is the 1986 reconstruction by Catalan architects of the **Pavelló Mies van der Rohe** (daily 10am–8pm; guided visits Wed & Fri 5–7pm; €4; ☎934 234 016, ❾www.miesbcn.com), which recalls part of the German contribution to the 1929 Exhibition. Originally designed by Mies van der Rohe and used as a reception room during the Exhibition, it's considered a major example of modern rationalist architecture. The pavilion has a startlingly beautiful conjunction of hard straight lines with watery surfaces, its dark-green polished onyx alternating with shining glass. It's open to visitors but unless there's an exhibition in place (a fairly regular occurrence), there is nothing to see inside save Mies van der Rohe's iconic tubular steel *Barcelona Chair*, though you can buy postcards and books from the small shop and debate quite how much you want a Mies mousepad or a "Less is More" T-shirt.

# Poble Espanyol

A five-minute walk up Avinguda del Marquès de Comillas brings you to the **Poble Espanyol**, or Spanish Village (Mon 9am–8pm, Tues–Thurs 9am–2am, Fri 9am–4am, Sat 9am–5am, Sun 9am–midnight; €8, night ticket €5, combined ticket with MNAC €12; ☎935 086 300, ❾www.poble-espanyol.com). This was an inspired concept for the International Exhibition of 1929 – a complete village consisting of streets and squares with reconstructions of famous or characteristic buildings from all over Spain, such as the fairy-tale medieval walls of Ávila through which you enter. "Get to know Spain in one hour" is what's promised and it's nowhere near as cheesy as you might think. It works well as a crash-course introduction to Spanish architecture – everything is well labelled and at least reasonably accurate. The echoing main square is lined with cafés, while the surrounding streets, alleys and buildings contain around forty workshops (daily 10am–6/8pm, depending on season), where you can see engraving, weaving, pottery and other crafts. Inevitably, it's all one huge shopping experience – castanets to Lladró porcelain, religious icons to Barcelona soccer shirts – and prices are inflated, but children will love it (and you can let them run free as there's no traffic). Your ticket also gets you entry to the **Fran Daurel Col.leccío d'Art Contemporani** museum so you might as well drop in to see the minor Tàpies and Miró lithographs and the series of Picasso ceramics.

Get to the village as it opens if you want to enjoy it in relatively crowd-free circumstances – once the tour groups arrive, it becomes a bit of a scrum. You could, of course, always come at the end of the day, when the village transforms into a vibrant centre of Barcelona nightlife. Two of Barcelona's hippest designers, Alfredo Arribas and Xavier Mariscal, installed a club in the Ávila gate in the early 1990s (the *Torres de Avila*). Other fashionable venues followed and, this being Barcelona, the whole complex now stays open until the small hours.

# Museu Nacional d'Art de Catalunya

The towering, domed **Palau Nacional**, set back on Montjuïc at the top of the long flight of steps from the fountains, was the flagship building of Barcelona's 1929 International Exhibition. Partly the work of Pere Domènech i Roura (son of the more famous Lluís Domènech i Montaner), its massive frescoed oval hall hosted the opening ceremony of the Exhibition, providing a fittingly grandiose backdrop for the city's biggest show since the Universal Exhibition of 1888. The palace was due to be demolished once the exhibition was over, but gained a reprieve and ultimately became home to one of Spain's great museums.

The **Museu Nacional d'Art de Catalunya** (**MNAC**; Tues–Sat 10am–7pm, Sun & hols 10am–2.30pm; €8.50, ticket valid 48hr, annual pass €14, first Sun of the month free; ☎936 220 376, ⓦ www.mnac.cat) is the city's most renowned art experience, showcasing a thousand years of Catalan art in stupendous surroundings. For first-time visitors, it can be difficult to know where to start, but if time is limited it's recommended that you concentrate on the medieval collection. This is split into two main sections, one dedicated to Romanesque art and the other to Gothic – periods in which Catalunya's artists were pre-eminent in Spain. The collection of Romanesque frescoes in particular is the museum's pride and joy, and is perhaps the best collection of its kind in the world. MNAC also has impressive holdings of European Renaissance and Baroque art, as well as an unsurpassed collection of "modern" (ie nineteenth- and twentieth-century) Catalan art up until the 1940s – everything from the 1950s and later is covered by MACBA in the Raval. In addition, there are priceless collections of Catalan photography, drawings and engravings, and a numismatic section, items from which are either displayed as part of the general collection or sometimes appear in **temporary exhibitions** (separate admission charge, varies), which change every two to four months. Finally, there's a **café–bar**, gift shop and art **bookshop** in the gloriously restored oval hall, and a superior museum **restaurant** called *Oleum* (Tues–Sun lunch only) on the upper floor with views over the city.

## The Romanesque collection

Great numbers of Romanesque churches were built in the Catalan Pyrenees as the Christian Reconquest spread. Medieval Catalan studios decorated the churches with frescoes depicting biblical events, and even the most remote Pyrenean valleys could boast lavish masterpieces. However, by the nineteenth century many of these churches had either been ruined by later renovations or lay abandoned, prone to theft and damage. Not until 1919 was a concerted effort made to remove the frescoes to the museum, where they could be better preserved and displayed.

Six remarkable sections present the **frescoes** in a reconstruction of their original setting, so you can see their size and where they would have been placed in the church buildings. Full explanatory notes (in English) cover the artistic techniques, interpretation and iconography of the paintings, which for the most part have a vibrant, raw quality, best exemplified by those taken from churches in the Boí valley in the Catalan Pyrenees. In the apse of the early twelfth-century church of Sant Climent in Taüll, the so-called **Master of Taüll** painted an extraordinarily powerful *Christ in Majesty*, combining a Byzantine hierarchical composition with the imposing colours and strong outlines of contemporary manuscript illuminators. Look out for details such as the leper, to the left of the Sant Climent altar, patiently allowing a dog to lick his sores. Frescoes from other churches explore a variety of themes, from heaven to hell, with the displays complemented by sculptures, altar panels, woodcarvings, religious objects and furniture retrieved from the mouldering churches themselves.

## The Gothic collection

The evolution from the Romanesque to the Gothic period was marked by a move from murals to painting on wood, and by the depiction of more naturalistic figures in scenes showing the lives of the saints, and later in portraits of kings and patrons of the arts. In the early part of the period, the Catalan and Valencian schools particularly were influenced by contemporary Italian styles, and you'll see some outstanding altarpieces, tombs and church decoration. Later began the International Gothic or "1400" style in which the influences became more widespread; the important figures of this movement were the fifteenth-century artists **Jaume Huguet** and **Lluís Dalmau**. Works from the end of this period show the strong influence of contemporary Flemish painting, in the use of denser colours, the depiction of crowd scenes and a concern for perspective. The last Catalan artist of note here is the so-called **Master of La Seu d'Urgell**, represented by a number of works, including a fine series of six paintings (Christ, the Virgin Mary, Saints Peter, Paul and Sebastian, and Mary Magdalene) that once formed the covers of an organ.

## The Renaissance and Baroque collections

Many of the **Renaissance** and **Baroque** works on display have come from private collections bequeathed to the museum, notably by conservative politician Francesc Cambó and Madrid's Thyssen-Bornemisza. Selections from these bequests rate their own rooms in the Renaissance and Baroque galleries, while other rooms here trace artistic development from the early sixteenth to the eighteenth century. Major European artists displayed include Peter Paul Rubens, Giovanni Battista Tiepolo, Jean Honoré Fragonard, Francisco de Goya, El Greco, Francisco de Zurbarán and Diego Velázquez, though the museum is of course keen to play up Catalan works of the period, which largely absorbed the prevailing European influences – thus Barcelona artist **Antoni Viladomat** (1678–1755), whose twenty paintings of St Francis, executed for a monastery, are shown here in their entirety. However, more familiar to most will be the masterpieces of the Spanish Golden Age, notably Velázquez's *Saint Paul* and Zurbarán's *Immaculate Conception.*

## The modern art collection

MNAC ends on a high note with its unsurpassed **nineteenth- and twentieth-century Catalan art** collection, which is particularly good on *modernista* and *noucentista* painting and sculpture, the two dominant schools of the period. Rooms highlight individual artists and genres, shedding light on the development of art in an exciting period of Catalunya's history, while there are fascinating diversions into *modernista* interior design (with some pieces by Gaudí), avant-garde sculpture and historical photography.

Although he died young, in 1874, **Marià Fortuny i Marsal** is often regarded as the earliest *modernista* artist; he was certainly the first Catalan painter known widely abroad, having exhibited to great acclaim in Paris and Rome. He specialized in minutely detailed pictures, often of exotic subjects – his set-piece *Battle of Tetuan* was based on a visit to Morocco in 1859 to observe the war there. Closer to home are the intricate street and market scenes of El Born neighbourhood the work of the main name in Catalan Realism, Ramon Martí i Alsina, while the master of nineteenth-century Catalan landscape painting was **Joaquim Veyreda i Vila**, founder of the "Olot School" (Olot being a town in northern Catalunya), whose members were influenced both by the work of the early Impressionists and by the distinctive volcanic scenery of the Olot region. However, it wasn't until the later emergence of **Ramon Casas i Carbó** (whose famous picture of himself and Pere Romeu on a tandem once hung on the walls of *Els Quatre Gats*) and **Santiago Rusiñol i Prats** that Catalan art acquired a progressive sheen, taking its cue from the very latest in European styles, whether the symbolism of Whistler or the vibrant social observation of Toulouse-Lautrec. Hot on their heels came a new generation of *modernista* artists – Josep Maria Sert, Marià Pidelaserra i Brias, Ricard Canals i Llambí and others – who were strongly influenced by the scene in contemporary Paris. The two brightest stars of the period, though, were **Joaquim Mir i Trinxet**, whose highly charged landscapes tended towards the abstract, and **Isidre Nonell i Monturiol**, who from 1902 until his early death in 1911 painted sombre naturalistic studies of impoverished gypsy communities.

*Noucentisme* was a style at once more classical and less consciously flamboyant than *modernisme* – witness the portraits and landscapes of **Joaquim Sunyer i Miró**, perhaps the best known *noucentista* artist, and the work of sculptors like **Pau Gargallo i Catalán**. This was also a period when the Barcelona art world flourished under the patronage of private galleries like the Galeries Dalmau, whose important shows in the city after World War I promoted Cubism and avant-garde works to a wider audience.

# Museu Etnològic

From MNAC, Passeig de Santa Madrona snakes downhill towards the Theatre City and Poble Sec, first passing the **Museu Etnològic** (June–Sept Tues–Sat noon–8pm, Sun 11am–3pm; Oct–May Tues & Thurs 10am–7pm, Wed & Fri–Sun

10am–2pm; €3.50, free 1st Sun of month; ☎934 246 807, ⓦwww.museuetnologic .bcn.cat), the city's ethnological museum. This boasts extensive cultural collections from across the globe, particularly the Amazon region, Papua New Guinea, pre-Hispanic America, Australia, Morocco and Ethiopia. However, there are simply too many pieces to show at any one time, so the museum has rotating exhibitions, which usually last for a year or two and concentrate on a particular subject or geographical area. Refreshingly, Spain and its regions aren't neglected, which means that there's usually a focus on the minutiae of rural Spanish life or an examination of subjects like medieval carving or early industrialization. For these exhibits, the museum draws on the work of Spanish ethnographers such as Ramon Violant who spent much of the 1940s recording the daily routine of inhabitants in the Pyrenees. In addition, the museum has opened up its **reserved rooms**, where the conservers and staff have generally worked, and it's a real treat to walk past the storage cabinets, piled high with anything from African masks to Spanish fans.

# Museu d'Arqueològia de Catalunya

Further down Passeig de Santa Madrona from the ethnological museum is the impressive **Museu d'Arqueològia de Catalunya** (Tues–Sat 9.30am–7pm, Sun & hols 10am–2.30pm; €3; ☎934 246 577, ⓦwww.mac.cat), whose array of relics spans the centuries from the Stone Age to the time of the Visigoths, with the Roman and Greek periods particularly well represented. The sections dealing with prehistoric, Stone and Bronze Age periods are the most disappointing, with any interest well hidden by the old-fashioned case-by-case presentation – though to be fair some exhibits are gradually being updated. However, there's no such reservation about the displays in the central rotunda, which concentrate on sixth- and seventh-century BC finds from the Greek site at Empúries on the Costa Brava, some beautiful figures from the Carthaginian settlements in Ibiza, and ceramics from the Iberian era, including tablets bearing inscriptions in an indecipherable script. The highlights are many and varied, including a notable marble statue of Asclepius, Greek god of medicine, which dominates the hall. The Second Punic War (218–201 BC) saw the Carthaginians expelled from Iberia by the Romans, who made their provincial capital at Tarragona (Tarraco), with a secondary outpost at Barcelona (Barcino). There's some fine Roman glassware and mosaic work on display, while an upper floor interprets life in **Barcino** itself through a collection of tombstones, statues, inscriptions and friezes found all over the city. Some of the stonework is remarkably vivid, depicting the faces of some of Barcino's inhabitants as clearly as the day they were carved.

# La Ciutat del Teatre

At the foot of Montjuïc, on the eastern slopes, the theatre area known as **La Ciutat del Teatre** occupies a back corner of the old working-class neighbourhood of Poble Sec. Passeig de Santa Madrona runs down here from MNAC, passing the ethnological and archeological museums, or there are more direct steps descending the hillside.

The theatre buildings that make up La Ciutat del Teatre sit in a tight huddle off c/de Lleida, with the **Mercat de les Flores** theatre – once a flower market – and progressive **Teatre Lliure** occupying the spaghetti-western-style Palau de l'Agricultura premises built for the 1929 Exhibition. Walk through the terracotta arch from c/de Lleida, and off to the left is the far sleeker **Institut del Teatre**, with its sheer walls contrasting markedly with the neighbourhood's cheap housing, whose laundry is strung just metres away from the gleaming Theatre City. The institute brings together the city's major drama and dance schools, and various conservatories, libraries and study centres. The "Theatre" section in Chapter 13 has more details about performances, events and festivals at all these venues.

# Poble Sec

Lying immediately below Montjuïc, confined by the hill on one side and the busy Avinguda del Paral.lel on the other, is the neighbourhood of **Poble Sec** (Ⓜ Poble Sec), or "dry village", so called because it had no water supply until the nineteenth century. It's a complete contrast to the landscaped slopes behind it – a grid of contoured narrow streets, down-to-earth grocery stores, bakeries, local shops and good-value restaurants. Asian immigrants have stamped their mark on many of the neighbourhood stores and businesses, while Poble Sec is also slowly becoming a bit of a "new Raval" as a walk along the main, pedestrianized **Carrer de Blai** shows – quite a few fashionable bars have opened here recently. Meanwhile, the Montjuïc **funicular** has its lower station on the southern fringe of the neighbourhood (access from Ⓜ Paral.lel).

Many visitors never set foot in Poble Sec, though the opening of one of the city's old Civil War air-raid shelters provides a compelling reason to make the short journey across town. **Refugi 307**, at c/Nou de la Rambla 169 (guided visits Sat & Sun at 11am, noon & 1pm; €3; ☏ 932 562 122, Ⓦ www.museu historia.bcn.cat), was dug into the Montjuïc hillside by local people from

## The city under siege

During the Civil War years Poble Sec – like many inner-city neighbourhoods — suffered grievously from Nationalist bombing raids, a foretaste of what was to come in Europe during World War II. From 1936 onwards, the city authorities planned for a system of communal **air-raid shelters** and many had been excavated by the time that the first raids hit Barcelona in early 1937. The raids were particularly savage in March 1938, and by the end of the war three thousand inhabitants had died in the bombings, with many more injured and thousands of buildings destroyed. Even so, the shelters undoubtedly saved many lives, with most constructed in working-class areas (like Poble Sec, Barceloneta and Gràcia) where the locals hadn't been able to leave the city or couldn't reach the relative safety of either the metro tunnels or the Collserola hills. Altogether, around 1400 shelters were built in Barcelona (and another 2000 across Catalunya), some as simple as reinforced cellars, though many were larger collaborative efforts like Refugi 307, featuring vaulted brick-lined tunnels, ventilation, water supplies, and even infirmaries and play areas for children. In the wake of Republican defeat, after the war, many of the shelters were forgotten about, though the city council has latterly taken up their cause in the name of education and remembrance of Barcelona's often overlooked wartime history.

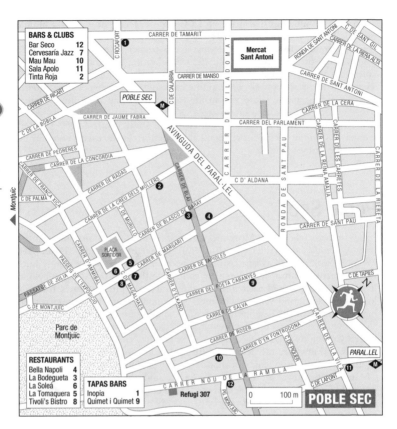

**BARS & CLUBS**

| | |
|---|---|
| Bar Seco | 12 |
| Cervesaria Jazz | 7 |
| Mau Mau | 10 |
| Sala Apolo | 11 |
| Tinta Roja | 2 |

**RESTAURANTS**

| | |
|---|---|
| Bella Napoli | 4 |
| La Bodegueta | 3 |
| La Soleá | 6 |
| La Tomaquera | 5 |
| Tivoli's Bistro | 8 |

**TAPAS BARS**

| | |
|---|---|
| Inopia | 1 |
| Quimet i Quimet | 9 |

Refugi 307

0          100 m

POBLE SEC

Mercat
Sant Antoni

Parc de
Montjuic

1936 onwards, and the 200 metres of tunnels could shelter up to 2000 people from Franco's bombing raids. With no radar to protect the city, they had two minutes from the sound of the sirens to get underground. The tours are in Spanish or Catalan, though there is usually someone on hand who speaks English, and you can just turn up on the day. Photographic storyboards at the start of the tour give a bit of background, and then it's hard hat on to follow your guide into the labyrinth to the sound of screaming sirens and droning warplanes.

# The Olympic area

From Poble Espanyol, the main road through Montjuïc climbs around the hill and up to the city's principal **Olympic area**, sometimes known as the Anella Olímpica (Olympic Ring). The 1992 Olympics were the second planned for Montjuïc. The first, in 1936 – the "People's Olympics" – were organized as an alternative to the Nazis' infamous Berlin games of that year, but the day before the official opening, Franco's army revolt triggered the Civil War and scuppered the Barcelona games. Some of the 25,000 athletes and spectators who had turned up stayed on to join the Republican forces.

Avinguda del Estadi leads you right past some of Barcelona's most celebrated sporting edifices – like Ricardo Bofill's **Institut Nacional d'Educació Física de Catalunya** (**INEF**; a sports university), the **Piscines Bernat Picornell** (swimming pools and sports complex) and the Japanese-designed, steel-and-glass **Palau Sant Jordi**. Opened in 1990 with Luciano Pavarotti in attendance, this sports and concert hall seats 17,000 people and is overshadowed only by the Olympic stadium itself, the **Estadi Olímpic**, which comfortably holds 65,000. Built originally for the 1929 Exhibition, and completely refitted to accommodate the 1992 opening and closing ceremonies, it's a marvellously spacious stadium, its original Neoclassical facade left untouched by the Catalan architects in charge of the project. Between the stadium and the Palau Sant Jordi, a vast *terrassa* provides one of the finest vantage points in the city. Long water-fed troughs break the concrete and marble expanse, while the confident, space-age curve of Santiago Calatrava's **communications tower** dominates the skyline.

Around the other side, just across the road from the stadium, the history of the Games themselves – and Barcelona's successful hosting – are covered in the **Museu Olímpic i de l'Esport**, Avgda. de l'Estadi 21 (Mon & Wed–Sat 10am–6pm, Sun

▲ Montjuïc's communications tower

& hols 10am–2.30pm; €4; ☎934 262 089, ⓦwww.fundaciobarcelonaolimpica.es).
It's a fully interactive experience, with lots of Olympic memorabilia and sports gear
on display, plus sporting videos and an audiovisual presentation, but even so is
probably one for hardcore sports fans only.

# Fundació Joan Miró

Montjuïc's highlight for many is the **Fundació Joan Miró** (Tues–Sat 10am–7pm,
July–Sept until 8pm, Thurs until 9.30pm, Sun & hols 10am–2.30pm; €8, exhibitions €4, price includes audio-guide; ☎934 439 470, ⓦwww.fundaciomiro-bcn.
org), possibly Barcelona's most adventurous art museum and certainly its most
attractive. The impressive white modernist structure is set in lovely gardens
overlooking the city, and it lies just a few minutes' walk from either the Olympic
stadium or the Montjuïc funicular and cable-car stations.

    **Joan Miró** (1893–1983) was one of the greatest of Catalan artists, estab-
lishing an international reputation while retaining links with his homeland.
He had his first exhibition in 1918 and subsequently spent his summers in
Catalunya and the rest of the time in France, before moving to Mallorca in
1956, where he died. His friend, the architect Josep-Luis Sert, designed the
building that now houses the museum, which comprises a permanent collection of paintings, graphics, tapestries and sculptures donated by Miró himself
and covering the period from 1914 to 1978. Aside from the permanent
collection on display, the Fundació sponsors excellent temporary exhibitions,
film shows, lectures and children's theatre, while summer music nights
(usually June and July) are a feature every year. Young experimental artists
have their own space in the **Espai 13** gallery. There's also a **library**, with
books and periodicals on contemporary art, a **bookshop** selling posters and
a **café-restaurant** (lunch 1.30–3pm, otherwise drinks, pastries and
sandwiches) with outdoor tables on a sunny patio – you don't have to pay to
get into the museum to use this.

## The collection

The **paintings and drawings** are instantly recognizable, among the chief links
between Surrealism and abstract art. Miró showed a childlike delight in colours
and shapes and developed a free, highly decorative style – one of his favourite
early techniques was to spill paint on the canvas and move his brush around in

it. Much of the collection is, in fact, of his later works, since the museum was only proposed – and works specifically set aside – in the 1960s, when Miró had already been painting for almost fifty years. But there are early Realist works from before the mid-1920s, like the effervescent *Portrait of a Young Girl* (1919), while other gaps are filled by a collection later donated by Miró's widow, Pilar Juncosa, which demonstrates Miró's preoccupations in the 1930s and 1940s. During this period he began his *Constellations* series, in which first appeared the colours, themes and symbols that later came to define his work – reds and blues, women, birds and tears, the sun, moon and stars, all eventually pared down to the minimalist basics. The same period also saw the fifty black-and-white lithographs of the *Barcelona Series* (1939–44), executed in the immediate aftermath of the Civil War. They are a dark reflection of the turmoil of the period; snarling faces and great black shapes and shadows dominate. For a rapid appraisal of Miró's entire *oeuvre* look in on the museum's **Sala K**, whose 23 works are on long-term loan from a Japanese collector. Here, in a kind of potted retrospective, you can trace Miró's development as an artist, from his early Impressionist landscapes (1914) to the minimal renderings of the 1970s.

Perhaps the most innovative room of all is one full of work by other artists in homage to Miró, including fine pieces by Henri Matisse, Henry Moore, Max Ernst, Richard Serra, Robert Motherwell and Eduardo Chillida. The single most compelling exhibit in this section however, has to be Alexander Calder's **Mercury Fountain**, which he built for the Republican pavilion at the Paris Universal Exhibition of 1936–37 – the same exhibition for which Picasso painted *Guernica*. Like *Guernica*, it's a tribute to a town, this time the mercury-mining town of Almáden – its name spelled out in dangling metal letters above the fountain – which saw saturation bombing during the Civil War.

Other exhibits include Miró's enormous bright **tapestries** (he donated nine to the museum), pencil drawings (particularly of misshapen women and gawky ballerinas) and **sculpture** outside in the gardens. All these started life in the form of **sketches and notes**, and the museum has retained five thousand separate examples, of which it usually displays a selection. From a doodle on a scrap of old newspaper or on the back of a postcard, it's possible to trace the development of shapes and themes that later evolved into full-blown works of art.

# Castell de Montjuïc

Marking the top of the hill and the end of the line is Barcelona's castle – and the best way up is by the Telefèric de Montjuïc (cable car) which tacks up the hillside, offering magnificent views on the way, before depositing you within the eighteenth-century walls. The outer defences of the **Castell de Montjuïc** (grounds open daily 7am–8pm; free) were constructed as a series of angular concentric perimeters, designed for artillery deflection, while the inner part of the fort served as a military base and prison for many years. It was here that the last president of the pre-war Generalitat, **Lluís Companys i Jover**, was executed on Franco's orders on October 15, 1940 – he had been in exile in Paris after the Civil War, but was handed over to Franco by the Germans upon their capture of the French capital. He's buried in the nearby Cementiri del Sud-Oest.

The ramparts and grounds are free to enter, and you can skirt the outer walls of the bastion as well, where the locals come at weekends to practise archery in the moat. There are open-air film screenings here in summer too. You have to pay to go inside the inner keep, where there's a splendid *mirador* (viewpoint) and **Museu Militar** (April–Oct Tues–Sun 9.30am–8pm; Nov–March Tues–Fri 9.30am–5/6pm, Sat & Sun until 7/8pm; €3, *mirador* only €1; ☎933 298 613, ⓦwww.museomilitarmontjuic.es), which presents endless swords, guns, medals, uniforms, armour, model castles, maps and portraits in a series of rooms around the parade ground and down on the lower level of the bastion. The fortress is army (and therefore state) property and its museum has long been considered an anachronism by the city – there was an equestrian statue of Franco here for many years, and even now there's barely a hint in the museum displays (other than some Republican uniforms and weaponry) that Barcelona was ripped apart by Civil War. However, the Spanish government recently decided to hand the fortress over to the city and it will eventually be converted into a Peace Museum.

Below the castle walls, a panoramic pathway – the **Camí del Mar** – has been cut from the cliff edge, providing magnificent views, first across to Port Olímpic and the northern beaches, and then southwest as the path swings around the castle. This is an unfamiliar view of the city, of the sprawling docks and container yards, and cruise ships and tankers are usually visible negotiating the busy sea lanes. The path is just over 1km long and ends at the back of the castle battlements near the **Mirador del Migdia**, where there's a great open-air chill-out bar, *La Caseta del Migdia* (weekends all year from 10 or 11am, plus summer weekend DJ nights, ⓦwww.lacaseta.org). Down through the trees is the *mirador* itself, a balcony with extensive views over the Baixa Llobregat industrial area. You can see across to the Olympic stadium from here, while in the immediate foreground is the extraordinary **Cementiri del Sud-Oest**, stretching along the ridge below, whose tombs are stacked like apartment blocks on great conifer-lined avenues.

# The gardens of Montjuïc

Montjuïc's main gardens are scattered across the southern and eastern reaches of the hill, below the castle. Principal among them is the **Jardí Botànic de Barcelona** (daily: June–Aug 10am–8pm; April, May & Sept 10am–7pm; Feb, March & Oct–March 10am–6pm; Nov–Jan 10am–5pm; €3.50, free last Sun of month; ☎934 264 935; ⓦwww.jardibotanic.bcn.es), on c/Dr Font i Quer, laid out on terraced slopes which offer fine views across the city. The Montjuïc buses run here directly, or the entrance is just a five-minute walk around the back of the Olympic stadium. It's a beautifully kept contemporary garden, where wide, easy-to-follow paths (fine for strollers and wheelchairs) wind through landscaped zones representing the flora of the Mediterranean, Canary Islands, California, Chile, North and South Africa and Australia. Just don't come in the full heat of the summer day, as there's very little shade. Guided tours in Spanish/Catalan every weekend (except August) show you the highlights, but you get an English-language audio-guide and map included in the entry fee in any case.

Signposted off Avinguda de Miramar, west of (and below) the Fundació Joan Miró, the terraces, clipped hedges and grottoes of the **Jardins Laribal** (daily 10am–dusk; free) date from 1918. They surround the spring of **Font del Gat**, which has been a picnic site since the nineteenth century. Josep Puig i Cadafalch built a restaurant here of the same name for the 1929 International Exhibition, and it's open now for lunch (1–4pm; closed Mon), with wonderful views from its terrace.

East of here, the Montjuïc cable car passes over the **Jardins de Mossèn Jacint Verdaguer** and adjacent **Jardins Joan Brossa** (both daily 10am–dusk; free), which tack up the hillside to the castle. Walking down through the gardens from the castle is a pleasant way to return to the lower slopes of Montjuïc, through what used to be the site of the old Montjuïc amusement park, though it's now fully landscaped, with children's play areas – halfway, there are sweeping city views from the **Mirador de l'Alcalde**.

Finally, outside the upper cross-harbour cable-car station, are the formal **Jardins de Miramar**, plus more fine views from the cable-car station café-*terrassa*. Steps lead down from a point close to the cable-car station into the precipitous cactus gardens of the **Jardins de Mossèn Costa i Llobera** (daily 10am–dusk; free), which look out over the port. The flourishing stands of Central and South American, Indian and African cacti, some over 6m high, make a dramatic scene, little experienced by most visitors to Montjuïc, though the people lounging on the steps and in the shade of the bigger specimens suggest it's something of an open secret among the locals.

# The Eixample

The **Eixample** – the gridded, nineteenth-century new-town area north of Plaça de Catalunya – is the city's main shopping and business district. It covers a vast expanse spreading north to the outlying hills and suburbs, though most of what there is to see lies within a few blocks of the two central, parallel thoroughfares, **Passeig de Gràcia** and **Rambla de Catalunya**. To visitors, the district's regular blocks and seemingly endless streets can appear offputting, while many locals experience only a fraction of the district on a daily basis. Indeed, the Eixample can't really be said to be a single neighbourhood at all – at least not in the same way that the old-town *barris* distinguish themselves – though its genesis lay in the increasingly crowded streets and alleys of the Ciutat Vella.

As Barcelona grew more industrialized throughout the nineteenth century, the old town became overcrowded and unsanitary. Conditions were such that in 1851 permission was given by the Spanish state to knock down the encircling walls so that the city could expand beyond its medieval limits, across the plain to the hills beyond the old town. Following a pioneering plan drawn up by engineer Ildefons Cerdà i Sunyer, work started in 1859 on what became known as the Ensanche in Castilian, and Eixample in Catalan – the "Extension" or "Widening".

As the money in the city moved north, so did a new class of **modernista architects**, who began to pepper the Eixample with ever-more-striking examples of their work, which were eagerly commissioned by status-conscious merchants and businessmen. These extraordinary buildings – most notably the work of Antoni Gaudí i Cornet, Lluís Domènech i Montaner and Josep Puig i Cadafalch (see colour section) provide the main attraction for visitors to the Eixample, turning it into a sort of open-air urban museum, particularly along the attractive central spine of Passeig de Gràcia. Almost everything else you're likely to want to see is found to the east of here in the area known as **Dreta de l'Eixample** (the right-hand side) where, aside from the architecture, attractions include museums concentrating on Egyptian antiquities, and Catalan art and ceramics, with a special draw provided by the gallery devoted to the works of Catalan artist Antoni Tàpies. Further east is Gaudí's extraordinary **Sagrada Família** church – the one building in the city to which a visit is virtually obligatory. A few blocks south of here, Barcelona's major avenues all meet at the swirling roundabout of **Glòries**, where a further set of attractions await, including the city's biggest flea market, its main concert hall and music museum, and Catalunya's flagship national theatre building.

There's rather less to get excited about on the western, or left-hand side – the so-called **Esquerra de l'Eixample** – which houses many of the public buildings contained within the original nineteenth-century plan. Nevertheless, certain areas provide an interesting contrast with the *modernista* flourishes over the way, particularly the urban park projects close to Barcelona Sants train station, notably the Parc Joan Miró.

As the Eixample covers a very large area, you won't be able to see everything described below as part of a single outing – all the relevant public transport details are given in the text. For a map and guide showing all the city's *modernista* sights, and for other benefits, the **Ruta del Modernisme** package might be of interest, while the Barcelona Card or the Articket also offer useful discounts (see p.31).

# Dreta de l'Eixample

It's the right-hand side of the Eixample – the so-called **Dreta de l'Eixample** – that has the bulk of the city's show-stopping *modernista* buildings. Most are contained within the triangle formed by the Passeig de Gràcia, Avinguda Diagonal and the Gran Via de les Corts Catalanes, and all are within a few blocks of each other. The stand-out sights are Gaudí's **La Pedrera** apartment building, as well as the so-called **Mansana de la Discòrdia**, or "Block of Discord", which gets its name because the three adjacent houses, casas Lleó Morera, Amatller and Batlló – built within a decade of each other by three different architects – show off wildly varying manifestations of the *modernista* style and spirit. Gaudí's first apartment building, the Casa Calvet, is also in the Dreta, along with various art galleries and museums, a great neighbourhood market and several interesting restored public spaces.

The main access is along the wide **Passeig de Gràcia**, which runs northwest from Plaça de Catalunya as far as the southern reaches of Gràcia. Laid out in its present form in 1827, it's a splendid, showy avenue, bisected by the other two main city boulevards, the Gran Via de les Corts Catalanes and Avinguda

---

## Design a city . . . designer city

When it came to building an entire new town in the nineteenth century, Barcelona then, as now, didn't do things by halves. The city authorities championed a fan-shaped plan by popular municipal architect **Antoni Rovira i Trias**, whose design radiated out from the existing shape of the old town. (His statue, in Gràcia's Plaça Rovira i Trias, sits on a bench with his Eixample plan set in the ground beneath him.) However, much to local chagrin, Rovira's elegant if conventional plan was passed over by the Spanish government in favour of a revolutionary blueprint drawn up by utopian engineer and urban planner **Ildefons Cerdà i Sunyer**. This was defiantly modern in style and scale – a grid-shaped new town marching off to the north, intersected by broad avenues cut on the diagonal. Districts would be divided into blocks, with buildings limited in height, and central gardens, schools, markets, hospitals and other services provided for the inhabitants. Space and light were part of the very fabric of the design, with Cerdà's characteristic wide streets and shaved corners of the blocks surviving today. However, he eventually saw most of his more radical social proposals ignored, as the Eixample rapidly became a fashionable area in which to live and speculators developed buildings on the proposed open spaces. Even today though, the underlying fabric of Cerdà's plan is always evident, while in certain quiet corners and gardens the original emphasis on social community within grand design lives on.

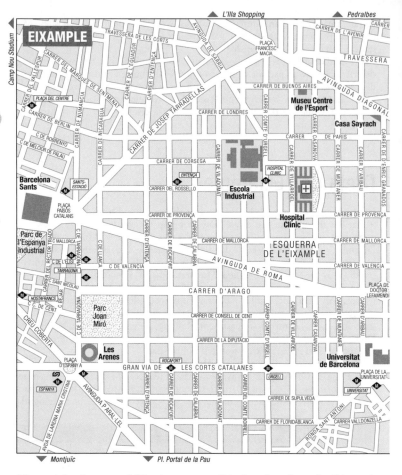

Diagonal. It takes around 25 minutes to stroll its length as far as the Diagonal. At intervals you can rest at the elaborate benches and lamps designed in 1900 by the city's municipal architect, Pere Falqués, and there are metro stations at either end.

## Casa Lleó Morera and the Museu del Perfum

On the corner with c/Consell de Cent, at Pg. de Gràcia 35, the six-storey **Casa Lleó Morera** was designed by Lluís Domènech i Montaner and completed in 1906. It's the least extravagant of the buildings in the block, and has suffered more than the others from "improvements" wrought by subsequent owners, which included removing the ground-floor arches and sculptures. The luxury leather goods store Loewe occupies the whole of the ground floor, while the main entrance to the building is resolutely guarded to prevent more than a peek inside. This is a pity, because it has a rich Art Nouveau interior, flush with ceramics and wood, as well as exquisite stained glass, while its semicircular jutting balconies are quite distinctive.

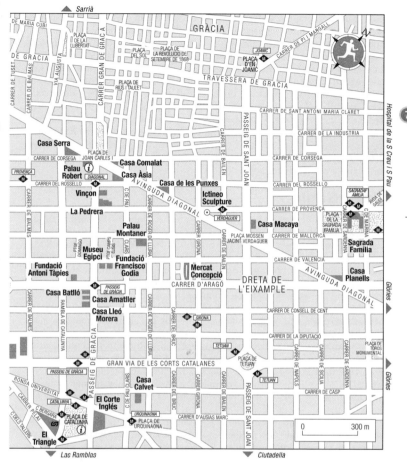

An oddity a couple of doors up is the **Museu del Perfum** (Mon–Fri 10.30am–1.30pm & 4.30–8pm, Sat 11am–2pm; €5; ☏ 932 160 121, Ⓦ www .museodelperfume.com), located in the back of the Regia perfume store at Pg. de Gràcia 39. They may have to turn the lights on for you, but there's no missing the exhibits as a rather cloying pong exudes from the room. It's a private collection of over five thousand perfume and essence bottles from Egyptian times onwards, and there are some exquisite pieces displayed, including Turkish filigree-and-crystal ware and bronze and silver Indian elephant flasks. More modern times are represented by scents made for Brigitte Bardot, Grace Kelly and Elizabeth Taylor, and if you're diligent enough to scan all the shelves you might be able to track down the perfume bottle designed by Salvador Dalí.

## Casa Amatller

Josep Puig i Cadafalch's striking **Casa Amatller** is at Pg. de Gràcia 41, an apartment block from 1900 created largely from the bones of an existing building and paid for by Antoni Amatller, a Catalan chocolate manufacturer, art collector, photographer and traveller. The facade rises in steps to a point, studded with coloured ceramic decoration and with heraldic sculptures over the doors and windows. Inside the hallway, the ceramic tiles continue along the walls, while twisted stone columns are interspersed by dragon lamps, all of which are further illuminated by fine stained-glass doors and an interior glass roof. There are **guided tours** of the house (Mon–Fri at 11am, noon, 5pm & 6pm, plus Sun at noon; €8; reservations at the house or call ☎934 877 217, ⓦwww.amatller .org), which include a visit to Amatller's photographic studio and chocolate-tasting in the original kitchen. Temporary exhibitions at the house are usually worth a look, too, with some based on the collections amassed by Amatller or by his daughter, who established the Amatller Institute of Hispanic Art here in 1941. The Institute promotes research into the history of Hispanic art, and maintains a photo library and archive in the house.

## Casa Batlló

Perhaps the most extraordinary creation on the Block of Discord is Antoni Gaudí's **Casa Batlló** at Pg. de Gràcia 43 (daily 9am–8pm, access occasionally restricted due to private events; €16.50; ☎932 160 306, ⓦwww.casabatllo.cat; advance sales also from TelEntrada, ☎902 101 212, ⓦwww.telentrada.com), designed for the industrialist Josep Batlló. The original apartment building was considered dull by contemporaries, so Gaudí was hired to give it a face-lift, completing the work by 1907. He contrived to create an undulating facade that Dalí later compared to "the tranquil waters of a lake". There's an animal motif at work here, too: the stone facade hangs in folds, like skin, and from below, the twisted balcony railings resemble malevolent eyes. The higher part of the facade is less abstruse and more decorative, pockmarked with circular ceramic buttons laid on a bright mosaic background and finished with a little tower topped with a three-dimensional cross. The sinuous interior, meanwhile, resembles the insides of some great organism, complete with snakeskin-patterned walls and window frames, fireplaces, doorways and staircases that display not a straight line between them.

**Self-guided audio tours** show you the main floor (including the salon overlooking Passeig de Gràcia), the patio and rear facade, the ribbed attic and the celebrated mosaic rooftop chimneys. It's best to reserve a ticket in advance (by phone or in person) as this is a very popular attraction – the scrum of aimless visitors, audio-stick glued to their ears, can be a frustrating business at peak times.

## Fundació Antoni Tàpies

Lluís Domènech i Montaner's first important building, the **Casa Montaner i Simon**, c/Aragó 255, was finished in 1880. This was one of the earliest of all *modernista* projects in Barcelona: like Gaudí after him, the architect incorporated Moorish-style flourishes into his iron-framed work, which consists of two floors, supported by cast-iron columns and with no dividing walls. The building originally served the publishing firm of Montaner i Simon, but, as the enormous aluminium tubular structure on the roof announces, it was converted in 1990 to house the **Fundació Antoni Tàpies** (Tues–Sun 10am–8pm; €6; ☎934 870 315, ⓦwww.fundaciotapies.org; Ⓜ Passeig de Gràcia).

It's a beautiful building dedicated to all aspects of the life and work of Catalunya's most eminent postwar artist. Tàpies' work rather divides opinion. It's not immediately accessible (in the way of, say, Miró) and you're either going to love or hate the gallery. Temporary exhibitions here focus on selections of

**DRETA DE L'EIXAMPLE**

| ACCOMMODATION | | | CAFÉS | | RESTAURANTS | |
|---|---|---|---|---|---|---|
| Centric Point | | Goya | I | Café del Centre | 4 | El Japonés | 1 |
| (hostel) | F | Granvía | G | Llaie Llibrería Café | 6 | O'Nabo de Lugo | 3 |
| Claris | D | Majestic | C | | | Tragaluz | 2 |
| Condes de | | Omm | A | TAPAS BARS | | | |
| Barcelona | B | Prestige | E | Casa Alfonso | 8 | CLUB | |
| D'Uxelles | H | San Remo | L | TapaÇ24 | 5 | Buda | |
| Girona | J | the5rooms | K | | | Restaurante | 7 |

Born in the city in 1923 (on c/de la Canuda in the Barri Gòtic), **Antoni Tàpies i Puig** left school to study law at the University of Barcelona in 1944, though he left before completing his degree. Drawn to art from an early age, and largely self-taught (though he studied briefly at Barcelona's Academia Valls), he was a founding member (1948) of the influential Dau al Set ("Die at Seven"), a grouping of seven artists producing a monthly avant-garde magazine of the same name which ran until 1956. His first major paintings date from as early as 1945, at which time he was already interested in collage (using newspaper, cardboard, silver wrapping, string and wire) and engraving techniques. In the Dau al Set period, after coming into contact with Miró, among others, he underwent a brief Surrealist phase. However, after a stay in Paris he found his feet with an **abstract style** that matured in the Fifties, during which time he held his first major exhibitions, including shows in New York and Europe. His large works are deceptively simple, though underlying messages and themes are signalled by the inclusion of everyday objects and symbols on the canvas. Tàpies has also continually experimented with unusual materials, like oil paint mixed with crushed marble, or employing sand, clay, cloth or straw in his collages. His work became increasingly **political** during the Sixties and Seventies. *A la memòria de Salvador Puig Antich, 1974 (In Memory of Salvador Puig Antich*, 1974) commemorates a Catalan anarchist executed by Franco's regime, while slogans splashed across other works, or the frequent use of the red bars of the Catalan flag, leave no doubt about his affiliations. His most recent works are more sombre still, featuring recurring images of earth, shrouds and bodies, as echoes of civil war and conflict.

Tàpies' work from every period, while three or four exhibitions a year highlight works and installations by other contemporary artists. The foundation also includes a peerless archive on Tàpies' work held in the gorgeous **library** on the upper floor fashioned from the original shelves of the publisher's warehouse. In his later years Tàpies himself has concentrated on public art and sculpture; important **outdoor works in Barcelona** include *Homenatge a Picasso* (*Homage to Picasso*; 1983), on Passeig de Picasso, outside the gates of the Parc de la Ciutadella, while the foundation building is capped by *Núvol i Cadira* (*Cloud and Chair*; 1990), a tangle of glass, wire and metal.

## Museu Egipci de Barcelona

Half a block east of Passeig de Gràcia, the **Museu Egipci de Barcelona**, at c/de València 284 (Mon–Sat 10am–8pm, Sun 10am–2pm; €7; ☎934 880 188, Ⓦwww.museuegipci.com; ⓂPasseig de Gràcia), is an exceptional private collection of artefacts from ancient Egypt, ranging from the earliest kingdoms to the era of Cleopatra. It was founded by hotelier and antiquity collector Jordi Clos – whose luxury *Hotel Claris*, a block away, still has its own private museum for guests – and displays a remarkable gathering of over six hundred objects, ranging from amulets to sarcophagi. The emphasis is on the shape and character of Egyptian society, and visitors are given a hugely detailed English-language guidebook, which enables you to nail down specific periods and descriptions, case by case, if you so wish. But the real pleasure here is a serendipitous wander, turning up items like a wood-and-leather bed of the First and Second Dynasties (2920–2649 BC), some examples of cat mummies of the Late Period (715–332 BC) or a rare figurine of a spoonbill (ibis) representing an Egyptian god (though archeologists aren't yet sure which). If you'd like to know more, an Egyptologist leads **guided tours** every Saturday at 11am

(Catalan) and 5pm (Spanish), included in the entry price – English-language tours may also be available if you contact the museum in advance. There are temporary exhibitions (extra charge sometimes levied), plus a library and a good book and gift shop on the lower floor, and a terrace café upstairs. The museum also hosts a full programme of study sessions, children's activities and themed evening events – the reception desk or website can provide details.

## Fundació Francisco Godia

The building next door to the Egyptian museum on c/de València houses the private art collection of the Fundació **Francisco Godia** (Mon & Wed–Sat 10am–2pm & 4–7pm, Sun 10am–2pm; €4.50; ℡932 723 180, Ⓦwww.fundacionfgodia .org; ⓂPasseig de Gràcia). Harnessing medieval art, ceramics and modern Catalan art, in many ways it serves as a taster for the huge collections at Montjuïc in MNAC, while its small size makes it immediately more accessible. The pieces here – displayed in hushed rooms where the only sound is the hum of the air conditioning – were collected by aesthete and 1950s racing driver Francisco Godia, whose medals and cups are the first things you encounter. Beyond lie selected Romanesque carvings and Gothic paintings, notably work by fifteenth-century artist Jaume Huguet, and then there's a jump to the *modernista* paintings of Isidre Nonell, Santiago Rusiñol and Ramon Casas, among others. There's a varied selection of ceramics on show, too, from most of the historically important production centres in Spain. From fifteenth-century Valencia originate the *socarrats*, decorated terracotta panels used to stud ceilings. Not all of the collection can be shown at any one time, so pieces are rotated on occasion, while special exhibitions also run in tandem, for which there's usually no extra charge.

## La Pedrera

Antoni Gaudí's weird apartment building at Pg. de Gràcia 92 (ⓂDiagonal) is simply not to be missed – though you can expect queues whenever you visit. Constructed as the Casa Milà between 1905 and 1911, and popularly known as

▲ La Pedrera

**La Pedrera** – "The Stone Quarry", it was declared a UNESCO World Heritage Site in 1984. Its hulking, rippled facade, curving around the street corner in one smooth sweep, is said to have been inspired by the mountain of Montserrat just outside Barcelona, while the apartments themselves, whose balconies of tangled metal drip over the facade, resemble eroded cave dwellings. Indeed, there's not a straight line to be seen – hence the contemporary joke that the new tenants would only be able to keep snakes as pets. The building, which Gaudí himself described as "more luminous than light", was his last secular commission – and one of his best – but even here he was injecting religious motifs and sculptures into the building until told to remove them. A sculpture of the Virgin Mary was planned to complete the roof, but the building's owners demurred, having been alarmed by the anti-religious fervour of the "Tragic Week" in Barcelona in 1909, when anarchist-sponsored rioting destroyed churches and religious foundations. Gaudí, by now working full-time on the Sagrada Família, was appalled, and determined in future to use his skills only for religious purposes.

The **self-guided visit** (entrance on c/Provença, March–Oct 9am–8pm, Nov–Feb daily 9am–6.30pm, closed first week Jan; ☏902 400 973, ⓦwww .lapedreraeducacio.org; €8) includes a trip up to the extraordinary *terrat* (roof terrace) to see at close quarters the enigmatic chimneys, as well as an informative exhibition about Gaudí's work installed under the 270 curved brick arches of the attic. El Pis ("the apartment") on the building's fourth floor re-creates the design and style of a *modernista*-era bourgeois apartment in a series of extraordinarily light rooms that flow seamlessly from one to another. The apartment is filled with period furniture and effects, while the moulded door and window frames, and even the brass door handles, all follow Gaudí's sinuous building design.

Casa Milà itself is still split into private apartments and is administered by the Fundació Caixa de Catalunya. Through the grand main entrance of the building you can access the Fundació's first-floor **exhibition hall** (daily 10am–8pm; free; ⓦwww.fundaciocaixacatalunya.org), which hosts temporary art shows of works by major international artists.

## Casa Ramon Casas: Vinçon

Right next to La Pedrera, in the same block on Passeig de Gràcia, the **Casa Ramon Casas** (1899) was built for the wealthy Barcelona artist Ramon Casas i Carbó (1866–1932). He had found early success in Paris with friends Santiago Rusiñol and Miquel Utrillo, and the three of them were later involved in *Els Quatre Gats* tavern, which Casas largely financed. In 1941, the **Vinçon** store (Mon–Sat 10am–8.30pm; ☏932 156 050, ⓦwww.vincon.com) was established in the building, which emerged in the Sixties as the country's pre-eminent purveyor of furniture and design, a reputation today's department store still maintains. There are several entrances – at Pg. de Gràcia 96, c/Provença 273 and c/Pau Claris 175 – and apart from checking out the extraordinary furniture floor, which gives access to a terrace with views of the interior of La Pedrera, you should try and make time for **La Sala Vinçon** (open same hours as the store). This is Vinçon's exhibition hall and art gallery, located in Casas' original studio, and it puts on excellent shows of graphic and industrial design and contemporary furniture.

## Along Avinguda Diagonal

At the top of Passeig de Gràcia you'll find the **Palau Robert**, Pg. de Gràcia 107 (Mon–Sat 10am–7pm, Sun 10am–2.30pm; ⓣ932 388 091, ⓦwww.gencat.cat/palaurobert; free; ⓂDiagonal), the information centre for the region of Catalunya, which hosts changing exhibitions on all matters Catalan, from art to business; the pretty gardens around the back are a popular meeting point for the local nannies and their charges.

Across the Diagonal from here stands **Casa Comalat** (1909), Avgda. Diagonal 442, at the junction with c/de Corsega, a tricky corner plot, handled with aplomb by the architect Salvador Valeri i Pupurull, who gave it two very different *modernista* facades. On the other side of the avenue, at no. 373, the almost Gothic Palau Quadras (a Josep Puig i Cadafalch work from 1904) has a new lease of life as **Casa Àsia** (Tues–Sat 10am–8pm, Sun 10am–2pm; free; ⓣ932 837 337, ⓦwww.casaasia.es), a cultural and arts centre for Asia and the Pacific Region. You can check the website for current exhibitions, but it's always worth calling in anyway as there's a good café on the ground floor and, best of all, the Jardi d'Orient roof terrace. Take the elevator up, and you'll get views of the Sagrada Família towers rising behind Puig i Cadafalch's largest work, the soaring Casa Terrades, a little further down Diagonal, on the left at nos. 416–420. This is more usually known as the **Casa de les Punxes** (House of Spikes) because of its red-tiled turrets and steep gables. Built in 1903 for three sisters, and converted from three separate houses spreading around an entire corner of a block, the crenellated structure is almost northern European in style.

Keep to the avenue and you'll pass a sculpture of the **Ictineo** (Diagonal at c/de Provença), the world's earliest powered submarine, courtesy of the Catalans (see p.89), before turning up Passeig de Sant Joan to see Puig i Cadafalch's palatial **Casa Macaya** (ⓂVerdaguer). Dating from 1898–1900, it's a superbly ornamental building with a Gothic-inspired courtyard and canopied staircase from which griffins spring. You might be able to poke your head inside for a look, since the house has been used in the past as a gallery run by the Fundació La Caixa, but even from the outside it's worth pausing to view the unusual exterior carvings by craftsman Eusebi Arnau – like the angel with a "box" Brownie camera or the sculptor himself on his way to work by bike. You're only four blocks west of the Sagrada Família at this point, but you might as well stay with the Diagonal until you reach Josep Maria Jujol i Gilbert's **Casa Planells** at Avgda. Diagonal 332. Jujol was one of Gaudí's early collaborators, responsible for La Pedrera's undulating balconies and much of the mosaic work in the Parc Güell. Built in 1923–24, this apartment block – a sinuous solution to an acute-corner building – simplifies many of the themes that Gaudí exaggerated in his own work.

## Palau Montaner

A couple of blocks south of the Diagonal, the **Palau Montaner,** c/de Mallorca 278, was built in 1896 for a member of the Montaner i Simon publishing family – after the original architect quit, the *modernista* architect Lluís Domènech i Montaner took over halfway through construction, and the top half of the facade is clearly more elaborate than the lower part. Meanwhile, the period's most celebrated craftsmen were set to work on the interior, which sports rich mosaic floors, painted glass, carved woodwork and a monumental staircase. The building is now the seat of the Madrid government's delegation to Catalunya, but there are **guided tours** at the weekend (Sat at 10.30am in English, plus others in Spanish/Catalan at 11.30am & 12.30pm and Sun at 10.30am, 11.30am & 12.30pm in Spanish/Catalan; €5; ☏933 177 652, ⓦwww .rutadelmodernisme.com) which explain something of the house's history and show you the public rooms, grand dining room and courtyard. It's unusual to be able to get inside a private *modernista* house of the period, so it's definitely worth the effort.

## Mercat de la Concepció and around

The Dreta's finest neighbourhood market, the **Mercat de la Concepció** (Mon 8am–3pm, Tues–Fri 8am–8pm, Sat 8am–4pm; July & Aug closes 3pm; ⓦwww .laconcepcio.com), was inaugurated in 1888, its iron-and-glass tram-shed structure reminiscent of others in the city. Flowers, shrubs, trees and plants are a Concepció speciality (the florists on c/de Valencia are open 24 hours a day), and there are a couple of good snack bars inside the market and a few outdoor cafés to the side.

The market takes its name from the nearby church of **La Concepció** (entrance on c/Roger de Llúria; daily 8am–1pm & 5–9pm; free), whose quiet cloister is a surprising haven of slender columns and orange trees. This was part of a fifteenth-century Gothic convent that once stood in the old town. It was abandoned in the early nineteenth century and then transferred here brick by brick in the 1870s, along with the Romanesque belfry from another old-town church.

A couple of restored corners showing something of the spirit of the original Eixample plan are found just to the south, by walking down c/Roger de Llúria. At no. 56, between carrers Consell de Cent and Diputació, a herringbone-brick tunnel leads into the **Jardins de les Torres de les Aigües** (daily 10am–dusk; free), an enclosed square centred on a Moorish-style water tower. The plan was for all the city's nineteenth-century inhabitants to have access to such gardens and public spaces, and it has been handsomely restored by the city council, who turn it into a backyard beach every summer, complete with sand and paddling pool. Another example of the old Eixample lies directly opposite, across c/Roger de Llúria, where the cobbled **Passatge del Permanyer** cuts across an Eixample block, lined by candy-coloured single-storey townhouses.

## Casa Calvet

Gaudí fans will want to finish an Eixample tour by crossing the Gran Via de les Corts Catalanes to tick off the great man's earliest commissioned townhouse building, erected for a prominent local textile family. **Casa Calvet**, at c/de Casp 48 (Ⓜ Urquinaona/Catalunya), dates from 1899 and, though fairly conventional in style, the Baroque inspiration on display in the sculpted facade and church-like lobby was to surface again in his later, more elaborate buildings on Passeig de Gràcia. If you want a closer look inside, you'll have to book a table in the fancy restaurant, *Casa Calvet* (ⓦwww.casacalvet.es), that now occupies the premises.

# Sagrada Família and Glòries

The easternmost reaches of the Dreta de l'Eixample are dominated by the one building that is an essential stop on any visit to Barcelona – Antoni Gaudí's great church of the **Sagrada Família**. Most visitors make a special journey out by metro to see the church and then head back into the centre, but it's worth diverting the few blocks south to the area known as **Glòries** where you can visit the city's sprawling flea market, the national theatre building, music museum and the sole surviving bullring in Barcelona. This is an area destined for dramatic redevelopment over the next few years, as part of the city council's ongoing attempt to breathe new life into peripheral urban areas.

## Sagrada Família

Nothing – really, nothing – prepares you for the impact of the **Temple Expiatori de la Sagrada Família** (daily: April–Sept 9am–8pm; Oct–March 9am–6pm; €8, €11.50 including guided tour, audio-guide €3.50; ℡932 073 031, ⓦwww.sagradafamilia.org; ⓜSagrada Família), which occupies an entire city block between c/de Mallorca and c/de Provença, north of the Diagonal; the metro drops you right outside.

In many ways the overpowering church of the "Sacred Family" has become a kind of symbol for the city, and was one of the few churches (along with the cathedral, La Seu) left untouched by the orgy of church-burning which accompanied both the 1909 "Tragic Week" rioting and the 1936 revolution. More than any building in the Barri Gòtic, it speaks volumes about the Catalan urge to glorify uniqueness and endeavour. It is the most fantastic of the modern architectural creations in which Barcelona excels – even the coldest hearts will find the Sagrada Família inspirational in form and spirit.

### Some history

Begun in 1882 by public subscription, the Sagrada Família was originally intended by its progenitor, the Catalan publisher Josep Bocabella, to be an expiatory building that would atone for the city's increasingly revolutionary ideas. Bocabella appointed the architect Francesc de Paula Villar to the work, and his plan was for a modest church in an orthodox neo-Gothic style. Two years later, after arguments between the two men, Gaudí – only 31 years of age – took charge and changed the direction and scale of the project almost immediately, seeing in the Sagrada Família an opportunity to reflect his own deepening spiritual and nationalist feelings. He spent most of the rest of his life working on the church. Indeed, after he finished the Parc Güell in 1911, Gaudí vowed never to work again on secular art, but to devote himself solely to the Sagrada Família (where, eventually, he lived in a workshop on site), and he was adapting the plans ceaselessly right up to his untimely death. Run over by a tram on the Gran Via on June 7, 1926, he died in hospital three days later – initially unrecognized, for he had become a virtual recluse, rarely leaving his small studio. His death was treated as a Catalan national disaster, and all of Barcelona turned out for his funeral procession. Following papal dispensation, he was buried in the Sagrada Família crypt.

Work on the church was slow, even in Gaudí's day, mainly due to a persistent lack of funds. It took four years to finish the crypt (1901) and the first full plan of the building wasn't published until 1917. The first tower was erected the following year, but by the time of Gaudí's death only one facade was complete.

**SAGRADA FAMILIA & GLÒRIES**

**BAR**
Michael Collins · · · · · · · · 2

**ACCOMMODATION**
Eurostars Gaudí · · · · · · · · A

**RESTAURANTS**
Alkimia · · · · · · · · · · · · · 1
Gorria · · · · · · · · · · · · · · 4
Piazzenza · · · · · · · · · · · · 2

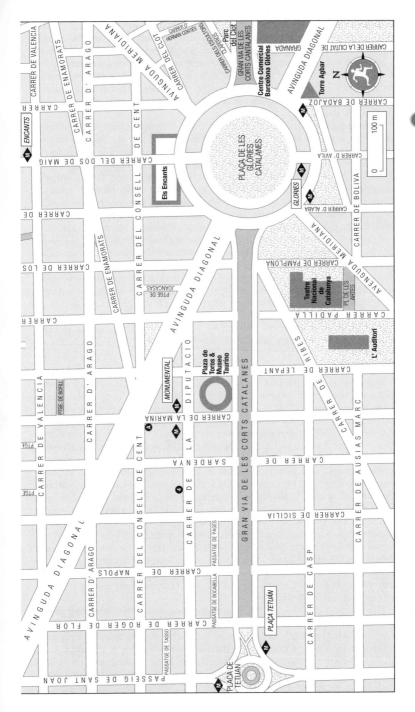

Although the church building survived the Civil War, Gaudí's plans and models were destroyed in 1936 by the anarchists, who regarded Gaudí and his church as conservative religious relics that the new Barcelona could do without. George Orwell – whose sympathies were very much with the anarchists during the Civil War – remarked that the Sagrada Família had been spared because of its supposed artistic value, but added that it was "one of the most hideous buildings in the world" and that the anarchists "showed bad taste in not blowing it up when they had the chance".

Work restarted in the late 1950s amid great controversy, and has continued ever since – as have the arguments. Some maintained that the Sagrada Família should be left incomplete as a memorial to Gaudí, others that the architect intended it to be the work of several generations, each continuing in its own style. On balance it's probably safe enough to assume that Gaudí saw the struggle to finish the building as at least as important as the method and style. Construction is financed by private funding and ticket sales, not by government or church, and for many years the work has been overseen by chief architect Jordi Bonet, the son of one of Gaudí's assistants. His vision has attracted no little criticism for infringing Gaudí's original spirit, not least the work on the Passion facade, commissioned from sculptor Josep María Subirachs. Computer-aided design and high-tech construction techniques have also proved controversial, though they have undoubtedly speeded up the work in recent years. Meanwhile, tunnelling under the temple for the high-speed AVE train line has kicked up a huge stink among critics who claim that the church will be put at risk (not so, say the tunnel engineers). All in all, though the project might be drawing inexorably towards realization, no one is yet prepared to put forward a definite completion date, leaving plenty more time for argument.

## The building

The size alone is startling – Gaudí's original plan was to build a church capable of seating over 10,000 people. In particular, twelve extraordinary **spires** rise to over 100m. They have been likened to everything from perforated cigars to celestial billiard cues, but for Gaudí they were symbolic of the twelve apostles. A precise symbolism also pervades the facades, each of which is divided into three porches devoted to Faith, Hope and Charity, and each uniquely sculpted. Gaudí made extensive use of human, plant and animal models (posing them in his workshop), as well as taking casts and photographs, in order to produce exactly the likenesses he sought for the sculptural groups. The eastern **Nativity facade** (facing c/de la Marina) was the first to be completed and is alive with fecund detail, its very columns resting on the backs of giant tortoises. Contrast this with the Cubist austerity of Subirachs' work on the western **Passion facade** (c/de Sardenya), where the brutal story of the Crucifixion is played out across the harsh mountain stone. Gaudí meant the so-far unfinished south facade, the **Gloria**, to be the culmination of the Temple – designed (he said), to show "the religious realities of present and future life . . . man's origin, his end". Everything from the Creation to Heaven and Hell, in short, is to be included in one magnificent ensemble.

The reality is that the place is a giant building site, with scaffolding, pallets, dressed stone, cranes, tarpaulins and fencing scattered about, and contractors hard at work. However, construction of the vaults over the side-aisles began in 1995 and for the first time a recognizable church interior is starting to take shape. In 2001 the vaults of the central nave were finished, and the whole church is due to be roofed in due course, with a 170-metre-high central dome and tower to follow (which will make the church the tallest building in

Barcelona). Extraordinary columns branch towards the spreading stone leaves of the roof, a favourite Gaudí motif inspired by the city's plane trees – he envisaged the temple interior as a forest from very early days.

**Elevators** (open same hours as the church; €2) run up the towers of the Passion and Nativity facades, from where you'll be rewarded by partial views of the city through an extraordinary jumble of latticed stonework, ceramic decoration, carved buttresses and sculpture. Your entrance ticket also gives you access to the **crypt**, where a **museum** (timing as for the church) traces the career of the architect and the history of the church. Models, sketches and photographs help to make some sense of the work going on around you, and you can see sculptors and model-makers at work in the plaster workshop. The 45-minute **guided tours** run hourly in season (May to Oct, in English at 11am, 1pm, 3pm & 5pm), mornings only the rest of the year, and you can book a place on the next one when you turn up.

## Hospital de la Santa Creu i de Sant Pau

While you're in the neighbourhood, it would be a shame not to stroll from the Sagrada Família to Lluís Domènech i Montaner's innovative **Hospital de la Santa Creu i de Sant Pau** (ⓂHospital de Sant Pau), possibly the one building that can rival the church for size and invention. The hospital has its own metro stop, but it's far better to walk up the four-block-long Avinguda de Gaudí, which gives terrific views back over the spires of the Sagrada Família.

Work started on the hospital in 1902, the brief being to replace the city's medieval hospital buildings in the Raval with a modern series of departments and wards. Domènech i Montaner spent ten years working on the building and left his trademarks all over it: thumbing his nose at Cerdà, the buildings are aligned diagonally to the Eixample, surrounded by gardens; and everywhere, whimsical pavilions, turrets and towers sport bright ceramic tiles and little domes. Domènech retired in 1912, once funds had run out, and the building wasn't fully completed until 1930, seven years after his death, though the latter stages were overseen by Domènech's son Pere, ensuring a certain continuity of style. Craftsmen adorned every inch with sculpture, mosaics, stained glass and ironwork, while much of the actual business of running a hospital was hidden away in underground corridors which connect the buildings together. It's a stunning, harmonious achievement – that it's a hospital seems almost incidental, which is doubtless the effect that the architect intended.

The *modernista* hospital buildings are deemed to have served their purpose; behind them spreads the high-tech central block of the new hospital. The pavilions have been turned over to educational and cultural use (a Museum of Medicine is mooted), and include the **Centre del Modernisme** (daily 10am–2pm; ☎933 177 652, Ⓦwww.rutadelmodernisme.com), where you can find out about and buy the city's Ruta del Modernisme sightseeing package. You can also sign up here for informative **guided tours** of the complex (daily at 10.15am & 12.15pm in English, plus others in Spanish/Catalan; €5), which can tell you more about the six-hundred-year history of the hospital.

## Plaça de les Glòries Catalanes and around

Barcelona's major arterial routes all meet at the **Plaça de les Glòries Catalanes** (ⓂGlòries), named for and dedicated to the "Catalan glories", from architecture to literature. Although now stuck out at the eastern edge of the city centre, Glòries was conceived by nineteenth-century designer Ildefons Cerdà as the nucleus of his Eixample blueprint. This never materialized and for years it's been no more than a swirling traffic roundabout, though current plans put Glòries at the heart of the city's latest wave of regeneration. By 2012, the roundabout traffic is to be tunnelled underground, thus opening up a grand pedestrianized park which will contain a cultural and design centre to house the city's municipal museum collections.

Glòries is already positioned as a gateway to the Diagonal Mar district, with trams running down Avinguda Diagonal to the Diagonal Mar shopping centre and Fòrum site. Meanwhile, the signature building on the roundabout is French architect Jean Nouvel's cigar-shaped **Torre Agbar** (142m), the headquarters of the local water company, which is a highly distinctive aluminium-and-glass tower with no less than 4000 windows, its shape inspired by the rocky protuberances of Montserrat. A huge shopping mall lies across the Diagonal from here, while further across the Gran Via the park and play areas of **Parc del Clot** show what can be done in an urban setting within the remains of a razed factory site. Meanwhile, Jean Nouvel also designed the new **Parc del Centre del Poble Nou** further down the Diagonal, an eye-catching contemporary park of giant ferns, herb gardens, green spaces, sculptures and play areas set between carrers Bilbao, Bac de Roda and Marroc.

On the north side of Glòries, on c/Dos de Maig, the open-air **Els Encants** (Mon, Wed, Fri & Sat 9am–6pm, plus Dec 1–Jan 5 Sun 9am–3pm; ⓂEncants/Glòries) is an absolute must for flea market addicts. It takes up the entire block below c/Consell de Cent, and you name it, you can buy it: old sewing machines, cheese graters, photograph albums, cutlery, lawnmowers, clothes, shoes, CDs, antiques, furniture and out-and-out junk. Go in the morning to see it at its best – haggling is de rigueur, but you're up against experts.

## Teatre Nacional de Catalunya

Off to the southwest of Glòries, the **Teatre Nacional de Catalunya** (ⓂGlòries) makes another dramatic statement. Catalunya´s national theatre, designed by local architect Ricardo Bofill, presents the neighbourhood with a soaring glass box encased within a Greek temple on a raised dais, surrounded by manicured lawns. There are guided building and backstage **tours** for anyone interested in learning more (currently Tues & Thurs; €3; reservations required; see website for details, Ⓦwww.tnc.cat).

## L'Auditori and the Museu de la Música

Set a block over from the national theatre, and forming a sort of cultural enclave, **L'Auditori** is the city's contemporary city concert hall, built in 1999. Housed within it, on the c/Padilla side, is the **Museu de la Música** (Mon & Wed–Fri 11am–9pm, Sat, Sun & hols 10am–7pm; €4, free first Sun of month; ☎932 563 650, Ⓦwww.museumusica.bcn.cat; ⓂGlòries/Marina), which displays a remarkable collection of instruments and musical devices, from seventeenth-century serpent horns to reel-to-reel cassette decks. It's all very impressive, with soaring glass-walled cases letting you view the pieces from all sides, and yet it struggles to engage, partly because of the sheer number and variety of instruments and partly because of the impenetrable commentary, with sections called things like "The humanist spirit and the predominance of polyphony". Make of that what you will, or the chronological "timeline" that runs from Pythagoras in the fifth century BC to 2007 when "the Rolling Stones continue to play". Still, there's a bit of big-screen Elvis here and African drumming there, and if you ever wanted to pluck at a harp without anyone shouting at you, this is the place.

## Plaza de Toros Monumental

The city's only surviving bullring, the **Plaza de Toros Monumental**, stands three blocks west of Glòries, at Gran Via de les Corts Catalanes 749 (ⓂMonumental). Its brick facade, Moorish egg-shaped domes, polychromatic decoration and *sol y sombra* ("sun and shade") seating sections provide a taste of Andalucía in a city where the bullfight doesn't have much of a following – tellingly, the ring is one part of Barcelona where not a word of Catalan is seen. The city authorities are minded to ban bullfighting altogether, so its days may be numbered anyway. Matador costumes, photographs, posters and the stuffed heads of vanquished bulls occupy the small **Museo Taurino** (Mon–Sat 10.30am–2pm & 4–7pm, Sun 11am–1pm; €4; ☎932 455 804) – enter at the corner with c/de la Marina – while an overhead walkway provides a view into the bull pens.

# Esquerra de l'Eixample

The long streets west of Rambla de Catalunya as far as Barcelona Sants train station – making up the **Esquerra de l'Eixample** – are perhaps the least visited on any city sightseeing trip. With all the major architectural highlights found on the Eixample's eastern (or right-hand) side, the Esquerra (left-hand side) was intended by its nineteenth-century planners for public buildings, institutions and industrial concerns, many of which still stand. However, the Esquerra does have its pockets of interest, not least the city university and an eye-catching public park or two, while it's here that some of the city's best bars and clubs are found, particularly in the gay-friendly streets of the so-called Gaixample district, near the university.

## Universitat de Barcelona and around

Built in the 1860s, the grand Neoclassical main building of the **Universitat de Barcelona**, at Plaça de la Universitat (ⓂUniversitat), is now mainly used for ceremonies and administration purposes, but no one minds if you stroll through the doors. There's usually an exhibition in the echoing main hall, while beyond lie two fine arcaded courtyards and extensive gardens, providing a welcome escape from the traffic. Students eat at the self-service café and bar in the basement, though the traditional meeting point is the *Bar Estudiantil*, outside in Plaça Universitat, where you can usually grab a pavement table.

In the streets behind the university – particularly around carrers Muntaner, Casanova and Consell de Cent – Barcelona has its own gay district, known as the **Gaixample**. Gay-friendly bars, clubs, restaurants and businesses have mushroomed here over the last decade (the best are reviewed in Chapter 14), though if you're expecting the overt street scene of San Francisco's Castro or even London's Soho, you'll be disappointed.

## Along Avinguda Diagonal

The most interest lies in the buildings on and off the upper reaches of Avinguda Diagonal (ⓂDiagonal). At the top of Rambla de Catalunya, Puig i Cadafalch's pseudo-medieval **Casa Serra** (1903) has been much altered, though it retains its original tiles, canopies and jaunty tower. A bronze statue of Sant Jordi, patron saint of Catalunya, guards the Diagonal side of the

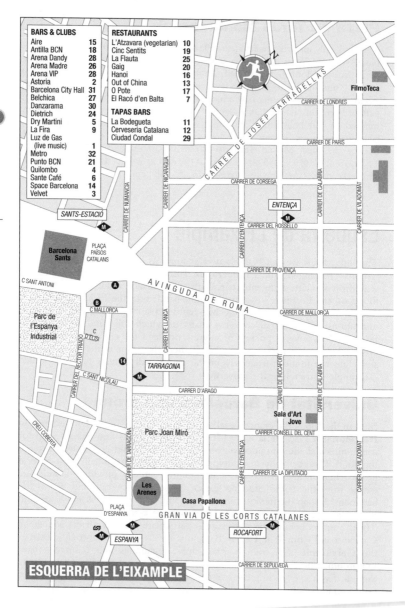

| BARS & CLUBS | | RESTAURANTS | |
|---|---|---|---|
| Aire | 15 | L'Atzavara (vegetarian) | 10 |
| Antilla BCN | 18 | Cinc Sentits | 19 |
| Arena Dandy | 28 | La Flauta | 25 |
| Arena Madre | 26 | Gaig | 20 |
| Arena VIP | 28 | Hanoi | 16 |
| Astoria | 2 | Out of China | 13 |
| Barcelona City Hall | 31 | O Pote | 17 |
| Belchica | 27 | El Racó d'en Balta | 7 |
| Danzarama | 30 | | |
| Dietrich | 24 | **TAPAS BARS** | |
| Dry Martini | 5 | La Bodegueta | 11 |
| La Fira | 9 | Cerveseria Catalana | 12 |
| Luz de Gas | | Ciudad Condal | 29 |
| (live music) | 1 | | |
| Metro | 32 | | |
| Punto BCN | 21 | | |
| Quilombo | 4 | | |
| Sante Café | 6 | | |
| Space Barcelona | 14 | | |
| Velvet | 3 | | |

**ESQUERRA DE L'EIXAMPLE**

building, now used as offices. Further up the Diagonal, also on the left, at no. 423 at the junction with c/Enric Granados, **Casa Sayrach** (1918) flows around its corner site, a vision of pink granite and marble, with a central tower topped by a cupola and a Pedrera-style roof.

Three blocks west you'll find the quirky **Museu i Centre d'Estudis de l'Esport** (June–Sept Mon–Fri 8am–3pm; rest of the year Mon–Fri

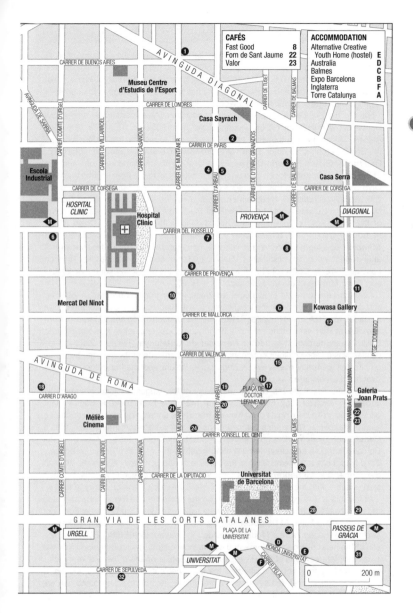

| CAFÉS | |
|---|---|
| Fast Good | 8 |
| Forn de Sant Jaume | 22 |
| Valor | 23 |

| ACCOMMODATION | |
|---|---|
| Alternative Creative Youth Home (hostel) | E |
| Australia | D |
| Balmes | C |
| Expo Barcelona | B |
| Inglaterra | F |
| Torre Catalunya | A |

10am–2pm & 3–7pm; free; ☎934 192 232; Ⓜ Hospital Clinic), at c/de Buenos Aires 56–58. Built as the Casa Pere Companys in 1911 by Josep Puig i Cadafalch, the little cream-coloured house contains probably the most unassuming sporting hall of fame found anywhere in the world. In a couple of quiet, wood-panelled rooms photographs of 1920s Catalan rally drivers and footballers are displayed alongside a motley collection of memorabilia,

## Contemporary architecture

It's easy to get sidetracked by the *modernista* architecture of the Eixample, and to forget that Barcelona also boasts plenty of contemporary wonders. Following the death of Franco, there was a feeling among architects that Barcelona had a lot of catching up to do, but subsequently the city has taken centre stage in the matter of urban design and renewal. Now the world looks to Barcelona for inspiration.

Even in the Franco years, exciting work had taken place, particularly among the Rationalist school of architects working from the 1950s to the 1970s, like José Antonio Coderch. From the latter part of this period, too, dates the earliest work by the Catalan architects – among them **Oriol Bohigas**, **Carlos Buxadé, Joan Margarit**, **Ricardo Bofill** and **Frederic Correa** – who later transformed the very look and feel of the city. The impetus for change on a substantial level came from hosting the **1992 Olympics**. Nothing less than the redesign of whole city neighbourhoods would do, with decaying industrial areas either swept away or transformed. While Correa, Margarit and Buxadé worked on the refit of the Estadi Olímpic, Bofill was in charge of INEF (the Sports University) and had a hand in the airport refit. Down at the harbour, Bohigas and others were responsible for creating the visionary **Vila Olímpica** development, carving residential, commercial and leisure facilities out of abandoned industrial blackspots. New city landmarks appeared, like Norman Foster's **Torre de Collserola** tower at Tibidabo, and the twin towers of the *Hotel Arts* and **Torre Mapfre** at the Port Olímpic.

Attention later turned to other neglected areas, with signature buildings announcing a planned transformation of the local environment. Richard Meier's contemporary art museum, **MACBA**, in the Raval, and Helio Piñon and Alberto Viaplana's **Maremàgnum** complex at Port Vell, anchored those neighbourhoods' respective revivals. Ricardo Bofill's Greek-temple-style **Teatre Nacional de Catalunya** (TNC) at Plaça de les Glòries was an early indicator of change on the eastern side of the city, and the same architect is currently overseeing a huge hotel, leisure and marina complex by the beach at Barceloneta.

It's around **Plaça de les Glòries** that many of the biggest projects are currently underway. Anchored by the eye-catching 142-metre-high **Torre Agbar**, a giant glowing cigar of a building by Jean Nouvel, the area is undergoing radical restructuring as a public plaza. There are advanced plans for a new transport interchange, plus a **Centre del Disseny** (Design Centre) by MBM (architects Josep Martorell, Oriol Bohigas and David Mackay) that will bring together the city's applied art collections. Zaha Hadid has a "Cinema City" in the pipeline at nearby Plaça de les Arts, while to the northeast at **La Sagrera** work is underway on the city's second AVE (high-speed train) station, with the dramatic 34-storey Torre Sagrera by Frank O. Gehry to follow.

At the foot of Avinguda Diagonal, down on the shoreline, the former industrial area of Poble Nou was transformed by the works associated with the Universal Forum of Cultures held in 2004. At **Diagonal Mar**, as the area is now known, Jacques Herzog (architect of London's Tate Modern) provided the centrepiece **Edifici Fòrum**, which sits at the heart of a new business and commercial district linking Barcelona with the once-desolate environs of the River Besòs. Meanwhile, on the other side of the city, it's Richard Rogers who is revitalizing the city's neglected bullring, **Les Arenes** at Plaça d'Espanya, intended as a gateway landmark, incorporating a domed garden, viewing platform and leisure centre.

from a signed water polo ball used in the 1992 Olympics to Everest mountaineer Carles Vàlles' ice pick

Beyond here Avinguda Diagonal flows on to **Plaça Francesc Macià** and the uptown shopping and business district – you can catch a tram from the *plaça* along the avenue up to L'Illa shopping centre, or just walk the short distance north up Avinguda Pau Casals to **Turó Parc** (daily 10am–dusk), a good place to rest weary feet, with a small lake and a café kiosk.

# Avinguda Diagonal to Barcelona Sants

South of the Diagonal stand several much larger examples of the *modernista* and Neoclassical spirit which infused public buildings of the nineteenth century. The Batlló textile mill on the corner of c/del Comte d'Urgell and c/del Rossello underwent major refurbishment in 1908 to emerge as the **Escola Industrial** (ⓂHospital Clinic). It occupies four entire Eixample blocks, with later academic buildings added in the 1920s, including a chapel by Joan Rubió i Bellvér, who worked with Antoni Gaudí. Students usually fill the courtyards, and no one minds if you take a stroll through. A block to the east is the massive **Hospital Clinic** (1904), with its fine pedimented portico, while the neighbourhood **Mercat del Ninot** (Mon 7am–2pm, Tues–Thurs 7am–2pm & 5.30–8.30pm, Fri 7am–8pm, Sat 7am–3pm; Ⓦwww.mercatdelninot.com), built in 1892, takes up a large area to the south, between carrers Villaroel and Casanova. This is almost entirely tourist-free, with produce, meat and fish inside and rows of shops around the block outside selling clothes, jewellery, accessories and homeware.

# Barcelona Sants to Plaça d'Espanya

Basque architect Luis Peña Ganchegui's **Parc de l'Espanya Industrial** (daily 10am–dusk; ⓂSants Estació) lies two minutes' walk away around the southern side of Barcelona Sants station. Built on the site of an old textile factory, it has a line of red-and-yellow-striped lighthouses at the top of glaring white steps, with an incongruously classical Neptune in the water below. Altogether, six sculptors are represented here and, along with the boating lake, café kiosk, playground and sports facilities provided, the park takes a decent stab at reconciling local interests with the mundane nature of the surroundings.

To the south, down c/de Tarragona, **Parc Joan Miró** (daily 10am–dusk; ⓂTarragona) was laid out on the site of the nineteenth-century municipal slaughterhouse. It features a raised piazza whose main feature is Joan Miró's gigantic mosaic sculpture *Dona i Ocell* (*Woman and Bird*), towering above a shallow reflecting pool. It's a familiar symbol if you've studied Miró's other works, but the sculpture is known locally by several other names – all of them easy to guess when you consider its erect, helmeted shape. The rear of the park is given over to games areas and landscaped sections of palms and firs, with a kiosk café and some outdoor tables found in amongst the trees. The children's playground here is one of the best in the city, with a climbing frame and aerial runway as well as swings and slides.

The former **Les Arenes** bullring (ⓂEspanya) backing Parc Joan Miró is undergoing a massive Richard Rogers-inspired refit, to convert it into a leisure and retail complex with enormous roof terrace, while retaining the circular Moorish facade of 1900. Also spared the wrecker's ball is the six-storey *modernista* **Casa Papallona** (1912), on the eastern side of Les Arenes on c/de Llança. It's one of the city's favourite house facades, crowned by a huge ceramic butterfly.

**8**

# The northern suburbs

U
ntil the Eixample stretched out across the plain to meet them, a string of small towns and villages ringed the city to the north. Today, they're firmly entrenched as suburbs of Barcelona, but most still retain an individual identity worth investigating even on a short visit to the city. Some of the sights will figure on most people's tours of the city, while others are more specialized, but taken together they do help to counter the notion that Barcelona begins and ends on the Ramblas.

**Gràcia** – the closest neighbourhood to the Eixample – is still very much the liberal, almost bohemian stronghold it was in the nineteenth century. Visits tend to revolve around browsing in the neighbourhood market or sipping a drink in one of the quiet squares, though Gràcia also has an active cultural scene and nightlife of its own. Antoni Gaudí's surreal **Parc Güell**, on the northeastern fringes of Gràcia, is the single biggest draw, while in neigh-bouring **Horta** ("garden", named for the gardens and country estates that once characterized the area) a couple more distinctive parks attract the curious with an hour or two to spare, notably the **Parc del Laberint** and its renowned maze.

To the northwest of the city centre, what was once the village of **Les Corts** is now indistinguishable from the rest of the modern city, save for the hallowed precincts of **Camp Nou**, FC Barcelona's stupendous football stadium and museum. North of here, past the university and across Avinguda Diagonal, the **Palau Reial de Pedralbes** combines three applied art museums, while a half-day's excursion can be made of the trip by walking from the palace, past the Gaudí dragon gate at **Pavellons Güell** to the Gothic **Monestir de Pedralbes**. Meanwhile, **Sarrià** just to the east, is still more like a small town than a suburb, with a pretty main street and market to explore.

Perhaps the only rival to Parc Güell as a single-destination visit out of the centre is the city's new science museum, **CosmoCaixa**, which opened in 2005. This lies just below the ring road (the Ronda de Dalt), beyond which extend the Collserola hills whose highest peak – **Tibidabo**, reached by tram and funicular – should really be saved for a clear day. The views are the draw here, from the amusement park, peak-top church or nearby **Torre de Collserola**, while a pleasant walk winds west to **Vallvidrera**, a hilltop village with another funicular connection back towards the city. Finally, from the information centre of the nearby **Parc de Collserola**, you can hike in the pinewoods high above Barcelona and see scarcely a soul – perhaps the greatest surprise in this most surprising of cities.

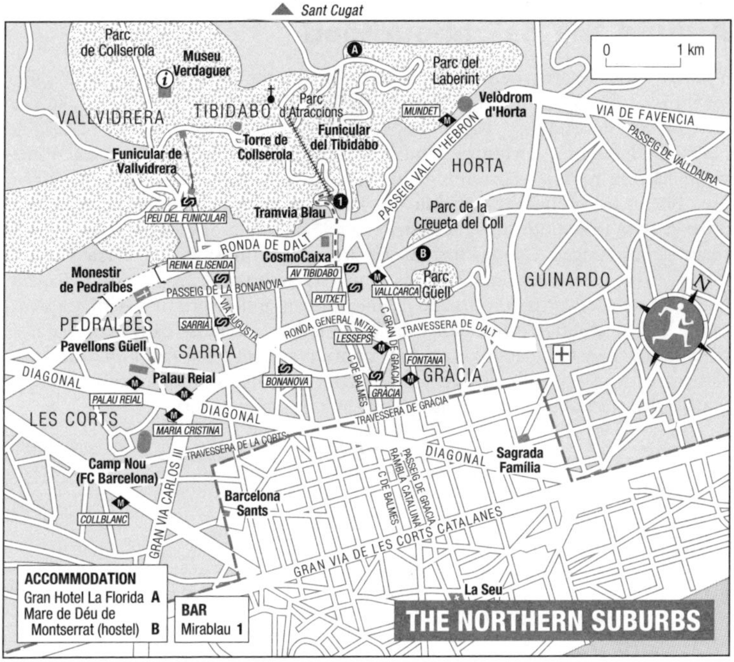




# Gràcia

Named after a long-destroyed fifteenth-century monastery, **Gràcia** was a village for much of its early existence before being annexed as a fully fledged suburb of the city in the late nineteenth century. Beginning at the top of Passeig de Gràcia, and bordered roughly by c/Balmes to the west and the streets above the Sagrada Família to the east, it's traditionally been home to arty and political types, students and the intelligentsia, though Gràcia also has a genuine local population (including one of the city's biggest Romany communities) that even today lends it an attractive small-town atmosphere. Consequently, its traditional annual summer festival, the Festa Major every August – a week's worth of concerts, parades, fireworks and parties – has no peer in any other neighbourhood. Actual sights are few and far between, but much of the pleasure to be had here is serendipitous; wander the narrow, gridded eighteenth- and nineteenth-century streets, park yourself on a bench under a plane tree, catch a film or otherwise take time out from the rigours of city-centre life. You'll soon get the feel of a neighbourhood that – unlike some in Barcelona – still has a soul.

Gràcia is around a thirty-minute hike from Plaça de Catalunya. **Getting there** by public transport means taking the FGC train from Plaça de Catalunya to Gràcia station, or buses 22 or 24 from Plaça de Catalunya up c/Gran de Gràcia, or the metro to either ⓂDiagonal (south) or ⓂFontana (north). From any of the stations, it's around a five-hundred-metre walk to Gràcia's two central squares, Plaça del Sol and Plaça Rius i Taulet, in the network of gridded streets off the eastern side of c/Gran de Gràcia.

# Around the neighbourhood

You may as well start where the locals start – first thing in the morning, shopping for bread and provisions in the **Mercat de la Llibertat**, a block west of c/Gran de Gràcia. The building was revamped in 1893 by a former pupil of Gaudí, Francesc Berenguer i Mestrès, who sheltered its food stalls under a *modernista* wrought-iron roof. It's currently being restored, but is due to re-open by 2009. Two blocks to the north, **Rambla del Prat** has the finest surviving collection of *modernista* townhouses in the district, while a couple of blocks further north again stands Antoni Gaudí's first major private commission, the **Casa Vicens** (1883–85) at c/les Carolines 24 (ⓂFontana). Here he took inspiration from the Moorish style, covering the facade in linear green-and-white tiles with a flower motif. The decorative iron railings are a reminder of Gaudí's early training as a metalsmith and, to further prove his versatility – and how Art Nouveau cuts across art forms – Gaudí also designed much of the mansion's furniture (though as it's a private house, unfortunately you can't get in to see it).

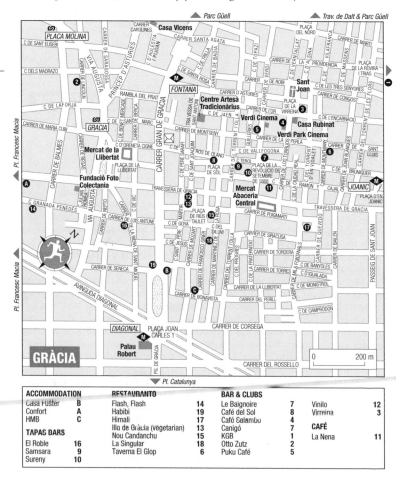

| ACCOMMODATION | | RESTAURANTS | | BAR & CLUBS | | | |
|---|---|---|---|---|---|---|---|
| Casa Fúster | B | Flash, Flash | 14 | Le Baignoire | 7 | Vinilo | 12 |
| Confort | A | Habibi | 19 | Café del Sol | 8 | Virreina | 3 |
| HMB | C | Himali | 17 | Café Salambo | 4 | | |
| | | Illa de Gràcia (vegetarian) | 13 | Canigó | 7 | **CAFÉ** | |
| **TAPAS BARS** | | Nou Candanchu | 15 | KGB | 1 | La Nena | 11 |
| El Roble | 16 | La Singular | 18 | Otto Zutz | 2 | | |
| Samsara | 9 | Taverna El Glop | 6 | Puku Café | 5 | | |
| Sureny | 10 | | | | | | |

From Casa Vicens, it's a five-minute walk east along c/Santa Agata, c/de la Providencia and then south into pretty **Plaça de la Virreina**, backed by its much-restored parish church of Sant Joan. This is one of Gràcia's favourite squares, with the *Virreina Bar* and others providing drinks and a place to rest and admire the handsome houses, most notably **Casa Rubinat** (1909), c/de l'Or 44, the last major work of Francesc Berenguer. Children and dogs, meanwhile, scamper around the small drinking fountain. In the streets around here, between carrers Torrijos and Verdi, are most of the neighbourhood's boutiques, galleries, cinemas and cafés, with c/Verdi in particular always worth a stroll.

Another short walk to the southwest, **Plaça del Sol** is the beating heart of much of the district's nightlife, though it's not quite so appealing during the day. It was redesigned rather soullessly in the 1980s, losing much of its attraction for older locals at least. Far more in keeping with Gràcia's overall tenor is **Plaça Rius i Taulet**, just to the south across Travessera de Gràcia. The thirty-metre-high clock tower was a rallying point for nineteenth-century radicals – whose twenty-first-century counterparts prefer to meet for brunch at the popular café *terrassas*.

At Plaça Rius i Taulet you're close to the main c/Gran de Gràcia. Walk south, and where the street becomes Passeig de Gràcia stands the **Casa Fuster**, on the left at no. 132 (Ⓜ Diagonal). Designed by Lluís Domènech i Montaner in 1908 (and now a luxury hotel, Ⓦ www.hotelcasafuster.com) it sports many of Domènech's most characteristic design features: a multi-columned building with chunky floral capitals, and – designed to fit the awkward corner it's built on – one concave and one convex tower.

# Parc Güell

From 1900 to 1914 Antoni Gaudí worked for Eusebi Güell (patron of Gaudí's Palau Güell, off the Ramblas) on the **Parc Güell** (daily: May–Aug 10am–9pm; April & Sept 10am–8pm; March & Oct 10am–7pm; Nov–Feb 10am–6pm; free), on the outskirts of Gràcia. This was Gaudí's most ambitious project after the Sagrada Família – on which he was engaged at the same time, commissioned as a private housing estate of sixty dwellings and furnished with paths, recreational areas and decorative monuments. It was conceived as a "Garden City" of the type popular at the time in England – indeed, Gaudí's original plans used the English spelling "Park Güell". In the end, only two houses were actually built, and the park was officially opened to the public instead in 1922.

Laid out on a hill, which provides fabulous views back across the city, the park is an almost hallucinatory expression of the imagination. Pavilions of contorted stone, giant decorative lizards, meandering rustic viaducts, a vast Hall of Columns (intended to be the estate's market), carved stone trees – all combine in one manic swirl of ideas and excesses, reminiscent of an amusement park. The Hall of Columns, for example, was described by the art critic Sacheverell Sitwell (in *Spain*) as "at once a fun fair, a petrified forest, and the great temple of Amun at Karnak, itself drunk, and reeling in an eccentric earthquake". Perhaps the most famous element – certainly the most widely photographed – is the long, meandering **ceramic bench** that snakes along the edge of the terrace above the columned hall. It's entirely decorated with a brightly coloured broken tile-and-glass mosaic (a method known as *trencadís*) that forms a dizzying sequence of abstract motifs, symbols, words and pictures. The ceramic mosaics and decorations found throughout the park were mostly executed by Josep Maria Jujol, who assisted on several of Gaudí's projects.

There are terrific views from the self-service **café**, which operates from one of the caverns adjoining the main terrace, but to escape the milling crowds you'll need to climb away from here, up into the wooded, landscaped gardens. At the very highest point – follow signs for "**Turó de les Tres Creus**" – on the spot where Gaudí had planned to place a chapel, three stone crosses top a stepped tumulus. It's from here that a 360-degree city panorama unfolds in all its glory.

At the main entrance on c/Olot, the former porter's lodge – and never can a porter have had more whimsical lodgings – is now the **Centre d'Interpretació** (Tues–Sun 11am–3pm; €2.30, combined ticket with City History Museum €6; ⓣ932 856 899, ⓦwww.museuhistoria.bcn.cat), offering a rather perfunctory introduction to the park's history, design and building methods used. Far better is the **Casa Museu Gaudí** (daily: April–Sept 10am–8pm; Oct–March 10am–6pm; €4; ⓣ932 193 811, ⓦwww.casamuseugaudi.org), a little way inside the park, designed and built in 1904 by one of Gaudí's other collaborators, Francesc Berenguer, and in which Gaudí was persuaded to live until he left to camp out at the Sagrada Família for good. Gaudí's ascetic study and bedroom have been kept much as they were in his day – there's an inkling of his personality in the displayed religious texts and pictures, along with a silver coffee cup and his death mask, made at the Sant Pau hospital where he died. Other rooms display a diverting collection of furniture he designed for other projects – a typical mixture of wild originality and brilliant engineering, as well as plans and objects relating to the park and to Gaudí's life.

## Park practicalities

If you have a choice, it's probably best to visit Parc Güell during the week, as weekends can be very busy indeed. The park straddles a steep hill and however you get there will involve an ascent on foot of some kind to reach the main section (see colour map 7 for approaches). The most direct route is on **bus #24** from Plaça de Catalunya, Passeig de Gràcia or c/Gran de Gràcia, which drops you on Carretera del Carmel at the eastern side gate by the car park. From ⓜVallcarca you have to walk a few hundred metres down Avinguda de l'Hospital Militar until you see the mechanical escalators on your left, ascending Baixada de la Glória. Follow these – and the short sections of stepped path in between – right to the western-side park entrance (15min), from where you wind down a path to the main terrace. **Walking from Gràcia** (and ⓜLesseps), turn right along Travessera de Dalt and then left up steep c/Larrard, which leads straight to the main entrance of the park on c/Olot (10min). The **Bus Turístic** stops at the bottom end of c/Larrard on c/la Mare de Deu de la Salut.

You'll have to walk back down c/Larrard to Travessera de Dalt for bus or metro connections back to the city, though **taxis** do hang about the main gates on c/Olot. There's a **café** with terrace seats in the park, while Carrer Larrard has several other little cafés, if you want to refuel on your way up or down, as well as a mini-market for picnic supplies.

# Parc de la Creueta del Coll

There couldn't be a greater contrast with Parc Güell than Horta's **Parc de la Creueta del Coll** (daily 10am–dusk; free), a *nou urbanisme* development by Olympic architects Martorell and Mackay, that was laid out on the site of an old quarry. There's a stand of palm trees by a small artificial lake, and concrete promenades under the sheer quarry walls, but lately it's all been allowed to go to the dogs (and feral cats) a bit and could do with a spruce-up. Still, you're greeted at the top of the park steps by an Ellsworth Kelly metal spike, while suspended by steel cables over a water-filled quarry is a massive concrete claw by the Basque artist Eduardo Chillida. **Bus** #28 from Plaça de Catalunya, up Passeig de Gràcia, stops just 100m from the park steps, or you can walk up Passeig de la Mare de Deu del Coll from Ⓜ Vallcarca in about twenty minutes (there's a neighbourhood map at the metro station).

Combining the park with a visit to Parc Güell is easy, too, though you'll need a keen sense of direction to find it from the rear exit of Parc Güell – it helps if you've climbed to the top of Güell's three-crosses hill and fixed in mind the quarry walls, which you can see across the valley. It's far easier to visit Parc de la Creueta del Coll first, then walk back down the main Passeig de la Mare de Deu del Coll until you see the signpost pointing down c/Balears (on your left) – from there, signposts guide you into Parc Güell the back way.

## Parc del Laberint

Confronted by the roaring traffic on the Passeig Vall d'Hebron, it seems inconceivable that there's any kind of sanctuary to hand, but just a couple of minutes' walk from Ⓜ Mundet metro puts you at the gates of the **Parc del Laberint** (daily 10am–dusk; €2, free Wed & Sun). The former estate mansion is undergoing long term restoration but the late eighteenth-century gardens are open for visits and are an enchanting spectacle. A series of paths, terraces, pavilions and water features embrace the hillside, merging with the pine forest beyond. At the very heart of the park is the famed topiary maze, El Laberint, created by the Marquis de Llupià i Alfarràs and designed as an Enlightenment puzzle concerning the forms of love. A statue of Eros in the centre is the reward for successfully negotiating the maze. Near the park entrance are a drinks kiosk, picnic area and children's playground.

▲ Parc del Laberint

At ⓂMundet, use the Passeig Vall d'Hebron (Muntanya) exit. Walk up the main road against the traffic flow for one minute and turn left into the car park and grounds of the Velòdrom – the park entrance is immediately behind the cycle stadium, up the green slope.

# Camp Nou and FC Barcelona

Within the city's Les Corts area, behind the university buildings, the magnificent **Camp Nou** football stadium will be high on the visiting list of any sports fan. It's no exaggeration to say that football in Barcelona is a genuine obsession, with support for the local giants **FC (Futbol Club) Barcelona** raised to an art form. "More than just a club" is the proud boast, and certainly during the dictatorship years the club stood as a Catalan symbol around which people could rally. Arch-rivals, Real Madrid, on the other hand, were always seen as Franco's club. Moreover, unlike any other professional team, the famous "blaugrana" (claret and blue) shirts remained unsullied by sponsors' names for a century – until, in a typically Catalan statement of intent, the Unicef logo was chosen.

The team – European champions in 1992 and 2006, home to the great names of Cruyff, Maradona, Stoichkof, Lineker and Ronaldinho – plays at the magnificent Camp Nou stadium. This was built in 1957, and enlarged for the 1982

## It's only a game?

Some people believe football is a matter of life or death . . . I can assure you it is much, much more important than that.

Bill Shankly

There isn't a Catalan football supporter who wouldn't agree with Liverpool legend and quip-meister Bill Shankly. These are fans who routinely boo their own team if they think the performance isn't up to scratch, thousands of white handkerchiefs waving along in disapproval. A disappointing season is seen as a slur on the Catalan nation, and if success goes instead to bitter rivals Real Madrid, then the pain is almost too much to bear. When team figurehead and captain **Luis Figo** was transferred to Madrid in 2000 (one of only a handful to have played for both clubs), the outrage was almost comical in its ferocity – at a later match between the two sides, a pig's head was thrown onto the pitch as Figo prepared to take a corner. Recent seasons have been testing for the fans, to say the least. Having finally wrestled the initiative back from the "Galacticos" of Real Madrid (Ronaldo, Zidane, Beckham, et al), and winning the Spanish league in 2005 and 2006, and the European Champions League in 2006, Barça – under Dutch coach Frank Rijkaard – imploded. From being the most exciting in Spain, featuring international superstars like **Ronaldinho** and **Samuel Eto'o** and the new Argentinian wonder-kid **Lionel Messi**, the team became – well, only the second most exciting in Barcelona, after Espanyol as player tensions erupted and the team lost ground again to Real Madrid, who won the league in both 2007 and 2008. An end-of-season 4-1 drubbing by the *madrileños* was the last straw, and Rijkaard lost his job in favour of former Barça player, B-team coach and all-Catalan hero, **Pep Guardiola**. Interesting times are promised, but whether there will be more boos and white hankies along the way depends on the swagger of the team and the mood of the crowd.

World Cup semi-final to accommodate 98,000 people– a second remodelling has just been announced, to be overseen by architect Norman Foster. The stadium provides one of the best football-watching experiences in the world and the matches can be an invigorating introduction to Catalan passions. The football season runs from August until May, with games usually played on Sundays – see p.238 for details on how to get a ticket. The stadium complex also hosts basketball, handball and hockey games with FC Barcelona's other professional teams, and there's also a public ice rink here.

Together, the stadium and the club's **Museu del Futbol** (April–Oct Mon–Sat 10am–8pm, rest of the year until 6.30pm, Sun 10am–3pm; museum only €8.50, including tour €13; ☎902 189 900 or 934 963 600, ⓦwww .fcbarcelona.com) provide a splendid celebration of Spain's national sport. The entrance is on Avinguda Arístides Maillol, through Gates (*Accés*) 7 and 9 (ⓜCollblanc/Maria Cristina & 10min walk); the Bus Turístic stops outside. The all-inclusive ticket allows you on the **self-guided tour**, winding into the bowels of the stadium, through the changing rooms, out onto the pitch side and up to the press gallery and directors' box for stunning views. The **museum** is jammed full of silverware, memorabilia, paintings and sculpture, while photograph displays and archive footage trace the history of the club back to 1901. Finally, you're directed into the **FC Botiga Megastore**, where you can buy anything from a replica shirt down to a branded bottle of wine.

# Palau Reial de Pedralbes

Opposite the university on Avinguda Diagonal, formal grounds stretch up to the Italianate **Palau Reial de Pedralbes** (ⓜPalau Reial) – basically a large villa with pretensions. It was built for the use of the royal family on their visits to Barcelona, with funds raised by public subscription, and received its first such visit in 1926. However, within five years the king had abdicated and the palace somewhat lost its role. Franco kept it on as a presidential residence and it later passed to the city, which now uses its rooms to show off its **applied art collections**. Until the projected Centre del Disseny (Design Centre) at Glòries is completed – which means for the foreseeable future – the palace contains separate **museums** of ceramics, decorative arts, and textiles and clothing (all Tues–Sat 10am–6pm, Sun & hols 10am–3pm, €4.20, free first Sun of the month), which can be visited on the same ticket; free first sun of the month. The **gardens** (10am–dusk, free entry), meanwhile, are a calm oasis, where – hidden in a bamboo thicket, to the left-centre of the facade – is the "Hercules fountain" (1884), an early work by Antoni Gaudí.

## Museu de Ceràmica

The collection at the **Museu de Ceràmica** (ⓦwww.museuceramica.bcn.cat) ranges from the thirteenth to the nineteenth century, and includes fine Moorish-influenced tiles and plates from the Aragonese town of Teruel, as well as a series of fifteenth- and sixteenth-century *socarrats* (decorated terra-cotta panels) from Paterno displaying demons and erotic scenes. Catalunya, too, has a long ceramics tradition, and there are entire rooms here of Catalan water stoups, jars, dishes, plates and bowls. Perhaps the most vivid examples of the polychromatic work coming out of Barcelona and Lleida workshops of

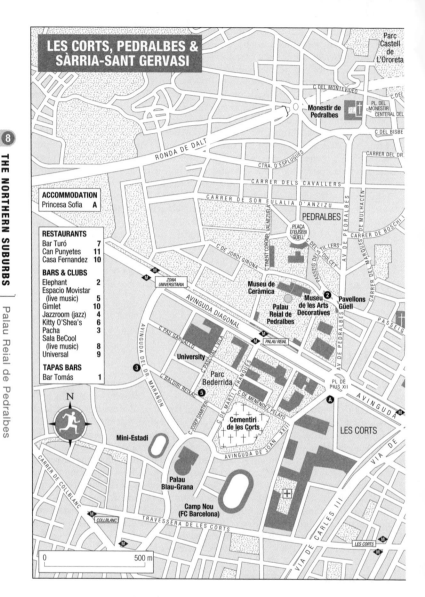

LES CORTS, PEDRALBES &
SÀRRIA-SANT GERVASI

**ACCOMMODATION**
Princesa Sofia     A

**RESTAURANTS**
Bar Turó                    7
Can Punyetes            11
Casa Fernandez         10

**BARS & CLUBS**
Elephant                    2
Espacio Movistar
(live music)             5
Gimlet                      10
Jazzroom (jazz)         4
Kitty O'Shea's           6
Pacha                       3
Sala BeCool
(live music)             8
Universal                   9

**TAPAS BARS**
Bar Tomás                 1

the time are the two extensive *azulejo* (ceramic tile) panels of 1710, one showing a Madrid bullfight, the other the feasting and dancing taking place at a party centred on the craze of the period – hot-chocolate-drinking. In the modern section, Picasso, Miró and the *modernista* artist Antoni Serra i Fiter are all represented. The whole display is considerably more interesting than the bare recital of exhibits suggests, particularly if you're already fascinated by the diverse ceramic designs and embellishments that adorn so many of the city's buildings, old and new.

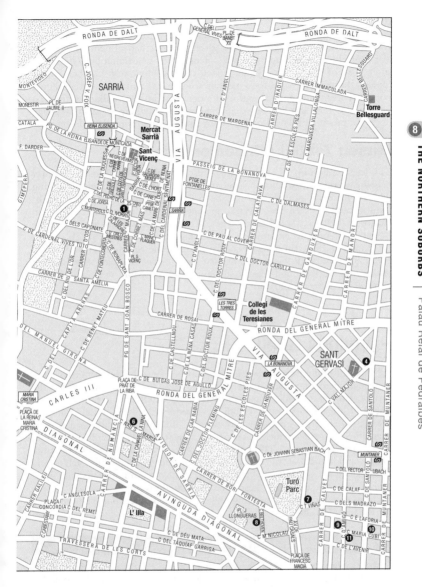

## Museu de les Arts Decoratives

The **Museu de les Arts Decoratives** (ⓦ www.museuartsdecoratives.bcn
.cat) provides a fair old romp from Romanesque art through to contemporary
Catalan design, but there are some beautiful pieces here, starting with a pair
of delicate thirteenth-century Andalusian boxes showing clear Arabic traits –
these are two of the very earliest pieces in the collection. Side rooms showcase
the various periods under the spotlight, with displays of highly polished

Baroque and Neoclassical furniture contrasting with the varied Art Deco and *modernista* holdings. The highlight here has to be the four-metre-high stained-glass window of 1900, depicting the *sardana* (a circle dance) being performed in a scene that looks back to medieval times for its inspiration. The entire latter half of the gallery concentrates on contemporary Catalan *disseny* (design), from chairs to espresso machines, lighting to sink taps, though there's not much context provided and in the end it's a bit like walking through a furnishings store and not being allowed to buy anything. English-language notes are provided if you'd prefer to put some names to goods and objects.

## Museu Textil i d'Indumentaria

The latest collection to arrive at the palace is that of the **Museu Textil i d'Indumentaria** (ⓦ www.museutextil.bcn.cat), the textile and clothing museum formerly located in La Ribera. Its layout was undecided at the time of writing, but the extensive collection presents selected items from late-Roman fabrics to 1930s cocktail dresses, while demonstrating the art and technique behind cloth-making, embroidery, lace and tapestry work. There are also pieces by Spanish and Catalan designers of the 1970s to the current day, like those of Pedro Rodríguez (1895–1990), the first *haute couture* designer to establish a studio in Barcelona, and Catalan designer Antonio Miró, who has recently donated pieces to the museum.

# Pavellons Güell

A block east of the Palau Reial gardens, Avinguda Pedralbes heads north off the Diagonal up to the Monestir de Pedralbes. Just a couple of minutes up the avenue, you'll pass Gaudí's remarkable **Pavellons Güell** on your left. As an early test of his capabilities, Antoni Gaudí was asked by his patron, Eusebi Güell, to rework the entrance, gatehouse and stables of the Güell summer residence, on a large working estate which was sited well away from the filth and unruly mobs of downtown Barcelona. The summer house itself was later given to the royal family, and rebuilt as the Palau Reial, but the brick-and-tile stables and outbuildings survive as Gaudí created them, frothy, whimsical affairs with more than a Moorish touch to them. The *trencadís* (broken tile mosaics) on the minarets were first experimented with here by Gaudí, a technique he then used for the rest of his life.

---

### Here be dragons

The slavering beast on Gaudí's dragon gate at the Pavellons Güell is not the vanquished dragon of Sant Jordi (St George), the Catalan patron saint, but the one that appears in the Labours of Hercules myth, a familiar Catalan theme in the nineteenth century. Gaudí's design was based on a work by the Catalan renaissance poet Jacint Verdaguer, a friend of the Güell family, who had reworked the myth in his epic poem, *L'Atlàntida* – thus, the dragon guarding golden apples in the Gardens of Hesperides is here protecting instead an orange tree (considered a more Catalan fruit). Gaudí's gate indeed can be read as an homage to Verdaguer, with its stencilled roses representing those traditionally given to the winner of the Catalan poetry competition, the Jocs Floral, which the poet won in 1877.

However, it's the gateway that's the most famous element. An extraordinary winged dragon made of twisted iron snarls at the passers-by, its razor-toothed jaws spread wide in a fearsome roar. Backing up to pose for a photograph suddenly doesn't seem like such a good idea. During the week you can't go any further than the gate, but it's well worth coinciding with the **guided visits** (Mon, Fri, Sat & Sun at 10.15am & 12.15pm in English, plus 11.15am & 1.15pm in Spanish/Catalan €5; ☎933 177 652, ⓦwww.rutadelmodernisme .com), especially to see inside Gaudí's innovative stables, now used as a library by the university's historical architecture department.

# Monestir de Pedralbes

At the end of Avinguda Pedralbes, the Gothic **Monestir de Pedralbes** (Tues–Sat 10am–2pm, June–Sept 10am–5pm, Sun & holidays 10am–3pm; combined ticket with City History Museum €6, free first Sun of the month; ☎932 563 434, ⓦwww.museuhistoria.bcn.cat) is reached up a cobbled street that passes through a small archway set back from the road. Founded in 1326 for the nuns of the Order of St Clare, this is, in effect, an entire monastic village preserved on the outskirts of the city, within medieval walls and gateways that completely shut out the noise and clamour of the twenty-first century. It's a twenty-minute walk from ⓜPalau Reial, or ten minutes from FGC Reina Elisenda (frequent trains from Plaça de Catalunya). Alternatively, you can go directly by bus from the city centre (30min): the 22 from Plaça de Catalunya and Passeig de Gràcia stops outside, while the 64 from Ronda Sant Antoni and c/Aribau ends its run at the monastery.

## The monastery

It took the medieval craftsmen a little over a year to prepare Pedralbes (from the Latin *petras albas*, "white stones") for its first community of nuns. The speed of the initial construction and the subsequent uninterrupted habitation by the Order helps explain the extreme architectural harmony. After 600 years of isolation the monastery was sequestered by the Generalitat during the Civil War and it later opened as a museum in 1983 – a new adjacent convent was built as part of the deal, where the Clare nuns still reside. The ensemble now forms part of the City History Museum.

The **cloisters** in particular are the finest in the city, built on three levels and adorned by the slenderest of columns, with the only sound the tinkling water from the fountain. Rooms opening off the cloisters give a clear impression of convent life, from the chapter house and austere refectory to a fully equipped kitchen and infirmary. Alcoves and day cells display restored frescoes, religious artefacts, furniture and utensils, while in the nuns' former dormitory – now given a black marble floor and soaring oak-beamed ceiling – is a selection of the rarer **treasures**. Whilst the nuns themselves eschewed personal trappings, the monastery acquired valuable art and other possessions over the centuries – including pieces of Gothic furniture claimed to be part of the founding queen's endowment. There are paintings by Flemish artists, an impressive series of so-called "factitious" altarpieces of the sixteenth century (made up of sections of different style and provenance) and some outstanding illuminated choir books.

The adjacent **church** (usually 11am–1pm & 5–8pm) is a simple, single-naved structure, which retains some of its original fourteenth-century stained glass. In the chancel, to the right of the altar, the foundation's sponsor, Elisenda de Montcada, wife of Jaume II, lies in a superb carved marble tomb. Widowed in 1327, six months after the inauguration of the monastery, Elisenda retired to an adjacent palace, where she lived until her death in 1364.

# Sarrià

If *modernista* buildings are high on your agenda, the exteriors of a couple of other important Gaudí buildings can be seen in the **Sarrià** district, east of Pedralbes. Not far from the science museum, the **Torre Bellesguard** (c/Bellesguard 16–20; FGC Avgda. del Tibidabo), built from 1900 to 1909 on the site of the early fifteenth-century palace of King Martin I (the last of the Catalan kings), is a neo-Gothic house of unremarkable proportions; the **Col. legi de les Teresianes** (c/Ganduxer 85; FGC Bonanova) was a convent school, embellished in 1888 by Gaudí with an iron gate and parabolic arches.

If you are going to poke around these nether reaches of Barcelona, you may as well venture into the heart of Sarrià itself. At the northern end of its narrow main street – c/Major de Sarrià (FGC Sarrià; c/Mare de Deu de Núria exit) – stands the much-restored church of **Sant Vicenç** (at Plaça de Sarrià; bus #64 from Pedralbes/ Plaça Universitat also stops here on its way to and from the monastery). This flanks the main Passeig de la Reina Elisenda de Montcada, across which lies the neighbourhood market, **Mercat Sarrià**, housed in a 1911 *modernista* red-brick building. Traffic-free c/Major de Sarrià runs downhill from here, past other surviving old-town squares, prettiest of which is **Plaça Sant Vicenç** (off c/Mañe i Flaquer), where there's a statue of the saint. If you make it this way, don't miss the *Bar Tomás*, just around the corner on c/Major de Sarrià, for the world's best *patatas bravas*.

# CosmoCaixa

A dramatic refurbishment in 2005 transformed the city's science museum into a must-see attraction, certainly if you've got children in tow – it's an easy place to spend a couple of hours, and can be seen on your way to or from Tibidabo. Partly housed in a converted *modernista* hospice (built in 1904–09 by Josep Domènech i Estapà), **CosmoCaixa** (Tues–Sun 10am–8pm; €3, first Sun of month free, children's activities €2, planetarium €2; ☎932 126 050, Ⓦwww.fundacio.lacaixa.es) retains the original building but has added a stylish, light-filled public concourse and a huge underground extension with four subterranean levels. The main exhibits are all down on the bottom floor, centred on the enormous open-plan Sala de la Matèria (Matter Room), where hands-on experiments and displays investigate life, the universe and everything, "from bacteria to Shakespeare". Many of the exhibits, and their densely worded explanations, require a very large thinking cap – younger children are soon going to be zooming around the open spaces. But there's no denying the overall pull of the two big draws, namely the 100 tonnes of "sliced" rock in the Mur Geològic (Geological Wall) and, best of all, the **Bosc**

**Inundat** – nothing less than a thousand square metres of r
rainforest, complete with croc-filled mangroves, anacondas, gia
dozy capybaras (the world's largest rodent, the size of a family do
Other lower levels of the museum are devoted to **children's a**
**activities**, such as Toca Toca! (Touch Touch!) – handling animals, i
plants – Clik (ages 3–6) and Flash (7–10), where science games and exp
are presented in a fun way. These activities all tend to be held at weeke
during school holidays – pick up a schedule when you arrive, or che... the
website. There are also daily shows in the **planetarium** (Spanish and Catalan
only, but worth experiencing), a great gift shop, and a café-restaurant with
outdoor seating beneath the restored hospital facade.

CosmoCaixa is at c/Teodor Roviralta 47–51, just below the city ring road, the
Ronda del Dalt. The easiest way to get there is by FGC train from Plaça de
Catalunya to **Avinguda del Tibidabo station**, and then walk up the avenue,
turning left just before the ring road (10min) – or the Tramvia Blau or Bus
Turístic can drop you close by.

# Tibidabo

If the views from the Castell de Montjuïc are good, those from the heights of
**Tibidabo** (550m) – which forms the northwestern boundary of the city – are
legendary. On one of those mythical clear days, you can see across to Montserrat
and the Pyrenees, and out to sea even as far as Mallorca. The very name is based
on this view, taken from the Temptations of Christ in the wilderness, when
Satan led him to a high place and offered him everything that could be seen:
*Haec omnia tibi dabo si cadens adoraberis me* ("All these things will I give thee, if
thou wilt fall down and worship me").

The views aside, what many people make the trip for is the rather wonderful
**Parc d'Atraccions** (days and hours vary, check website, but basically June–Sept
& hols Wed–Sun; rest of the year weekends only; closed Jan & Feb; open from
noon until 7–11pm depending on season; ☎932 117 942, ⓦwww.tibidabo.es;
Skywalk ticket €11, full admission €24, plus family/discount tickets), Barcelona's
funfair, that's been thrilling the citizens for over a century. The self-styled
"magic mountain" is a mix of traditional rides and a few more high-tech attractions, laid out around several levels of the mountaintop, connected by landscaped
paths and gardens. Some of the more famous attractions are grouped under the
"Skywalk Promenade" ticket, including the aeroplane ride, a Barcelona institution that's been spinning since 1928, the carousel and the Museu d'Autòmates,
a collection of coin-operated antique fairground machines in working order.
There are amazing views from everywhere, and they are even more extensive if
you climb the shining steps of the neighbouring **Templo Expiatorio de**
**España** to the dramatic, wide balcony. Inside the church, also known as the
Sagrat Cor (Sacred Heart), a lift (*ascensor*; daily 10am–2pm & 3–7pm; €2) takes
you higher still, to just under the feet of Christ, from where the city, surrounding
hills and sea shimmer in the distance.

## Practicalities

Getting there can be a convoluted matter but it is also half the fun, since you'll
need to combine several forms of transport. It takes up to an hour, all told, from
the city centre.

.., take the FGC train (Tibidabo line 7) from Plaça de Catalunya station , **Avinguda del Tibidabo** (the last stop). Emerging from the station escalators, cross the road to the tram/bus shelter at the bottom of the tree-lined avenue; the Bus Turistic stops here, too. An antique tram service, the **Tramvia Blau** (mid-June to mid-Sept daily 10am–8pm, rest of year weekends & hols, plus Christmas and Easter weeks 10am–6pm, departures every 15–30min; €2.60 one way, €3.90 return) then runs you up the hill to Plaça Doctor Andreu; there's a bus service instead out of season during the week. By the tram and bus stop on Plaça Doctor Andreu there are several café-bars and restaurants, where you change to the **Funicular del Tibidabo**, with connections every 15min to Tibidabo at the top (operates when the Parc d'Attracions is open, €3 return, reimbursed with park admission ticket). Alternatively, the special **Tibibus** runs direct to Tibidabo from Plaça de

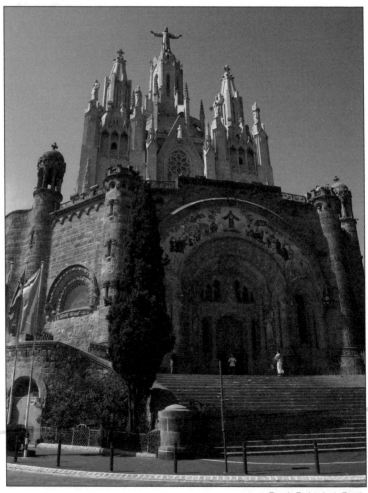

▲ Templo Expiatorio de España

Catalunya, outside El Corte Inglés (from 10.30am, every day that the parl
open; €2.50, reimbursed with park admission ticket).

**Drinks and meals** inside the park are pricey. Immediately outside the upp .
funicular station and park there's another restaurant, which is packed with
families on Sundays. It's not that great, though it does have outdoor terrace seats.
The best choice for a sandwich or simple meal is the *Marisa*, an inexpensive
bar-restaurant on the road to Vallvidrera just below the Tibidabo car park. It's a
three-minute walk from the upper funicular station and has a little concrete
patio to the side with sweeping views.

# Torre de Collserola and Vallvidrera

Follow the road from the Tibidabo car park and it's only a few minutes' walk to
Norman Foster's **Torre de Collserola** (Wed–Sun 11am–2.30pm & 3.30–7pm;
July–Sept until 8pm; €5; ☎934 069 354, ⓦwww.torredecollserola.com), a
soaring communications tower high above the tree line, with a glass lift that
whisks you up ten floors (115m) for yet more stunning views – 70km, they
claim, on a good day.

Afterwards, you could just head back to Tibidabo for the funicular-and-tram
ride back to the city, but to complete a circular tour it's more interesting to
follow the cobbled path near the tower's car park, which brings you out on the
pine-clad edges of **Vallvidrera**, a wealthy suburban village perched on the flank
of the Collserola hills – a twenty-minute walk all told from Tibidabo. There's
another **funicular** station here (6am–midnight every 6–10min), connecting to
Peu del Funicular, an FGC station on the Sabadell and Terrassa line from Plaça
de Catalunya.

Vallvidrera's main square isn't obvious – if you turn left out of the funicular
station and walk down the steep steps, Plaça de Vallvidrera is the traffic roundabout
at the bottom. There are a couple of local **bar-restaurants** on its fringes, the most
striking being *Can Josean* (closed Tues) with a simple bar at the front and a dining
room at the rear, with views out over the city from the back tables.

# Parc de Collserola

The **Parc de Collserola**, encompassing Tibidabo (its highest peak), is one of
Barcelona's best-kept secrets. While many make the ascent to the amusement
park and church, few realize that beyond stretches an area of peaks and wooded
valleys roughly 17km by 18km, threaded by rivers, roads and paths. You can, in
fact, walk into the park from Tibidabo and the Torre de Collserola, but it's better
to start from the park's information centre, across to the east, above Vallvidrera,
where hiking-trail leaflets and other information are available.

The **Centre d'Informació** (daily 10am–3pm; ☎932 803 552, ⓦwww
.parccollserola.net) lies in oak and pinewoods, an easy, signposted ten-minute
stepped walk up through the trees from the FGC Baixada de Vallvidrera station
(Sabadell and Terrassa line from Pl. de Catalunya; 15min). There's an exhibition
here on the park's history, flora and fauna, while the staff hand out English-
language leaflets detailing the various walks you can make from the centre,
ranging from a fifteen-minute stroll to the Vallvidrera dam to a couple of hours

circling the hills. A bar-restaurant (with an outdoor terrace) provides snacks and meals, and sells bottles of water for hikers and cyclists.

If you're here at the weekend, before you head off you might as well have a quick look inside the **Museu-Casa Verdaguer** (Sat, Sun & hols 10am–2pm; free; ℡932 047 805), housed in the Villa Joana, which sits just below the information centre. Jacint Verdaguer i Santaló (1845–1902), the Catalan Renaissance poet and priest, lived here briefly before his death, and the house has been preserved as an example of well-to-do nineteenth-century Catalan life. Extracts from his poetry enliven the climb up from the FGC station to the information centre and house.

Well-marked **paths** radiate from the information centre into the hills and valleys. Some – like the oak-forest walk – soon gain height for marvellous views over the tree canopy, while others descend through the valley bottoms to springs and shaded picnic areas. The walk touted as the most diverse is that to the **Font de la Buderalla**, a landscaped spring deep in the woods, beneath the Torre de Collserola. It's about an hour if you circle back to the information centre from here, but a good idea is to follow the signs for the Torre de Collserola and Vallvidrera once you reach the *font* (a further 20min). That way, you can return to Barcelona instead via the funicular from the village of Vallvidrera, or even take in the views from the Collserola tower or Tibidabo before going back.

# Out of the city

lthough there are plenty of traditional coastal bolt holes close to
Barcelona, like Castelldefels to the south or the small towns of the
Costa Maresme to the north, unquestionably the best local seaside
destination is **Sitges**, half an hour to the south along the Costa
Daurada. It's a charming resort with an international reputation, extremely
popular with gay visitors and chic city-dwellers. Otherwise, the one essential
excursion is to **Montserrat**, the extraordinary mountain and monastery 40km
northwest of Barcelona, reached by a precipitous cable-car or mountain
railway ride. However short your trip to the city, this is worth making time for,
as it's a place of great significance for Catalans, not to mention being a terrific
place for a hike in the hills.

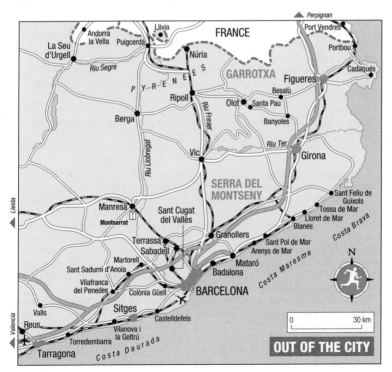

149

## Regional festivals

**February–March**
**Carnival** Sitges has Catalunya's best Carnival celebrations.

**March–April**
International jazz festival in Reus sees acts playing in clubs and old-town squares.

**May**
11 Cremada del Dimoni at Badalona: demon-burning, dancing and fireworks.

**Third week** Fires i Festes de la Santa Creu in Figueres – processions and music. Also Trapezi, the international circus fair in Reus, with street performances and spectacle.

**Corpus Christi** (moveable feast, sometimes falls in early June): Festa de Corpus Christi in Sitges – big processions and streets decorated with flowers.

**June**
24 Dia de Sant Joan celebrated everywhere; watch out for things shutting down for a day on either side.

**Last week** Annual festival at Canet de Mar and Sant Cugat del Vallès. Also Festa Major de Sant Pere in Reus, the town's biggest annual bash.

**July**
**Second week** Annual festival at Arenys de Mar.

**August**
15 Annual festival at Castelldefels.
19 Festa de Sant Magi in Tarragona.

**Last week** Festa Major in Sitges, to honour the town's patron saint, Sant Bartolomeu.

**29 & 30** Festa Major in Vilafranca del Penedès, dedicated to Sant Felix, with human towers, dancing and processions – continues into the first two days of September.

**September**
**Second Sunday** Fira Gran in Sant Sadurní d'Anoia, the town's big annual festival.
23 Festa de Sant Tecla in Tarragona, with processions of *gegants* and human castles.

**October**
**Second week** The Setmana del Cava – a sort of *cava* festival – is held in Sant Sadurní d'Anoia.

If you enjoy Barcelona's varied church architecture, there's more to come, starting with Gaudí's inspired work at the **Colònia Güell**, a late nineteenth-century idealistic community established by the architect's patron Eusebi Güell. This is a half-day's outing, while a second half-day can be spent visiting the Benedictine monastery at **Sant Cugat del Vallès** and the complex of early medieval churches at **Terrassa**, all of them largely unsung and utterly fascinating. Another route out of the city, due west, leads through the wine-producing towns of **Sant Sadurní d'Anoia** and **Vilafranca del Penedès**, both of which can be seen in a day's excursion with enough time for a wine-tasting tour.

It's also straightforward to see something of Barcelona's neighbouring cities, all very different from the Catalan capital. To the south of Barcelona, beyond Sitges, lies **Tarragona**, with a compact old town and an amazing series of Roman remains. Nearby **Reus** was the birthplace of Gaudí and features an interpretative museum that's the last word on the man and his work. To the north, inland from the coast, sits medieval **Girona**, perhaps the most beautiful of all Catalan cities, with its river, fortified walls and golden buildings. These three destinations are an hour or so from Barcelona, and it's only the extreme northern town of **Figueres** that requires any lengthier a journey – entirely justified for anyone interested in seeing Catalunya's most indescribable museum, the renowned **Museu Dalí**.

Full **public transport** details are given below for each destination. Local and regional trains provide the most reliable service, and you can check current timetables with RENFE (☎902 240 202, ⓦwww.renfe.es) or FGC (☎932 051 515, ⓦwww.fgc.es). There are buses to most regional destinations, too, from the Barcelona Nord bus station, though these usually take longer than the train. It really isn't worth renting a car unless you want to see a lot of what's described above in a short time. Each account also includes some **café and restaurant** recommendations, while if you feel like spending the night away from Barcelona it's best to contact the local tourist offices, whose details are provided. A visit to Barcelona's **Centre d'Informació de Catalunya** at Palau Robert, Pg. de Gràcia 107 (☎932 388, 091, ⓦwww.gencat.cat/palaurobert) might also be in order, to pick up maps, information and advice before you go.

# Sitges

The seaside town of **SITGES**, 36km south of Barcelona, is definitely the highlight of the Costa Daurada – the great weekend escape for young Barcelonans, who have created a resort very much in their own image. It's also a noted gay holiday destination, with a nightlife to match and between June and September it seems like there's one nonstop party going on – which, in a way, there is. During the heat of the day, though, the tempo drops as everyone hits the beach, while out of season Sitges is delightful: far less crowded, and with a temperate climate that encourages promenade strolls and old-town exploration.

▲ Sitges beach

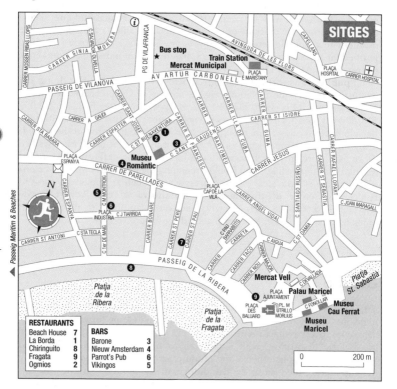

SITGES

Bus stop
Train Station
Mercat Municipal
Museu Romàntic
Mercat Vell
Palau Maricel
Museu Cau Ferrat
Museu Maricel

Platja de la Ribera
Platja de la Fragata
Platja St. Sabastià

| RESTAURANTS | | BARS | |
|---|---|---|---|
| Beach House | 7 | Barone | 3 |
| La Borda | 1 | Nieuw Amsterdam | 4 |
| Chiringuito | 8 | Parrot's Pub | 6 |
| Fragata | 9 | Vikingos | 5 |
| Ogmios | 2 | | |

0          200 m

Note that Monday isn't the best day to come, as the three museums and many restaurants are closed.

## The Town

There are clean sand **beaches** either side of the old-town headland – though these become extremely crowded in high season. For more space it's best to keep walking west along the promenade, passing a series of eight interlinked beaches that runs a couple of kilometres down the coast as far as the *Hotel Terramar*. There are breakwaters, beach bars, restaurants, showers and watersports facilities along the way, with the more notorious gay nudist beaches found at the far end – for these, keep on past *L'Antlantida* disco to the *Sun Beach Garden* (10min) and the small coves beyond.

Scores of handsome restored **mansions** in town were built in the nineteenth century by successful local merchants (known as "Americanos") who returned from Cuba and Puerto Rico. A walk along the seafront promenade reveals the best of them, adorned with wrought-iron balconies, stained-glass windows and ceramic decoration. The knoll overlooking the town beaches and marina is topped by the landmark Baroque **parish church** dedicated to Sant Bartolomeu, whose annual festival is celebrated in town in the last week of August. Behind, in the narrow streets of the old town, you'll find a series of late-medieval white-washed mansions as well as the brick **Mercat Vell** (Old Market), the latter now

an exhibition hall. One house on c/Fonollar contains the **Museu**
(June–SeptTues–Sat 9.30am–2pm & 4–7pm, Sun 10am–3pm; Oct–N
9.30am–2pm & 3.30–6.30pm, Sun 10am–3pm; €3.50, combined t
museums €6.40; ℡938 940 364), the former house and workshop of t
writer **Santiago Rusiñol i Prats** (1861–1931), who moved here in
flourished as an important *modernista* centre under his patronage
organized five *modernista* festivals between 1892 and 1899 – and the house
contains a mixture of his own works and those by contemporaries, as well as
various collected odds and ends, like the decorative ironwork Rusiñol brought
back in bulk from the Pyrenees. Nearby, the **Museu Maricel** (same hours, price
and contact details as Cau Ferrat) contains minor artworks, ranging from medieval
to modern, and maintains an impressive collection of Catalan ceramics and
sculpture. In July and August (usually two evenings a week) the main part of the
mansion itself is open for guided tours, a short concert and drinks – ask at the
tourist office for the current schedule.

The **Museu Romàntic** in the centre of town at c/Sant Gaudenci 1, off
c/Sant Josep (same hours and price as Cau Ferrat; ℡938 942 969), occupies the
stately rooms of Can Llopis, a bourgeois home completed in 1793. Admission
is by guided tour only (every hour, English sometimes spoken) and demonstrates the lifestyle of a rich Sitges family in the eighteenth and nineteenth
centuries by displaying a wealth of period furniture and possessions, from divans
to dolls.

# Practicalities

**Trains** to Sitges leave Passeig de Gràcia or Barcelona Sants stations every
twenty minutes, more frequently at peak times (destination Vilanova or
St Vicenç) and it's a thirty- to forty-minute ride depending on the service.
There's also a direct **bus from Barcelona Airport** (Mon–Fri hourly 7.40am–
11.40pm, Sat & Sun every 2–3hr with Mon-Bus, ℡938 937 060, ⓦwww
.monbus.cat), which takes around thirty minutes. Although the Sitges nightlife
might be legendary, the trains do you no favours, with the last departure back
to Barcelona at around 10.30pm (though they do start again at around 5am).
However, there is an hourly **nightbus** from Passeig deVilafranca by the tourist
office (currently between midnight and 3am) which drops passengers on Ronda
Universitat in Barcelona 50 minutes later. A taxi will cost at least €50.

The main **Oficina de Turisme** at c/Sinia Morera 1 (mid-June to mid-Sept
daily 9am–8pm; mid-Sept to mid-June Mon–Fri 9am–2pm & 4–6.30pm; ℡938
109 340, ⓦwww.sitgestour.com, ⓦwww.bestsitges.cat) is behind the Oasis
shopping centre, up Passeig deVilafranca, five minutes' walk from the station.

---

## Carnival time

Carnival in Sitges (*Carnestoltes* in Catalan; Feb/March) is outrageous, thanks largely
to the strong gay presence. It opens on the so-called Fat Thursday with the arrival of
the Carnival King, following which there's a full programme of parades, masked balls,
concerts, beach parties and sausage sizzles. The traditional *xatónada* gala dinners
are named for the carnival dish, *xató*, a kind of salt-cod salad, which originates in
Sitges. There's a children's procession on Sunday, while Carnival climaxes in Sunday
night's Debauchery Parade and the even bigger Tuesday-night Extermination Parade,
in which exquisitely dressed drag queens swan about the streets in high heels,
twirling lacy parasols and coyly fanning themselves. Bar doors stand wide open,
bands play, and processions and celebrations go on until dawn.

r picnic supplies visit the **Mercat Municipal** (Mon–Thurs 8am–2pm, Fri & Sat 8am–2pm & 5.30–8.30pm), close to the train station on Avinguda Artur Carbonell. Every **restaurant** along the front does a paella with a promenade view, while typical of the new wave of classier seafood places is *Fragata*, Pg. de la Ribera 1 (☎938 941 086, ⓦwww.restaurantefragata.com), where catch-of-the-day choices like monkfish casserole, shellfish and rice, tuna tartare or grilled local prawns cost €17–25. Alternatively, the *Chiringuito*, Pg. de la Ribera (☎938 947 596), claims to be Spain's oldest beach bar, offering grilled sardines, fried calamari, sandwiches and snacks at budget prices. At *Beach House*, c/Sant Pau 34 (☎938 949 029, ⓦwww.beachhousesitges.com, closed Dec to Easter), there's a *table d'hôte* menu €25) that changes every day and offers four courses of the best in Asian-Med fusion food. Modern French cuisine gets an airing at stylish *Ogmios*, c/Sant Buenaventura 17 (☎938 947 135; dinner only, though open Sat & Sun lunch, also closed Tues) – things like salmon and anchovy salad, and sea bass with almonds, from €25 – while just down the road at c/Sant Buenaventura 5, *La Borda* (☎938 112 002, closed Thurs in winter) is a cheery old-style Catalan restaurant with good-value, all-inclusive menus between €15 and €20.

The epicentre of local **nightlife** is c/Primer de Maig and c/Montroig, where café-*terrassas* like *Vikingos* and the staunchly gay *Parrot's Pub* (ⓦwww .parrots-sitges.com) are local fixtures. *Parrot's* also now has a stylish Mediter-ranean restaurant next door (dinner only). For more of a pub atmosphere, there's the longstanding Dutch bar *Nieuw Amsterdam*, c/de les Parellades 70, a fixture for over 40 years, serving foreign beers and Indonesian and Dutch food specialities. And there's also the *Barone* on c/Sant Gaudenci, definitely not a style bar, but a real slice of Sitges nonetheless – a cubbyhole of a tavern that's the favoured haunt of a cross-section of locals, all smoking away furiously amid the faded black-and-white photos.

# Montserrat

The mountain of **Montserrat**, with its weirdly shaped crags of rock, vast monastery and hermitage caves, stands just 40km northwest of Barcelona, off the road to Lleida. It's the most popular day-trip from the city, reached in around ninety minutes by train and then cable car or rack railway for a thrilling ride up to the monastery. Once there, you can visit the basilica and monastery buildings, and complete your day with a walk around the woods and crags, using the two funicular railways that depart from the monastery complex.

Legends hang easily upon Montserrat. Fifty years after the birth of Christ, St Peter is said to have deposited an image of the Virgin (known as La Moreneta, the Black Virgin), carved by St Luke, in one of the mountain caves. The icon was lost in the early eighth century after being hidden during the Moorish invasion, but reappeared in 880, accompanied by the customary visions and celestial music. A chapel was built to house it, and in 976 this was superseded by a Benedictine **monastery**, set at an altitude of nearly 1000m. Miracles abounded and the Virgin of Montserrat soon became the chief cult-image of Catalunya and a pilgrimage centre second in Spain only to Santiago de Compostela in Galicia – the main **pilgrimages** to Montserrat take place on April 27 and September 8.

For centuries, the monastery enjoyed outrageous prosperity, having its own flag and a form of extraterritorial independence along the lines of the Vatican

City, and its fortunes declined only in the nineteenth century. In 1811 Napoleon's troops devastated the buildings, stole many of the treasures and "hunted the hermits like chamois along the cliffs". In 1835 the monastery was suppressed for supporting the wrong side in the civil war known as the First Carlist War. Monks were allowed to return nine years later, but by 1882 their numbers had fallen to nineteen. However, over the twentieth century Montserrat's popularity again became established. In addition to the tourists, tens of thousands of newly married couples come here to seek La Moreneta's blessing, while Montserrat has also become something of an important nationalist symbol for Catalans.

## The monastery

The monastery itself is of no particular architectural interest, save perhaps in its monstrous bulk. Its various buildings – including hotel, post office, souvenir shop and even supermarket – fan out around an open square, and there are extraordinary mountain views from the terrace as well as from various other vantage points scattered around the complex.

Of the religious buildings, only the **Basilica** (daily 7.30am–8pm; free), dating largely from 1560 to 1592, is open to the public. **La Moreneta** (access 8–10.30am & noon–6.30pm), blackened by the smoke of countless candles, stands above the high altar – reached from behind, by way of an entrance to the right of the basilica's main entrance. The approach to this beautiful icon reveals the enormous wealth of the monastery, as you queue along a corridor leading through the back of the basilica's rich side-chapels. Signs at head height command "SILENCE" in various languages, but nothing quietens the line to climb the stairs behind the altar and kiss the image's hands and feet. The best time to visit the basilica is when Montserrat's world-famous **boys' choir** sings (Mon–Fri at 1pm & 6.45pm, Sun at noon & 6.45pm, *not* Sat and *not* during school holidays at Christmas/New Year and from late June to mid-Aug). The boys belong to Montserrat's Escolania, a choral school established in the fourteenth century and unchanged in musical style since its foundation.

Near the entrance to the basilica, the **Museu de Montserrat** (Mon–Fri 10am–5.45pm, Sat & Sun 9am–7pm; €6.50) presents a few archeological finds brought back by travelling monks together with painting and sculpture dating from as early as the thirteenth century, including works by Caravaggio, El Greco, Tiepolo, Picasso, Dalí, Monet and Degas. Religious items are in short supply, as most of the monastery's valuables were carried off by Napoleon's troops. There's also the **Espai Audiovisual** (Mon–Fri 10am–5.45pm, Sat & Sun 9am–7pm; €2), near the information office, which tells you something of the life of a Benedictine community.

## Walks on the mountain

After you've poked around the monastery grounds, it's the walks around the woods and mountainside of Montserrat that are the real attraction. Following the tracks to various caves and the thirteen different hermitages, you can contemplate what Goethe wrote in 1816: "Nowhere but in his own Montserrat will a man find happiness and peace." The going is pretty good on all the tracks – most have been graded and some concreted – and the signposting is clear, but take a bottle of water and keep away from the edges. A map with walking notes is available from the Montserrat tourist office.

Two separate funiculars run from points close to the cable-car station, with departures every twenty minutes (daily 10am–6pm; weekends only Oct to

**getation** of the lower slopes of Montserrat is essentially Mediterranean forest re fires have occasionally swept through, the burned patches have since been onized by Spanish gorse, rosemary and a profusion of grape hyacinths, early le orchids and martagon lilies. Higher up, although apparently barren of vegetation, Montserrat's rounded turrets support a wide variety of fissure plants, not least of which is the lime-encrusting saxifrage *Saxifraga callosa* ssp. *catalaunica* – known to grow only at Montserrat and on the hills near Marseille. Plants more typical of the high Pyrenees also make their home here, including botanical gems such as ramonda and the handsome Pyrenean bellflower.

**Birds** of Montserrat include Bonelli's warblers, nightingales, serins and firecrests in the woodlands, while the burned areas provide refuge for Sardinian warblers and good hunting for Bonelli's eagles. Sant Jeroni, the highest point of Montserrat, is an excellent place to watch for peregrines, crag martins and black redstarts all year round, with the addition of alpine swifts in the summer and alpine accentors in the winter. On sunny days Iberian wall lizards emerge from the crevices to bask on rock faces.

March). One drops to the path for **Santa Cova** (€2.70 return), a seventeenth-century chapel built where the icon is said originally to have been found. It's an easy walk there and back, which takes less than an hour. The other funicular rises steeply to the hermitage of **Sant Joan** (€6.60 return, joint ticket for both funiculars €7.50), from where it's a tougher forty-five-minute walk to the **Sant Jeroni** hermitage, and another fifteen minutes to the Sant Jeroni summit at 1236m. Several other walks are also possible from the Sant Joan funicular; perhaps the nicest is the simple (but steep) forty-five-minute circuit around the ridge that leads back down to the monastery.

## Practicalities

To reach the Montserrat cable-car and rack-railway stations, take the **FGC train** (line R5, direction Manresa), which leaves from Plaça d'Espanya (ⓂEspanya) daily at hourly intervals from 8.36am. Get off at Montserrat Aeri (52min) for the connecting cable car, the **Aeri de Montserrat** (☎938 350 005, Ⓦwww.aeridemontserrat.com) – you may have to queue for fifteen minutes or so, but then it's an exhilarating five-minute swoop up the sheer mountainside to a terrace just below the monastery. The alternative approach is by cog-wheel mountain railway, the **Cremallera de Montserrat** (☎902 312 020, Ⓦwww.cremallerademontserrat.cat), which departs from Monistrol de Montserrat (the next stop after Montserrat Aeri, another 4min); again, services connect with train arrivals from Barcelona, and take about twenty minutes to climb to the monastery. **Returning to Barcelona**, the R5 trains depart hourly from Monistrol de Montserrat (from 9.33am) and Montserrat Aeri (from 9.37am).

A desk and information board at Plaça d'Espanya station details all the combined fare options. Currently, a **return ticket** from Barcelona costs €15 (either for train and cable car or train and *cremallera*), and there are also two combined tickets: the **Trans Montserrat** (€21), which includes the metro, train, cable car/cremallera, unlimited use of the two funiculars and entry to the audiovisual exhibit; and the **Tot Montserrat** (€35), which includes the same plus museum entry and a self-service cafeteria lunch. Both tickets are also available at the Plaça de Catalunya tourist office in Barcelona.

**Drivers** should take the A2 motorway as far as the Martorell exit, and then follow the N11 and C55 to the Montserrat turn-off – or they can park at either the cable-car or the rack-railway station and take the rides up instead. All-in cable-car/*cremallera*/Montserrat attraction combo tickets are available at the station for drivers who park-and-ride.

There's a **visitor centre** at Montserrat, just up from the *cremallera* station (daily 9am–5.45pm, July–Sept until 7pm; ☎938 777 701, ⓦwww.montserratvisita .com), where you can pick up maps of the complex and mountain. They can also advise you about the accommodation options, from camping to staying at the three-star *Abat Cisneros* hotel.

There are plenty of places to eat, but all are relatively pricey and none particularly inspiring. They are also very busy at peak times. The most expensive **restaurant** is inside the *Hotel Abat Cisneros*, opposite the basilica, which is reasonably good but overpriced (meals €30–40). Cheaper, and boasting the best views, is the *Restaurant de Montserrat* (meals €25) in the cliff-edge building near the car park, though here and in the **self-service restaurant**, one floor up and with the same good views, there's no à la carte choice – that is, you have to order a full meal – and the food can at best be described as adequate. The self-service restaurant is where you eat with the all-inclusive Tot Montserrat ticket. Or try the self-service cafeteria near the upper cable-car station, the bar in the square further up, which also has a patisserie and a supermarket. There's a lot to be said for taking your own picnic and striking off up the mountainside.

# Sant Cugat and Terrassa

A series of remarkable churches lies on the commuter line out of the city to the northwest, the first in the dormitory town of **Sant Cugat del Vallès** – just twenty-five minutes from Barcelona – and the second (actually a group of three) another fifteen minutes beyond in the industrial city of **Terrassa**. You can easily see all the churches in a morning, but throw in lunch and this just about stretches to a day-trip, and it's not a bad ride in any case – after Sarrià, the train emerges from the city tunnels and chugs down the wooded valley into Sant Cugat. FGC trains run on the S1 line from Plaça de Catalunya, also stopping in Gràcia, with departures every ten to fifteen minutes.

## Sant Cugat del Vallès

At **SANT CUGAT DEL VALLÈS**, the Benedictine **Reial Monestir** (Royal Monastery) was founded as far back as the ninth century, though most of the surviving buildings date from three or four hundred years later. Its fawn stone facade and triple-decker bell tower make a lovely sight as you approach from the square outside, through the gate, past the renovated Bishop's Palace and under a splendid rose window. Finest of all, though, is the beautiful twelfth-century Romanesque **cloister**, with noteworthy capital carvings of mythical beasts and biblical scenes. They have an unusual homogeneity, since they were all done by a single sculptor, Arnau Gatell. The main church is free to visit (Mon–Sat 9am–noon & 6–8pm, Sun open for Mass from 9am), but entrance to the cloister is to the side of the church, as part of the **Museu de Sant Cugat** (Tues–Sat 10am–1.30pm & 3–7pm, June–Sept until 8pm, Sun and hols all year 10am–2.30pm; €3), which also includes the restored dormitory, kitchen and refectory of the monastery, along with exhibitions about its history and monastic life. What were once the monastery's kitchen gardens lie across from the Bishop's Palace, though the formerly lush plots that sustained the brothers are now mere dusty gardens, albeit with views over the low walls to Tibidabo and the Collserola hills.

To reach the monastery, walk straight ahead out of the train station and down the pedestrianized c/Valldoreix, taking the first right and then the first left (it's still c/Valldoreix), and then keep straight along the shopping street (c/Santa Maria and then c/Santiago Rusiñol) until you see the monastery bell tower (10min). You'll pass plenty of places to eat on your way, while Plaça Octavia, outside the monastery, has a weekly **market** every Thursday.

## Terrassa

**TERRASSA**, a large city with a population of 150,000, about 20km out of Barcelona, hides its treasures in the older part of town, a twenty-minute walk from the station (get off at Terrassa-Rambla, the last stop). Here, three pre-Romanesque churches, dating from the fifth to the tenth centuries, form an unusual complex built on the site of the former Roman town of Egara. It's known as the **Conjunt Monumental de les Esglésies de Sant Pere** (Tues–Sat 10am–1.30pm & 4–7pm, Sun 11am–2pm; free; ☎937 833 702) – not that you'll see any signs – and excavations and improvement works are still ongoing. But the church doors are usually open for visits and someone should be around to give you an explanatory leaflet.

The largest church, **Sant Pere**, is the least interesting, with just a badly faded Gothic mural and a tenth-century mosaic fragment on view within its walls. **Santa Maria** is far better endowed, starting with a mosaic pavement outside that dates from the fifth century. The same date is given to the sunken baptismal font inside, while much later Gothic (fourteenth- and fifteenth-century) murals and altarpieces – one by Catalan master Jaume Huguet – are also on display. But it's the intervening building, the fifth-century baptistry of **Sant Miquel**, that's the most fascinating here. A tiny, square building of rough masonry, steeped in gloom, it has eight assorted columns supporting the dome, each with carved Roman or Visigothic capitals. Underneath sits the partially reconstructed baptismal bath, while steps lead down into a simple crypt.

To get there, turn right out of the station (Rambla d'Egara exit) and immediately right again into Plaça de Clavé, following c/Major up to Plaça Vella, where there are some outdoor **cafés**. The route then crosses the square, turns up c/Gavatxons and follows c/Sant Pere, c/Nou de Sant Pere and c/de la Creu Gran, finally crossing a viaduct to arrive at the entrance to the church complex.

Terrassa is also known for its *modernista*-style **industrial buildings** – the town was an important textile producer in the nineteenth century, and the Catalan Museum of Science and Technology (Rambla d'Egara 270, ⊛www.mnactec .cat) is housed in one of its grandest factories. Barcelona's Ruta del Modernisme package provides an "industrial and *modernista* route" through town, while the local tourist office organizes guided tours (Raval de Montserrat 14, ☎937 397 019, ⊛www.terrassa.org/turisme).

# Colònia Güell

Before work at the Parc Güell got under way, Antoni Gaudí had already been charged with the design of parts of Eusebi Güell's earliest attempts to establish a Utopian industrial estate, or *colònia* (colony), on the western outskirts of

Barcelona. The **Colònia Güell** was very much of its time – more than seventy similar colonies were established along Catalan rivers in the late nineteenth century, using water power to drive the textile mills The concept was a familiar one in Britain, where enlightened Victorian entrepreneurs had long created idealistic towns (Saltaire, Bournville) to house their workers.

The Colònia Güell at Santa Coloma de Cervelló was begun in 1890 and, by 1920, incorporated over one hundred houses, a school, theatre and cultural association, plus the chapel and crypt for which Gaudí was responsible. The buildings were predominantly of brick and iron, sporting typical *modernista* Gothic and Moorish-style flourishes. The Güell company was taken over in 1945 and the whole complex closed as a going concern in 1973, though the buildings have since been restored – and, indeed, many are still lived in today.

There's an exhibition (with English notes) at the visitor centre, but by far the best way of appreciating the site is simply to stroll the streets, past the rows of terraced houses, whose front gardens are tended lovingly by the current inhabitants. Brick towers, ceramic panels and stained glass elevate many of the houses above the ordinary – like the private Ca l'Espinal (1900) by Gaudí's contemporary, Joan Rubió i Bellver. It is, though, Gaudí's **church** (May–Oct Mon–Sat 10am–2pm & 3–7pm, Sun 10am–3pm; Nov–April daily 10am–3pm), built into the pine-clad hillside above the colony, which alone deserves to be called a masterpiece. The crypt was designed to carry the weight of the chapel above, its palm-tree-like columns supporting a brick vault, and the whole lot resembling a labyrinth of caves fashioned from a variety of different stone and brick. The more extraordinary features of Gaudí's flights of fancy presage his later work on the Sagrada Família – like the original scalloped pews, the conch shells used as water stoups, the vivid stained glass, and the window that opens up like the wings of a butterfly. Despite appearances, the church was never actually finished – Gaudí stopped work on it in 1914 – and continuing restoration work aims to complete the outer walls, though Gaudí's planned forty-metre-high central dome is unlikely ever to be realized.

## Practicalities

Take the **FGC train** S8 (direction Martorell; roughly every 15min) from Plaça d'Espanya to the small Colònia Güell station; the ride takes twenty minutes. From here, follow the painted blue footprints across the highway and into the *colònia* to the visitor centre (10min), the **Centre d'Acollida de Visitants** (May–Oct Mon–Fri 10am–2pm & 3–7pm, Sat, Sun & holidays 10am–3pm; Nov–April daily 10am–3pm; ☎936 305 807, ⓦwww.elbaixllo bregat.net/coloniaguell). You can walk around the *colònia* and see the church from the outside for free, though to visit the church interior you'll have to buy a ticket (€4) at the visitor centre – the church is open during the hours detailed above, but closed for visits during Mass on Sundays (11am & 1pm). There are **guided tours** available daily throughout the year, of either the church and estate (€8; 2hr) or the church on its own (€5; 1hr), but you'll need to call the visitor centre in advance about the possibility since the service is only for groups.

It's a working village, so you'll find a bank and pharmacy, as well as two or three cafés and restaurants.

# The wine region: L'Alt Penedès

Trains (Mon–Fri every 30min, Sat & Sun every 60min) from Plaça de Catalunya or Barcelona Sants run west from Barcelona into **L'Alt Penedès** (ⓦwww .altpenedes.net), a region roughly halfway between the city and Tarragona, devoted to wine production. It's the largest Catalan producer of still and sparkling wines, which becomes increasingly clear the further the train heads into the region, with vines as far as the eye can see on both sides of the track. There are two main towns to visit, both of which can easily be seen in a single day: **Sant Sadurní d'Anoia**, the closer to Barcelona (40min), is the self-styled Capital del Cava, home to around fifty producers of sparkling wine; **Vilafranca del Penedès**, ten minutes down the line, is the region's administrative capital and produces mostly still wine, red and white.

If you're serious about **visiting vineyards** it's a trip better done by car, as many of the more interesting boutique producers lie out in the countryside. Either of the towns' tourist offices can provide a good map pinpointing all the local vineyards as well as the rural farmhouse restaurants that are a feature of this region. Local tour operators also have various organized trips out into the wine region, like **Spanish Trails Adventures** (ⓣ935 001 616, ⓦwww.spanish-trails .com), who run full-day, small-group escorted Penedès wine tours (from €85, transport and lunch included), including a cycling-wine tour option that lets you bike the quiet country lanes while visiting two or three wineries.

## Sant Sadurní d'Anoia

**SANT SADURNÍ D'ANOIA**, built on land watered by the Riu Noya, has been an important centre of wine production since the eighteenth century. When, at the end of the nineteenth century, French vineyards suffered heavily from philoxera, Sant Sadurní prospered, though later it too succumbed to the

▲ Freixenet cava factory, Sant Sadurní d'Anoia

Cava is a naturally sparkling wine made using the *méthode champenoise,* the traditional method for making Champagne. The basic **grape** varieties of L'Alt Penedès are
*macabeu, xarel.lo* and *parellada,* which are fermented to produce a wine base and
then mixed with sugar and yeast before being bottled: a process known as **tiratge**.
The bottles are then sealed hermetically – the **tapat** – and laid flat in cellars – the
**criança** – for up to nine months, to ferment for a second time. The wine is later
decanted to get rid of the sediment before being corked.

The *cava* is then **classified** according to the amount of sugar used in the fermentation: either *Brut* (less than 20g a litre) or *Sec* (20–30g); *Semisec* (30–50g) or *Dolç*
(more than 50g). This is the first thing to take note of before buying or drinking: *Brut*
and *Sec* are to most people's tastes and are excellent with almost any food, or as an
aperitif; *Semisec* and *Dolç* are better used as dessert wines.

same wasting disease – something remembered still in the annual September
festival by the parade of a representation of the feared philoxera parasite. The
production of *cava*, for which the town is now famous, began only in the 1870s
– an industry that went hand in hand with the Catalan cork business, established
in the forests of the hinterland. Today, a hundred million bottles a year of *cava* –
the Catalan *méthode champenoise* – are turned out by dozens of companies, many
of which are only too happy to escort you around their premises, show you the
fermentation process, and let you taste a glass or two.

The town itself is of little interest, but it hardly matters, since most people
never get any further than the most prominent and most famous company,
**Freixenet** (☎938 917 000, ⓦwww.freixenet.es) – producer of those distinctive
black bottles – whose building is right outside the train station. They offer daily
90-minute **tours** and tastings (Mon–Thurs 10am–1pm & 3–4.30pm, Fri–Sun
10am–1pm; €5) for which it's best to call and reserve a place. Many other
companies have similar arrangements, including the out-of-town **Codorníu**
(Mon–Fri 9am–5pm, Sat, Sun & hols 9am–1pm; ☎938 913 342, ⓦwww
.codorniu.com) – the region's earliest *cava* producer – which has a fine building
by *modernista* architect Josep Puig i Cadafalch as an added attraction. There are
four dozen other *caves* or cellars in and around town, all shown on a map
available at the Sant Sadurní **tourist office**, at c/Hospital 26 (Tues–Fri 10am–
2pm & 4.30–6.30pm, Sat, Sun & hols 10am–2pm; ☎938 913 188, ⓦwww
.santsadurni.cat), and also on their website. The office is in the centre of town,
a fifteen-minute walk from the train station, and you can rent bikes here too if
you fancied cycling to some of the out-of-town producers.

## Vilafranca del Penedès

As a town, **VILAFRANCA DEL PENEDÈS** is rather more interesting than
Sant Sadurní. Founded in the eleventh century in an attempt to attract settlers
to land retaken from the expelled Moors, it became a prosperous market
centre. This character is still in evidence today, with a compact old town at
whose heart lie narrow streets and arcaded squares adorned with restored
medieval mansions.

From the train station, walk up to the main Rambla de Nostra Senyora and cut
to the right up c/de Sant Joan to the enclosed Plaça de Sant Joan, which has a small
daily produce **market**. A rather larger affair takes place every Saturday, when the
stalls also stock clothes, household goods, handicrafts and agricultural gear. There's
a **tourist office** at the back of the square, at c/Cort 14 (Mon 4–7pm, Tues–Fri

9am–1pm & 4–7pm, Sat 10am–1pm; ☎938 181 254, Ⓦwww.turismevilafranca .com). Behind here, in Plaça Jaume I, opposite the much-restored Gothic church of Santa Maria, the **Museu de Vilafranca** (Tues–Sat 10am–2pm & 4–7pm, Sun 10am–2pm; €3) is housed in a twelfth-century palace and worth visiting largely for its section on the region's wine industry. The experience culminates with a visit to the museum's tavern for a tasting.

The vineyards of Vilafranca are all out of town, though the largest and best known, **Torres** (Mon–Fri 9am–5pm, Sat 9am–6pm, Sun & hols 9am–1pm; tours €5; ☎938 177 487, Ⓦwww.torres.es), is only a three-kilometre taxi ride to the northwest, on the Sant Martí de Sarroca road. Also owned by Torres is boutique winemaker **Jean Leon** (Mon–Sat 9.30am–5.30pm, Sun & hols 9.30am–1pm; tours €6; ☎938 995 512, Ⓦwww.jeanleon.com) at Torrelavit, closer to Sant Sadurní, whose American-modernist-inspired visitor centre is set in particularly bucolic surroundings.

The most agreeable place in town to **wine-taste** is *Inzolia*, c/de la Palma 21 (Mon 5–10pm, Tues–Sat 10am–2pm & 5–10pm; ☎938 181 938, Ⓦwww .inzolia.com), just off c/de Sant Joan, where a range of *cavas* and wines are sold by the glass, and there's a good wine shop attached. There are plenty of **restaurants** – the tourist office has a list – with the moderately priced *L'Hereu*, c/Casal 1 (☎938 902 217) particularly recommended, serving generous portions of country-style food with local wines. The restaurant is across the *rambla* from c/de Sant Joan, through the passageway.

The **Festa Major** (Ⓦwww.festamajor.info), at the end of August and the first couple of days in September, brings the place to a standstill: dances and parades clog the streets, while the festival is most widely known for its display of *castellers* – teams of people competing to build human towers.

# Tarragona

Majestically sited on a rocky hill, 100km southwest of Barcelona and sited sheer above the sea, **TARRAGONA** is an ancient place: settled originally by Iberians and then Carthaginians, it was later used as the base for the Roman conquest of the peninsula, which began in 218 BC with Scipio's march south against Hannibal. The fortified city became an imperial resort and, under Augustus, "Tarraco" was the most elegant and cultured city of Roman Spain, boasting at its peak a quarter of a million inhabitants. The modern city provides a fine setting for some splendid Roman remains, and there's an attractive medieval part, too, while the rocky coastline below conceals a couple of reasonable beaches. It's worth noting that almost all Tarragona's sights and museums are **closed on Mondays**, though the old town and the exterior of some of the Roman remains can still be seen should you decide to visit then.

## The City

The heart of the upper town is the sweeping **Rambla Nova**, lined with cafés and restaurants, while the parallel **Rambla Vella** marks the start of the old town. To either side of the *ramblas* are scattered a profusion of relics from Tarragona's Roman past, including various temples, and parts of the forum, theatre, circus and amphitheatre. The old encircling **Roman walls** still stand too, largely dating from the third and second century BC though erected on even older

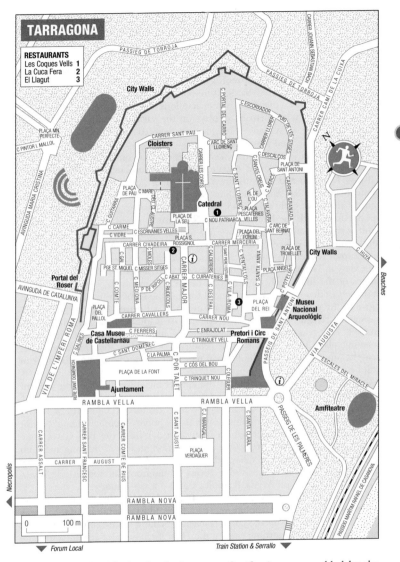

**TARRAGONA**

**RESTAURANTS**
Les Coques Vells 1
La Cuca Fera 2
El Llagut 3

City Walls

Cloisters

Catedral ❶

Portal del Roser

Casa Museu de Castellarnau

Pretori i Circ Romans

Ajuntament

Museu Nacional Arqueològic

City Walls

Beaches

Amfiteatre

Necropolis

Forum Local

Train Station & Serrallo

0  100 m

Iberian megalithic blocks; the sloping outer fortifications were added by the British in 1707 to secure the city during the War of the Spanish Succession.

At the heart of Tarragona lies the medieval old town, with the **Catedral** its focal point (Mon–Sat: June to mid-Oct 10am–7pm; mid-Oct to mid-Nov 10am–5pm; mid-Nov to mid-March 10am–2pm; mid-March to May 10am–6pm; €3.50). It's a site of great antiquity, as the Christian church was built over the site of the provincial Roman forum – and in the main facade, a soaring Gothic portal is framed by Romanesque doors, surmounted by a cross and an elaborate rose window. Except for during services, entrance to the cathedral is

163

through the lovely **cloisters** (*claustre*; signposted up a street to the left of the facade), where among several oddly sculpted capitals, one represents a cat's funeral being directed by rats.

Tarragona has several museums – dedicated to modern art, old weapons, port and harbour, and the noble Castellarnau family – but the only essential visit is to the **Museu Nacional Arqueològic** (June–Sept Tues–Sat 9.30am–8pm, Sun 10am–2pm; Oct–May Tues–Sat 9.30am–6pm, Sun 10am–2pm; €2.40), off Plaça del Rei. The huge collection is a marvellous reflection of the richness of imperial Tarraco, with thematic displays on the various remains and buildings around the city, as well as whole rooms devoted to inscriptions, mosaics, sculpture, ceramics and jewellery.

The archeological museum is likely to set you off on the trail of the local Roman sites, most grouped together under the umbrella of the Tarragona History Museum and all with the same opening hours and admission details (June–Sept Tues–Sat 9am–9pm, Sun 9am–3pm; Oct–May Tues–Sat 9am–5pm, Sun 10am–3pm; each site €2.45, joint ticket to all €9.25). These start most spectacularly with the **Pretori i Circ Romans** (entered from Plaça del Rei), built at the end of the first century AD to hold chariot races. The circus vaults and chambers have been restored to spectacular effect, while the Pretori tower was a royal residence in medieval times. A lift takes you up to the roof for the best view in Tarragona, looking down over the **Amfiteatre**, built into the green slopes of the hill nearby, to the coast below. As provincial capital, Tarragona sustained both a ceremonial provincial forum (the scant remnants of which lie close to the cathedral in Plaça del Fòrum) and a **Fòrum Local**, whose more substantial remains are on the western side of Rambla Nova, near the central market. This was the commercial centre of imperial Tarraco and the main meeting place for locals for three centuries – the evocative remains of the temple, some small shops, the Roman road and various house foundations can still be seen.

Other remains lie further out of the centre, including those of the ancient **necropolis**, where both pagan and Christian tombs have been uncovered, spanning a period from the third to the sixth century AD. The site is largely closed, with only a small exhibition open to the public. More rewarding is a visit to the **Roman Aqueduct**, which brought water from the Riu Gayo, some 32km distant. The most impressive extant section, nearly 220m long and 26m high, lies in an overgrown valley, off the main road, in the middle of nowhere: take the bus marked "Sant Salvador" (every 20min from the stop outside Avgda. Prat de la Riba 11, off Avgda. Ramon i Cajal) – a ten-minute ride.

The closest beach to town is the long **Platja del Miracle**, over the rail lines below the amphitheatre, though nicer by far is **Platja Arrabassada**, a couple of kilometres further up the coast, reached by taking Via Augusta (off the end of Rambla Vella) and turning right at the *Hotel Astari* – a pleasant thirty-minute walk with gradually unfolding views of the beach and a few beach bars when you get there.

## Practicalities

The hourly AVE (high-speed) trains from Barcelona Sants have cut journey times to Tarragona to just 35 minutes, but tickets are expensive and the **Camp de Tarragona** AVE station is ten minutes out of town, which adds on the price of a taxi ride into the centre. Otherwise, there are regular trains every thirty minutes from Passeig de Gràcia and Barcelona Sants and the journey takes just over an hour, stopping at the main **train station** in the lower town:

turn right out of the station and climb the steps ahead of you to reach the Rambla Nova, by the statue of Roger de Llúria (10min), from where the Rambla Vella and the old town are just a short walk around the balcony promenade. There are **taxis** outside the station. The **Oficina de Turisme** is at c/Major 39 in the old town (July–Sept Mon–Sat 9am–9pm, Sun 10am–3pm; Oct–June Mon–Sat 10am–2pm & 4–7pm, Sun 10am–2pm; ☎977 250 795, ⓦ www.tarragonaturisme.cat).

The pretty old-town squares, like Plaça del Rei, Plaça del Fòrum and Plaça de la Font are the best places for outdoor drinks. The latter in particular features more than a dozen **cafés**, **bars and restaurants** serving everything from tapas to pizzas. *La Cuca Fera*, Pl. Santiago Rossignol 5 (☎977 242 007; closed Tues, Wed & three weeks in Feb) serves moderately priced Catalan dishes with tables below the cathedral in one of Tarragona's loveliest backdrops. *El Llagut*, c/Natzaret 10 (☎977 228 938), on Plaça del Rei, is good for seafood and rice dishes. Pricier is *Les Coques Vells*, c/Nou Patriarca (☎977 228 300; closed Sun & July), at around €40 a head for fine dining. Otherwise, a good place for lunch is down in **Serrallo**, Tarragona's so-called fishermen's quarter, a fifteen-minute walk west along the industrial harbourfront from the train station. You'll get a tasty paella down here – try along c/Sant Pere, one block back from the harbour, at places like *Cal Marti* at no. 12 (☎977 212 384; closed Sun dinner) and *Cal Brut* at no. 14 (☎977 241 405; closed Wed, and Sun dinner).

# Reus

Fourteen kilometres northwest of Tarragona, and 100km southwest of Barcelona, the small city of **REUS** was the birthplace of architect Antoni Gaudí, who was born here in 1852. There was little in his early life in Reus to indicate what was to come. He was born to a humble family of boilermakers and coppersmiths, and left for Barcelona when he was 16 years old. Consequently, there are no Gaudí buildings in Reus itself, but there is a fascinating interpretative centre dedicated to the city's most famous son that's essential viewing for anyone interested in his life and work. You can easily see the centre and the rest of the sights in Reus in a day out from Barcelona – actually, it's a charming small city of 100,000, full of pretty squares, good restaurants and handsome pedestrianized shopping streets.

## The City

The **Gaudí Centre**, in the central Plaça del Mercadal (Mon–Sat 10am–2pm & 4–8pm, mid-June to mid-Sept 10am–8pm, Sun all year 10am–2pm; €6; ⓦ www .gaudicentre.com), is a gleaming box of a building, converted from a former bank, that throws much light on the inspiration behind Gaudí's work. It's not really a museum as such, though there are exhibits including his former school reports, his only surviving manuscript notebook and a reproduction of the architect's study-workshop at the Sagrada Família. Instead, the centre cleverly investigates the architectural techniques pioneered by Gaudí, with hands-on demonstration models and audiovisual aids that show how he created wave roofs and spiral towers, for example. If you ever wondered why none of Gaudí's door frames are straight, or what trees, ferns and snails have to do with architecture, the centre is undoubtedly the place to find out.

The Gaudí Centre itself forms part of the city's **Ruta del Modernisme**, a marked trail around the many buildings and mansions erected in the *modernista* style at the end of the nineteenth century and beginning of the twentieth. This was a period when Reus was Catalunya's second city (after Barcelona), with a merchant class made wealthy by the trade in wine and olive oil and, later, textiles, fabrics and ceramics. Gaudí may never have built here, but his contemporary, Lluís Domènech i Montaner did. His **Casa Navàs** (1901), across Plaça Mercadal from the Centre, is considered Reus' finest townhouse – still privately owned, it's usually open two or three times a week (including every Saturday) for tours of the virtually intact period interior. The same architect's **Institute Pere Mata** (1898), a *modernista* sanatorium on the edge of the city centre, is also often open for visits – it was one of the Domènech i Montaner's biggest projects and prefigures his equally dramatic Barcelona Hospital de la Santa Creu i de Sant Pau. You might as well also divert the few minutes from the commercial centre to see **Gaudí's birthplace** (c/Sant Vicenç 4): the house is not original, but a plaque marks the site while, just down the street, outside a school, is a rather touching sculpture of the young Gaudí playing marbles.

Almost everything else to see lies within a clearly defined circuit of boulevards. The main church is that of the city's patron saint, **Sant Pere**, a couple of minutes' walk from the Gaudí Centre. This is where Gaudí was baptized (there's a plaque by the baptismal chapel, to the left of the main entrance) and the church also boasts the heart of Reus' Number Two Son, *modernista* artist Marià Fortuny i Marsal (the plaque here reads "he gave his soul to heaven, his fame to the world, and his heart to his country"). Behind the church is an arcaded square with cafés, **Plaça de les Peixateries Velles**, that was once the fish market, while **Plaça del Mercadal** itself used to be the site of the general market – the numbers you can see etched in the square's paving indicated the position of the stalls. Nowadays, the daily market takes place at the **Mercat Central** on c/Sant Joan, not far from the train station.

## Practicalities

Ryanair arrivals at **Reus airport**, 3km outside town, can catch connecting buses direct to Barcelona or down to the coast, while local bus #50 runs into town, via the train station. There are hourly trains to Reus (via Tarragona) from Passeig de Gràcia and Barcelona Sants, and the journey takes an hour and 20 minutes. It's a fifteen-minute walk from the **train station** into the centre, or there are taxis outside the station.

The **Oficina de Turisme** is inside the Gaudí Centre on Plaça del Mercadal (Mon–Sat 10am–2pm & 4–8pm, mid-June to mid-Sept 10am–8pm, Sun all year 10am–2pm; ☎977 010 670 or 902 360 200, ⓦwww.reus.cat/turisme), where you can pick up a good map of town. Ask here about **guided tours** (not always in English) that include the centre and the Ruta del Modernisme, giving access to the buildings mentioned above and others that are normally closed to the public.

**Restaurants** are plentiful; all those reviewed below are right in the centre. *Cerveseria Ferreteria*, Pl. de la Farinera 10 (☎977 340 326), is a popular place for tapas and grills – the interesting interior is a converted nineteenth-century ironmonger's and there's a pretty *terrassa* in the square outside. There's another good beer-and-tapas place round the corner, *La Cerveseria*, c/de les Vallroquetes 4 (☎658 771 841; opens 5pm), which brews its own beers. Traditional places, with market-led Catalan cuisine and good-value *menús del dia* day and night (€20–25), include *Florida*, c/Metge Fortuny 2, at Plaça del Mercadal (☎977 342 077), and

*La Glorieta del Castell*, Pl. del Castell 2 (☎977 340 826; closed Sun dinner). For fancier, contemporary cuisine – main courses €20 to €30, set menus at €30 and €50 – there's *Restaurant Joan Urgellès*, c/Aleus 7 (☎977 342 178), and the renowned *GaudíR de Diego*, on the top floor of the Gaudí Centre (☎977 127 702; closed Sun, & Mon dinner), the latter considered the best in town and especially good for fish and rice.

# Girona

The ancient walled city of **GIRONA** stands on a fortress-like hill, high above the Riu Onyar. It's been fought over in almost every century since it was the Roman fortress of Gerunda on the Via Augusta and perhaps more than any other place in Catalunya it retains the distinct flavour of its erstwhile inhabitants. Following the Moorish conquest of Spain, Girona was an Arab town for over two hundred years, a fact apparent in the maze of narrow streets in the centre, and there was also a continuous Jewish presence here for six hundred years. By the eighteenth century, Girona had been besieged on 21 occasions, and in the nineteenth century it earned itself the nickname "Immortal" by surviving five attacks, of which the longest was a seven-month assault by the French in 1809. Not surprisingly, all this attention has bequeathed the city a hotchpotch of architectural styles, yet the overall impression for the visitor is of an overwhelmingly beautiful medieval city. Its attraction is heightened by its setting, with the old and new towns divided by the river, which is crisscrossed by footbridges, with pastel-coloured houses reflected in the waters below.

## The City

Although the bulk of modern Girona lies on the west side of the Riu Onyar, most visitors spend nearly all their time in the **old city**, over the river. This thin wedge of land contains all the sights and monuments, and it takes only half an hour or so to walk from end to end. It's worth noting that most of the museums and sights are **closed on Mondays**, though the city is emphatically still worth a visit if that's the only day you can manage.

Centrepiece of the old city is the **Catedral** (Tues–Fri 10am–8pm, Nov–March 10am–7pm, Sat 10am–4.30pm, Sun 10am–2pm; €5, cloister and treasury free Sun; Ⓦwww.catedraldegirona.org), a mighty Gothic structure approached by a magnificent flight of seventeenth-century Baroque steps. Inside, there are no aisles, just one tremendous Gothic nave vault with a span of 22m, the largest in the world. This emphasis on width and height is a feature of Catalan-Gothic, with its "hall churches", of which, unsurprisingly, Girona's is the ultimate example. The displayed treasures of the cathedral include the famous eleventh-century Creation Tapestry – the best piece of Romanesque textile in existence. But it's the exquisite Romanesque **cloisters** (1180–1210) that make the strongest impression, boasting minutely carved figures and scenes on double columns.

Through the twin-towered Portal de Sobreportas, below the cathedral, are Girona's so-called **Banys Arabs** (April–Sept Mon–Sat 10am–7pm, Sun 10am–2pm; Oct–March daily 10am–2pm; €1.80; ☎972 21 3 262, Ⓦwww .banysarabs.org), probably designed by Moorish craftsmen in the thirteenth century, a couple of hundred years after the Moors' occupation of Girona had

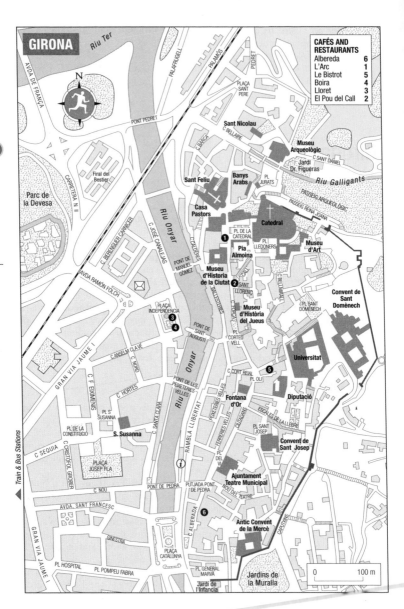

CAFÉS AND
RESTAURANTS
Albereda          6
L'Arc             1
Le Bistrot        5
Boira             4
Lloret            3
El Pou del Call   2

ended. They are the best-preserved ancient baths in Spain after those at Granada, featuring three principal rooms for different temperatures, with an underfloor heating system.

From the cathedral square, the main street, Pujada Rei Marti, leads downhill to the Riu Galligants, a small tributary of the Onyar. The **Museu Arqueològic** (June–Sept Tues–Sat 10.30am–1.30pm & 4–7pm, Sun 10am–2pm; Oct–May Tues–Sat 10am–2pm & 4–6pm, Sun 10am–2pm; €1.80; Ⓦwww.mac.es) stands on the far bank in the former church of Sant Pere de Galligants, a harmonious setting for displays of Roman statuary, sarcophagi and mosaics. The beautiful Romanesque cloisters contain heavier medieval relics, such as inscribed tablets and stones, including some bearing Jewish inscriptions. From the museum you can gain access to the **Passeig Arqueològic**, where steps and landscaped grounds lead up to the walls of the old city. There are fine views out over the rooftops and the cathedral, and endless little diversions into old watchtowers, down blind dead ends and around crumpled sections of masonry.

Quite apart from its Roman remains and Arab influences, Girona also contains one of the best-preserved Jewish quarters in western Europe, home at its height to around three hundred people who formed a sort of independent town within Girona, protected by the king in return for payment. From the eleventh century onwards, however, the Jewish community suffered systematic persecution and, until the expulsion of the Jews from Spain in 1492, the quarter was effectively a ghetto, its residents restricted to its limits and forced to wear distinguishing clothing if they did leave. For an impression of the cultural and social life of Girona's medieval Jewish community visit the **Museu d'Història dels Jueus** (May–Oct Mon–Sat 10am–8pm; Nov–April Mon–Sat 10am–6pm; Sun all year 10am–3pm; €2; ☎972 216 761), signposted (Call Jueu) up the skinniest of stepped streets off c/de la Força. Amid the complex of rooms, staircases, courtyards and adjoining buildings were the synagogue, the butcher's shop, the baths and other community buildings and services.

# Practicalities

Regular bus services run from **Girona airport**, 13km south of the city, to Girona, Barcelona or the Costa Brava. Trains run every hour from Barcelona Sants (currently at 25 past the hour), calling at Passeig de Gràcia station, and take between 1hr 15min and 1hr 30min. Girona's **train station** lies across the river in the modern part of the city – walk down to Gran Via Jaume I and then turn right down c/Nou to reach the Pont de Pedra and the base of the old town (10min). There's also a taxi rank at the station.

The **Oficina de Turisme** (Mon–Fri 8am–8pm, Sat 8am–2pm & 4–8pm, Sun 9am–2pm; ☎972 226 575, ⓦwww.ajuntament.gi/turisme) is at Rambla de la Llibertat 1, on the river, near the Pont de Pedra. They can give you a useful map and have bus and train timetables for all onward and return services.

Girona's chic bars and restaurants are grouped on c/de la Força in the centre of the old city, as well as on and around Rambla de la Llibertat and on the parallel Plaça del Vi – the last two places being where you'll also find the best daytime **cafés** with outdoor seating. *L'Arc*, Pl. de la Catedral 9 (☎972 203 087), is a friendly bar serving snacks and sandwiches at the foot of the cathedral steps. Favoured old-town **restaurants** include *El Pou del Call*, c/de la Força 14 (☎972 223 774; closed Sun dinner), in the Jewish quarter, and the cheaper *Le Bistrot*, Pujada de Sant Domènec (☎972 218 803), which often has tables outside on the steps below the church. Considerably more expensive is the *Albereda*, c/Albereda 7 (☎972 226 002, ⓦwww.restaurantalbereda.com closed all Sun, Mon dinner & Aug), for very fine Catalan dining. There's another dozen or so restaurants, serving sushi to seafood, just over the river in pretty **Plaça Independència**. *Boira*, Pl. de la Independencia 17 (☎972 219 605), has arcade tables and upmarket Catalan food, while you won't score a cheaper *menú del dia* than at *Lloret*, Pl. de la Independencia 14 (☎972 213 671) – the food's reasonable enough, and the upstairs dining room has river and cathedral views. ▾

# Figueres and the Dalí museum

**FIGUERES**, a provincial town in the north of Catalunya with a population of some thirty thousand, would pass almost unnoticed were it not for the Museu Dalí, installed by Salvador Dalí in a building as surreal as the exhibits within. It's a popular day-trip from Barcelona, though you should make a reasonably early start since even the fastest trains take an hour and forty minutes to reach the town.

The museum is very much the main event in town (it's signposted from just about everywhere), though a circuit of the impressive walls of the seventeenth-century Castell de Sant Fernand, 1km northwest of the centre, the last bastion of the Republicans in the Civil War, helps fill in any spare time. The town is also only half an hour by bus from the coast at Roses, or an hour from prettier Cadaqués. In the centre, pavement cafés line the tree-shaded *rambla* and you can browse around the art galleries, clothes stores and gift shops in the pedestrianized streets and squares. There are a couple of other museums, too. The Museu de l'Empordà has some local Roman finds and work by local artists, while the Museu del Joguet is a toy museum with over three thousand exhibits from all over Catalunya, but really these are small beer when compared to the Dalí extravaganza.

## Museu Dalí

The **Museu Dalí** (July–Sept daily 9am–7.15pm; Aug daily 9am–7.15pm & 10pm–12.30am; Oct–June Tues–Sun 9.30am–5.15pm; €11, night visits €12; ☏972 677 500; ⓦwww.salvador-dali.org) appeals to everyone's innate love of fantasy, absurdity and participation. The museum is not a collection of Dalí's greatest hits – those are scattered far and wide. Nonetheless, what you do get beggars description and is not to be missed.

The building (a former theatre on Plaça Gala i Salvador Dalí) is an exhibit in itself, topped by a huge metallic dome and decorated with a line of luminous

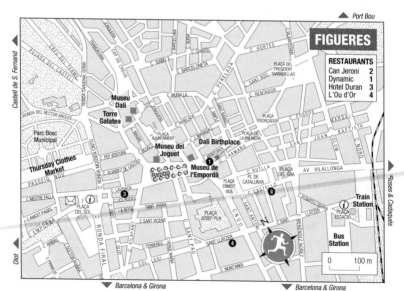

## Surreal Salvador

**Salvador Dalí i Domènech** (1904–89) was born in Figueres – you can see the exterior of the house he was born in at c/Monturiol 6 (there's a plaque) and that of the next house in which the Dalí family lived (at no. 10). He gave his first exhibition in the town when he was just fourteen and, after a stint at the Royal Academy of Art in Madrid (he was expelled), he made his way to Paris, where he established himself at the forefront of the Surrealist movement. A celebrity artist in the US in the 1940s and 1950s, he returned eventually to Europe where, among other projects, he set about reconstructing Figueres' old municipal theatre, where he had held his first boyhood exhibition. This opened as the Museu Dalí in 1974, which Dalí then fashioned into an inspired repository for some of his most bizarre works. A frail man by 1980, controversy surrounds the artist's final years, particularly after he suffered severe burns in a fire in 1984, following which he moved into the Torre Galatea, the tower adjacent to the museum. Spanish government officials and friends fear that, in his senile condition, he was being manipulated. In particular, it's alleged that he was made to sign blank canvases – and this has inevitably led to the questioning of the authenticity of some of his later works. Dalí died in Figueres on January 23, 1989. His body now lies behind a simple granite slab inside the museum.

egg shapes. Outlandish sculptures and statues adorn the square and facade and it gets even crazier inside, where the walls of the circular courtyard are ringed by stylized mannequins preparing to dive from the heights – below sits the famous *Rainy Cadillac*, where you can water the snail-encrusted occupants of a steamy Cadillac by feeding it with coins. In the Mae West Room an unnerving portrait of the actress is revealed by peering through a mirror at giant nostrils, red lips and hanging tresses, while elsewhere there's a complete life-sized orchestra, some of Dalí's extraordinary furniture (like the fish-tail bed), and ranks of Surrealist paintings – including one room dominated by the ceiling fresco of the huge feet of Dalí and Gala (his Russian wife and muse). The museum also contains many of Dalí's collected works by other artists, from Catalan contemporaries to El Greco, and there are temporary exhibitions, too, while your ticket also allows admission to see the **Dalí-Joies** – a collection of extraordinary jewels, designed in the Forties for an American millionaire and displayed here with Dalí's original drawings.

## Practicalities

**Trains** depart hourly from Barcelona Sants and Passeig de Gràcia and take up to two hours to reach Figueres, depending on the service. Currently, the 7.45am, 9.25am or 10.25am from Sants (each taking 1hr 40min) are the best day-trip options. Alternatively, Figueres is just thirty to forty minutes by train from Girona, if you feel like combining the two towns. Arriving at the train station, you reach the centre of town simply by following the "Museu Dalí" signs (10min). The main **Turisme** is at the top of town on Plaça del Sol (July–Sept Mon–Sat 9am–8pm, Sun 9am–3pm; Aug–June Mon–Fri 10am–2pm, Sat 10am–2pm & 3–6pm, Sun 10am–2pm; ☎972 503 155, ⓦwww.figueresciutat.com), in front of the post office building.

A gaggle of tourist **restaurants** is crowded into the narrow streets around the Dalí museum, and there are more cafés and restaurants overlooking the *rambla*. To eat with the locals seek out *Can Jeroni*, c/Castelló 36 (☎972 500 983; closed Sun), a tiled tavern with country-style dishes and grills, or the *L'Ou d'Or*, c/Sant Llatzer 16 (☎972 503 765, ⓦwww.loudor.com; closed Sun), where an uncomplicated *menú del dia* is served day and night – in either you'll be able to eat for around €20. There's creative tapas in a contemporary setting at *Dynamic*, c/Monturiol 2 (☎972 500 003; closed Sun), while the *Hotel Duran*, at c/Lausaca 5 (☎972 501 250, ⓦwww.hotelduran.com) is the top choice in town, known for its excellent regional cuisine; it's expensive though there is a reasonable lunchtime *menú del dia*. On Tuesday, Thursday and Saturday, you'll coincide with the **fruit and veg market** in Plaça de Catalunya – if you have a choice, Thursday is best since there's also a huge **clothes market** on Passeig Nou.

# Listings

# Listings

# Accommodation

Finding a hotel vacancy in Barcelona can be very difficult, especially at Easter, in summer and during festivals or trade fairs. You're advised to book in advance – several weeks at peak times – especially if you want to stay at a particular place.

Places to stay go under various names – *pension, residencia, hostal, hotel* – though these are an anachronism and only **hotels and pensions** are recognized as official categories. These are all star-rated (hotels, one- to five-star; pensions, one- or two-star), but the rating is not necessarily a guide to cost or ambience. Some of the smaller, boutique-style pensions and hotels have services and facilities that belie their star rating; some four- and five-star hotels have disappointingly small rooms and an impersonal feel. Meanwhile, the number of private **"bed-and-breakfast"** establishments (advertised as such) is on the increase, and while some are simply the traditional room in someone's house, others are very stylish and pricey home-from-homes.

**Room rates** vary wildly. The absolute cheapest double/twin rooms in a simple family-run pension, sharing a shower and toilet, cost around €50 (singles from €30), though it's more realistic to budget on a minimum of €70 a night. If you want heating, air conditioning, soundproofing, a TV and a lift to your room, there's a fair amount of choice around the €100 mark, while up to €200 gets you the run of decent hotels in most city areas. For Barcelona's most fashionable and exclusive hotels, room rates are set at European capital norms – from €250 to €400 a night. Right at the other end of the scale is the burgeoning number of city **youth hostels**, where a dorm bed goes for between €20 and €30, depending on the season. A youth hostel, incidentally, is an *albergue*; *hostal* is the word for a pension.

The **room rates** given at the end of the reviews reflect the official quoted cost of a double/twin room in high season (basically Easter to the end of October, plus major trade fairs, festivals and other events) – there's also a seven-percent tax, **IVA**, that is added to all accommodation bills. Some places offer **discounts** in January, February and November, or for longer stays, while larger hotels have special rates in August (when business travel is scarce) or at weekends. Many hotels also have special Internet rates, while if you don't mind arriving without a booking, same-day walk-in rates can offer substantial savings.

**Breakfast** isn't usually included in the price, unless specifically stated in our reviews – and occasionally it is offered as part of a special deal. However, it's usually available for an extra charge and, in many hotels, breakfast can be the most lavish of buffet spreads. These are not cheap though (around €10–15 per person), so if all you want is coffee and a croissant it's better to go out to a café.

**Credit cards** are accepted almost everywhere, even in very modest places (though American Express isn't always) – pensions or hotels that don't accept cards are highlighted in the reviews.

## Balconies, views and noise

Almost all hotels and pensions in Barcelona have at least some rooms with a **balcony** over the street or square. These tend to be the brightest rooms in the building and, because of the obvious inherent attraction, they sometimes cost a little more than the other rooms. However, it can't be stressed enough that rooms facing onto Barcelona's streets are often noisy. Traffic is a constant presence (including the dawn street-cleaners) and, in a city where people are just getting ready to go out at 10pm, you can be assured of a fair amount of pedestrian noise too, particularly in the old town, and especially at weekends. Soundproofed windows and double-glazing deal partly with the problem, but you tend not to have this luxury in cheaper pensions – where throwing open the windows may be the only way to get some air in the height of summer anyway. Bring earplugs if you're at all concerned about having a sleepless night.

Alternatively, ask for an **internal room** (*habitación interior*). It's true that most buildings are built around a central air or lift shaft, and your view could simply be a lime-green wall 1m away and someone's washing line. However, some places are built instead around an internal patio, so your room might overlook a pot-plant terrace or garden – and you shouldn't get any street noise.

Finally, don't be afraid to **ask to see the room** before you part with any money – even the swankiest places won't balk at showing you around. Standards vary greatly between places in the same category and it does no harm to check that you're not being stuck at the back in an airless box.

## Making a reservation

You can book accommodation at the **city tourist offices**, but only in person and on the day. However, you can book online through the tourist office website, or contact one of the other **reservation agencies** listed below.

Some agencies specialize in **apartment rentals**, available by the night, week or month. Prices for these compare well with mid-range hotels (starting at around €100 a night for a two-person studio), but make sure you're happy with the location (some are out in the more mundane suburbs) and understand all the costs – seasonal premiums, cleaning charges, utility bills and taxes can all push up the attractive quoted figure.

When booking directly at hotels and pensions, you may be asked for a **credit card** number to secure a room. At most hotels, the price won't be charged against your card until your stay, though some smaller pensions may take a deposit or charge you in advance.

### Reservation agencies

**Barcelona Apartment Rentals** UK ☎0117/907 5060, ⊛www.barcelonaapartmentrentals.co.uk. A small range of quality apartments, mainly in the Eixample (some near the Sagrada Família) and Gràcia. Friendly, English-speaking service and advice from a born-and-bred *barcelonina*; airport pick-ups available.
**Barcelona On-Line** Barcelona ☎902 887 017 or 933 437 993, ⊛www.barcelona-on-line.es.

Commission-free reservations for hotels, pensions and apartments in Barcelona and the surrounding area. Call or use the online database.
**Inside-BCN** Barcelona ☎932 682 868 or 699 840 808, ⊛www.inside-bcn.com. Small selection of stylishly renovated apartments (sleeping two to six) available in the Born or on Plaça Reial.
**My Favourite Things** Barcelona ☎637 265 405, ⊛www.myft.net. Barcelona-based agency

with an eye for unusual and offbeat accommodation, from boutique hotels to private bed and breakfasts in the city, or rural homestays and country retreats.

**Tourist Flats BCN Barcelona** ☎650 925 252, ⓦ www.flatsbcn.com. Old-town apartments sleeping two to ten, especially on and around the Ramblas.

**Turisme de Barcelona Offices in Barcelona at Pl. de Catalunya; Pl. de Sant Jaume; Barcelona** Sants; Barcelona Airport ☎932 853 832, ⓦwww .hotelsbcn.com. Same-day, commission-free accommodation bookings, in person only, or on the website. For office opening hours, see p.32.

**Visit BCN.com** UK ☎0871/990 3045, Barcelona ☎933 152 265, ⓦwww.visit-bcn.com. Wide range of private apartments for rent (by the night or longer), from lofts to *modernista* buildings.

# Hotels and pensions

First things first: if you hanker after a **Ramblas** view, you're going to pay heavily for the privilege – generally speaking, there are much better deals to be had either side of the famous boulevard, often just a minute's walk away. Alongside some classy boutique choices, most of the very cheapest city accommodation is found in the **Barri Gòtic** old town area, where there are loads of options ranging from basic pensions to three-star hotels. It's a heavily touristed district, but you should still be careful (without being paranoid) when coming and going after dark.

The other main location for budget accommodation is on the west side of the Ramblas in **El Raval**, which still has its rough edges but is changing fast as the whole neighbourhood undergoes a massive face-lift. East of the Barri Gòtic, in **Sant Pere** and **La Ribera**, there are a number of safely sited budget, mid-range and boutique options, handy for the Picasso museum and Born nightlife area. North of Plaça de Catalunya, the central spine of the Eixample is the **Passeig de Gràcia**, which has some of the city's most fashionable and luxurious hotels, often housed in converted palaces and mansions. The Eixample itself splits into Right (**Dreta**) and Left (**Esquerra**), and on either side there are some comparative bargains just a few minutes' walk from the *modernista* architectural masterpieces. Hotels near **Sants** station are convenient for Montjuïc and the metro system, and those further north in **Les Corts** for the Avinguda Diagonal shopping district. For waterfront views look at hotels in **Port Vell** at the end of the Ramblas, and at the **Port Olímpic** southeast of the old town – while new four- and five-stars abound much further out on the metro at the rather soulless **Diagonal Mar** conference and events site. If you don't mind being a metro ride from the museums and buildings, and like the idea of suburban living, then the northern district of **Gràcia** is probably the best base, as you're only ever a short walk away from excellent bars, restaurants and clubs.

## The Ramblas

For locations, see map, p.46.

🏃 **Benidorm Ramblas** 37 ☎933 022 054, ⓦwww.hostalbenidorm.com; ⓜ**Drassanes**. Refurbished pension opposite Plaça Reial that offers real value for money, hence the tribes of young tourists. Plain rooms available for one to five people, all with bathtubs or showers, and a balcony and Ramblas view if you're lucky (and prepared to pay a bit more). English spoken and left-luggage service available. From €69.

**H1898 Ramblas** 109 ☎935 529 552, ⓦwww .nnhotels.es; ⓜCatalunya. One of the grander buildings on the Ramblas, the former HQ of the Philippines Tobacco Company has been given an eye-poppingly boutique refit. There are four grades of rooms (the standard is "Classic") all decorated in deep red, green or black, and all beautifully appointed. Public areas reflect the original construction period – 1898 – but there are some stunningly updated spaces, like the neo-colonial hall and lounge (and the fanciest *Starbucks* in town), while facilities include outdoor pool and spa, gym, bar and restaurant. Some suites even have their own private pool, Jacuzzi and garden. Walk-in rates €150, otherwise from €250.

**Lloret Ramblas 125** ℡ 933 173 366, ⓦ www .hlloret.com; Ⓜ Catalunya. Gilt mirrors, old paintings and wrinkled leather sofas in the lounge speak of a faded glory for this one-star hotel, though some rooms, bathrooms and tile floors have been upgraded. But it's a fine building in a good location, and many rooms have Ramblas-facing balconies – as does the dining room where continental breakfast is available (not included). From €85.

**Mare Nostrum Ramblas 67, entrance on c/Sant Pau** ℡ 933 185 340, ⓦ www.hostalmarenostrum .com; Ⓜ Liceu. Cheery two-star *pension* whose English-speaking management offers comfortable double, triple and family rooms with satellite TV and a/c. There's nothing flashy, but rooms are reasonably modern, well kept and double-glazed against the noise. Some rooms come with balconies and street views and a simple breakfast is included. Their new one-star hotel, *Hotel Curious* (ⓦ www.hotelcurious.com), offers funkier rooms nearby, a couple of blocks up in the Raval on c/del Carme. €75, en suite €85, *Curious* €110.

**Oriente Ramblas 45** ℡ 933 022 558, ⓦ www .hotelhusaoriente.com; Ⓜ Liceu. If you're looking for somewhere traditional but not too pricey on the Ramblas, this historic three-star hotel is your best bet. Converted from a former convent, there's mid-nineteenth-century style in the grand public rooms and a mix of bedrooms, all tastefully updated, some very contemporary. A fair few have Ramblas views, though the quieter rooms face inwards. From €100.

**Rivoli Ramblas Ramblas 128** ℡ 934 817 676, ⓦ www.hotelrivoliramblas.com; Ⓜ Catalunya. The elegant, soundproofed rooms in this stylish four-star hotel near the top of the avenue are variously furnished (Art Deco to contemporary), but all come with spacious marble bathrooms. The front ones have Ramblas views, and there's also a lovely rooftop terrace and bar. From €200.

## Barri Gòtic

For locations, see map, pp.54–55.

**Alamar c/Comtessa de Sobradiel 1** ℡ 933 025 012, ⓦ www.pensioalamar.com; Ⓜ Drassanes. If you don't mind sharing a bathroom then this simply furnished pension makes a convenient base. Twelve rooms (including five singles) have basins and double-glazing; most also have little balconies. Space is tight, but there's a friendly welcome, laundry service and use of a small kitchen. No noise requested after midnight, so it suits early-birds and sightseers rather than partygoers. No credit cards. From €36, July & Aug from €45.

**Cantón c/Nou de Sant Francesc 40** ℡ 933 173 019, ⓦ www.hotelcanton-bcn.com; Ⓜ Drassanes. Refurbished one-star hotel that's only two blocks off the Ramblas and close to the harbour and Port Vell. Forty rooms feature uniform blue-and-white trim curtains and bedspreads, high wooden headboards, central heating and a/c, fridge and wardrobe. Some bathrooms are a bit smarter than others, and a few rooms have balconies (though they don't have much of a view) – all are well insulated against street noise. A buffet continental breakfast is available, served in a stone-walled dining room, and room prices drop a good bit out of season. €85.

**Colón Avgda. Catedral 7** ℡ 933 011 404, ⓦ www.hotelcolon.es; Ⓜ Jaume I. Splendidly situated four-star hotel opposite the La Seu cathedral – rooms at the front throw open their windows onto balconies with superb views, while a pavement *terrassa* takes full advantage of its position. It's an old-money kind of place, with faithful-retainer staff and huge public salons. "Superior" rooms have an Edwardian lounge area and highly floral decor, though other rooms are more contemporary. Check the website for the best rates, otherwise from €200.

**Fernando c/de Ferran 31** ℡ 933 017 993, ⓦ www.hfernando.com; Ⓜ Liceu. Rooms at these prices fill quickly around here; that they're also light, modern and well kept by friendly people is a real bonus. All come with basin, shower and TV (some singles share facilities), while dorm accommodation is available on the top floor in rooms that sleep four to eight, some with attached bathroom. All accommodation is a few euros cheaper outside July & Aug. Dorms €25, rooms €70.

**El Jardí** Pl. Sant Josep Oriol 1 ☎933 015 900, ⓦwww.hoteljardi-barcelona.com; ⓜLiceu. The hotel's location, overlooking the charming Plaça del Pi, is what sells this place – and explains the steepish prices for rooms that, though smart and modern, can be a bit bare and even poky. But the bathrooms have been nicely done and some rooms (the top ones have terraces) look directly onto the square. You can have breakfast here (not included), but the *Bar del Pi* in the square is a better bet. From €89, terrace or balcony €106.

**Levante** Bxda. Sant Miquel 2 ☎933 179 565, ⓦwww.hostallevante.com; ⓜJaume I. A budget favourite, with fifty rooms – singles, doubles, twins, triples – on two rambling floors. Some rooms are much better than others (with newer pine furniture, en-suite bathrooms and balconies). The comings and goings aren't to everyone s liking (*tranquilo* it isn't), but prices are reasonable. Six apartments with kitchen and washing machine also available nearby, sleeping five to seven people. €60, en suite €70, apartments from €30 per person per night.

🏃 **Mari-Luz** c/del Palau 4, 2 ☎933 173 463, ⓦwww.pensionmariluz.com; ⓜJaume I/Liceu. This old mansion, on a quieter-than-usual Barri Gòtic street, has a more personal touch than the huge new hostels in town. Someone's been to IKEA for furniture and there are contemporary art prints on the walls, a useful noticeboard, central heating and a/c, laundry facilities and a small kitchen. It can be a tight squeeze when full as there are five dorm rooms (sleeping 4–6 people), two of these en suite, plus six inexpensive doubles and a triple with shared bathrooms. A dozen nicely restored apartments (sleeping 2–6; ⓦwww.apartaments-unio.com) a few minutes' walk away in the Raval offer more

privacy. Dorms €15–22, rooms €37–57, apartments from €70–100.

**Metropol** c/Ample 31 ☎933 105 100, ⓦwww .hesperia-metropol.com; ⓜDrassanes. Slightly off the beaten old-town track – and consequently, prices are better value than similar three-star places on the nearby Ramblas. The lobby is a masterpiece of contemporary design, while rooms are understated but comfortable. Street noise isn't too bad either, so opening the shutters onto c/Ample doesn't blast the eardrums first thing in the morning. From €120.

🏃 **Neri** c/de Sant Sever 5 ☎933 040 655, ⓦwww.hotelneri.com; ⓜLiceu/Jaume I. A delightful eighteenth-century palace close to the cathedral houses this stunning boutique hotel of just 22 individually styled rooms and suites. Swags of flowing material, rescued timber, subdued colours, granite-toned bathrooms and lofty proportions provide a common theme. In the public areas, Catalan designers have created eye-catching effects, like a boa constrictor sofa and a tapestry that falls four floors through the central atrium. A beamed library and stylish roof terrace provide a tranquil escape, while breakfast is served bento-box style, either out in the courtyard in summer or in chef Jordi Ruiz's fine contemporary Mediterranean restaurant. From €285.

**Racó del Pi** c/del Pi 7 ☎933 426 190, ⓦwww .h10.es; ⓜLiceu. Some imagination went into the conversion of this old-town mansion, and the result is a stylish three-star hotel in a great location. Rooms – some with balconies over the street - have wood floors and granite-and-mosaic bathrooms. There's a glass of *cava* on check-in, and although breakfast is extra there's free coffee and pastries during the day in the bar. Low-season last-minute rates as low as €110, otherwise from €150.

---

## Best places for …

**Dorm delight** *Alternative Creative Youth Home* (p.187), *Centric Point* (p.187), *Mari-Luz* (p.179).

**Great value** *Australia* (p.185), *Grau* (p.180), *Rembrandt* (p.180).

**More than just B&B** *Marina View* (p.182), *Pensió 2000* (p.181), *thefiverooms* (p.184).

**Old-world lodgings** *D'Uxelles* (p.183), *Meson Castilla* (p.180), *Peninsular* (p.181).

**Style on a budget** *Gat Raval/Xino* (p.180), *Goya* (p.184), *Market* (p.180).

**Rembrandt** c/Portaferrissa 23 ☏ 933 181
011, ⒲ www.hostalrembrandt.com;
Ⓜ **Liceu**. A clean, safe, old-town budget
pension that has been smartened up over
the years by friendly English-speaking
owners, who request "pin-drop silence"
after 11pm. Simple tile-floored rooms (with
or without private bathroom, no TVs) have a
street-side balcony or little patio, while larger
rooms are more versatile and can sleep up
to four. Apartments also available nearby
(c/Canudua 13, ⒲ www.apartrembrandt
.com) offering en-suite single and double
rooms with balcony, a/c, satellite TV and
daily housekeeping. From €55, en suite €65,
apartment rooms €70–100.

## El Raval

For locations, see map, pp.66–67.

**Abba Rambla** Rambla de Raval 4 ☏ 935 055
400, ⒲ www.abbaramblahotel.com; Ⓜ **Sant
Antoni/Liceu**. Three-star style on the Raval's
up-and-coming *rambla*. Public areas,
including the bar, are pretty cool and
contemporary, rooms less so, though they
are pleasing enough with wall-mounted flat-
screen TVs and decent bathrooms. Rooms,
bar and coffee shop all face the *rambla*.
From €105.

**Cèntric** c/Casanova 13 ☏ 934 267 573 or 902 014
881, ⒲ www.hostalcentric.com; Ⓜ **Universitat**. A
good upper-budget choice, just a couple of
minutes' walk from the Raval proper. Most
rooms feature wood panelling and reasonable furniture, decent beds, and plenty of
light; cheaper ones on the upper floors (no
lift) share bathrooms, while some of the more
expensive en-suite ones also have a/c.
There's a sunny terrace at the rear. €63, en
suite from €86.

**Gat Raval** c/Joaquín Costa 44, 2 ☏ 934
816 670, ⒲ www.gataccommodation.com;
Ⓜ **Universitat**. Going for the boutique end of
the budget market, the *Gat Raval* has done
its fashionable best with a rambling
townhouse. Lime green is a recurring
theme, from doors to bedspreads, while
each room is broken down to fundamentals
– chair, basin, wall-mounted TV, fan and
heating, and signature book-lit street photograph and artwork that doubles as a
reading light. Only six of the twenty-four
rooms are en suite, but communal facilities
are good, and there are internal or street
and MACBA views, Internet access, drinks

machine and staff on duty 24/7. €75, en
suite €85.

**Gat Xino** c/Hospital 149–155 ☏ 933 248
833, ⒲ www.gataccommodation.com;
Ⓜ **Sant Antoni**. The sister hotel to the *Gat
Raval* shares the same signature style, facilities and colour scheme, but all 35 rooms
here are en suite, while four suites have
much more space, bigger bathrooms and
less street noise (and one has a terrace).
You also get a coffee, cereal and toast
breakfast served in a patio area; there's
24hr staff and security. €100, suite €118,
terrace suite €139.

**Grau** c/Ramelleres 27 ☏ 933 018 135,
⒲ www.hostalgrau.com; Ⓜ **Catalunya**. A
really friendly pension, with attractive,
colour-coordinated rooms on several floors
(no lift); renovated superior rooms also have
balconies, a/c, new bathrooms and a touch
of modern Catalan style. There's a little
rustic-chic lounge area, wireless Internet
access, and breakfast available weekdays in
the adjacent café-bar (included in room
rates in Jan & Feb). Six small private apartments in the same building (sleeping 2 to 5,
available by the night) offer a bit more
independence, and prices out of season for
all rooms drop by quite a bit. €70, en suite
from €90, apartments from €95.

**Market** c/Comte Borrell 68, at Ptge. Sant
Antoni Abat ☏ 933 251 205, ⒲ www
.markethotel.com.es; Ⓜ **Sant Antoni**. Just a
stone's throw from Sant Antoni market and
the Raval, the designer-budget *Market* hotel
makes a definite splash with its part-
Japanese, part neo-colonial look. Very
fetching jet-black rooms feature hardwood
floors, wooden screen-cladding and
shutters, bathrooms with a faux-bamboo
towel radiator and boxy wardrobes topped
with travel trunks. It's a feel that flows
through the building and down into the
impressive restaurant, which is a really
dramatic space in which to dine – and the
food here is exceptionally good value too.
Breakfast included in the rate. From €100.

**Meson Castilla** c/Valldonzella 5 ☏ 933 182 182,
⒲ www.mesoncastilla.com; Ⓜ **Universitat**. A
throwback to 1960s rural Spain, with every
inch carved, painted and stencilled, from the
grandfather clock in reception to the
wardrobe in your room. Large rooms with
a/c (some with terraces), filled with country-
style furniture, a vast rustic dining room
(buffet breakfast included) and – best of

all – a lovely tiled rear patio on which to read in the sun. Parking available. €140, terrace room €155.

**Peninsular** c/de Sant Pau 34 ☎933 023 138, ⓦwww.hotelpeninsular.net; Ⓜ Liceu. This interesting old building originally belonged to a priestly order, which explains the slightly cell-like quality of the rooms. However, there's nothing spartan about the attractive galleried inner courtyard (around which the rooms are ranged), hung with dozens of tumbling houseplants, while breakfast is served in the arcaded dining room. €78.

**Ramos** c/de l'Hospital 36 ☎933 020 723, ⓦwww.hostalramos.com; Ⓜ Liceu. The best rooms here in this family-run pension overlook either the quiet marble internal patio or the attractive Pl. de Sant Agustí. Partitioning has spoiled the proportions of some (those facing the square are the largest), but all have either half- or full-size bathtubs, polished tile floors and TV. It's something of a haven and very popular; some English is spoken. €72.

**Sant Agustí** Pl. Sant Agustí 3 ☎933 181 658, ⓦwww.hotelsa.com; Ⓜ Liceu. Barcelona's oldest hotel occupies a former seventeenth-century convent building, with balconies overlooking a restored square and namesake church. It's of three-star standard, with appealing rooms that have been modernized and air-conditioned – the best are located right in the attic (supplement charged), from where there are rooftop views. Breakfast included. From €160.

**La Terrassa** c/Junta del Comerç 11 ☎933 025 174, ⓦwww.laterrassa-barcelona.com; Ⓜ Liceu. A popular Raval budget choice where 45 rooms on various floors (there's a lift) have built-in closets, modern shower rooms, effective double-glazing, ceiling fans and heaters. They are fairly plain, and "basic-interior" rooms don't have much natural light, but "basic-" and "standard-exterior" rooms either face the street or the sunny courtyard (open to all guests), and some are more spacious than others. Interior rooms €53–58, basic and standard exterior €60–74, large exterior €78.

## Sant Pere

For locations, see map, p.74.

**Ciutat** c/de la Princesa 35 ☎932 697 475, ⓦwww.ciutatbarcelona.com; Ⓜ Jaume 1. Contemporary three-star hotel that's well sited

for old-town sightseeing. Colour-coordinated rooms are stylish and soundproofed against street noise, if a bit tight on space. There's a cute deck and small pool for lounging about, and a handsome restaurant attached. From €125.

**Grand Hotel Central** Via Laietana 30 ☎932 957 900 ⓦwww.grandhotelcentral.com; Ⓜ Jaume I. It might be on one of the city's noisiest thoroughfares, but the soundproofing does its job handsomely in this wham-glam designer hotel. Spacious, ever-so-lovely rooms hit all the right buttons – hardwood floors, massage-showers, flat-screen TVs, MP3 players – and up on the roof there are amazing views from the sundeck and infinity pool. Meanwhile, the chic hotel restaurant, *Actual*, showcases the new-wave Catalan cooking of chef Ramón Freixa. From €200.

**Pensió 2000** c/Sant Pere Més Alt 6, 1 ☎933 107 466, ⓦwww.pensio2000.com; Ⓜ Urquinaona. As close to a family-run bed and breakfast as Barcelona gets – seven huge rooms (some overlook the Palau de la Música Catalana, across the street) in a welcoming mansion apartment strewn with books, plants and pictures. A third person could easily share most rooms (€23 supplement), while a choice of breakfasts (not included) is served either in your room or on the internal patio. Laundry service available. €62, en suite €80.

## La Ribera

For locations, see map, p.78.

**Banys Orientals** c/de l'Argenteria 37 ☎932 688 460, ⓦwww.hotelbanysorientals.com; Ⓜ Jaume I. Funky boutique hotel with 43 minimalist rooms and some more spacious duplex suites nearby. Hardwood floors, crisp white sheets, sharp marble bathrooms and urban-chic decor – not to mention bargain prices for this sort of style – make it a hugely popular choice. The attached restaurant, *Senyor Parellada*, is a great find too. €100, suites €130.

**Chic & Basic** c/de la Princesa 50 ☎932 954 652, ⓦwww.chicandbasic.com; Ⓜ Jaume I. From the babbling blurb above reception ("it's fresh, it's cool, it's fusion") to the open-plan, all-in-white rooms, everything is punchily boutique and in-your-face. But it works really well, as 31 decent-sized rooms mix glamour and comfort with laugh-aloud conceits like adjustable mood-lighting, sashaying plastic curtains and mirrored walls. Chic, certainly – basic, not at all, though the concept eschews room service, mini-bars and tons of staff at your beck and call, so it won't suit everyone. Bikes and Internet are available, and there's a tiny fitness room, while meals are courtesy of the attached – also effortlessly cool – *thewhitebar* restaurant. There's a more budget *Chic & Basic* on c/Tallers (near Pl. Universitat, El Raval) and Barri Gòtic apartments too (details on the website). From €110, larger rooms from €135.

🏃 **Nuevo Colón** **Avgda. Marquès de l'Argentera 19, 1** ☏ **933 195 077,** Ⓦ **www.hostalnuevocolon.com;** Ⓜ **Barceloneta.** In the hands of the same friendly family for over seventy years, the well-kept pension sports twenty-six spacious rooms painted yellow and kitted out with directors' chairs and double glazing. Front rooms are very sunny, as is the lounge and terrace, all with side views to Ciutadella park. There are also three self-catering apartments available (by the night) in the same building, which sleep up to six. €47, en suite €67, apartments €155.

**Park** **Avgda. Marquès de l'Argentera 11** ☏ **933 196 000,** Ⓦ **www.parkhotelbarcelona.com;** Ⓜ **Barceloneta.** A classy update for this elegant, modernist 1950s building starts with the chic bar and lounge, and runs up the feature period stairway to rooms in fawn and brown with parquet floors, marble bathrooms and beds with angular reading lights. It's pricey for a three-star, but there's real style here. From €150.

## Port Vell

For locations, see the map, p.91.

🏃 **Duquesa de Cardona** **Pg. de Colom 12** ☏ **932 689 090,** Ⓦ **www.hduquesade cardona.com;** Ⓜ **Drassanes.** Step of the busy harbourfront highway into this soothing four-star haven, remodelled from a sixteenth-century mansion. The rooms are calm and quiet, decorated in earth tones and immaculately appointed. Not all the "classic" (ie standard) rooms have views, but everyone has access to the stylish roof-deck overlooking the harbour. It's great for sundowner drinks and boasts (if that's the word) probably the city's smallest outdoor pool. From €180.

**Grand Marina** **World Trade Centre, Moll de Barcelona** ☏ **936 039 000,** Ⓦ **www.grand marinahotel.com;** Ⓜ **Drassanes.** Five-star comforts on eight floors overlooking the port. Most of the rooms have enormous marble bathrooms with Jacuzzi baths and a separate dressing area. Public areas draw gasps, with commissioned works by Catalan artists and a rooftop pool with fantastic views. Advance website bookings offer good deals. From €200.

**Marina View B&B** **Pg. de Colom** ☏ **609 206 493,** Ⓦ **www.marinaviewbcn.com;** Ⓜ **Drassanes.** A classy, personally run place in a great location – the two front rooms have terrific harbour views. There's far more of a hotel feel here than a simple B&B, with the five rooms featuring stylish linen, bold colours, excellent bathrooms, mini-bars (with normal drinks prices), hospitality trays, satellite TV and wi-fi access – then again, these aren't exactly run-of-the-mill B&B prices. Breakfast is included (served in the room). Advance reservations are essential (contact for directions), and a two-night minimum stay is usually required. From €120, harbour views €135.

## Port Olímpic

For location, see map, p.93.

**Arts Barcelona** **c/Marina 19–21, Port Olímpic** ☏ **932 211 000,** Ⓦ **www.ritzcarlton.com/hotels /barcelona;** Ⓜ **Ciutadella-Vila Olímpica.** The city benchmark for five-star designer luxury. Service and standards are first-rate, and the classy rooms feature enormous marble bathrooms and floor-to-ceiling windows with fabulous views of the port and sea. Stunning duplex apartments have their own perks (24hr butler service, personal Mini Cooper) and dining options range from the open-air terrace restaurant to Michelin-starred chef Sergi Arola's contemporary tapas place, *Arola* (closed Mon & Tues). You're only a hop from the beach, but seafront gardens encompass a swimming pool and hot tub, while the jaw-dropping Six Senses spa occupies the top two floors. Special rates start at around €200, otherwise from €300.

## Montjuïc

For location, see map, p.96.

**AC Miramar** **Plaza Carlos Ibañez 3** ☏ **932 811 600,** Ⓦ **www.hotelacmiramar.com;** Ⓜ **Paral.lel,**

## Best hotels for …

**Boutique beauty** *Banys Orientals* (p.181), *Chic & Basic* (p.181), *Neri* (p.179).

**Money no object** *Arts Barcelona* (p.182), *Claris* (p.183), *Omm* (p.184).

**Rooftop pools** *Duquesa de Cardona* (p.182), *Grand Marina* (p.182), *Majestic* (p.184).

**Rooms with a view** *Condes de Barcelona* (p.183), *AC Miramar* (p.182), *Torre Catalunya* (p.185).

**Staying put** *Gran Hotel La Florida* (p.186), *H1898* (p.177), *Princesa Sofia* (p.186).

**and Funicular de Montjuïc.** Quite the grandest location in the city for a hotel, with views to knock your socks off. The remodelled *Miramar* – first built for the 1929 International Exhibition – has 75 super-stylish rooms wrapped around the kernel of the original building, all with sweeping vistas. From the architecture books in the soaring lobby to the terrace-Jacuzzi that comes with each room, you're clearly in designer heaven; the wi-fi access, plasma TVs, iPod connections and stunning pool, garden and deck come as no surprise. True, you're not in the city centre, but it's only a 10min taxi ride from most downtown destinations. From €260.

### Dreta de l'Eixample

For locations, see map, p.115.

**Claris** c/Pau Claris 150 ⓣ 934 876 262, ⓦ www .derbyhotels.es; Ⓜ Passeig de Gràcia. Very select five-star-deluxe hotel, from the incense-scented marble lobby complete with authentic Roman mosaics to the hugely appealing rooms ranged around a soaring, water-washed atrium. It even has its own private antiquities museum. If there's a gripe, it's that there's not a lot of

▼ The Claris's rooftop pool

room space for your euro, but the staff couldn't be more accommodating and there's a stylish rooftop terrace pool. The bar is a cool hangout in its own right, while in the hotel restaurant, *East 47*, you eat creative Mediterranean cuisine under the gaze of a line of Warhol self-portraits. From €275.

**Condes de Barcelona** Pg. de Gràcia 73–75 ⓣ 934 450 000, ⓦ www.condesdebarcelona .com; Ⓜ Passeig de Gràcia. Straddling two sides of c/Mallorca, the *Condes* is fashioned from two former palaces; the north side has kept its interior marblework and wrought-iron balconies, but there's little difference between the rooms in either building. All are classily turned out in contemporary style, some with Jacuzzi and balcony, and some with views of Gaudí's La Pedrera. The best deals are those on the south-side seventh-floor exterior, with fantastic private terraces but charging standard room rates. There's also a pretty roof terrace and plunge pool, while Michelin-starred Basque chef Martín Berasategui is at the helm in the acclaimed *Lasarte* restaurant. Book through the website for the best rates. From €200.

**D'Uxelles** Gran Via de les Corts Catalanes 688 ⓣ 932 652 560, ⓦ www .hotelduxelles.com; Ⓜ Girona/Tetuan. Elegant nineteenth-century townhouse rooms feature high ceilings, wrought-iron bedsteads, antique mirrors, typical tiled floors and country-decor bathrooms – some also have balconies and little private patios (it's quietest at the back of the building). Prices are very reasonable, especially in winter, and extra beds can be placed in many rooms – a few rooms are also available in another building at Gran Via 667. €100.

**Girona** c/Girona 24, 1 ⓣ 932 650 259, ⓦ www.hostalgirona.com; Ⓜ Urquinaona. Delightful and friendly family-run pension with a wide range of cosy, traditional rooms, plus corridors laid with rugs, polished wooden doors, paintings and restored furniture throughout. Some rooms share a bathroom, others have a shower or full bath, while the biggest and best rooms have a/c and balconies, though you can expect some noise. Prices vary considerably, but from €50, full en suite €75

**Goya** c/de Pau Claris 74, 1 ⊕ 933 022 565, ⓦ www.hostalgoya.com; Ⓜ **Urquinaona.** Refurbishment has raised the game at this boutique-style pension, now offering a dozen fabulous rooms in *Hostal Goya* and seven more on the floor below in *Goya Principal*, all stylishly decorated and with excellent bathrooms. There's a fair range of options, with the best rooms opening directly onto a balcony or a terrace. There are comfortable sitting areas, and free coffee and tea available on both floors. From €90, balcony/terrace rooms €105.

**Granvía** Gran Via de les Corts Catalanes 642 ⊕ 933 181 900, ⓦ www.nnhotels.com; Ⓜ **Catalunya/ Passeig de Gràcia.** An attractive townhouse, built for a nineteenth-century banking family, with swish lobby and public rooms exuding old-style comfort. You may be less lucky with your own room, as some of the accommodation is cramped, but there's a lovely roof terrace. Prices are pretty reasonable for a three-star hotel given that a/c, full bath and satellite TV come as standard. €130.

**Majestic** Pg. de Gràcia 68 ⊕ 934 881 717, ⓦ www.hotelmajestic.es; Ⓜ **Passeig de Gràcia.** Traditional grand-dame hotel, first opened in 1918, though refitted in unthreatening contemporary style to provide a tranquil city-centre base. Big-ticket original art adorns the public areas (it's known for its art collection), and the rooms – larger than many in this price range – have been pleasantly refurbished. The absolute clincher is the rooftop pool and deck, with amazing views over to the Sagrada Família. The *Drolma* restaurant is highly rated too, while the high quoted room rates can almost always be beaten, either simply by asking or by checking the website. From €300.

**Omm** c/Rosselló 265 ⊕ 934 454 000, ⓦ www .hotelomm.es; Ⓜ **Diagonal.** Barcelona's most fashionable restaurant group, Tragaluz, has entered the hotel game with the designer experience that is *Omm*. Expect minimalist, open-plan rooms in muted colours, a studiously chic bar, the Michelin-starred *Moo*

restaurant, plus terrace, pool and Spaciomm "relaxation centre", not to mention fearsomely handsome staff. It's not to everyone's taste – it's probably fair to say that the less annoyed you are by the website, the more you'll like the hotel. From €300.

**Prestige** Pg. de Gràcia 62 ⊕ 932 724 180 or 902 200 414, ⓦ www.prestigepaseodegracia.com; Ⓜ **Passeig de Gràcia.** A sharp redesign of a 1930s Eixample building has added achingly fashionable minimalist rooms, an Oriental-style internal patio garden and the Zeroom, a lounge with wireless Internet facility and style library. It's almost a parody of itself it's so cool, but the staff keep things real and pride themselves on their city know-how. "Functional" (standard) rooms are a bit less impressive (no views), so upgrade if you can. Advance deals from €170, otherwise from €250.

**San Remo** c/Ausias Marc 19, 2 ⊕ 933 021 989, ⓦ www.hostalsanremo.com; Ⓜ **Urquinaona.** As *pensions* go, the doubles aren't a bad size for the money and the small tiled bathrooms are pretty good for this price range. There's a/c and double-glazing, but even so you'll get more peace at the back – though the internal rooms aren't nearly as appealing as those with balconies. The seven rooms include one decently priced single. €56–62.

**the5Rooms** c/Pau Claris 72, 2 ⊕ 933 427 880, ⓦ www.thefiverooms.com; Ⓜ **Urquinaona.** The luxury B&B concept has suddenly taken off in Barcelona and the impeccably tasteful *5 rooms* set the standard. The owner's fashion background is evident in gorgeous contemporary-styled rooms that are spacious and light-filled, with original artwork above each bed, exposed brick walls and terrific bathrooms. Despite the high-spec surroundings, the feel is house-party rather than hotel – breakfast is served whenever you like, drinks are always available, and owner Jessica is happy to sit down and talk you through her favourite bars, restaurants and galleries. Two apartments are also available, sleeping up to 4 people. €135–165, apartments from €175 for 2 people.

## Sagrada Família and Glòries

For location, see map, pp.122–123.

**Eurostars Gaudí** c/Consell de Cent 498-500 ⊕ 932 320 288, ⓦ www.eurostarshotels .com; Ⓜ **Monumental.** An excellent-value four-star choice within walking distance of the Sagrada Familia. The hotel doesn't overdo the Gaudí theme, staff are really helpful and the comfortable rooms feature contemporary furniture, marble bathrooms, black-out curtains and flat-screen TV. Junior suites on the eighth floor boast a terrace with loungers and views of the Gaudí church and distant hills. Buffet breakfast included. From €110, suites €120–200.

## Esquerra de l'Eixample

For locations, see map, pp.128–129.

**Australia** Ronda Universitat 11, 4 ☏933 174 177, ⓦwww.residenciaustralia.com; ⓂUniversitat. A very welcoming budget pension, overseen by Thomas, fount of city knowledge, musician and cheery host. Three of the four rooms have basins and balconies, and share two nice bathrooms (hairdryers provided); the other is classed as a suite with private bathroom, a/c, TV, fridge and kettle for tea and coffee. There's wi-fi access throughout. Just down the street in another building are some more tidy suites, also with full facilities. €59, suites €85.

**Balmes** c/Mallorca 216 ☏934 511 914, ⓦwww.derbyhotels.es; ⓂPasseig de Gràcia. From the same stable as the luxury Claris, this boutique three-star has sharp-as-a-knife dining and bar facilities, classy rooms with parquet floors and leather sofas, and some larger duplexes available. A couple of ground-floor rooms have their own terrace overlooking the lush patio garden, complete with swimming pool and bar, and on your way in and out every day you can browse the African art and sculpture in the lobby. Last-minute rates as low as €100, otherwise from €160.

**Expo Barcelona** c/Mallorca 1-23 ☏936 003 020, ⓦwww.expogrupo.com; ⓂSants-Estació. Bright, spacious rooms at a good-value four-star hotel. Each has a sliding window onto a capacious terrace and the best have views across to Montjuïc. There's also a rooftop pool, a good buffet breakfast, and the metro right on your doorstep (it's just a minute from Sants station). From €90.

**Inglaterra** c/Pelai 14 ☏935 051 100, ⓦwww.hotel-inglaterra.com; ⓂUniversitat. The boutique little sister to the Majestic has an excellent location, and harmoniously toned rooms and snazzy bathrooms. Space is at a premium, but some rooms have cute private terraces, others street-side balconies (and very effective double-glazing). Best of all is the romantic roof-terrace – and guests can use the Majestic's pool. Four-nights-for-three offers available in July–Aug, otherwise from €130.

**Torre Catalunya** Avgda. de Roma 2–4 ☏936 006 999, ⓦwww.expogrupo.com; ⓂSants-Estació. The landmark four-star-deluxe hotel outside Sants station towers over the surrounding buildings, which means the large, light rooms have sweeping views from all sides. Rooms above the twelfth floor are superior in terms of views and services, but all are elegantly turned out in earth tones and feature huge beds, flat-screen TVs and very good bathrooms. Breakfast is a buzz – an extensive buffet served on the twenty-third floor, accompanied by panoramic views – with the adjacent contemporary Catalan restaurant, Visual, another reason to linger. There's a spa with indoor pool, and guests can also use the sister Expo's outdoor pool. The website has the best rates, often remarkably low for this class of hotel. From €100, superior rooms from €125.

## Gràcia

For locations, see map, p.134.

**Casa Fuster** Pg. de Gràcia 132 ☏932 553 000, ⓦwww.hotelcasafuster.com; ⓂDiagonal. Modernista architect Domènech i Montaner's magnificent Casa Fuster (1908) is the backdrop for five-star-deluxe luxury with service to match. Rooms are in earth tones, with huge beds, smart bathrooms, flat-screen TVs and remote-controlled light and heat, while public areas make full use of the architectural heritage – from the magnificent pillared lobby bar to the panoramic roof terrace and pool. There's also a contemporary restaurant, Galaxó, plus fitness centre, sauna and 24hr room service. From €250.

**Confort** Trav. de Gràcia 72 ☏932 386 828, ⓦwww.mediumhoteles.com; ⓂFGC Gràcia/Fontana. Handy for uptown shopping or Gràcia nightlife, this modern two-star has far more character than most, with chic little rooms, a dining room (buffet breakfast served) and attractive terrace. Good advance rates, otherwise €120.

**HMB** c/Bonavista 21 ☏933 682 013, ⓦwww.hostalhmb.com; ⓂDiagonal. Tucked away at the bottom of Gràcia is this chic little budget pension, with just a dozen rooms with flat-screen TVs, coordinated furnishings and decent bathrooms. It's a safe, well-run choice, and good value for money. From €70.

## Les Corts

For location, see map, pp.140–141.

**Princesa Sofia** **Pl. Pius XII 4** ☎935 081 000, ⓦwww.expogrupo.com; ⓂMaria Cristina. A classic – one of the first five-star hotels in town thirty years ago – and well placed for shoppers, with wide-ranging city views from the upper floors. It still exudes old-school charm (the concierges know everything) though the warm-toned rooms, massages and treatments in the Aqua Diagonal Wellness Centre, pool (with retractable roof) and superior club rooms and lounges offer a more contemporary experience – the Barcelona football team stays and eats here before every home match. An immense buffet breakfast is served in the *Contraste* restaurant – which also has a pretty patio for summer dining. From €140, club rooms from €210.

## Tibidabo

For location, see map, p.133.

**Gran Hotel La Florida** **Carretera Vallvidrera a Tibidabo 83–93, 7km from the centre** ☎932 593 000, ⓦwww.hotellaflorida.com. Describing itself as an "urban resort", the five-star, hillside *Gran Hotel La Florida* re-creates the glory days of the 1950s, when it was at the centre of Barcelona high society. Its terraces and pool all have amazing views, while some rooms and suites have a private garden or terrace and a Jacuzzi – sea-view rooms are charged at a premium. There's also a spa, restaurant and poolside bar. Book in advance online from €175, otherwise from €400.

# Youth hostels

The number of youth hostels in Barcelona has expanded rapidly in recent years. Some traditional backpacker dives survive here and there, but they have largely been superseded by purpose-built modern hostels with en-suite dorm rooms as well as private rooms. They compare well in price with budget rooms in the very cheapest pensions, and Internet access, self-catering kitchens, common rooms and laundry facilities are standard. If you don't have your own sleeping bag or sheet sleeping bag, most places can rent them to you. Security is pretty good at most hostels, with staffed reception desks and 24hr access commonplace, but you should still always use the lockers or safes provided. You only need an International Youth Hostel Federation (IYHF) card for a couple of places, but you can join on check-in. Rates given below indicate the low-season and high-season range, and some places offer discounts for longer stays.

## Barri Gòtic

For locations, see map, pp.54–55.

**Itaca** **c/Ripoll 21** ☎933 019 751, ⓦwww.itacahostel.com; ⓂJaume I. Bright and breezy converted house close to the cathedral, with spacious rooms (sleeping eight or twelve) with balconies. Dorms are mixed, though you can also reserve a private room or apartment (sleeps up to 6). With a hostel capacity of only 30 it doesn't feel at all institutional. There's a kitchen and book-exchange service, and coffee and breakfast available. Dorms €18–26, private rooms €50–65, apartments €100–120.

**Kabul** **Pl. Reial 17** ☎933 185 190, ⓦwww.kabul-hostel.com; ⓂLiceu. A budget travellers' haven in the heart of the old town, with pool table and terrace, and weekly pub crawls to help you get acquainted. A big, monastic-style common room-cum-bar overlooks the square. It has a reputation as a bit of a party place, but it's safe and welcoming enough. Rooms vary in size and number of beds (sleeping four to twenty, no private rooms) and the price includes breakfast and free Internet access. No phone reservations in summer. €20–27.

## El Raval

For locations, see map, pp.66–67.

**Barcelona Mar** **c/de Sant Pau 80** ☎933 248 530, ⓦwww.youthostel-barcelona.com;

Ⓜ **Paral.lel/Drassanes.** Large, rather clinically furnished hostel with lots of beds, on the fringe of the Rambla de Raval. Dorms – in six-, eight-, ten-, fourteen- or sixteen-bedded rooms – are mixed, and beds are ship's-bunk-style with a little curtain for privacy. It's a good location for night owls, and a secure place with 24hr reception. €18–27, includes continental breakfast.

**Center Ramblas** c/Hospital 63 ☎934 124 069, ⓦwww.center-ramblas.com; Ⓜ **Liceu.** Very popular 200-bed hostel, 100m from the Ramblas, and equipped with lounge, bar, laundry, Internet access, travel library, luggage storage and more. Heated and a/c dorms – sleeping three to ten – have stone-flagged floors and individual lockers. Price includes breakfast. No credit cards. Under-25s €17–21, over-25s €21–25, non-IYHF members €2 extra.

## La Ribera

For location, see map, p.78.

**Gothic Point** c/Vigatans 5, book online at ⓦwww.equity-point.com; Ⓜ **Jaume I.** Of the three Equity Point hostels, this is the most backpacker-orientated, which might or might not be a good thing, depending on your view, age and capacity for company. Rooms have fourteen bunks and integral shower rooms, and each bed has its own bedside cabinet and reading light. Lockers, left-luggage and tours available. Open 24hr. Dorms €18–23, includes breakfast and free Internet.

## Barceloneta

For location, see map, p.91.

**Sea Point** Pl. del Mar 1–4, book online at ⓦwww.equity-point.com; Ⓜ **Barceloneta.** The budget beachside choice. Neat little modern bunk rooms sleep six or seven, with an en-suite shower-bathroom in each one. The attached café, where you have breakfast, looks right out onto the boardwalk and palm trees. Open 24hr. Dorms €18–23, includes breakfast and free Internet.

## Dreta de l'Eixample

For location, see map, p.115.

**Centric Point** Pg. de Gràcia 33 ☎932 156 538 ⓦwww.equity-point.com; Ⓜ **Passeig de Gràcia.** Bills itself as "one of

the most spectacular hostels ᴉ. and it's hard to disagree, with arou. beds spread across several floors of a refurbished *modernista* building in a swish midtown location. Private twins, doubles, triples and quads available, all with wardrobe, shower room, balcony and views, while dorms (all en suite, most also with balcony) sleep up to 12. Facilities are first-rate, with bar, kitchen, wireless Internet, laundry and roof terrace with spectacular views. Prices include continental breakfast and free Internet access. Dorms from €17–24, private rooms from €80–125.

## Esquerra de l'Eixample

For location, see map, pp.128–129.

**Alternative Creative Youth Home** Ronda Universitat ☎635 669 021, ⓦwww.alternative-barcelona.com; Ⓜ **Catalunya.** A self-selecting art and counter-culture crowd make their way to this highly individual hostel – you don't even find out the exact address until you book, and once there you can expect a stylishly refurbished space with wireless Internet, projection lounge and cool music. The regular hostel stuff is well designed, if on the small side, with a maximum of 24 people spread across 3 small dorms. There's a walk-in kitchen, lockers and laundry, and plenty of information from the city-savvy staff. €20–32.

## Horta

For location, see map, p.133.

**Mare de Déu de Montserrat** Pg. de la Mare de Déu del Coll 41–51 ☎932 105 151, reservations on ☎934 838 363, ⓦwww.xanascat.cat; Ⓜ **Vallcarca** (follow Avgda. República d'Argentina, c/Viaducte de Vallcarca and then signs) or bus #28 from Pl. de Catalunya stops just across the street. Stunning converted mansion with tile and stained-glass interior, gardens, terrace and city views – a long way out, but close to Parc Güell. Dorms sleep four, six, eight or twelve, and there are all the usual facilities plus a local restaurant just around the corner or meals provided. IYHF membership required; five-night maximum stay; reception open 8am–3pm & 4.30–11pm; main door closes at midnight, but opens every 30min thereafter. Dorms €17–25, includes breakfast.

# 11

# Cafés, tapas bars and restaurants

Good cafés, tapas bars and restaurants are easily found all over the city, though you'll probably do most of your eating where you do most of your sightseeing, in the old town, particularly in the **Barri Gòtic**. However, if you step no further than the **Ramblas** or the streets around the cathedral, you are not going to experience the best of the city's cuisine – in the main tourist areas food and service can be indifferent and prices high. You need to be a bit more adventurous, and explore the backstreets of neighbourhoods like **Sant Pere**, **La Ribera**, **El Raval** and **Poble Sec**, where you'll find excellent restaurants, some little more than hole-in-the-wall cafés or traditional taverns, others surprisingly funky and chic. Most, but not all, of the big-ticket, destination-dining restaurants are found in the **Eixample**, though here you'll also discover plenty of bargains in places aimed at lunching workers. **Gràcia**, further out, is a nice village-like place to spend the evening, with plenty of good mid-range restaurants. For fish and seafood you're best off in the harbourside **Barceloneta** district or at the **Port Olímpic**.

## Cafés and fast food

There are thousands of **cafés** in Barcelona and you're rarely more than a step away from a coffee fix or a quick sandwich. In terms of what's available to eat

### Starting the day

Unless you're staying somewhere with a decent buffet breakfast spread, you may as well pass up the overpriced coffee-and-croissant option in your hotel and join the locals in the bars, cafés and patisseries. Two or three euros should get you a hot drink and a brioche, croissant or sandwich just about anywhere – many advertised deals run until noon. *Ensaimadas* (pastry spirals) are a popular choice, while *xocolata amb xurros* (chocolate con churros – long, fried tubular doughnuts with thick drinking chocolate) is a good cold-weather starter. The traditional country breakfast is *pa amb tomàquet* (pan con tomate) – bread rubbed with tomato, olive oil and garlic, perhaps topped with some cured ham or sliced cheese. Otherwise, breakfast sandwiches are whatever can be stuffed inside a *flauta* (thin baguette), from ham to *truita* (tortilla). For toast, ask for *torrades* (tostadas).

**Al fresco dining** *Agua* (p.205), *El Cangrejo Loco* (p.205), *La Soleá* (p.206).
**Breakfast** *Ciudad Condal* (p.196), *Kasparo* (p.190), *Laie Llibreria Café* (p.191).
**Cheap eats** *Bar Salvador* (p.203), *L'Económic* (p.201), *Romesco* (p.200).
**Catch of the day** *Can Majo* (p.204), *Can Maño* (p.204), *Els Pescadors* (p.205).
**Classy café society** *Café d'Estiu* (p.190), *Café de l'Opera* (p.189), *Textil Café* (p.191).
**Ethnic artistry** *Himali* (p.209), *Shunka* (p.199), *Wushu* (p.203).
**Fusion sensations** *Ànima* (p.200), *Biblioteca* (p.201), *Limbo* (p.198).
**Money no object** *Alkimia* (p.207), *Comerç 24* (p.202), *Gaig* (p.208).
**Romantic assignations** *Café de l'Acadèmia* (p.198), *La Singular* (p.209), *Senyor Parellada* (p.203).
**New-school tapas** *Sureny* (p.96); *Santa Maria* (p.194); *TapaÇ24* (p.195).
**Old-school tapas** *Bodega La Plata* (p.193), *Cal Pep* (p.194), *Inopia* (p.195).
**Unique experiences** *Casa Fernandez* (p.209), *Espai Sucre* (p.202), *Flash, Flash* (p.208).

and drink, there's often little difference between a bar and a café, but the places detailed in this section have been chosen for their food or ambience. You might be able to get a full meal, but they are more geared towards breakfast, snacks and sightseeing stops. Most places are open long hours – from 7 or 8am until midnight, or much later in some cases – so whether it's coffee first thing or a late-night nibble, you'll find somewhere to cater for you.

Many establishments are classics of their kind – century-old cafés or unique neighbourhood haunts – while others specialize in certain types of food and drink. A **forn** is a bakery, a **pastisseria** a cake and pastry shop, both often with cafés attached. A **xocolateria** specializes in chocolate, including the drinking kind. In a **granja** or **orxateria**, more like milk bars than regular cafés, you'll be able to sample traditional delights like *orxata* (*horchata*, tiger-nut drink), ice cream, and *granissat* (*granizado*, a crushed-ice drink flavoured with orange, lemon or coffee).

**Pizza**, **burger**, **felafel** and **kebab** and **cappuccino** joints are ubiquitous, especially around the Ramblas and on the main streets in the Eixample. Most major international chains are represented, while **local and Spanish chains** include *Pans & Company* and *Bocatta*, for hot and cold baguette-based sandwiches and salads; *Fresh and Ready* for deli, sandwiches and juices; and the coffee chains *Il Caffe di Roma*, *Aroma* and *Café di Francesco*.

### Ramblas

For locations, see map, p.46.

**Antiga Casa Figueras** Ramblas 83 ☎933 016 027, ⓦwww.escriba.es; Ⓜ Liceu. Serves glorious pastries from the renowned Escribà family business in a *modernista*-designed pastry shop, with a few tables inside and out. Many people rate this as the best bakery in Barcelona. Mon–Sat 9am–3pm & 5–8.30pm.

**Café de l'Opera** Ramblas 74 ☎933 177 585, ⓦwww.cafeoperabcn.com; Ⓜ Liceu. If you're going to pay through the nose for a Ramblas seat, it may as well be at this famous old café-bar opposite the opera house, which retains its late nineteenth-century decor as well as a bank of sought-after pavement tables. It's not a complete tourist-fest, though – locals pop in throughout the day and night for coffee, cakes, snacks and tapas. Daily 8.30am–2am.

**Café Zurich** Pl. Catalunya 1 ☎933 179 153, ⓦwww.cafezurich.com; Ⓜ Catalunya. The most famous meet-and-greet café in town, right at the top of the Ramblas underneath El Triangle shopping centre. It's good for croissants and breakfast sandwiches and there's a huge terrace, but sit inside if you don't want to be bothered by endless rounds of buskers and beggars. Mon–Fri 8am–11pm, Sat & Sun 10am–11pm, June–Sept open until 1am.

## Barri Gòtic

For locations, see map, pp.54–55.

**Caelum** c/Palla 8 ☎ 933 026 993; Ⓜ **Liceu.** The lovingly packaged confections in this upscale café-cum-deli are made in convents and monasteries across Spain. Choose from *frutas de almendra* (marzipan sweeties) from Seville, Benedictine preserves or Cistercian cookies. Tues–Sun 10.30am–8.30pm; closed two weeks in Aug.

**Café d'Estiu** Pl. de Sant Iu 5–6 ☎ 932 682 598; Ⓜ **Jaume I.** The summer outpost of La Ribera's *Tèxtil Café* is housed on the delightful interior terrace of the Museu Marès, under the spreading boughs of the orange tree. Relax with the newspapers during the day, or come for the candlelit evenings. April–Oct Tues–Sun 10am–10pm.

**Dulcinea** c/Petritxol 2 ☎ 932 311 756; Ⓜ **Liceu.** One of the old town's traditional treats is to come here for a thick hot chocolate, slathered in cream if you like it that way. Then if you've still got room, try one of their pastries or perhaps a dish of *mel i mato* (curd cheese with honey). A dickie-bow-wearing waiter patrols the beamed and panelled room bearing a silver tray. Daily 9am–1pm & 5–9pm; closed Aug.

**Mesón del Cafe** c/Llibreteria 16 ☎ 933 150 754; Ⓜ **Jaume I.** Offbeat locals' café where you'll probably have to stand to sample the pastries and the excellent coffee – including a cappuccino laden with fresh cream – though there is a sort of cubbyhole at the back with a few tables. Mon–Sat 7am–11pm.

## El Raval

For locations, see map, pp.66–67.

**Granja de Gavà** c/Joaquim Costa 37 ☎ 933 175 883; Ⓜ **Universitat.** This traditionally tiled café has an arty air – witness the daubs on the walls, the 3m-high woman on the bar and the weekly poetry readings and other events. It's a thoroughly relaxed spot – proclaiming "No TV, just good music"

– and serves up breakfast, sandwiches, crêpes, salads, juices and shakes. Mon–Fri 8am–1am, Sat 8am–2.30am.

**Granja M. Viader** c/Xuclà 4–6 ☎ 933 183 486; Ⓜ **Liceu.** The oldest milk bar (*granja*) in town is tucked away down a narrow alley just off c/del Carmé, with a pavement plaque outside for services to the city. Sr. Viader was the proud inventor of "Cacaolat" (a popular chocolate drink, but you could also try the *mel i mató* (curd cheese and honey) or *llet Mallorquina* (fresh milk with cinnamon and lemon rind) for a taste of the old days. Mon 5–8.45pm, Tues–Sat 9am–1.45pm & 5–8.45pm; closed two weeks in Aug.

**Kasparo** Pl. Vicenç Martorell 4 ☎ 933 022 072; Ⓜ **Catalunya.** Sited in the arcaded corner of a quiet square off c/Bonsuccés, this tiny café and *terrassa* is popular with locals who come to let their kids play in the adjacent playground. There's muesli, Greek yoghurt, and toast and jam for early birds, while later in the day sandwiches, tapas and assorted *platos del dia* are on offer – things like hummus and bread, vegetable quiche, couscous or pasta. Daily 9am–10pm, until midnight in summer; closed Jan.

**Mendizábal** c/Junta de Comerç 2, no phone; Ⓜ **Liceu.** Don't look for a bar – there isn't

▲ Mesón del Cafe

## Coffee and tea

**Coffee** is invariably espresso – ask for a *café sol* (*café solo*) or simply *un café*. A slightly weaker large black coffee is called a *café americano*. A *tallat* (*cortado*) is a small strong black coffee with a dash of steamed milk; a larger cup with more hot milk is a *café amb llet* (*café con leche*). Black coffee is also frequently mixed with brandy, cognac or whisky, all such concoctions being called *cigaló* (*carajillo*); liqueur mixed with white coffee is a *trifásico*. Decaffeinated coffee (*descafeinat*, *descafeinado*) is available, usually in sachet form, though increasingly you can get the real thing – ask for it *de màquina* (from the machine).

**Tea** comes without milk unless you ask for it, and is often insipid (often just a teabag in a cup of hot water). If you do ask for milk, chances are it'll be hot and UHT. Better are the infusions that you can get in most bars, like mint *(menta),* camomile (*camomila*) and lime *(tila).*

one. This cheery stand-up counter opposite the Hospital de la Santa Creu dispenses juices, shakes, beer and sandwiches to passing punters. The lucky ones grab a table over the road in the shady little square. Daily 10am–midnight, June–Sept until 1am.

### La Ribera

For locations, see map, p.78.
**Café del Born Pl. Comercial 10** ☎932 683 272; Ⓜ Jaume I. No gimmicks, no fusion food, and dodgy local art kept at a bare minimum – this is the recipe for success at this always popular neighbourhood café-bar. There's a simple Mediterranean menu on offer, while Sunday brunch is the big draw. Mon–Thurs & Sun 9am–1am, Fri & Sat 9am–3.30am.

**Rosal Pg. del Born 27, no phone;** Ⓜ Jaume I. The *terrassa* at the end of the Born gets the sun all day, making it a popular meeting place, though it's also packed on summer nights. Menu specials here are couscous or curry combinations, and if you can raise a smile from the staff you're on a roll. Daily 9am–2am.

🏃 **Tèxtil Café c/de Montcada 12–14** ☎932 682 598, Ⓦ www.textilcafe.com; Ⓜ Jaume I. Everyone loves this relaxed boho café, set inside a shady, cobbled medieval courtyard on the neighbourhood's most visited street (the Picasso museum is just up the road). The food's great for sharing – there's hummus, guacamole, baba ganoush and tapenade, as well as things like quiche, salads, chilli, lasagne and big sandwiches. And there's also a lunchtime and evening *menú del dia*, and live swing and jazz most Sun nights. Tues & Wed 10am–8.30pm,

Thurs 10am–midnight, Fri & Sat 10am–1am, Sun 10am–midnight; Tues–Thurs in winter daytime only.

### Poble Nou

For location, see map, p.85.
**El Tío Ché Rambla Poble Nou 44–46** ☎933 091 872, Ⓦ www.eltioche.com; Ⓜ Poble Nou, or bus #36 from Ⓜ Barceloneta. A down-to-earth café in a down-to-earth neighbourhood, run by the same family for four generations. The specialities are orange or lemon *granissat* (crushed ice) and their famous *orxata* (tiger-nut drink), but there are also *torrons* (almond fudge), hot chocolate, coffee, croissants and sandwiches. It's a bit off the beaten track, though you can stroll up easily enough from Bogatell beach (15min) or down the *rambla* from Poble Nou metro (10min). Daily 10am–midnight; reduced hours in winter.

### Dreta de l'Eixample

For locations, see map, p.115.
**Café del Centre c/Girona 69** ☎934 881 101; Ⓜ Girona. Formerly a casino, later converted into a café, but retaining its elegant *modernista* decor, which is the main reason for a visit. It's only three blocks from the tourist sights on the Passeig de Gràcia, but largely invisible as far as most visitors are concerned, so good to know about for a quiet coffee or lunch. Mon–Fri noon–2am, Sat 7.30pm–2am.

🏃 **Laie Llibreria Café c/Pau Claris 85** ☎933 027 310, Ⓦ www.laie.es; Ⓜ Urquinaona. The city's first and best bookshop café, and a great place to drop in on any time, with a bar and mezzanine seating or a roomier salon at the back. The weekday buffet breakfast spread is popular, and there are set lunch and dinner deals, à la carte dining, and magazines (*National Geographic* to *Marie Claire*) to browse. Also branches in the Caixa Forum art gallery and L'Illa shopping centre. Mon 8.30am–9pm, Tues–Fri 8.30am–1am, Sat 10am–1am.

## Esquerra de l'Eixample

For locations, see map, pp.128–129.
**Fast Good c/Balmes 127** ☎ **934 522 374,** Ⓦ **www.fast-good.com;** Ⓜ **Provença.** The concept is familiar – help-yourself ready-made salads, fancy sandwiches and fruit bowls – but since this is fast food Ferran Adrià style (ie, triple Michelin-starred chef on a mission), quality and sourcing is all. Gourmet burgers, classy egg and chips, and proper children's meals are on the menu too, all at realistic prices – just a shame the dining area looks like an airport departure lounge. Daily noon–midnight.
**Forn de Sant Jaume Rambla de Catalunya 50** ☎ **932 160 229;** Ⓜ **Passeig de Gràcia.** The

windows are piled high with goodies at this classic old *patisseria* and *bomboneria* – croissants, cakes and sweets are either to take away or eat at the busy little adjacent café. Mon–Sat 9am–9pm.
**Valor Rambla de Catalunya 46** ☎ **934 876 246;** Ⓜ **Passeig de Gràcia.** Ornate uptown chocolate specialist, serving the gentle folk since 1881. A warming hot choc and *xurros* sends you happily on your way on a chilly morning. Mon–Thurs 8.30am–1pm & 3.30–11pm, Fri–Sun 9am–midnight.

## Gràcia

For location, see map, p.134.
🏃 **La Nena c/Ramon i Cajal 36** ☎ **932 851 476;** Ⓜ **Fontana.** First and foremost, it's the food at "the little girl" that's the main attraction – fantastic home-made cakes, plus waffles, quiches, organic ice cream, squeezed juices and the like. But parents love it too, as it's very child-friendly, down to little seats for little people and games and puzzles to keep them occupied. Daily 9am–2pm & 4–10pm.

# Tapas bars

If you've ever been disappointed in tapas – microwaved *patatas bravas* and frozen calamari, at an outrageous mark-up – it's time to re-evaluate, at least in Barcelona where the tapas boom shows no sign of abating. In recent years, it seems that every bar and restaurant has been quick to rustle up its own little menu of small dishes, and you can eat really well just dining on tapas, especially in some of the new-wave places that are deadly serious about their food.

The current fascination is odd because tapas is not a particularly Catalan phenomenon at all. Indeed, the best of the old-style city tapas bars tend to concentrate on specialities from other Spanish regions, like octopus, peppers and seafood from Galicia; cider, cured meats and cheese from Asturias; or the ubiquitous Basque-style *pintxos*, which are bite-sized concoctions on a slice of bread, held together with a cocktail stick (you're charged by the number of sticks on your plate when you've finished). More contemporary tapas bars serve "creative tapas" – you're as likely to get a samosa or a yucca chip as a garlic mushroom these days in Barcelona – while a few stand-out places offer classy, restaurant-standard experiences that are still truly tapas at heart.

By the way, don't expect eating tapas to be cheap. Jumping from bar to bar for dinner is going to cost you at least as much as eating in a medium-priced restaurant, say €25 a head, and twice as much in the really good places. Also, apart from the fancier restaurant-style tapas places, you generally won't be able to pay with a credit card.

## Ramblas

For locations, see map, p.46.

**Amaya Ramblas** 20–24 ☎ 933 026 138 (bar), 933 021 037 (restaurant), ⓦ www.restauranteamaya.com; ⓜ Drassanes. A Ramblas fixture since 1941 – restaurant on one side, tapas bar on the other, both serving Basque seafood specialities including octopus, baby squid, clams, mussels, anchovies and prawns. The bar offers the cheapest and most enjoyable introduction to the cuisine, otherwise main dishes in the restaurant cost €14–20. Bar daily 10am–12.30am; restaurant daily 1.30–4pm & 8.30pm–midnight.

**Bar Central La Boqueria Mercat de la Boqueria, Ramblas 91, no phone;** ⓜ Liceu. This gleaming, chrome stand-up bar in the market's central aisle is the venue for ultra-fresh market produce, served by black-T-shirted staff who work at a fair lick. Breakfast, snack or lunch, it's all the same to them – salmon cutlets, sardines, calamari, razor clams, hake fillets, sausages, pork steaks, asparagus spears and the rest, plunked on the griddle and sprinkled with salt. Breakfast costs just a few euros or it's €5–15 for some tapas or a main dish and a drink. Mon–Sat 6.30am–4pm.

🏃 **Bar Pinotxo Mercat de la Boqueria, Ramblas 91** ☎ 933 171 731; ⓜ Liceu. The market's most renowned refuelling stop – just inside the main entrance on the right – attracts traders, chefs, tourists and celebs, who stand three deep at busy times. A coffee, a grilled sandwich and a glass of cava (no, really) is the local breakfast of choice, or let the cheery staff steer you towards the tapas and daily specials, anything from a slice of tortilla to fried baby squid. Mon–Sat 6am–5pm; closed Aug.

## Barri Gòtic

For locations, see map, pp.54–55.

**Bar Celta Pulperia c/de la Mercè 16** ☎ 933 150 006; ⓜ Drassanes. This no-nonsense, brightly lit Galician tapas bar specializes in typical *gallego* dishes like octopus and fried green *pimientos* (peppers), washed down with heady regional wine. You eat at the U-shaped bar or at tables in the back room, and while it's not one for a long, lazy meal, it's just right to kick off a bout of bar-hopping. Tues–Sat noon–midnight.

🏃 **Bodega La Plata c/de la Mercè 28** ☎ 933 151 009; ⓜ Drassanes. An old-town classic with a marble counter open to the street and cheap wine straight from the barrel. Anchovies are the speciality (marinaded or deep-fried like whitebait), attracting an enthusiastic local crowd, from businessmen to pre-clubbers. Daily 10am–4pm & 8–11pm.

**Ginger c/Palma Sant Just 1** ☎ 933 105 309; ⓜ Jaume I. Cocktails and creative tapas in a slickly updated 1970s-style setting. It's a world away from *patatas bravas* and battered squid – think roast duck vinaigrette, tuna tartare and vegetarian satay. Tues–Sat 7pm–3am; closed two weeks in Aug.

**La Pineda c/del Pi 16** ☎ 933 024 393; ⓜ Liceu. On a street of boutiques and gift shops survives this old-fashioned grocery store, with a tiny bar and a few tables at the back where the old guys and curious tourists hang out. Selections from the regional cured hams and sausages suspended over the counter are the things to eat. Mon–Sat 9am–3pm & 6–10pm.

**Taller de Tapas Pl. Sant Josep Oriol 9** ☎ 933 018 020, ⓦ www.tallerdetapas.com; ⓜ Liceu. More restaurant than bar, the "tapas workshop"

## No such thing as a free lunch …

…except, once upon a time, in southern Spain. **Tapas** (from *tapar*, to cover) originated as free snacks given away as covers for drinks' glasses, perhaps to keep the flies off in the baking sun. It's still a much more southern, Andalusian thing, though the Basques, *gallegos* and other northerners, all with their own tapas tradition, might disagree. In some parts of Spain, tapas still comes for free with drinks – a dish of olives, a bite of omelette, some fried peppers. But in Barcelona you can expect to pay for every mouthful … unless you count the restaurants which kick off proceedings with an *amuse-gueule* shot glass of soup or designer canapé – free to anyone just about to pay €80 for dinner.

sucks in tourists with its pretty location by the church of Santa Maria del Pi – there's a year-round outdoor terrace. The open kitchen turns out market-fresh tapas, with fish a speciality at dinner, so you might get griddled tuna, sautéed razor clams, anchovies from L'Escala or cod fish-cakes. Prices are on the high side, but the food's generally reliable. There is another similarly busy branch in the Born at c/Argenteria 51, and a rather less atmospheric outlet in the upper Barri Gòtic at c/Comtal 28, which serves the same range of tapas but also boasts *cerveseria* (beer house) credentials, with a range of 20 international bottled beers. Mon–Sat 9.30am–midnight, Sun noon–midnight.

🏃 **La Viñatería del Call** **c/Sant Domènec del Call 9** ☎ **933 026 092;** Ⓜ **Jaume I.** The wood-table tavern is principally an eating place – with a long menu of cheese and ham platters, *escalivada*, smoked fish, fried peppers and much more – but it's also a great late-night bar, with a serious wine list and jazz and flamenco sounds as a backdrop. If you want to eat, especially at weekends, it's best to reserve a table. Mon–Sat 6pm–1am.

## El Raval

For location, see map, pp.66–67.

🏃 **Mam i Teca** **c/de la Lluna 4** ☎ **934 413 335;** Ⓜ **Sant Antoni.** An intimate (code for very small) place for superior tapas and fine wines, run by a wine-loving gourmet. All the meat is organic, the regional cheeses are well chosen, and market-fresh ingredients are the basis for the daily pasta dishes, a platter of grilled vegetables or a simple serving of lamb cutlets. Finish with chocolate truffles or home-made ice cream. There are only three or four tables, or you can perch at the bar. Mon, Wed–Fri & Sun 1–4pm & 8.30pm–midnight, Sat 8.30pm–midnight.

## Sant Pere

For locations, see map, p.74.

🏃 **El Bitxo** **c/Verdaguer i Callis 9** ☎ **932 681 700,** Ⓜ **Urquinaona.** This is a great find for drinks and tapas, close to the Palau de la Música Catalana. It's tiny (four small wooden tables and a line of bar stools) but there's a friendly welcome, and the food is very good, especially the cured and smoked

meats and sausages, and regional cheeses. Mon–Sat 1pm–1am.

🏃 **Mosquito** **c/dels Carders 46** ☎ **932 687 569,** Ⓦ **www.mosquitotapas.com;** Ⓜ **Jaume 1.** The sculpted dive-bombing mozzies above the door herald "tapas exóticas", which turn out to be delicious pan-Asian tapas, things like Balinese chicken wings, Singapore noodles, potato *chaat* and crispy *pakoras*, each around €3–5. There's a sushi and sashimi menu too, and if you factor in the friendly service, Fair Trade coffee and world music you've got a winning combination. Tues–Sun 5pm–1am, Fri & Sat until 2.30am.

**Santa Maria** **c/Comerç 17** ☎ **933 151 227,** Ⓦ **www.santamania.info;** Ⓜ **Jaume I.** Paco Guzmán's new-wave tapas bar has a glass-fronted kitchen turning out taste sensations – such as Catalan sushi, octopus confit, yucca chips, or quail with salsa. Around €40 should get you a good range of dishes, finishing on a high note with the famous "Dracula" dessert – a shot glass of strawberry and vanilla cream flavours with pop-rocks that sets off crackles in your mouth. Tues–Sat 1.30–3.30pm & 8.30pm–12.30am; closed two weeks in Aug.

## La Ribera

For locations, see map, p.78.

🏃 **Cal Pep** **Pl. de les Olles 8** ☎ **933 107 961,** Ⓦ **www.calpep.com;** Ⓜ **Barceloneta.** There's no equal in town for fresh-off-the-boat and out-of-the-market tapas, and if you don't want to queue, get there on opening for a seat at the counter. Prices can be high for what's effectively a bar meal (up to €40 a head) but it's definitely worth it. After a quick tutorial from the waiter, sit back and enjoy fried shrimp, hot green peppers, grilled sea bass, Catalan sausage and beans, baby squid and chickpeas, and other classics – the whole show overseen by Pep himself bustling up and down the counter. Mon 8–11.45pm, Tues–Fri 1.15–4pm & 8–11.45pm, Sat 1.30–4pm; closed Aug.

**Euskal Etxea** **Pl. de Montcada 1–3** ☎ **933 102 185;** Ⓜ **Jaume I/Barceloneta.** The bar at the front of the local Basque community centre is great for *pintxos*-picking – these pint-sized tapas are displayed along the counter, so just point to what you want (and keep

⑪

the sticks so that the bill can be tallied at the end). There's a pricier restaurant out back with more good Basque specialities. Mon 6.30pm–midnight, Tues–Sat noon–4pm & 6.30pm–midnight; restaurant opens 1.30pm & 8.30pm.

**El Xampanyet** c/de Montcada 22 ☎933 197 003; Ⓜ Jaume I/Barceloneta. Traditional blue-tiled bar doing a roaring trade in sweet sparkling *cava* and *sidra*. Salted anchovies are the house speciality, but there's also marinaded tuna, spicy mussels, sun-dried tomatoes, sliced meats and cheese. As is often the way, the drinks are cheap and the tapas turn out to be rather pricey, but there's usually a good buzz about the place. Tues–Sat noon–4pm & 6.30–11pm, Sun noon–4pm; closed Aug.

## Barceloneta

For locations, see map, p.91.

🏃 **Cova Fumada** c/Baluard 56 ☎932 214 061; Ⓜ Barceloneta. A good place for a gregarious lunch – the busy, old-style bar is behind the brown wooden doors on Barceloneta's market square (there's no sign). The seafood is straight from the market's fish stalls, though the house speciality is the *bomba* (spicy potato-meatball), a dish you can get all over Barcelona these days but which the *Cova Fumada* claims as its own. Mon–Fri 9am–3pm & 6–8pm, Sat 9am–3pm; closed Aug.

🏃 **Jai-Ca** c/Ginebra 13 ☎932 683 265; Ⓜ Barceloneta. Always a great choice, at any time of the day, with seafood platters piled on the bar, from bundles of razor clams to plump anchovies. Meanwhile, the fryers in the kitchen work overtime, turning out crisp baby squid, fried shrimp and little green peppers scattered with rock-salt. Take your haul to a tile-topped cane table, or outside onto the tiny street-corner patio. Daily 10am–11pm.

**Vaso de Oro** c/Balboa 6 ☎933 193 098; Ⓜ Barceloneta. If you can get in this corridor of a bar you're doing well (Sun lunch is particularly busy), and there's no menu, so order the *patatas bravas*, some thick slices of fried sausage and a dollop of tuna salad and you've touched all the bases. Unusually, they also brew their own beer, which comes in tall schooners, either light or dark. Daily 9am–midnight.

## Poble Sec

For locations, see map, p.104.

🏃 **Inopia** c/Tamarit 104 ☎934 245 231, Ⓦ www.barinopia.com; Ⓜ Poble Sec. You'll have to make a special trip to this sleek, in-the-know tapas bar, stuck in sight-seer's no-man's-land, but it's unquestionably worth it. It's the brainchild of Albert Adrià, brother of Ferran Adrià (of best-restaurant-in-the-world fame, *El Bulli*), and it's always standing room only for the best "classic tapas" in town. Regional wines are very reasonably priced, and don't miss the signature-dish *patatas bravas*, the griddled tuna, lamb brochettes or the *fritura de verdura* (vegetable tempura). You can eat and drink for around €25. Tues–Fri 7–11pm, Sat 1.30–3.30pm & 7–11pm.

🏃 **Quimet i Quimet** c/Poeta Cabanyes 25 ☎934 423 142; Ⓜ Paral.lel. At busy times here everyone has to breathe in to squeeze another punter through the door. The bottles are stacked five shelves high – there's a chalkboard menu of wines by the glass – while little plates of classy finger food are dished out from the minuscule counter, things like roast onions, marinaded mushrooms, stuffed cherry tomatoes, grilled aubergine or anchovy-wrapped olives. Tues–Sat noon–4pm & 7–11pm, Sun noon–4pm; closed Aug.

## Dreta de l'Eixample

For locations, see map, p.115.

**Casa Alfonso** c/Roger de Llúria 6 ☎933 019 783, Ⓦ www.casaalfonso.com; Ⓜ Urquinaona. It's about half-past 1930 in *Alfonso*'s – bar and *xarcuteria* up front, country-style wood-panelled dining room at the rear. Alongside the tapas are two-person platters (like mixed cheeses or smoked fish) or selections from the grill, served with garlic or *romesco* sauces. Mon–Fri 9am–1am, Sat noon–1am.

🏃 **Tapaç24** c/Diputació 269 ☎934 880 977, Ⓦ www.carlesabellan.com; Ⓜ Passeig de Gràcia. Carles Abellan, king of pared-down designer cuisine at his famed restaurant *Comerç 24*, offers a simpler tapas menu at this retro basement bar-diner. There's a reassuringly traditional feel that's echoed in the menu – *patatas bravas*, Andalucian-style fried fish, *bombas* (meatballs), *chorizo* sausage and fried eggs. But the kitchen updates the classics too, so there's also *calamares romana* (fried squid) dyed black with squid ink or a burger with *foie gras*. Most tapas cost €6–14. There's always a rush and a bustle at meal times, and you might well have to queue. Daily 8am–midnight.

## Esquerra de l'Eixample

For locations, see map, pp.128–129.

**La Bodegueta Rambla Catalunya 100** ℡**932 154 894;** ⓜ**Diagonal.** This long-established basement bodega serves *cava* by the glass, a serious range of other wines, and good ham, cheese, anchovies and other tapas to soak it all up. In summer you can sit outside at the *rambla* tables. Daily 8am–2am; closed mornings in Aug.

**Cerveseria Catalana c/de Mallorca 236** ℡**932 160 368;** ⓜ**Passeig de Gràcia.** A place that is serious about its tapas and beer – the counters are piled high, supplemented by a blackboard list of daily specials, while the walls are lined with bottled brews from around the world. It's mostly an after-work kind of place, though lunchtime is always busy too. Daily 9am–1am.

🏃 **Ciudad Condal Rambla de Catalunya 18** ℡**933 181 997;** ⓜ**Passeig de Gràcia.** A really handy city-centre pit stop that caters for all needs, and the best of the large uptown tapas-hall-style places. Breakfast sees the bar groan under the weight of a dozen types of crispy baguette sandwich, piled high on platters, supplemented by a cabinet of croissants and pastries, while the daily changing tapas selection ranges far and wide, *patatas bravas* to octopus. It can be standing room only at lunchtime (and not much of that either), so get there early for a seat at the bar or in the rear dining room. Daily 7.30am–1.30am.

## Gràcia

For locations, see map, p.134.

**El Roble c/Luis Antunez 7** ℡**932 187 387;** ⓜ**Diagonal.** Roomy L-shaped bar on a busy corner with locals popping in for a snack

and a chat. It's a traditional place, with a large tapas selection served promptly to your table (order at the bar; there's a list on the wall) or nudge your way up to the counter and peruse the day's specials. Mon–Sat 7am–midnight; closed Aug.

🏃 **Samsara c/Terol 6** ℡**932 853 688;** ⓜ**Fontana.** Low tables, low lighting, and painted concrete walls hung with artworks and photos provide the backdrop for a laid-back place offering contemporary tapas and "platillos" (little plates). The menu changes daily, but typical dishes are brochettes of asparagus tempura, mini hamburgers and inventive salads, most costing €5–6. It's totally Gràcia – yes, that's a chill-out soundtrack and yes, there's a projection screen above the bar. Mon–Thurs & Sun 8.30pm–1.30am, Fri & Sat 8.30pm–3am.

🏃 **Sureny Pl. de la Revolució 17** ℡**932 137 556;** ⓜ**Fontana.** For a more gourmet experience in Gràcia – it's still a tapas place, but you're served by amiable staff at restaurant tables with inventive dishes from a seasonally changing menu. For around €7 or €8 a time you can sample clever concoctions like venison tartare with pineapple preserve, a scallop swimming in pumpkin soup or monkfish on baby asparagus. Or a tasting menu (around €35) gets you seven of the best plus dessert. Tues–Sat 8.30pm–midnight, Sun 1–3.30pm & 8.30pm–midnight.

## Sarrià

For location, see map, pp.140–141.

🏃 **Bar Tomás c/Major de Sarrià 49** ℡**932 031 077; FGC Sarrià.** The best *patatas bravas* in the city? Everyone points you here, to this utterly unassuming, white-formica-table bar in the 'burbs (12min by train from Pl. Catalunya FGC station) for a taste of their unrivalled spicy fried potatoes with garlic mayo and *salsa picante*. They fry between noon and 3pm and 6pm and closing so if it's *bravas* you want, note the hours. Daily except Wed 8am–10pm; closed Aug.

# Restaurants

Most restaurants in Barcelona serve a mixture of local Catalan and more mainstream Spanish food, with the best concentrating on seasonal market produce. (The features on p.202 and p.204 provide a rundown of trends and specialities, while for a menu reader turn to pp.294–298) Regional Spanish and colonial Spanish cuisine is fairly well represented, too, from Basque and Galician to Cuban and Filipino, while traditionally the fancier local restaurants tended towards a refined Catalan-French style of dining. This has been superseded recently by the two dominant trends in **contemporary Spanish cooking**, namely the food-as-chemistry approach pioneered by superchef Ferran Adrià and the more accessible tendency towards so-called **fusion** cuisine (basically Mediterranean flavours with exotic touches). The range of **foreign and ethnic** restaurants is not as wide as in other European cities, with Italian, Chinese, Middle Eastern and Indian and Pakistani food providing the main choices, though the cuisines of Latin America, North Africa, Southeast Asia and Japan are also represented.

Nearly all restaurants offer a weekday (ie Monday to Friday) three-course **menú del dia** (menu of the day) at lunchtime, with the cheapest starting at about €9, rising to €12–15 in fancier places. In many restaurants the price includes a drink, so this can be a real bargain. At night, the set menus are rarely available but eating out is still pretty good value and you'll be able to dine in a huge variety of restaurants for around €25–30 a head – though you can, of course, pay a lot more. If your main criteria are price and quantity, look for a **buffet restaurant** (*Fresc Co* has several outlets, and there are many others), where €9 or €10 gets you unlimited access to the hot and cold *buffet lliure* (free buffet). In other bars or cafés, budget meals often come in the form of a *plat combinat* (*plato combinado,* combined plate), of things like eggs, steak, calamari or chicken with fries and salad. Be warned that many cheaper restaurants and cafés might not provide a written **menu**, with the waiter merely reeling off the day's dishes at bewildering speed. To ask for a menu, request *la carta*.

**Opening hours** for restaurants are generally 1 to 4pm and 8.30 to 11pm, though most locals don't eat lunch until at least 2pm and dinner after 9 or even 10pm. However, in tourist and entertainment zones like Maremàgnum and the Port Olímpic, restaurants tend to stay open all day and will serve on request. A lot of restaurants **close on Sundays or Mondays, on public holidays and throughout August** – check the listings for specific details but expect changes, since many places imaginatively interpret their own posted opening days and times.

If there's somewhere you'd particularly like to eat – certainly at the more fashionable end of the market – you should **reserve a table**. Some places are booked solid for days, or weeks, in advance. Finally, all restaurant menus should make it clear whether the seven-percent **IVA** tax is included in the prices or not.

---

## Restaurant prices

The restaurant listings in this chapter are divided into price categories. As a rough guide, you'll get a **three-course meal (per person)** excluding drinks for:
**Inexpensive** Under €15
**Moderate** €15–30
**Expensive** €30–50
**Very expensive** Over €50
Bear in mind that the lunchtime *menú del dia* usually allows you to eat for much less than the price category might lead you to expect (and often includes a drink).

## Barri Gòtic

For locations, see map, pp.54–55.

### Inexpensive

**Venus Delicatessen** c/Avinyó 25 ☏ 933 011 585; Ⓜ Liceu/Jaume I. Not a deli, despite the name, but it's a handy place for Carrer d'Avinyo boutique shoppers, serving Mediterranean bistro cuisine throughout the day and night. It's also good for vegetarians, with things like lasagne, couscous, moussaka and salads mostly meat-free, and all costing around €7–10. No credit cards. Daily noon–midnight.

### Moderate

🏃 **Arc Café** c/Carabassa 19 ☏ 933 025 204, Ⓦ www.arccafe.com; Ⓜ Drassanes. Setting the standard for the chilled-out bistro-bars seemingly now on every corner, the *Arc* does substance *and* style. Drop in just for a drink by all means – it's a neighbourhood stalwart – but the seasonally changing menu is great value, and the kitchen's open all day. There are Greek salad, spring rolls, home-made burgers and Thai curries (with Thurs & Fri nights designated Thai food nights). A la carte main dishes are around €10. Mon–Thurs 10am–1am, Fri 10am–3am, Sat 11am–3am, Sun 11am–1am.

**Can Culleretes** c/Quintana 5 ☏ 933 173 022, Ⓦ www.culleretes.com; Ⓜ Liceu. Supposedly Barcelona's oldest restaurant (founded in 1786), serving straight-up Catalan food (*botifarra* sausage and beans, salt cod, game stews) in cosy, traditional surroundings. Local families come in droves, especially for celebrations or for Sun lunch, and there are really good-value set seafood meals available at both lunch and dinner. Tues–Sat 1.30–4pm & 9–11pm, Sun 1.30–4pm; closed July.

🏃 **Matsuri** Pl. Regomir 1 ☏ 932 681 535, Ⓦ www.matsuri-restaurante.com; Ⓜ Jaume I. *Matsuri*'s creative Southeast Asian cuisine concentrates on Thai-style noodles, soups, curries, salads, plus sushi and sashimi. Tastes are very definitely Catalan in execution – nothing too spicy or adventurous – but the service is friendly and the Indonesian-style furniture and terracotta colours make for a relaxed meal. Around €25 a head. Mon–Thurs 1.30–3.30pm & 8.30–11.30pm, Fri 1.30–3.30pm & 8.30pm–midnight, Sat 8.30pm–midnight.

**El Salón** c/L'Hostal d'en Sol 6–8 ☏ 933 152 159; Ⓜ Jaume I. Changes at *El Salón* have brightened the interior and lightened the mood, but the modern Mediterranean food still cuts the mustard. The menu changes seasonally, with inventive salads giving way to things like a confit of cod with spinach, pine nuts and raisins, and most mains are in the range €10–14. Mon–Sat 8.30pm–midnight; closed two weeks in Aug.

### Expensive

🏃 **Café de l'Acadèmia** c/Lledó 1 ☏ 933 198 253; Ⓜ Jaume I. Great for a date or a lazy lunch, with creative Catalan cooking served in a romantic stone-flagged restaurant or on a lovely summer *terrassa* in the medieval square outside, lit by candles at night. Seasonal dishes range from confit of *bacallà* (salt cod) with spinach and pine kernels to aubergine terrine with goat's cheese, plus grills, fresh fish and rice. Prices are pretty reasonable (mains €11–18) and it's always busy, so dinner reservations are essential. A no-choice *menú del dia* is a bargain for the quality (it's even cheaper eaten at the bar); a nice breakfast is served too. Mon–Fri 9am–noon, 1.30–4pm & 8.45–11.30pm; closed two weeks in Aug.

**Los Caracoles** c/Escudellers 14 ☏ 933 023 185; Ⓜ Liceu/Drassanes. A cavernous Barcelona landmark with spit-roast chickens turning on grills outside, dining rooms on various floors adorned with chandeliers and oil paintings, and an open kitchen straight out of Mervyn Peake's *Gormenghast*. The restaurant name means "snails", a house speciality, and the chicken's good too. There's a full Catalan/Spanish menu in a multitude of languages. However, prices are beginning to look exploitative (€16.50 for chicken and chips), service can be chaotic, to say the least, and the best that can be said about the whole affair sometimes is that it's been an experience – you certainly won't forget it. Daily 1pm–midnight.

**Limbo** c/de la Mercè 13 ☏ 933 107 699; Ⓜ Liceu. Designer restaurant that manages an intimate feel within a warehouse-style interior of exposed brick and wooden beams. The menu is market-led, and there are Asian influences, so you can expect things like swordfish tartare with red onion marmalade and wasabi, though there's also a pasta of the week and locally sourced meat. Most dishes cost between €7 and

The restaurants listed below are the pick of the specifically vegetaria[n] Barcelona, but you'll also be able to eat well in many tapas bars and mo[dern] brasseries and restaurants. Some salads and vegetable dishes are strictly [veg –] *espinacs a la Catalana* (spinach, pine nuts and raisins) and *escaliva[da]* [(grilled] aubergine, onions and peppers). Otherwise, there are plenty of Middle Eas[tern] and Pakistani restaurants, where you can order veg curries or a felafel-stuffed pitta. The ⓦwww.sincarne.net **website** is useful for listings and reviews in Barcelona.

**L'Atzavara** c/Muntaner 109, Eixample ⓣ934 545 925; ⓜProvença, map, pp.128–129. This lunch-only spot is a bit more gourmet than many similar places. For a fixed price you choose from half a dozen starters and soups, and three or four mains (stuffed peppers, say, or a vegetarian *fideuà*) and puds. Even with drinks and coffee, it should come to well under €15. Mon–Sat 1–4pm. Inexpensive.

🏃 **La Báscula** c/Flassaders 30, La Ribera ⓣ933 199 866; ⓜJaume I, map, p.78. An old chocolate factory in the back-streets has been given a hippy-chic makeover, by a local cooperative and serves up speciality pastas, gourmet sandwiches, crêpes and salads, plus dozens of teas, coffees, organic wines, juices and shakes. Their original café, *La Cererfa* (Bxda. Sant Miquel 3–5, Wed–Sat 7pm–midnight, ⓣ933 018 510), is also now open again for more of the same in the Barri Gòtic. No credit cards. Wed–Fri 7pm–midnight, Sat 1pm–midnight. Moderate.

🏃 **Biocenter** c/Pintor Fortuny 25, El Raval ⓣ933 014 583, dinner reservations ⓣ667 042 313, ⓦwww.restaurantebiocenter.es; ⓜLiceu, map, pp.66–67. One of the longest-running Raval veggie places, with a restaurant-bar across the road from the original health-food store. The fixed-price *menú del dia* starts serving at 1pm, with soup and a trawl through the salad bar for a first course, followed by market-fresh mains. For dinner, they dim the lights, add candles and sounds, and turn out a few more exotic dishes, from red veg curry to ginger tofu (mains €7–10). Daily 1–4pm, plus dinner Thurs–Sat 8–11.15pm. Inexpensive.

**Illa de Gràcia** c/Sant Domènec 19, Gràcia ⓣ932 380 229, ⓦwww.illadegracia.com; ⓜDiagonal, map, p.134. Sleek vegetarian dining room where the food is a cut above – think grilled tofu, stuffed aubergine gratin or wholewheat spaghetti *carbonara*. The veggie lasagne is a weekend special and the tofu burger also comes highly recommended. Tues–Fri 1–4pm & 9pm–midnight, Sat & Sun 2–4pm & 9pm–midnight; closed mid-Aug to mid-Sept. Inexpensive.

**Juicy Jones** c/Cardenal Casañas 7, Barri Gòtic ⓣ933 024 330; ⓜLiceu, map, pp.54–55. Veggie and vegan restaurant and juice bar with a *menú del día* that touches all corners of the world – cashew, carrot and coriander soup could be followed by pumpkin-stuffed gnocchi. The restaurant inhabits a mural-and-graffiti-splashed cellar at the back – juices are squeezed and soya milkshakes whizzed at the front bar. Another outlet in the Raval (c/de l'Hospital 74) offers more space, a similar menu and the same young, funky vibe. No credit cards. Daily 10am–midnight. Inexpensive.

**Sesamo** c/Sant Antoni Abat 52, El Raval ⓣ934 416 411, ⓦwww.sesamo-bcn.com; ⓜSant Antoni, map, pp.66–67. Innovative yet inexpensive vegetarian cooking that relies on fresh, mostly organic ingredients and influences from all over the globe. Set lunch is a steal, though even eating á la carte at night, you're unlikely to top €25. Meals are served 1–3.30pm & 9–11.30pm, but outside kitchen times it's open as a bar. Mon & Wed–Sat 1–5pm & 8pm–1am, Sun 8pm–1am. Moderate.

€18, though if you come for weekday lunch there's a really good-value *menú del dia*. Mon–Thurs 1.30–4pm & 8.30pm–midnight, Fri 1.30–4pm & 8.30pm–1am, Sat 8.30pm–1am, Sun 8.30pm–midnight.

**Shunka** c/Sagristans 5 ⓣ934 124 991; ⓜJaume I. Locals think this is the best Japanese restaurant in the old town – it's certainly always busy, so it's best to make an advance reservation, though you might lucky on spec if you're prepared to eat early or late. The open kitchen and the bustling staff are half the show, while the food – sushi to udon noodles – is really good. You can eat for around €30. Tues–Fri 1.30–3.30pm & 8.30–11.30pm, Sat & Sun 2–4pm & 8.30–11.30pm; closed two weeks in Aug.

## El Raval

For locations, see map, pp.66–67.

### Inexpensive

**Elisabets c/d'Elisabets 2** ☎933 175 826; Ⓜ**Catalunya**. Reliable Catalan home cooking served at cramped tables in a jovial brick-walled dining room. Chain-smoking locals breakfast on a sandwich and a glass of wine, the hearty lunchtime *menú del dia* is hard to beat for price, or you can just have tapas, sandwiches and drinks at the bar. No credit cards. Meals Mon–Sat 1–4pm, bar open Mon–Sat 8am–11pm; closed Aug.

**Mesón David c/de les Carretes 63** ☎934 415 934; Ⓜ**Paral.lel**. This down-to-earth Galician bar-restaurant is a firm favourite with neighbourhood families who bring their kids before they can even walk. The weekday *menú* is a steal – maybe some lentil broth followed by a grilled, butterflied trout and home-made *flan* – though it's the octopus and the *combinado Gallego* ("ham, salami, ear") that has the locals purring. There's a bang on the clog-gong for anyone who tips. Daily except Mon 1–4pm & 8pm–midnight.

**Pollo Rico c/de Sant Pau 31** ☎934 413 184; Ⓜ**Liceu**. Barcelona's original "greasy spoon" has been here forever and, while it's not to everyone's taste, if you're in the mood for good spit-roast chicken and a glass of rot-gut wine, served in double-quick time, this is the place. The upstairs dining room is a tad more sophisticated (only a tad) – either way, you'll be hard pushed to spend €15 from a long menu of Spanish and Catalan staples. No credit cards. Daily 10am–midnight; closed Wed.

**Romesco c/de l'Arc de Sant Agustí s/n** ☎934 189 381; Ⓜ**Liceu**. Old Barcelona hands talk lovingly of the *Romesco* – and as long as you accept its limitations (dining in a strip-lit corridor, Billy Goat Gruff waiters) you can hardly go wrong, as the most expensive thing on the menu is a grilled sirloin at €8

and most dishes go for €5 or less. It's basic but good, with big salads, country broths and grilled veg to start, followed by things like tuna steak, lamb chops or grilled prawns from the market, scattered with parsley and chopped garlic. If you spend more than €15 each you've probably eaten someone else's dinner as well. No credit cards. Mon–Sat 1–11.30pm; closed Aug.

### Moderate

**Ànima c/dels Angels 6** ☎933 424 912; Ⓜ**Liceu**. Sleek and arty, but also informal, this attracts a youngish crowd who come for the immaculately presented, seasonally influenced fusion cooking – courgette flowers and mussels tempura, followed by monkfish with a garlic and pistachio crust are typical summer dishes, with most mains costing around €14. It's an especially good deal at lunchtime, and the staff are unfailingly charming. Mon–Sat 1–4pm & 9pm–midnight.

**Bar Ra Pl. de la Garduña 3** ☎615 959 872, Ⓦ**www.ratown.com**; Ⓜ**Liceu**. Extremely hip place behind the Boqueria market, with a groove-ridden music policy, a funky feel and a sunny *terrassa*. "It's not a restaurant", they proclaim, but who are they kidding? Breakfast runs from 10am, there's a *menú del dia* served every day (weekends as well) from 1–4pm, with dinner from 9pm until

▲ Bar Ra

midnight. The menu is eclectic to say the least – Thai spring rolls to Catalan sausage – but with the market on the doorstep it's all good stuff. Daily 9am–2am.

**Ca l'Estevet c/Valldonzella 46 ☎933 024 186; ⓂUniversitat.** It's had its heyday, with scarcely a celebrity photo dating later than the 1980s (including a fresh-faced Gary Lineker, from his time with FC Barcelona). But the chatty English-speaking owner works the room with gusto, glad-handing locals and tourists alike, and talking up the short menu. Entrecôte and the *cabrito* (goat) are the house specials, otherwise it's a market-led daily changing menu, with most mains around €10–15. Portions aren't huge, but this is a reliable place for a decent meal. Tues–Sat 1.30–4pm & 8.30–11.30pm, Sun 1.30–4pm; closed two weeks in Aug.

**Fil. Manila c/de les Ramelleres 3 ☎933 186 487; ⓂCatalunya.** There's a token effort at bamboo cladding, but this resolute mom-and-pop Filipino establishment is little more than an extension of the family kitchen – the radio or TV provides background, and the kids are fed alongside customers. Sizzling is what the menu does best, but there are warming soups, grilled fish in banana leaves, sautéed meat or fish with garlic sauce, barbecued pork ribs – all good and hearty dishes. No credit cards. Daily except Tues 11am–4.30pm & 7.30pm–1am.

**Moti Mahal c/de Sant Pau 103 ☎933 293 252, ⓦwww.motimahalbcn.com; ⓂParal.lel.** Indian restaurants have sprouted all over the Raval in recent years, and most don't really make the grade, as the spice level is toned down for the local market. But the *Moti Mahal* is considered one of the more authentic places with a typical menu of biryanis, tandoori dishes and curries in various styles and strengths, all around €8 to €12. It's not much to look at, but what proper curryhouse is? In any case, if it's good enough for Harrison Ford, whose picture is proudly displayed, it's good enough for us. Daily except Tues noon–3.30pm & 8pm–midnight.

**La Verònica Ramba de Raval 2–4 ☎933 293 303; ⓂLiceu/Sant Antoni.** Funky, retro pizzeria *La Verònica* fits right into the new-look Rambla de Raval. There are loads of crispy pizzas (mostly vegetarian, between €10 and €14) and inventive salads, enjoyed by a resolutely young and up-for-a-night-out crowd. Daily noon–1am; closed 2 weeks in Aug.

### Expensive

**Biblioteca c/Junta del Comerç 28 ☎934 126 221, ⓦwww.bibliotecarestaurant. com; ⓂLiceu.** One of the most agreeable places to sample what Barcelona tends to call "creative cuisine", where the market-led, seasonally changing menu never fails to impress. The name's a nod to the library of cookbooks on display, and from the open kitchen emerge fish dishes that might be cooked Japanese- or Basque-style, robust lamb given the local treatment (with parsnip and turnip), or the signature dish of venison pie with flaky pastry served with a zippy veg purée of the day. Meals cost around €40, and clued-up English-speaking staff make for enjoyable, hassle-free dining. Mon–Fri 8pm–midnight, Sat 1–3.30pm & 8pm–midnight; closed two weeks in Aug.

### Sant Pere

For locations, see map, p.74.

### Inexpensive

**L'Econòmic Pl. de Sant Agusti Vell 13 ☎933 196 494; ⓂJaume I.** The beautifully tiled dining room dates back to 1932, an eye-catching backdrop for a hearty three-course set lunch, served up, as the name implies, for a very reasonable price. Well-cooked standards (grilled pork or chicken escalopes, a fish of the day) alternate with finer fare – like a pasta salad with black olive paste and salmon. You may have to wait under the arcades outside until a table becomes available. No credit cards. Mon–Fri 12.30–4.30pm; closed Aug.

**Lar O'Marulo c/Bou de Sant Pere 13 ☎933 105 798; ⓂUrquinaona.** A popular lunchtime-only place for local workers. It's a set meal, with a choice of eight starters and eight mains, plus dessert and wine, at a knock-down price. The food is straightforward and Spanish, fresh from the market, served in a busy, chatter-filled dining room. Mon–Fri 12.30–4.30pm.

### Moderate

**Cuines Santa Caterina Mercat Santa Caterina, Avgda. Francesc Cambó s/n ☎932 689 918, ⓦwww.cuinessantacaterina.com; ⓂJaume I.** The neighbourhood market has a ravishing open-plan restaurant, with tables set under soaring wooden rafters. The food touches all bases – pasta to sushi, Catalan rice dishes

CAFÉS, TAPAS BARS AND RESTAURANTS | Restaurants

to Thai curries – with daily specials rolling along an airport-style departure board above the open kitchen. Portions aren't enormous, but they're not expensive either (most things cost €9–12) – or you can just drink and munch superior tapas at the horseshoe bar. Bar daily 8am–midnight; restaurant 1–4pm & 8–11.30pm, Thurs–Sat until 12.30am.

**Pla de la Garsa** c/Assaonadors 13 ☎933 152 413; Ⓜ Jaume I. Seventeenth-century stone-and-beam house that's a relaxing place to sip wine, and eat pâté, cheese, sliced meats and other refined fare. Dishes run from €5 to €10, or there are various tasting menus available. Daily 8pm–2am.

### Expensive

 *page 74*

**Espai Sucre** c/de la Princesa 53 ☎932 681 630, Ⓦ www.espaisucre.com; Ⓜ Jaume I. The "Sugar Space" takes the current fad for food deconstruction off at a tangent by serving pretty much just dessert – these are inspired creations by Jordi Butrón, who assembles flavours and textures with the skill of a magician. There's a three-course or five-course seasonally changing pudding menu, with a small selection of savoury "mains" to pad out the experience. And check the website for a schedule of dessert demos and hands-on courses. Tues–Thurs 9–11.30pm, Fri & Sat sittings at 8.30pm & 11pm; closed Aug.

### Very expensive

**Comerç 24** c/Comerc 24 ☎933 192 102, Ⓦ www.carlesabellan.com; Ⓜ Jaume I. Chef Carles Abellan presents "glocal" cooking (ie, global + local): dishes from around the world, interpreted locally by a master of invention. In an oh-so-cool stripped-down warehouse interior the meal comes tapas-style, mixing flavours and textures with seeming abandon but to calculated effect (such as *foie gras* and truffle hamburger, shot glasses of frothy

---

## Catalan food and dishes

Traditional Catalan food places heavy emphasis on meat, olive oil, garlic, fruit and salad. The cuisine is typified by a willingness to mix flavours, so savoury dishes cooked with nuts or fruit are common, as are salads using both cooked and raw ingredients.

**Meat** is usually grilled and served with a few fried potatoes or salad, though Catalan sausage served with a pool of haricot beans is a classic menu item. Stewed veal and other casseroles are common, while poultry is sometimes mixed with seafood (chicken and prawns) or fruit (chicken or duck with prunes or pears) for tastes very definitely out of the Spanish mainstream. In season, **game** is also available, especially partridge, hare, rabbit and boar.

As for **fish and seafood**, you'll be offered hake, tuna, squid or cuttlefish even in cheap restaurants, and the local anchovies are superb. Cod is often salted and turns up in *esquiexada*, a summer salad of salt cod, tomatoes, onions and olives. Fish stews are a local speciality, though the mainstays of seafood restaurants are the rice-and noodle-based dishes. **Paella** comes originally from Valencia, but as that region was historically part of Catalunya, the dish has been enthusiastically adopted as Catalunya's own. More certainly Catalan is **fideuà**, thin noodles served with seafood – you stir in the fiery *all i olli* (garlic mayonnaise) provided. **Arròs negre** (black rice, cooked with squid ink) is another local delicacy.

**Vegetables** rarely amount to more than a few French fries or boiled potatoes, though there are some authentic Catalan vegetable dishes, like spinach tossed with raisins and pine nuts, or *samfaina*, a ratatouille-like stew. Spring is the season for **calçots**, huge spring onions, which are roasted whole and eaten with a spicy *romesco* dipping sauce. Autumn sees the arrival of **wild mushrooms**, mixed with rice, omelettes, salads or scrambled eggs. In winter, a dish of **stewed beans or lentils** is also a popular starter, almost certainly flavoured with bits of sausage, meat and fat.

For dessert, apart from fresh **fruit**, there's always *crème caramel* (flan in Catalan) – fantastic when home-made – though *crema Catalana* is the local choice, more like a crème brûlée, with a caramelized sugar coating. Or you might be offered *músic*, nuts and dried fruit served with a glass of sweet *moscatel* wine.

soup, tuna sashimi on pizza). Prices are high (around €70–80 a head), although you can have a cheaper, less formal meal at Abellan's Eixample tapas bar, *TapaÇ24*, where the food has something of the same panache. Tues–Sat 1.30–3.30pm & 8.30pm–12.30am; closed two weeks in Aug.

## La Ribera

For locations, see map, p.78.

### Inexpensive

**Bar Salvador** c/dels Canvis Nous 8 ☎933 101 041; Ⓜ Jaume I/Barceloneta. Almost everything in this simple workers' café costs between €4 and €7 which is why tables are packed at lunch, but you shouldn't have to wait in line long. Fillets of fish in egg batter, grilled steak with potato wedges, chickpeas with sausage, or garlic chicken are examples from a changing menu of six or seven starters and mains plus a few classic puds. Lunch starts at 1.30pm – before that, it's filled crusty sandwiches for Catalan breakfast. Mon–Fri 9am–5pm.

**Casa Delfín** Pg. del Born 36 ☎933 195 088; Ⓜ Jaume I/Barceloneta. On the Born's main drag, and rather out of place among the boutiques and delis, this old-school paper-tablecloth bar-restaurant packs in the locals for a cheap-and-cheerful *menú del dia*. Choose from up to ten fish and meat choices, from grills to stews, topped off by home-made desserts or fruit. Add a coffee and the whole blowout shouldn't top €12 per person. Mon–Sat 8am–5pm; closed Aug.

### Moderate

**Al Passatore** Pl. del Palau 8 ☎933 197 851; Ⓜ Barceloneta. The pizzas are immense, and definitely the main event as other dishes can be disappointing. In good weather you'll need to get your name on the list if you want an outdoor table – but the fast turnover means there's usually space here, or in the bigger branch across the square (enter at Pl. de les Olles), or at one of the other city locations (including Port Olímpic). Mon–Thurs 1pm–12.30am, Fri–Sun 1pm–1am.

**Mar de la Ribera** c/Sombrerers 7 ☎933 151 336; Ⓜ Jaume I. A cosy little place around the back of Santa Maria del Mar serving simple Galician-style seafood at decent prices (dishes €6–12). Try any of the steaks

and fillets – hake, salmon, tuna, sole, calamari – dressed with oil, garlic and chopped parsley, accompanied by tasty platters of grilled vegetables. Mixed fried fish and paella are also highly recommended. Mon 8–11.30pm, Tues–Sat 1–4pm & 8–11.30pm.

**Salero** c/Rec 60 ☎933 198 022; Ⓜ Barceloneta. A crisp, modern space fashioned from a former salt-cod warehouse – if white is your colour, you'll enjoy the experience. The food's Mediterranean-Asian, such as an aubergine, coconut and pumpkin curry or a *mee goreng* (fried noodle) of the day, with most dishes costing €10–17. Mon–Wed 1.30–4pm & 8.30pm–midnight, Thurs–Sun 1.30–4pm & 8.30pm–1am; closed 2 weeks in Aug.

**Senyor Parellada** c/Argenteria 37 ☎933 105 094; Ⓜ Jaume I. An utterly gorgeous renovation of an eighteenth-century building has kept the arcaded interior and splashed the walls yellow. Food is Catalan through and through – cuttlefish and cod, home-style cabbage rolls, duck with figs, a *papillote* of beans with herbs – served from a long menu that doesn't bother dividing starters from mains. Most dishes cost between €8 and €15, while more than a dozen puds await those who struggle through. Daily 1–4pm & 8.30pm–midnight.

**Wushu** Avgda. del Marquès de l'Argentera 1 ☎933 107 313, ⓦwww .wushu-restaurant.com; Ⓜ Barceloneta. If you're only going to eat one non-Catalan meal in Barcelona, this is where you should come – Aussie-chef Bradley's cool Asian wok bar, turning out super-authentic *pad Thais*, Malaysian *laksas*, Vietnamese rice paper rolls, red and green curries, Chinese *lo mein* noodles and the like. You can eat really well for around €25 or so, and the kitchen is always open during the adver-tised hours so it's one place in Barcelona where you don't have to wait until 10pm for your dinner. Tues–Sat 1pm–midnight, Sun 1–4pm.

### Expensive

**Set Portes** Pg. d'Isabel II 14 ☎933 192 950 or 933 193 033, ⓦwww.grup7portes.com; Ⓜ Barceloneta. A wood-panelled classic with the names of its famous clientele much to the fore – they've all eaten here, Errol Flynn to Yoko Ono. The decor in the "Seven Doors" has barely changed in almost 200

## What's cooking?

The best chef in the world, by common consent, is Catalan. **Ferran Adrià**, a self-taught chef from Barcelona, presides over *El Bulli* (Ⓦ www.elbulli.com), his triple-Michelin-starred restaurant just outside the town of Roses on the Costa Brava. Dinner here costs €200 a head, but it's barely worth worrying about the price because the tables are booked solid until the next millennium. It's strange, because what Adrià does is less like cooking and more like chemistry, spending the winter months each year when the restaurant is closed refining his techniques in his Barcelona "laboratory". He is the man responsible for breaking down dishes into their constituent ingredients and then playing with them – turning food into foam, distilling vegetable essence into gelatin blocks, injecting a seafood reduction into Rice Krispies, or adding herbs, cheese or even perfume to ice cream. You're either going to think this is fantastic or plain ridiculous but Adrià has spawned a generation of regional Spanish chefs – Jordi Vilà, Paco Guzmán, Andoni Luis Aduriz, Carles Abellan, Ramon Freixa, Xavier Pellicer, Sergi Arola – who are challenging contemporary tastes in an equally inventive fashion. Many are cooking right now in Barcelona, so go and see what the fuss is all about.

years and, while very elegant, it's not exclusive – you should book ahead, though, as the queues can be horrendous. The renowned rice dishes are fairly reasonably priced (€13–18), but for a full meal you're looking at more than €40 a head. Daily 1pm–1am.

### Barceloneta

For locations, see map, p.91.

#### Inexpensive

**Can Maño** c/Baluard 12 ℡ 933 193 082; Ⓜ Barceloneta. There's rarely a tourist in sight in this old-fashioned locals' diner, jam-packed with formica tables. Fried or grilled fish is the thing here, such as sardines, mullet or calamari, supplemented by a few daily seafood specials and basic meat dishes. Expect rough house wine and absolutely no frills, but it's an authentic experience, which is likely to cost you less than €12 a head. No credit cards. Mon–Fri 8am–5.30pm & 8–11pm, Sat noon–5pm; closed Aug.

#### Moderate

**Can Manel** Pg. Joan de Borbó 60 ℡ 932 215 013; Ⓜ Barceloneta. An institution since 1870, which fills very quickly, inside and out, because the food is both good and reasonably priced. If you want lunch outside on the shaded terrace, get here by 1.00pm. Paella, *fideuà* and *arròs a banda* are staples – from around €13 per person – while the catch of the day, usually simply grilled, ranges from cuttlefish to sole, bream or

hake (up to €22). A weekday lunchtime *menú* keeps the cost down, but there's usually not much fish or seafood on this. Daily 1–4pm & 8pm–midnight.

**Can Ros** c/Almirall Aixada 7 ℡ 932 215 049; Ⓜ Barceloneta. This has long been one of the best places to sample paella, *arròs negre* or a *fideuà*, all of which cost around €12 – as almost everywhere, rice servings are for a minimum of two people. The only real drawback is that there's no outside seating, and the tables are packed in close together, upstairs and down, but it's a comfortable, no-hurry kind of place. Daily except Wed 1–5pm & 8pm–midnight.

#### Expensive

**Antiga Casa Solé** c/Sant Carles 4 ℡ 932 215 012, Ⓦ www.restaurantcansole.com; Ⓜ Barceloneta. Founded in 1903, it was here – it's claimed – that *sarsuela* (Catalan fish stew) was invented. Since then, the quiet, formal *Casa Solé* has been dishing up market-fresh fish and seafood, either in stews or casseroles or simply grilled, sautéed or mixed with rice – baked squid and grilled cod are both house specialities. Count on a good €40 a head. Tues–Sat 1.30–4pm & 8.30–11pm, Sun 1.30–4pm; closed two weeks in Aug.

**Can Majo** c/Almirall Aixada 23 ℡ 932 215 818; Ⓜ Barceloneta. You can almost sit on the beach at this quality seafood restaurant – the summer *terrassa* is fringed by a blue picket fence, and the whole world saunters by as you tuck into reliably good rice, *fideuà*, fish stew or grilled fish. The menu changes daily according to what's off the boat; expect to spend €40–50 a head (and make a reservation if you want an outside table at the weekend). Tues–Sat 1–4pm & 8–11pm, Sun 1–4pm.

**Can Ramonet c/Maquinista 17 ☎933 193 064;** Ⓜ**Barceloneta.** Reputedly the oldest restaurant in the port area, it has the added attraction of a shady *terrassa* in front of the neighbourhood market. The food's good – splendid paella, plus whatever's fresh from the market that day – though with fish and seafood mains running at around €17–25 meals can turn out to be quite pricey. You can always opt instead for the rustic front bar where the tapas (from €8) are piled high on wooden barrels. Daily 1–4pm & 8pm– midnight; closed Sun dinner & Aug.

## Port Olímpic

For locations, see map, p.93.

### Moderate

**Agua Pg. Marítim 30 ☎932 251 272, ⓦwww .aguadeltragaluz.com;** Ⓜ**Ciutadella-Vila Olímpica.** Much the nicest boardwalk restaurant on the beachfront strip, perfect for brunch, though if the weather's iffy you can opt for the sleek, split-level dining room. The menu is seasonal, contemporary Mediterranean – grills, *risotti*, pasta, salads and tapas – and the prices are pretty fair (meals up to €30), so it's usually busy. Daily 1–4pm & 8–11.30pm, Fri & Sat until 12.30am.

### Expensive

**Bestial c/Ramon Trias Fargas 2–4 ☎932 240 407, ⓦwww.bestialdeltragaluz.com;** Ⓜ**Ciutadella-Vila Olímpica.** Right beside Frank Gehry's fish (under the wooden bridge) you'll find a stylish terrace-garden in front of the beach, great for an *al fresco* lunch. Inside the feel is sharp and minimalist, while the cooking's Mediterranean, mainly Italian, with dishes given an original twist. Rice, pasta and wood-fired pizzas are in the €9–14 range, with other dishes up to €21. At weekends there's DJ music and drinks until 2am. Daily 1–4pm & 8–11.30pm, Fri & Sat until 12.30am.

**El Cangrejo Loco Moll de Gregal 29–30, upper level ☎932 211 748, ⓦwww .elcangrejoloco.com;** Ⓜ**Ciutadella-Vila Olímpica.** The large outdoor terrace or huge picture windows at the "Crazy Crab" offer panoramas of the local coast and marina. The fish and shellfish are first-rate, with the

catch changing daily, but a mixed fried-fish plate or broad beans with prawns are typically Catalan starters. The paella can be thoroughly recommended too, and the service is spot-on. Daily 1pm–1am.

## Poble Nou

For locations, see map, p.85.

### Expensive

**Escribà Ronda del Litoral 42, Platja Bogatell ☎932 210 729, ⓦwww.escriba.es;** Ⓜ**Ciutadella-Vila Olímpica, or bus #36 from Port Vell.** Glorified beach shack – a *xiringuito* in the parlance – that's enough off the beaten track (a 15min walk along the prom from the Port Olímpic) to mark you out as in the know. The paellas and *fideuàs* (from €13–16) fly out of the kitchen, daily fish specials are more like €20, and there's a ten percent terrace surcharge, but what the hell – the food and views are great. Desserts are sensational cakes and pastries from the Escribà family patisserie. Tues–Sat 11am–1am, Sun 11am–4pm; restricted hours in winter, but usually open weekend lunch.

### Very expensive

**Els Pescadors Pl. del Prim 1 ☎932 252 018, ⓦwww.elspescadors.com;** Ⓜ**Poble Nou.** It's a difficult call, but if you had to choose just one top-class fish restaurant in Barcelona, this would be it. It's hidden away in a pretty square with gnarled trees in the back alleys of Rambla de Poble Nou, and lunch outside on a sunny day just can't be beaten (reservations advised). The daily changing menu runs to half a dozen or more fresh fish dishes, and half a dozen others involving rice or *fideuà*, with a whole separate section for the house special salt cod (try it with *samfaina*, like a Catalan ratatouille). Most dishes cost €10–25 and if you don't go mad you'll escape for around €50 a head, though it's easy to spend more. Daily 1–4pm & 8pm–midnight.

## Poble Sec

For locations, see map, p.104.

### Moderate

**Bella Napoli c/Margarit 14 ☎934 425 056;** Ⓜ**Paral.lel/Poble Sec.** Authentic Neapolitan pizzeria, right down to the cheery waiters and cheesy pop music. The pizzas – the best in the city – come straight from the depths of a beehive-shaped oven, or there's a big range of *antipasti*, pastas, *risotti* and veal *scaloppine,* with almost everything priced between €8 and €12. Tues 8.30pm–midnight, Wed–Sun 1.30–4.30pm & 8.30pm–midnight.

**La Bodegueta c/de Blai 47** ☎**934 420 846;** Ⓜ**Poble Sec.** Catalan taverna with food like mother used to make – a relaxed Sunday lunch here brings local families out in force. It's a good-natured, red-check-tablecloth-and-barrels kind of place, specializing in *torrades*, salads and grills – try the excellent grilled veg platter. Tues–Sun 1–4pm & 8.30pm–midnight.

🏃 **La Soleá Pl. del Sortidor 14** ☎**934 410 124;** Ⓜ**Poble Sec.** A great place for sunny days, with a *terrassa* in a tucked-away square – meanwhile, in the cheery if cramped interior, there's a backdrop of vibrant colours and young guns behind the counter singing along lustily to *flamenco nuevo* sounds. The food is international bistro-style, and pretty good value – salads and snacky stuff to start, followed by proper hamburgers, tandoori chicken, lasagne or a reassuringly old-fashioned Sunday plate of *fideuà* (Catalan noodles). No credit cards. Tues–Sat noon–midnight, Sun noon–5pm.

🏃 **La Tomaquera c/Margarit 58, no phone;** Ⓜ**Paral.lel/Poble Sec.** Sit down in this chatter-filled tavern and the bread arrives with a dish of olives and two quails' eggs – and any delicacy ends there as the chefs set to hacking steaks and chops from great sides and ribs of meat. It's not for the faint-hearted, but the grilled chicken will be the best you've ever had and the entrecôtes are enormous. Locals limber up with an appetizer of pan-fried snails with *chorizo* and tomato. Most main dishes cost €7–11. No credit cards. Tues–Sat 1.30–3.45pm & 8.30–10.45pm; closed Aug.

**Tivoli's Bistro c/Magalhaes 35** ☎**934 414 017,** Ⓦ**www.tivolisbistro.com;** Ⓜ**Paral.lel/Poble Sec.** Home-style Thai cuisine, toned down for local tastes but reasonably priced and run by a nice Catalan-Thai couple, who also organize cooking classes. A set meal (around €25 per person, dishes change weekly) is delivered to your table, usually incorporating a starter or two, a red or green curry, a vegetable and fish dish, and Thai noodles. Tues–Sat 9–11pm; closed 1st week Jan, & Aug to mid-Sept.

## Dreta de l'Eixample

For locations, see map, p.115.

### Moderate

**El Japonés Ptge. de la Concepció 2** ☎**934 872 592,** Ⓦ**www.eljaponesdeltragaluz.com;** Ⓜ**Diagonal.** Designer-style – gun-metal grey interior, black-clad staff, sharp service – at moderate prices gives this minimalist Japanese restaurant the edge over its more traditional city rivals. Tick your sushi, sashimi, tempura and noodle choices from the long menu and hand it to the waiter; average meal cost is around €25 a head. Mon–Thurs & Sun 1.30–4pm & 8.30pm–midnight, Fri & Sat 1.30–4pm & 8pm–1am.

### Expensive

**O'Nabo de Lugo c/de Pau Claris 169** ☎**932 153 047;** Ⓜ**Diagonal.** A la carte meals in this

## Room service

The hotels are where it's at for some some of the city's fanciest, often Michelin-starred, dining and if you're staying at any of the following you've got Barcelona's most exciting cooking right on the premises. Currently making waves is Joan Roca's **Moo** at the über-fashionable *Hotel Omm* (Ⓦwww.hotelomm.es), while Martín Berasategui brings his highly rated Basque style to **Lasarte** in the *Condes de Barcelona* (Ⓦwww.condesdebarcelona.com). Madrid-based chef Sergi Arola lends his name to the designer tapas place **Arola**, located at the glam waterfront *Arts Barcelona* (Ⓦwww.ritzcarlton.com/hotels/barcelona), and it's renowned Catalan chef Carles Gaig at the helm of **Gaig** in *Hotel Cram* (Ⓦwww.hotelcram.com). Graduates of Ferran Adrià's famed *El Bulli* restaurant are thick on the ground too, whether it's Jordi Ruiz at **Neri Restaurante** at the boutique *Hotel Neri* (Ⓦwww.hotelneri.com) or Ramon Freixa's **Actual** at the *Grand Hotel Central* (Ⓦwww.grandhotelcentral.com).

renowned Galician seafood restaurant can easily top €50, but arrive at lunch for the cut-price *menú del dia* and you'll get to sample standards like thick, meaty broth or *botifarra* (sausage) and potatoes; for more choice (and for some fish), trade up to the *menú especial*. It's the sort of place where the gruff, waistcoated waiters tend to know the lunching locals by name. Mon–Sat 1–4pm & 8.30pm–midnight.

**Tragaluz** Ptge. de la Concepció 5 ☎934 870 621, Ⓦwww.grupotragaluz.com/tragaluz; ⓂDiagonal. Attracts beautiful people by the score, and the classy Mediterranean-with-knobs-on cooking, served under a glass roof (*tragaluz* means "skylight"), doesn't disappoint. Mains cost €16–25, though cheaper eats are served downstairs courtesy of the *Tragarràpic* menu (served daily 1pm–midnight), where things like *fajitas* or a club sandwich cater for those fresh off the *modernista* trail (La Pedrera is just across the way). Daily 1.30–4pm & 8.30pm–midnight, Thurs–Sat until 1am.

## Sagrada Família and Glòries

For locations, see map, pp.122–123.

### Moderate

**Piazzenza** Avgda. Gaudí 27–29 ☎934 363 817; ⓂSagrada Família. A reliable standby just 5min walk from the Sagrada Família. There are tapas, drink and pizzas, served outdoors in summer, and you can eat for around €15–20. It's a pretty buzzy place at night, just as popular with locals as with tourists. Daily 1pm–1am; closed 2 weeks in Aug.

### Very expensive

**Alkimia** c/Indústria 79 ☎932 076 115; ⓂSagrada Família. Ask Barcelona foodies which is the best new-wave Catalan restaurant in town and once they've all stopped bickering, this is the one they'll probably plump for. "Alchemy" is what's promised by the name, and that's what chef Jordi Vilà delivers in bitingly minimalist style – think *pa amb tomàquet* (Catalan bread rubbed with tomato and olive oil), only liquidized and served in a shot glass. It's a Michelin-starred operation, so reservations are vital and the bill might reach €100 a head. Mon–Fri 1.30–3.30pm & 8.30–11pm; closed 2 weeks in Aug & Easter.

**Gorria** c/de la Diputacio 421 ☎932 451 164, Ⓦwww.restaurantegorria.com; ⓂMonumental. This elegant family-owned restaurant serves the finest seasonal Basque cuisine, like *pochas de Sanguesa* (a sort of white-bean stew), clams and hake in salsa verde, or wood-grilled lamb and suckling pig. Prices are on the high side (€50 a head and upwards), but this is regional Spanish cooking of the highest order. Mon 1–3.30pm, Tues–Sat 1–3.30pm & 9–11.30pm; closed Aug & Easter.

## Esquerra de l'Eixample ⑪

For locations, see map, pp.128–129.

### Inexpensive

**La Flauta** c/d'Aribau 23 ☎933 237 038; ⓂUniversitat. One of the city's best-value lunch menus sees potential diners queueing for tables daily – get there before 2pm to avoid the rush. It's a handsome bar-restaurant of dark wood and deep colours, and while the name recognizes the house speciality gourmet sandwiches (a *flauta* is a thin baguette), there's also tapas served all day and a really good *menú del dia* that depends on what's available at the market. Mon–Sat 8am–1am.

**O Pote** Pl. del Dr. Letamendi 29 ☎934 541 881, ⓂPasseig de Gràcia/Universitat. For a cheap uptown meal in a convivial atmosphere this family-run Galician bar-restaurant might just do the trick. Fried and grilled fish and seafood is the speciality, from baby squid to garlic prawns, served on paper tablecloths with absolutely no airs or graces. No credit cards. Mon–Sat 1–4pm & 8–11pm.

### Moderate

**Hanoi** Pl. Dr. Letamendi 27 ☎934 515 686, ⓂPasseig de Gràcia/Universitat. Ostensibly a Vietnamese restaurant, though many of the tasty dishes – from little baskets of *dim sum* to steamed bream with soy and ginger – tell of wider Southeast Asian sources. No matter, the daily weekday lunch is widely recognized as a good deal and the sleek restaurant fills quickly. There's another uptown branch, *Hanoi II*, further out, at Avgda. Sarrià 37, with a similar menu. Daily 12.30–4pm & 8.30pm–midnight.

**Out of China** c/Muntaner 100 ☎934 515 555; ⓂProvença. Most Chinese restaurants in Barcelona are pretty bland, which is not a

It's hardly surprising that, in a city that looks so good, restaurateurs have turned to some of Barcelona's extraordinary *modernista* buildings as backdrops to their businesses. Most famous is probably **El Quatre Gats** (c/Montsió 3, Barri Gòtic, ℡933 024 140, ⓦwww.4gats.com), the richly furnished old tavern that was the haunt of Picasso and his contemporaries. Now it's a mainstream Catalan restaurant and bar aimed squarely at tourists – the set lunch is your best bet for a reasonably priced meal here, which will give you plenty of time to take in the remarkable decor. That's also the case at the **Hotel España** (c/Sant Pau 9–11, El Raval, ℡933 181 758, ⓦwww.hotelespanya.com), where an amazing tiled dining room and elaborate Art Nouveau flourishes await expectant diners. Meanwhile, one of the best nights out is the glam experience at **Casa Calvet** (c/de Casp 48, Eixample, ℡934 124 012, ⓦwww.casacalvet.es), the wonderfully decorated townhouse that a young Antoni Gaudí built for a Catalan industrialist. Of the three, this is the only one with a serious reputation for its food – modern Catalan cuisine, and especially known for its desserts – where you can't expect much change out of €100.

charge you can level at the handsome space that is *Out of China*. The black tables, red chairs, frilly lanterns and jazz-lounge sounds set the tone for a contemporary Chinese menu that's particularly notable for its vegetarian options – wok-fried aubergine with market greens or tofu curry sit alongside soya chicken in ginger or crispy pork. The food doesn't always hit the heights, but the lunchtime *menú* is a good deal and even at night prices won't break the bank, with most dishes in the €8–10 range. Mon–Sat 1–4pm & 8pm–midnight, Sun 1–4pm.

**El Racó d'en Balta** c/Aribau 125 ℡934 531 044, ⓦwww.racodenbalta.com; Ⓜ**Provença**. This is a very funky place to eat, with a vibrant colour- and sculpture-splashed interior that petty much defies description. The weekday lunch is a good deal, otherwise you can eat for around €25 from a Mediterranean market-led menu; at night, the local hipsters lend the bar a certain style. Mon–Thurs 1–3.45pm & 9–11pm, Fri 1–3.45pm & 9–11.30pm, Sat 9–11.30pm; closed 1 week in Jan, 3 weeks in Aug & Easter.

### Very expensive

**Cinc Sentits** c/Aribau 58 ℡933 239 490, ⓦwww.cincsentits.com; Ⓜ**Passeig de Gràcia/ Universitat**. Dishes are assembled with great flair in this renowned contemporary "tasting kitchen" and though some find the whole experience a bit overly formal there's no doubting the skill at the "Five Senses". Fish with black-olive compôte and lemon marmalade is a typical offering, with most mains costing €20–25, though various

tasting menus (from €65) are the best way to get the measure of the place. Mon 1.30–3.30pm, Tues–Sat 1.30–3.30pm & 8.30–11pm.

**Gaig** c/Aragó 214 ℡934 291 017, ⓦwww .restaurantgaig.com; Ⓜ**Passeig de Gràcia/ Universitat**. The Gaig family restaurant was first founded in 1869 out in the Horta neighbourhood, but under fourth-generation family member, Carles Gaig, it has now found a sleek downtown home at the *Hotel Cram*. It's had a towering reputation (and a Michelin star) for years for quality reinterpretations of traditional Catalan dishes, so a typical *arròs* (rice) dish might combine *foie gras*, endive and citrus flavour. When starters can cost €35, and the *menú degustació* is €100 or so, you're talking about a true special-occasion place, and reservations are essential. Mon 9–11pm, Tues–Sat 1–3.30pm & 9–11pm; closed three weeks in Aug.

### Gràcia

For locations, see map, p.134.

### Inexpensive

🏃 **Flash, Flash** c/de la Granada del Penedès 25 ℡932 370 990, ⓦwww.grup7portes .com; Ⓜ**Diagonal**. A classic 1970s survivor, *Flash, Flash* does tortillas (most around €5–6) – served any way you like, from plain and simple to elaborately stuffed or doused in salsa, with sweet ones for dessert. If that doesn't grab you, there's a small menu of salads, soups and burgers. Either way,

# Festive Barcelona

Decorated floats and costumed giants inch down crowded streets, teams of red-shirted men clamber on each other's shoulders, sweets are hurled to children, fireworks burst into the sky and the drummers are going crazy – it's festival time in Barcelona, and you can forget all about a decent night's sleep. In a city with two patron saints, a dozen neighbourhoods each with their own *festa*, and a full cultural and music calendar, there will be something going on whenever you visit.

A gegant on parade ▲

# Festes de Santa Eulàlia

The depths of winter are interrupted by festivities in honour of Eulàlia, the young Barcelona girl who suffered a beastly martyrdom by the Romans for refusing to renounce her Christianity. She's a revered patron of the city and her saint's day falls on **February 12**, around which are held several days' worth of celebrations with a focus on children and families. Events take place in Plaça de Sant Jaume in the Barri Gòtic, where you'll be able to see the saint in parade with other *gegants* (giants), as well as the usual fire-running, dancing, concerts and firework displays throughout the neighbourhood. It's also an appropriate time to visit La Seu, Barcelona's old-town cathedral, whose crypt (open to view) contains the saint's venerated remains in a marble sarcophagus.

Teatre Grec ▼

# Barcelona Grec Festival

Since the 1970s, the summer's foremost **arts and music festival** has centred its performances on Montjuïc's open-air Greek theatre. Cut into the hillside on the site of an old quarry, this is a dramatic location for cutting-edge Shakespearean productions or events by Catalan avant-garde performance artists like La Fura del Baus, while music ranges from the likes of Phillip Glass to Taj Mahal, and African rap to Spanish singer-songwriters. There are also concerts, plays and dance productions at the CCCB and city theatres – in total, around fifty different events held over a six-week period from the end of June. The city council's cultural information office at Palau de la Virreïna on the Ramblas is the best stop for information and tickets.

## Celebrating Catalan-style

Central to any Catalan festival is the parade of **gegants**, the overblown five-metre-high giants with a costumed frame (to allow them to be carried) and papier-mâché or fibreglass heads. Barcelona has its own official city *gegants* of King Jaume and his queen, while each neighbourhood cherishes its own traditional figures, from elegant noblewomen to turban-clad sultans – the Barri Gòtic's church of Santa Maria del Pi has some of the most renowned. Come festival time they congregate in the city's squares, dancing cumbersomely to the sound of flutes and drums, and accompanied by smaller, more nimble figures known as **capgrossos** (bigheads) and by outsized lions and dragons. Also typically Catalan is the **correfoc** (fire-running), where brigades of drummers, fire-breathing dragons and demons with firework-flaring tridents cavort in the streets. It's as devilishly dangerous as it sounds, with intrepid onlookers attempting to stop the dragons passing, as firecrackers explode all around – approach with caution.

▲ Fire-runners take to the streets

▼ Barcelona lit up by fireworks

## Dia de Sant Joan

**St John's Day (June 24)** is the quietest saint's day of the year in the city – largely because everyone has been up all of the previous night for the famed **Nit del Foc** (Night of Fire), which involves massive bonfires and fireworks across the city. It marks a hedonistic welcome to summer, with *cava* (champagne) parties in full swing in every neighbourhood and pyrotechnics on Montjuïc and Tibidabo. The traditional place to end the night is on the beach, watching the sun come up, thankful that the dawning day is a public holiday.

# Festes de la Mercè

The biggest annual festival, held around September 24, is dedicated to **Our Lady of Mercy**, co-patroness of the city, whose image is paraded from the church of La Mercè near the port. It's an excuse for a week of merrymaking, culminating in spectacular pyrotechnics along the seafront. Every unique element of a Catalan festival can be seen at some stage during the Mercè – firework-toting demons chasing onlookers through the streets, human castle-builders reaching for the sky, processions of lumbering giants, and locals linking hands in the traditional circle-dance, the *sardana*. There are outdoor concerts across the city, bicycle races, children's events and family activities, and even free admission to city museums and galleries on the saint's day.

A team of castellers ▲

## Castles in the sky

Guaranteed to draw crowds at every festival are the teams of **castellers** – castle-makers – who pile person upon person, feet on shoulders, to see who can construct the highest, most aesthetically pleasing tower. It's an art that goes back over 200 years, combining individual strength with mutual cooperation – perhaps this is why it was discouraged as an activity under Franco. Nowadays, it's very popular once again, with societies known as *colles* in most Catalan towns who come together to perform at annual festivals and events. There's a real skill to assembling the *castell*, with operations directed by the *cap de colla* (society head) – the strongest members form the crowd at the base, known as the *pinya*, with the whole edifice topped by an agile child, the *anxaneta*, who lifts their palm above their head to "crown" the castle. Ten human storeys is the record.

you'll love the original white leatherette booths and monotone "models-with-cameras" cutouts – very Austin Powers. Daily 1pm–1.30am, bar open 11am–2am.

**Habibi c/Gran de Gràcia 7 ⊕ 932 179 545; Ⓜ Diagonal.** At this cheery Lebanese diner, the Plat Habibi gives you a taste of all the house specials – from a minty tabbouleh to lamb and chicken *schawarma* – and the *maghmour* (chickpeas with aubergine and mint) is excellent. Add a fresh-squeezed juice (there's no alcohol served), a home-made dessert and a mint tea and you're still only in for around €15. Mon–Fri 1pm–1am, Sat 2–4.30pm & 8pm–1am.

**Himali c/Milà i Fontanals 60 ⊕ 932 851 568; Ⓜ Joanic.** There's not much to suggest Barcelona's only Nepalese restaurant will be worth the trip – a few Nepalese flags and pictures adorn an otherwise unassuming neighbourhood restaurant, with stainless steel bar and TV to the fore. But the food differs from the downtown curry-house offerings, with *momo* (stuffed dumplings), grilled chicken with fragrant walnut curry sauce, and slow-cooked mutton and potato typical of the specialities spelled out in English on the menu, or explained by friendly English-speaking staff. Prices are really good value too, with most mains around €8–10, which includes rice and *naan* bread. Tues–Sun noon–4.30pm & 8pm–midnight.

**Nou Candanchu Pl. Rius i Taulet 9 ⊕ 932 377 362; Ⓜ Fontana.** Sit beneath the clock tower in summer and choose from the wide selection of local dishes – tapas and hot sandwiches but also steak and eggs, steamed clams and mussels, or cod and hake cooked plenty of different ways. It's managed by an affable bunch of young guys, and there's lots of choice for €8–12. Daily except Tues 7am–1am, Fri & Sat until 3am.

### Moderate

**La Singular c/Francesc Giner 50 ⊕ 932 375 098; Ⓜ Diagonal.** The tiniest of kitchens turns out refined Mediterranean food at moderate prices – say, aubergine and smoked fish salad, or chicken stuffed with dates and ham, with most dishes costing €8–14. There's always something appealing on the menu for veggies too. It's a cornerstone of the neighbourhood, with a

friendly atmosphere, but there are only nine tables, so go early or reserve. Mon–Thurs 1.30–4pm & 9pm–midnight, Fri 1.30–4pm & 9pm–1am, Sat 9pm–1am.

**Taverna El Glop c/Sant Lluís 24 ⊕ 932 137 058, Ⓦ www.tavernaelglop.com; Ⓜ Joanic.** The rusticity (stone-flagged floors, beams, baskets of garlic) stops just the right side of parody and the lunch *menú* is one of the city's best deals; otherwise expect to spend €15–25 a head for grills and other tavern specials, prepared in front of you on the open kitchen ranges. At the weekend you may have to wait for a table. There are other branches downtown in the Eixample (at Rambla de Catalunya 65 and c/de Casp 21) but this is the original and the best. Daily 1–4pm & 8pm–1am.

## Sant-Gervasi

For locations, see map, p.140–141.

### Moderate

**Bar Turó c/del Tenor Viñas 1 ⊕ 932 006 953, Ⓦ www.canpunyetes.com; FGC Muntaner.** A reliable place for tapas, fresh pasta and home-made pizzas, right by pretty Turó park. It's a contemporary place, with big windows that overlook a year-round street *terrassa*, and the food is pretty good value for uptown. Mon–Sat 9am–midnight, Sun 9am–4.30pm.

**Can Punyetes c/Marià Cubí 189 ⊕ 932 009 159, Ⓦ www.canpunyetes.com; FGC Gràcia.** Traditional grillhouse-tavern – well, since 1981 anyway – that offers slick city diners a taste of older times. There are simple salads and tapas, and open grills turning out sausage, lamb chops, chicken and pork, accompanied by grilled country bread, white beans and char-grilled potato halves. Prices are very reasonable (everything under €10) and locals love it. Daily 1–4pm & 8pm–midnight.

**Casa Fernandez c/Santaló 46 ⊕ 932 019 308, Ⓦ www.casafernandez.com; FGC Gràcia.** The long kitchen hours are a boon for the bar-crawlers in this neck of the woods. It's a contemporary place featuring market cuisine, though they are specialists in – of all things – fried eggs, either served straight with chips or add Catalan sausage, foie gras or other variations. Daily 1pm–1am.

# 12

# Bars and clubs

W hatever you're looking for from a night out, you'll find it somewhere in Barcelona – bohemian boozer, underground club, cocktail bar, summer dance palace, techno temple, Irish pub or designer bar, you name it. If all you want is a drink, then any café or bar can oblige. Some of the finest cafés are already covered in the previous chapter, Cafés, tapas and restaurants, and undoubtedly one of the city's greatest pleasures is to pull up a pavement seat and watch the world go by. However, the bar scene proper operates at a different pace, and with a different set of rules. Specialist **bars** in Barcelona include *bodegas* (specializing in wine), "pubs" and *cerveserías* (beer), *xampanyerías* (champagne and *cava*) and *coctelerías* (cocktails). Best known of the city's nightlife haunts are its hip **designer bars**, while there's a stylish **club scene** that goes from strength to strength fuelled by a potent mix of resident and guest DJs. For the lowdown on **gay and lesbian** nightlife in Barcelona, see Chapter 14.

The following list of bars and clubs provide a starting point for a decent night out in Barcelona, but the scene changes rapidly so don't be surprised to find that some places have subsequently changed hands or names, or closed down. In particular, there's an ongoing assault by the Ajuntament (city hall) against neighbourhood noise pollution, which has caused some high-profile casualties over the last couple of years as establishments have closed after local complaints. Local **listings magazines** (*Guía del Ocio*, Ⓦwww.guiadelociobcn.es, and *Time Out Barcelona*, Ⓦwww.timeout.cat) cover current openings, hours and club nights, and most bars, cafés, boutiques and music stores carry flyers and free magazines containing news and reviews.

It's worth noting that – unlike restaurants – most bars and clubs stay open throughout August.

## Bars

Generally, the bars in the old town are a mixture of traditional tourist haunts, local drinking places or fashionista hangouts. **La Ribera** is still one of the hottest destinations, with Passeig del Born the main focus, though a scene is developing up in the neighbouring *barri* of **Sant Pere** too. In the **Barri Gòtic**, it's the streets around Plaça Reial and Plaça George Orwell that have their share of the action. Over in **El Raval**, the most fashionable places are found in the upper part of the neighbourhood near MACBA, though you can still find tradition (and sleaze) further south, closer to the port, in the surviving bars of the old Barri Xines. The **Port Olímpic** and the **Port Vell** Maremàgnum complex are more mainstream summer-night playgrounds for locals and tourists

The **beer** (*cervesa* in Catalan, *cerveza* in Spanish) in Barcelona is lager, with the two main brands you'll see everywhere being Damm's Estrella and San Miguel. Voll Damm is a stronger lager, Bock Damm a darker one, or you might also see draught *cervesa negra*, a kind of black fizzy lager. Beer generally comes in 300ml bottles, while, on draught, a *caña* is a small glass, a *jarra* a larger one, whilst the *tubo* is a tall, cylindrical glass.

**Wine** (*vino, vi*), either red (*tinto, negre*), white (*blanco, blanc*) or rosé (*rosado, rosat*), is the invariable accompaniment to every meal. In bars, cafés and budget restaurants, it's whatever comes out of the barrel, or the house bottled special (ask for *vin* or *vi de la casa*). The Catalan wine industry is centred on the Alt Penedès and Priorat regions, notably the champagne-like *cava* from Sant Sadurní d'Anoia, with other local wine-making regions found in Empordà and around Lleida.

In mid-afternoon – or even at breakfast – many Catalans take a *copa* of **liqueur** with their coffee (for that matter, many of them drink wine and beer at breakfast, too). **Brandy** (*coñac*) is mostly from the south, though if you want a Catalan brandy look for Torres or Mascaró. For other spirits, always specify *nacional* unless you want a particular named foreign brand.

⑫

**BARS AND CLUBS** | Bars

alike. There are scores of bars in both these areas, all either themed or otherwise fairly mundane, but with the advantage that you can simply hop from one to another if you don't like your first choice. Other stylish designer bars or DJ-led music bars are concentrated mainly in the **Eixample** and the streets to the west of **Gràcia**, particularly on c/Santaló and c/Marià Cubí in **Sant Gervasi**.

Local bars are licensed to stay open usually until 11pm, although some keep going until 3am. Music bars usually go until 2.30 or 3am, after which you'll have to resort to a club.

### Ramblas

For locations, see map, p.46.

**Bosc de les Fades** Ptge. de la Banca 5 ☏ 933 172 649, ⓦ www.museocerabcn.com; Ⓜ Drassanes. Tucked away in an alley off the Ramblas, beside the entrance to the wax museum, the "Forest of the Fairies" is festooned with gnarled plaster tree trunks, hanging branches, fountains and stalactites. It's a bit cheesy, which is perhaps why it's a huge hit with the twenty-something crowd who huddle up in the dark recesses. Mon–Thurs & Sun 10.30am–1am, Fri & Sat 10.30am–3am.

**La Cazalla** Ramblas 25, no phone; Ⓜ Drassanes. An historic remnant of the old days, the hole-in-the-wall *Cazalla* (under the arch, at the beginning of c/de l'Arc del Teatre) first opened its hatch in 1912. It was closed for some years, but it's now back in business offering stand-up coffees, beers and shots to an assorted clientele of locals, cops, streetwalkers and the occasional stray tourist. Mon–Sat 10am–3am.

### Barri Gòtic

For locations, see map, p.54–55.

**L'Ascensor** c/Bellafila 3 ☏ 933 185 347; Ⓜ Jaume I. Sliding antique wooden elevator doors announce the entrance to "The Lift", but it's no theme bar – just an easy-going local hangout, great for a late-night drink. Daily 6.30pm–3am.

211

▲ L'Ascensor

**Bar del Pi Pl. Sant Josep Oriol 1 ☎933 022 123; Ⓜ Liceu.** Best known for its terrace tables in one of Barcelona's prettiest squares, which means it can be quite touristy, and service can be slow – not that anyone's in a hurry in this prime people-watching spot. But it's got a loyal local following too, with a one-up one-down gallery inside that gets nice and cosy in winter. Mon–Sat 9am–11pm, Sun 10am–10pm; closed two weeks in Jan & Aug.

🏃 **La Cerveteca c/Gignàs 25 ☎933 150 407, ⓦ www.lacerveteca.com; Ⓜ Jaume I/ Barceloneta.** Is it a bar, or is it the funkiest off-licence in town? What's for certain is that La Cerveteca offers the city's biggest and best beer selection from around the world, all correctly racked and shelved, and available to drink in or take out. Brews are taken seriously here but it's not a beard-and-sandals beer fest, more a modern art, Muddy Waters, Latino beat kind of place where beer-lovers gather round big stand-up barrels and swap stories. Mon & Tues 4–9pm, Wed & Thurs noon–9pm, Fri & Sat noon–10pm.

**Glaciar Pl. Reial 3 ☎933 021 163; Ⓜ Liceu.** At this traditional Barcelona meeting point the terrace seating in the square is packed most sunny evenings and at weekends. Mon–Thurs 4pm–2am, Fri & Sat 4pm–3am, Sun 9am–2am.

🏃 **Milk c/Gignàs 21 ☎932 680 922, ⓦ www .milkbarcelona.com; Ⓜ Jaume I.** Irish-owned bar and bistro that's quickly carved a niche as a welcoming neighbourhood hangout – nothing flashy, but decent food

and cocktails backed by a funky sound-track. Book at the weekends if you want to eat, and come early for the popular Sunday brunch. Mon–Sat 6.30pm–3am, Sun 11am–3am.

**Oviso c/Arai 5, Pl. George Orwell, no phone; Ⓜ Drassanes.** Holding a mirror on to the neighbourhood, the Oviso fits right in with the scruffy urban square outside – a shabby-chic mural-clad café-bar, popular with a hip young crowd. There's a sunny terrassa, and the salad and sandwiches are good too, available from breakfast onwards. Daily 10am–2.30am, Fri & Sat 10am until 3am.

**Pipa Club Pl. Reial 3 ☎933 024 732, ⓦ www .bpipaclub.com; Ⓜ Liceu.** A bit like a Victorian English pub, with its wood-panelled rooms, pool table and battery of regulars. Histori-cally a pipe-smoker's private club, it's a jazzy, late-night kind of place – ring the bell for admission and make your way up the stairs. Daily 11pm–3am.

**Schilling c/de Ferran 23 ☎933 176 787, ⓦ www.cafeschilling.com; Ⓜ Liceu.** In the European "grand-café" style, with high ceilings, big windows and an upmarket feel. It has a loyal gay following, but it's a mixed, chilled place to meet up, grab a bite and a copa and move on. Mon–Sat 10am–3am, Sun noon–3am.

**Travel Bar c/Boqueria 27 ☎933 425 252, ⓦ www.travelbar.com; Ⓜ Liceu.** Backpacking Catalans have brought their experiences home to provide a bar where travellers can hang out and meet like-minded souls, sign up for walking, biking or drinking

## Down the pub

Barcelona has embraced the "English" pub and "Irish" bar with a vengeance, and every *barri* has a place where the stag and hen groups can feel right at home. On the whole, there's little to choose between them, though they come into their own when only a pint of Guinness, a singalong-a-pub band or the match on the big screen will do. By common consent, the *Black Horse* (c/d'Allada Vermell 16, Sant Pere ☎932 683 338; Ⓜ Jaume I, map p.74) is best, with an off-the-beaten-track neighbourhood feel, despite being just a few minutes from the Picasso museum, while the same can be said of the *Michael Collins* (Pl. Sagrada Família 4, Dreta de l'Eixample ☎934 591 964; Ⓜ Sagrada Família, map pp.122–123), across from Gaudí's church. The old town pubs see a more transient tourist crowd – at least at *Molly's Fair City* (c/de Ferran 7–9, Barri Gòtic ☎933 424 026; Ⓜ Liceu, map pp.54–55) there's the original *modernista* decor to admire. Uptown expats and hotel guests favour *Kitty O'Shea's* (c/Nau Santa Maria 5–7, Les Corts ☎932 803 675; Ⓜ Maria Cristina, map pp.140–141), while for nightly knees-ups and big-screen sports make for the Port Olímpic's *Kennedy Irish Sailing Club* (Moll de Mestral, Port Olímpic ☎932 210 039; Ⓜ Ciutadella-Vila Olímpica, map p.93).

tours, check their email and generally chill out. It's solidly tourist-orientated, with footy on the TV and run-of-the-mill tapas, English breakfast and burgers are available – even so, it's more relaxed here than in the rowdy stag-friendly "Irish pubs" nearby, and is probably the most like an English pub that the city has to offer. Mon–Thurs & Sun 9am until 2am, Fri & Sat 9am until 3am.

## El Raval

For locations, see map, pp.66–67.

**Almirall c/de Joaquin Costa 33** ☎ **933 189 917;** Ⓜ **Universitat.** Dating from 1860, Barcelona's oldest bar – check out the *modernista* doors and counter – is a venerated leftist hangout. Not too young, not too loud, always good for a late-night drink. Daily 7pm–3am.

**Benidorm c/de Joaquin Costa 39** ☎ **933 178 052;** Ⓜ **Universitat.** Imagine … if your elderly aunt turned her parlour into a bar, dimmed the lights, and invited all her young friends. That, in a nutshell, is *Benidorm*, just a little bit cheesy and none the worse for that. Daily 7pm–3am.

🏃 **Café de les Delícies Rambla de Raval 47** ☎ **934 415 714;** Ⓜ **Liceu.** One of the first off the blocks in this revamped neighbourhood, and still perhaps the best – cute and cosy, mellow and arty, with a summer terrace and food for sharing. It feels more like someone's house than a bar, especially out back in the homely no-smoking lounge. Daily except Wed 6pm–2am, Fri & Sat until 3am; closed 2 weeks Aug.

**La Confitería c/de Sant Pau 128** ☎ **934 430 458;** Ⓜ **Paral.lel.** This old *modernista* bakery and confectioner's with a carved wood bar, murals, chandeliers and mirrored cabinets is now a popular meeting point. Mon–Sat 8pm–3am, Sun 7pm–2am.

**London Bar c/Nou de la Rambla 34** ☎ **933 185 261;** Ⓜ **Liceu.** Opened in 1910, this well-known bar attracts a mostly tourist clientele these days, but it's still worth looking in at least once. There's no longer any live music, and the big-screen TV at the back and the wireless Internet smack of "just-another-bar" syndrome, but nothing can dull the exuberant *modernista* decor (nor the authentic old town sleaze just up the street). Tues–Sat 7pm–4am; closed two weeks in Aug.

**Marsella c/de Sant Pau 65** ☎ **934 427 263;** Ⓜ **Liceu.** Authentic, atmospheric, 1930s bar – named for the French port of Marseilles – where absinthe is the drink of choice. It's frequented by a spirited mix of local characters and young trendies, all looking for a slice of the old Barri Xines. Mon–Sat 10pm–3am; closed 2 weeks in Aug.

**Muy Buenas c/del Carme 63** ☎ **934 425 053;** Ⓜ **Liceu.** Arguably the Raval's nicest traditional watering-hole, with a restored *modernista* interior and eager-to-please staff making things go with a swing. A long marble trough does duty as the bar, and the beer's pulled from antique beer taps. There are also tapas and meals. Tues–Sat 9am–3am.

🏃 **Resolis c/Riera Baixa 22** ☎ **934 412 948;** Ⓜ **Liceu/Sant Antoni.** The team behind *Ànima* restaurant rescued this decayed, century-old bar and turned it into a cool hangout with decent tapas. They didn't do much – a lick of paint, polish the panelling, patch up the brickwork – but now punters spill out of the door on to "secondhand clothes street" and a good time is had by all. There are superior tapas too, so if you only come to one bar in the Raval, come here. Mon–Sat 11am–1am.

🏃 **Zelig c/del Carme 116** ☎ **934 415 622,** ⓦ **www.zelig-barcelona.com;** Ⓜ **Sant Antoni.** The photo-frieze on granite walls and a fully stocked cocktail bar make it very much of its *barri* but *Zelig* stands out from the crowd – two Dutch owners offer a chatty welcome, a tendency towards 1980s sounds and a slight whiff of camp. Tues–Sun 7pm–2am, Fri & Sat 7pm–3am.

## Sant Pere

For location, see map, p.74.

🏃 **Casa Paco c/d'Allada Vermell 10** ☎ **935 073 719;** Ⓜ **Jaume I.** The *barri*'s signature bar is this cool-but-casual music joint that's a hit on the weekend DJ scene – the tagline "not a disco, just a bar with good music" says it all. There's a great *terrassa* under the trees, and if you can't get a table here there are half a dozen other *al fresco* bars down the traffic-free boulevard. Meanwhile, the associated *Pizza Paco* arcoss the way (also with its own terrace) means you don't have to go anywhere else for dinner. Mon–Thurs & Sun 9am–2am, Fri & Sat noon–3am, Oct to March opens daily at 6pm.

## La Ribera

For locations, see map, p.78.

**Berimbau** Pg. del Born 17 ☎ 933 195 378; Ⓜ Jaume I/Barceloneta. The oldest Brazilian bar in town, still a great place for authentic sounds and killer cocktails. Daily 6pm–2.30am.

🏃 **La Fianna** c/Banys Vells 19 ☎ 933 151 810, ⓦ www.lafianna.com; Ⓜ Jaume I. Flickering candelabras, parchment lampshades, rough plaster walls and deep colours set the Gothic mood in this stylish lounge-bar that's "putting the beat in the Born". Relax on the chill-out beds and velvet sofas, or book ahead to eat – the fusion-food restaurant is open from 8.30pm or it's a popular Sunday brunch spot. Mon–Wed & Sun 6pm–1.30am, Thurs–Sat 6pm–2.30am.

**Mudanzas** c/Vidrería 15 ☎ 933 191 137; Ⓜ Barceloneta. Locals like the relaxed feel (especially if you can hide yourself away in the cosy upper room), while those in the know come for the wide selection of rums, whiskies and vodkas from around the world. Daily 10am–2.30am, Aug opens at 6pm.

🏃 **El Nus** c/Mirallers 5 ☎ 933 195 355; Ⓜ Jaume I. Still has the feel of the shop it once was, down to the antique cash register, though it's now a kind of jazz bar-cum-gallery – a quiet, faintly old-fashioned, late-night place. Daily except Wed 7.30pm–2.30am.

**La Vinya del Senyor** Pl. Santa Maria 5 ☎ 933 103 379; Ⓜ Jaume I. There's no better view of the lovely church of Santa Maria del Mar than from the *terrassa* of this very popular wine bar. The wine list is really good – with a score or so available by the glass – and there are oysters, smoked salmon and other classy tapas. Tues–Thurs noon–1am, Fri & Sat noon–2am, Sun noon–midnight.

## Port Vell and Barceloneta

For locations, see map, p.91.

**Can Paixano** c/Reina Cristina 7 ☎ 933 100 839, ⓦ www.canpaixano.com; Ⓜ Barceloneta. A must on everyone's itinerary is this back-street joint where the drink of choice (all right, the only drink) is *cava* (Catalan champagne). Don't go thinking sophistication – it might come in traditional champagne saucers (the sort of thing Dean Martin used to stack in a pyramid and then pour wine over), but this is a counter-only joint where there's fizz, tapas and tapas-in-sandwiches, and that's your lot. And who could want more? Mon–Sat 9am–10.30pm; closed 2 weeks in Aug.

**Le Kasbah** Pl. Pau Vila, behind de Mar ☎ 932 380 722, ⓦ www.ottozutz.com; Ⓜ Barceloneta. The *terrassa* is the big summer draw here, when nothing but a reviving cocktail and a breath of fresh air will do, though the funky, sort-of-Oriental interior has a certain chilled-out charm. Tues–Sun 10pm–3am.

**Luz de Gas** Moll de Diposit, in front of Palau de Mar ☎ 932 097 711; Ⓜ Barceloneta. Sip a chilled drink on the polished deck of the moored boat, and soak up some great marina and harbour views. Queues form on hot days, when every parasol-shaded seat is taken, but it's especially nice at dusk as the city lights begin to twinkle. March–Oct daily noon–3am.

## Poble Sec

For locations, see map, p.104.

🏃 **Bar Seco** Pg. Montjuïc 74 ☎ 933 296 374; Ⓜ Paral.lel. It's just a bit out of the way in Poble Sec, but the Dry Village's Dry Bar is a local hit, especially for its quality veggie-friendly food and organic beers and wines. Big picture windows look out on to the corner plot, and there's *terrassa* seating over the road. Mon noon–2am, Tues–Sat 9am–2am, Sun 9am–midnight.

**Cervesería Jazz** c/Margarit 43 ☎ 934 433 259; Ⓜ Poble Sec. Grab a stool at the carved bar and shoot the breeze over an imported beer. It's an amiable place, and the music policy embraces reggae and other mellow sounds, not just jazz. Tues–Sat 7pm–2.30am.

🏃 **Tinta Roja** c/Creu dels Molers 17 ☎ 934 433 243, ⓦ www.tintaroja.net; Ⓜ Poble Sec. Highly theatrical tango bar with a succession of over-the-top crimson rooms leading to a stage at the back. There's cabaret and live music (tango, rumba, Cuban, flamenco) – often free – a couple of nights a week, though special shows are €10. Wed, Thurs & Sun 8pm–1.30am, Fri & Sat 8pm–3am; closed 2 weeks in Aug.

## Esquerra de l'Eixample

For locations, see map, pp.128–129.

**Belchica c/Villaroel 60 ☎625 814 001;** Ⓜ**Urgell.** Barcelona's first Belgian beer bar guarantees a range of decent brews that you can't get anywhere else. It's not a theme bar – unless you count drinking in what resembles a boiler room – just an enjoyable locale playing electronica, new jazz, lounge, reggae and other left-field sounds. Tues–Sat 6pm–3am, Sun & Mon 7pm–1am.

**Dry Martini c/Aribau 166 ☎932 175 072;** Ⓜ**Diagonal/Provença.** White-jacketed bar-tenders, dark wood and brass, a self-satisfied air – it could only be the city's legendary uptown cocktail bar. To be fair, though, no one mixes drinks better and the regulars aren't the one-dimensional business types you might expect. Mon–Thurs 1pm–2.30am, Fri & Sat 1pm–3am, Sun 6.30pm–2.30am.

**La Fira c/Provença 171, no phone;** Ⓜ**Provença.** One of the city's most bizarre drinking emporiums comes complete with old-fashioned fairground rides and circus paraphernalia. Sit at the bar fashioned from a circus awning or cosy up in the dodgem cars – but come at the weekend for any kind of crowd or atmosphere. Tues–Thurs & Sun 11pm–3am, Fri & Sat 11pm–5am.

**Quilombo c/d'Aribau 149 ☎934 395 406;** Ⓜ**Diagonal.** Unpretentious music bar – just a bare box of a room really – that's rolled with the years since 1971, featuring live guitarists, Latin American bands and a clientele that joins in enthusiastically. Mon–Thurs & Sun 9pm–3am, Fri & Sat 7.30pm–3.30am.

**Sante Café c/Comte d'Urgell 171 ☎933 237 832;** Ⓜ**Hospital Clinic.** A minimalist-style place that's more of a café during the day but chills out at night, with guest DJs at the weekend. Mon–Fri 9am–3am, Sat & Sun 5pm–3am; closed Aug.

## Gràcia

For locations, see map, p.134.

**La Baignoire c/Verdi 6, no phone;** Ⓜ**Fontana.** Cosy wine bar offering a small corner of sophistication – Ella Fitzgerald on the CD, a dozen good wines by the glass and cheesy nibbles. Mon–Thurs 7pm–1.30am, Fri & Sat 7pm–2.30am, Sun 6pm–1.30am.

**Café del Sol Pl. del Sol 16 ☎934 155 663;** Ⓜ**Fontana.** The grandaddy of the Plaça del Sol scene sees action day and night. On summer evenings, when the square is packed, there's not an outdoor table to be had, but even in winter this is a popular drinking den – the pubby interior has a back room and gallery, often rammed to the rafters. Daily 1pm–2.30am.

**Café Salambo c/Torrijos 51 ☎932 186 966,** Ⓦ**www.cafesalambo.com;** Ⓜ**Joanic/Fontana.** Where the pre- and post-cinema crowd meets (both Verdi cinemas are on the doorstep). It's a longstanding neighbourhood hangout, with something of a colonial feel, and there are lots of wines and *cava* by the glass and good food too. Tues–Thurs 4pm–1am, Fri & Sat noon–3am, Sun noon–9pm.

**Canigó Pl. de la Revolucio 10, no phone;** Ⓜ**Fontana.** Family-run neighbourhood bar now entering its third generation. It's not much to look at, but the drinks are as cheap as chips and it's a Gràcia institution, packed out at weekends with a young, hip and largely local crowd,

▲ Dry Martini

meeting to chew the fat. Tues–Sun
11am–midnight.
**Puku Café c/Guilleries 10** ℡ 933 682 573;
Ⓜ **Fontana.** Come early and it's a relaxed
place for a bite to eat and a drink, with
wines by the glass and things like salads,
platters and home-made ice cream. At
weekends it morphs into an equally chilled
electro-lounge as "indietronica" DJs take the
helm. Mon–Thurs & Sun–Wed 7pm–1am, Fri
& Sat 7pm–3am.

**Vinilo c/Matilde 2** ℡ 626 464 759;
Ⓜ **Diagonal/Fontana.** It's cunningly
simple to concoct a hit Gràcia bar – don't
shave, wear a beret, smoke like crazy, show
*Bladerunner* on the projection screen with
the sound down, play Jeff Buckley,
Radiohead and Morcheeba. To be fair, *Vinilo*
is a very cosy dive bar, with the lighting set
at a perpetual dusk – time easily slips away
in here. Daily 7pm–2am, Fri & Sat until 3am.
**Virreina Pl. de la Virreina 1** ℡ 932 379 880;
Ⓜ **Fontana.** Take time out in one of Gràcia's
loveliest squares at this popular local bar,
with seats inside and out. Mon–Thurs & Sun
10am–1am, Fri & Sat 10am–2am.

### Les Corts & Sant Gervasi

For location, see map, pp.140–141.
**Elephant Pg. dels Til.lers 1** ℡ 933 340 258,
Ⓦ www.elephantbcn.com; Ⓜ **Palau Reial.**

A gorgeous designer bar for gorgeous
designer people. There's dancing, but
mostly there's preening in a series of
ornamental, Oriental-style gardens.
Thurs–Sat 11pm–4am.
**Gimlet c/Santaló 46** ℡ 932 015 306; FGC
**Muntaner.** This favoured cocktail joint is
especially popular in summertime, when the
street-side tables offer a great vantage-point
for watching the party unfold. Daily
7.30pm–3am.
**Universal c/Marià Cubí 182** ℡ 932 013 596,
Ⓦ www.grupocostaeste.com; FGC **Muntaner.** A
classic designer bar that's been at the
cutting edge of Barcelona style since 1985
– and there are still queues. Be warned:
they operate a strict door policy here and if
your face doesn't fit you won't get in.
Mon–Thurs 11pm–3.30am, Fri & Sat
11pm–5am.

### Tibidabo

For location, see map, p.133.
**Mirablau Pl. del Dr Andrea, Avgda. Tibidabo**
℡ 934 185 879; FGC Avgda. del Tibidabo &
**Tramvia Blau or taxi.** Unbelievable city views
from a chic bar by the tram and funicular
terminus. By day a great place for coffee
and views, at night a rich-kid disco-tunes
stomping ground. Daily 11am–5am.

# Clubs

The main city-centre **neighbourhoods** for clubbing are the Barri Gòtic,
Raval, Eixample and Gràcia, though it's actually the peripheral areas where
you'll find the bulk of the big-name warehouse and designer venues. Poble
Nou, Poble Sec, Sants and Les Corts might not attract you during the day, but
they'll be high on the list of any seasoned clubber, as will the otherwise tourist
fantasy village of Poble Espanyol in Montjuïc. Meanwhile the Port Olímpic has
a number of high-profile clubs alongside the myriad music bars.

**Admission prices** are difficult to predict: some places are free or free before
a certain time, others charge a few token euros' entry, a few only charge if there's
live music, while in several entry depends on what you look like rather than how
much is in your pocket. Those that do charge tend to fall into the €10–20 range,
though this usually includes your first drink. If there is free entry, don't be
surprised to find that there's a minimum drinks' charge of anything up to €10.

Note that the distinction between a music-bar and a club is between a
closing time of 2 or 3am and at least 5am. Many of those listed below stay
open until 6 or 7am at weekends – fair enough, as they've usually barely got
started by 3am.

## Ramblas

For location, see map, p.46.
**Club Fellini** Ramblas 27 ☏932 724 980,
🕸www.clubfellini.com; Ⓜ Drassanes. Three
*salas* – Mirror Room, Red Room and Bad
Room – supply sounds from techno to soul
for "night victims, modernos and freaks". If
this sounds like you, look out for the flyers
– the various club nights are heavily publi-
cized. Mon–Sat midnight–5am, winter
usually Thurs–Sat only.

## Barri Gòtic

For locations, see map, pp.54–55
🚇 **Fantastico** Ptge. dels Escudellers 3 ☏933
175 411, 🕸www.fantasticoclub.com;
Ⓜ Drassanes. A cheery dive for the pop,
indie and electro crowd, listening to the
Kaiser Chiefs, The Killers, The Pigeon
Detectives, Get Cape and the like. Wed–Sat
11pm–3am.
🚇 **Fonfone** c/dels Escudellers 24 ☏933 171
424, 🕸www.fonfone.com; Ⓜ Drassanes.
Beautifully lit bar attracting a young crowd
into fast, hard music, though it changes
mood with satin soul, disco and best-of-
Eighties nights. Daily 10pm–3am.
**Karma** Pl. Reial 10 ☏933 025 680, 🕸www
.karmadisco.com; Ⓜ Liceu. A stalwart of the
scene, this old-school studenty basement
place can get claustrophobic at times.
Sounds are indie, Britpop and US college,
while a lively local crowd gathers at the
square-side bar and *terrassa* which is
open from 6pm. Tues–Sun
midnight–5.30am.
**La Macarena** c/Nou de Sant Francesc 5, no
phone 🕸www.macarenaclub.com;
Ⓜ Drassanes. A heaving, funky, electronic
temple with a tolerant crowd – they have to
be, as there's not much space. Mon–Thurs
& Sun midnight–4am, Fri & Sat
midnight–5am.

## El Raval

For locations, see map, p.66–67.
**La Concha** c/Guardia 14 ☏933 024 118;
Ⓜ Drassanes. The Arab–flamenco fusion
throws up a great atmosphere, worth
braving the slightly dodgy area for. It's a
rather kitsch, gay-friendly joint, with some
uninhibited dancing to flamenco and *rai* by
tourists and locals alike. Daily 5pm–3am.

🚇 **Moog** c/Arc del Teatre 3 ☏933 017 282,
🕸www.masimas.com; Ⓜ Drassanes.
Influential club with a minimalist look playing
techno, electro, drum 'n' bass, house, funk
and soul to an up-for-it crowd. Daily
midnight–5am.
**La Paloma** c/Tigre 27 ☏933 016 897, 🕸www
.lapaloma-bcn.com; Ⓜ Universitat. At the
time of writing, the best-known casualty of
the Ajuntament's crusade against late-
night noise, but it's hoped that closure
isn't permanent if they can sort out the
soundproofing. If and when it does re-
open, it's unmissable – a fabulous 1903-
era ballroom and concert venue where old
and young alike are put through their
rumba and cha-cha-cha steps, with DJs
kicking in after midnight on an assorted
roster of club nights.

## Port Olímpic

For location, see map, p.93.
**Club Catwalk** c/Ramon Trias Fargas 2–4
☏932 216 161, 🕸www.clubcatwalk.net;
Ⓜ Ciutadella-Vila Olímpica. The portside club
of choice for the beautiful of Barcelona,
playing house or funk and R&B to well-
heeled locals and visitors. It's under the
landmark *Hotel Arts Barcelona*. Wed–Sun
midnight–5am.

## Poble Nou

For location, see map, p.85.
**Razzmatazz** c/dels Almogavers 122 &
c/Pamplona 88 ☏932 720 910, 🕸www
.salarazzmatazz.com; Ⓜ Bogatell/Marina.
*Razzmatazz* hosts the biggest in-town rock
gigs (the concert hall capacity is 3000),
while at weekends the former warehouse
turns into "five clubs in one", spinning
indie, rock, pop, techno, electro, retro and
more in variously named bars like "The
Loft", "Pop Bar" or "Lolita". One price gets
you entrance to all the bars. Fri & Sat
1–6am.

## Montjuïc

For location, see map, p.96.
**La Terrrazza** Avgda. Marquès de Comillas, Poble
Espanyol ☏932 724 980, 🕸www.laterrrazza
.com; Ⓜ Espanya. Open-air summer club
that's *the* place to be in Barcelona. Nonstop
dance, house and techno, though don't get

there until at least 3am, and be prepared for the style police. May–Oct Thurs–Sat midnight–7am.

## Poble Sec

For locations, see map, p.104.

🏃 **Mau Mau** c/Fontrodona 33 ☎934 418 015; ⓦwww.maumaunderground.com; ⓂParal. lel. Great underground lounge-club, cultural centre and chill-out space with comfy sofas, nightly film and video projections, exhibitions, and a roster of guest DJs playing deep, soulful grooves. Strictly speaking it's a private club, but membership is only €5 and they tend to let foreign visitors in anyway. Thurs 11pm–2.30am, Fri & Sat 11pm–3.30am.

**Sala Apolo** c/Nou de la Rambla 113 ☎934 414 001, ⓦwww.sala-apolo.com; ⓂParal.lel. This old-time ballroom is now a hip concert venue with regular live gigs on two stages and an eclectic series of club nights, foremost of which is the weekends' long-running techno/electro Nitsa Club (ⓦwww.nitsa.com). Others prefer Wednesday night's Canibal Sound System (Latin/mestizo) and Thursday's Powder Room (funk). Wed midnight–5am, Thurs–Sat 12.30–5am.

## Esquerra de l'Eixample

For locations, see map, pp.128–129.

**Antilla BCN** c/Aragó 141–143 ☎934 512 151, ⓦwww.antillasalsa.com; ⓂHospital Clinic/Urgell. Latin and Caribbean tunes galore – rumba, son, salsa, merengue, mambo, you name it – for out-and-out good-time dancing. There are live bands, killer

cocktails and dance classes most nights. Daily 10.30pm–5am, weekends until 6am.

**Barcelona City Hall** Rambla de Catalunya 2–4 ☎932 380 722, ⓦwww.ottozutz.com; ⓂCatalunya. Very popular dance joint – the handy location helps – which hosts some of the most varied club nights around, from 80s' revival to electro. Daily midnight–6am.

**Space Barcelona** c/Tarragona 141–147 ☎934 530 582, ⓦwww.spacebarcelona.com; ⓂTarragona. With the Balearic beat big in Barcelona, it was no surprise when offshoots of the actual Ibiza clubs appeared on the scene. This was the first Space launched outside the island, and it's a thumpingly young, extremely posey joint. Fri & Sat midnight–6am, Sun 9pm–3am.

**Velvet** c/Balmes 161 ☎932 176 714; ⓂDiagonal. One of the few survivors of the first wave of stylish dance-bars in the 1980s, this lavish creation of designer Alfredo Arribas was inspired by the velveteen excesses of film-maker David Lynch. Daily 10.30pm–4.30am.

## Gràcia

For locations, see map, p.134.

**KGB** c/Alegre de Dalt 55 ☎932 105 906; ⓂJoanic. This warehouse bar and club was the first with the industrial look back in the 1980s. It was a well-known techno haunt, though current gigs and music policy aren't so rigid now, ranging from rumba to hip-hop. Thurs 1–4.30am, Fri & Sat 1–6am.

**Otto Zutz** c/de Lincoln 15 ☎932 380 722, ⓦwww.ottozutz.com; FGC Gràcia. It first opened in 1985 and has since lost some of its glam cachet, but this three-storey former

---

## This year's model

First it was bars in pool halls and archery ranges, followed in quick order by the invasion of the Irish bar and the gentle creep of the lounge scene. Barcelona always has another fad up its sleeve, and now it's upscale dining-and-dancing in extravagant gastro-clubs. The clientele is A-list celeb, footy player and WAG, well-heeled tourist and local rich kid, not adverse to dining out and kicking back in like-minded company. Down by the beach and port, the trend is exemplified by the beautiful-people hangouts **CDLC** (Pg. Marítim 32, Port Olímpic ☎932 240 470, ⓦwww.cdlcbarcelona.com, ⓂCiutadella-Vila Olímpica, map p.93) and **Shôko** (Pg. Marítim 36, Port Olímpic ☎932 259 200, ⓦwww.shoko.biz, ⓂCiutadella-Vila Olímpica, map p.93), while uptown venues include the glam **Danzarama** (Gran Via de les Corts Catalanes 604, Esquerra de l'Eixample ☎933 425 070, ⓦwww.danzarama.com, ⓂUniversitat, map p.128–129) and the **Buda Restaurante** (c/Pau Claris 92, Dreta de l'Eixample ☎933 184 252, ⓦwww.budarestaurante.com, ⓂCatalunya, map p.115).

textile factory still has a shed-load of pretensions. The sounds are basically hip-hop, R&B and house, and with the right clothes and face, you're in (you may or may not have to pay, depending on how impressive you are, the day of the week, the mood of the doorstaff, etc). Tues–Sat midnight–6am.

## Les Corts

For locations, see map, pp.140–141.

Bikini c/Deu i Mata 105, off Avgda. Diagonal ☎933 220 800, ⓦwww .bikinibcn.com; ⓜLes Corts/María Cristina. This traditional landmark of Barcelona nightlife

(behind the L'Illa shopping centre) offers a regular diet of great gigs followed by club sounds, from house to Brazilian, according to the night. Wed–Sun midnight–5am; closed Aug.

Pacha Avgda. Dr. Marañon 17 ☎933 343 233, ⓦwww.clubpachabcn.com; ⓜZona Universitaria. More Ibizan club culture in the latest superclub to transfer from beach to Barcelona. A roster of internationally known DJs are present year-round. June–Sept daily midnight–6am, winter Thurs–Sun midnight–6am.

# ⑬

# Entertainment

A s you would expect from a city of this size, Barcelona has a busy entertainment calendar – throughout the year there will always be
something worth catching, whether it's a rock gig, cabaret show or
night at the opera. The **music** scene is particularly strong, with jazz,
rock and flamenco to the fore. Catalans like their **cinema** and **theatre**, and
even if you don't speak Catalan or Spanish there's no need to miss out since
many cinemas show films in their original language. Catalan performers have
always steered away from the classics and gone for the innovative, so the city
boasts a long tradition of street and performance art. Barcelona excels in the
**visual arts**, too – from traditional exhibitions of paintings to contemporary
photography or installation works – and dozens of arts centres and galleries put
on varied shows throughout the year.

A useful first stop for tickets and information is the **Palau de la Virreina**,
Ramblas 99 (Mon–Sat 10am–8pm, Sun 11am–3pm; ☎933 161 000; Ⓜ Liceu).
**ServiCaixa** (☎902 332 211, Ⓦ www.servicaixa.com) and **TelEntrada** (☎902
101 212, Ⓦ www.telentrada.com) are the main advance booking agencies for
music, theatre, cinema and exhibition tickets. There's also a handy ticket desk on
the ground floor of **FNAC** (Mon–Sat 10am–10pm), the books and music
megastore in El Triangle shopping centre, Plaça de Catalunya.

The main clubs, concert halls and venues are listed below, but for up-to-date
art, music and culture information, the city council's Institute of Culture
website, Ⓦ **www.bcn.cat/cultura**, is invaluable – it covers every aspect of art
and culture in the city, with links to daily updated arts stories and a comprehensive calendar of events. Otherwise, the best **listings magazines** are the
weekly *Guía del Ocio* (Ⓦ www.guiadelociobcn.com) and *Time Out Barcelona*
(Ⓦ www.timeout.cat), online or from any newspaper stand. There's also a free
monthly "Cultural Agenda" guide in English available from tourist offices and
the Palau de la Virreina.

The year's big arts and culture festival is the summer **Festival de Barcelona
Grec**, featuring a wealth of music, theatre and dance. Other specific festivals are
highlighted in the relevant sections below – for full details turn to the festival
calendar in Chapter 15.

## Classical, contemporary and opera

Most of Barcelona's **classical** music concerts take place in the *modernista* Palau
de la Música Catalana or at the purpose-built, contemporary L'Auditori, while
**opera** is performed at its traditional home, the Gran Teatre del Liceu on the
Ramblas. Many of the city's churches, including the cathedral and Santa María

> The **locations of the venues** listed in this chapter are all marked on the neighbourhood maps in the Guide. Just check the address line for the relevant maps.

del Mar, also host concerts and recitals, while other interesting venues holding concerts include the historic Saló del Tinell in the Ajuntament, Palau Robert, FNAC Triangle at Plaça de Catalunya, Caixa Forum and the Fundació Joan Miró and CCCB (these two particularly for contemporary music).

Notable **festivals** include Nous Sons ("New Sounds"), the annual contemporary music festival (March–April), the Festival de Música Antiga (May), the Festa de la Música (June 21), and the Festival Opera Butxaca (Pocket Opera Festival; Nov), while there are free concerts in Barcelona's parks each July, the so-called **Clàssics als Parcs**.

**L'Auditori c/Lepant 150, Glòries** ☏ **932 479 300,** ⓦ **www.auditori.org;** Ⓜ **Marina/Monumental.** The city's main contemporary concert hall is home to the Orquestra Simfònica de Barcelona i Nacional de Catalunya (OBC), whose weekend concert season runs Sept–May. L'Auditori also puts on other orchestral and chamber works, jazz and world gigs, and music for children and families, while it's the main venue for the annual early music and contemporary music festivals. Under-26s with ID get fifty-percent discount on all tickets, 1hr before performances. The Bus de les Arts runs back to Pl. de Catalunya after concerts. Box office Mon–Sat noon–9pm, Sun 1hr before performance.

**Casa Elizalde c/València 302, Dreta de l'Eixample** ☏ **934 880 590,** ⓦ **www.casaelizalde .com;** Ⓜ **Passeig de Gràcia.** Small-scale classical concerts and recitals, plus more offbeat contemporary performances, held at the cultural centre, usually with free entry.

**Gran Teatre del Liceu Ramblas 51–59** ☏ **934 859 900; box office c/de Sant Pau 1** ☏ **934 859 913,** ⓦ **www.liceubarcelona.com;** Ⓜ **Liceu.** One of Europe's finest opera houses hosts a wide-ranging programme of opera and dance productions, plus other concerts and recitals including the extremely popular *sessions golfes* (late-night concerts). The season runs from Sept to June. Make bookings well in advance by phone or online – sales for the next season go on general sale in mid-July. Box office Mon–Fri 1.30–8pm, Sat & Sun 1hr before performance.

**Palau de la Música Catalana c/Palau de la Música 4-6, off c/Sant Pere Més Alt, Sant Pere** ☏ **932 957 200 or 902 442 882,** ⓦ **www .palaumusica.org;** Ⓜ **Urquinaona.** The extravagantly decorated Catalan concert hall is home to the Orfeó Català choral group, and venue for concerts by the Orquestra Ciutat de Barcelona among others, though there's a broad remit here – over a season you can catch anything, from *sardanes* to pop concerts. Concert season Sept–June. Box office Mon–Sat 10am–9pm, Sun 2hr before performance.

# Dance

Barcelona is very much a **contemporary dance** city, with regional, national and international performers and companies appearing regularly at theatre venues like the Mercat de les Flors, TNC, Teatre Lliure and Institut del Teatre – the latter, the city's theatre and dance school, has its own youth dance company, IT Dansa. The **Dies de Dansa** (Days of Dance) festival in July offers up brief (10- to 20-minute) contemporary dance performances of all kinds in courtyards at places like MACBA, CCCB, Caixa Forum and the Picasso and Miró museums.

For most visitors, however, dance in Barcelona means either watching (or joining in with) the Catalan national dance, the **sardana**, or catching a **flamenco** show. Although its home is indisputably Andalucia, flamenco also has deep roots in and around Barcelona, courtesy of its andaluz immigrants – unless you're looking for a showy night out, the pricey, tourist-oriented *tablaos* (flamenco and dinner shows) are best passed up in favour of the smaller clubs and restaurants that put on performances. If you're here at the end of April, don't miss the wild flamenco shows and parties of the **Feria de Abril de Catalunya**, a ten-day festival held down at the Fòrum site, and there are also two other flamenco festivals each year, in May and June.

## Dance venue

**Mercat de les Flors** c/de Lleida 59, Montjuïc ⊕ 934 261 875, ⓦ www.mercatflors.org; ⓜ **Poble Sec.** The city's old flower market serves as the "national centre for movement arts", with dance the central focus of its varied programme – from Asian performance art to European contemporary dance.

## Flamenco clubs

**El Tablao de Carmen** Poble Espanyol, Montjuïc ⊕ 933 256 895, ⓦ www.tablaodecarmen.com; ⓜ **Espanya.** The long-standing *tablao* in the Poble Espanyol at least looks the real deal, sited in a replica Andalucian street and featuring a variety of flamenco styles from both seasoned performers and new talent. Prices start at around €35 for the show and a drink, rising to €70 and upwards for the show plus dinner. Advance reservations essential. Tues–Sun, shows at 7.45pm & 10pm.

🏃 **Tarantos** Pl. Reial 17, Barri Gòtic ⊕ 933 191 789, ⓦ www.masimas.com; ⓜ Liceu. Some purists are sniffy about the experience, but for a cheap flamenco taster you can't beat *Tarantos* – a couple of rows of seats and a small bar in front of a stage where young singers, dancers and guitarists perform nightly at 8.30pm, 9.30pm & 10.30pm. Entry is just €6.

▲ Flamenco dancer at Tarantos

## Sardana performances

**Sardanes Populars** *Sardanes* are danced outside the cathedral, La Seu, in Plaça de la Seu (ⓜ Jaume I), every Sat at 6pm from Easter until the end of Nov You'll also see them danced at festivals and other public occasions.

# Film

All the latest films reach Barcelona fairly quickly, though at most of the larger cinemas and multiplexes (including the Maremàgnum screens at Port Vell) they're usually shown dubbed into Spanish or Catalan. However, several cinemas do show mostly **original-language** (*versión original* or V.O.) foreign films; the best are listed below. Tickets cost around €7, and most cinemas have one night (usually Mon or Wed) – *el día del espectador* – when entry is **discounted**, usually to around €5. Many cinemas also feature **late–night** screenings (*madrugadas*) on Friday and Saturday nights, which begin at 12.30 or 1am.

The city hosts several small **film festivals** throughout the year, including an international festival of independent short films, plus festivals devoted specifically to animation, women's, gay and lesbian, and African film. The Generalitat's FilmoTeca is often the venue for festival screenings. The sci-fi, horror and

## The sardana

The origins of the **sardana**, the Catalan national dance, are obscure, though similar folk dances in the Mediterranean date back hundreds if not thousands of years. It was established in its present form during the mid-nineteenth-century Renaixança (Renaissance), when Catalan arts and culture flourished, and was so identified with expressions of national identity that public dancing of *sardanes* was banned under the Franco regime. Sometimes mocked elsewhere in Spain, Catalans claim it to be truly democratic – a circle-dance open to all, danced in ordinary clothes (though some wear espadrilles) with no restriction in age or number. The dancers join hands, heads held high, arms raised, and though it looks deceptively simple and sedate it follows a precise pattern of steps, with shifts in pace and rhythm signalled by the accompanying *cobla* (band) of brass and wind instruments. This features typically Catalan instruments like the *flabiol* (a type of flute), and both tenor and soprano oboes, providing the characteristic high-pitched music. A strict etiquette applies to prevent the circle being broken in the wrong place, or a breakdown in the steps, and some of the more serious adherents may not welcome an intrusion into their circle by well-meaning first-timers. But usually visitors are encouraged to join the dance, especially at festival times, when the *sardana* breaks out spontaneously in the city's squares and parks. The **Federació Sardanista de Catalunya** (Ⓦ www.fed.sardanista .cat) publishes a calendar of dances and events on its website.

⑬ ENTERTAINMENT | Film

fantasy fest that is the **Festival Internacional de Cinema de Catalunya** (Ⓦ www.cinemasitges.com) is held in nearby Sitges in October.

## Cinemas

**Cine Maldà** c/del Pi 5, Barri Gòtic ℡ 934 813 704, Ⓜ Liceu. Hidden away in a little shopping centre just up from Plaça del Pi, the Maldà is a great place for independent movies and festival winners, all in V.O. Usually four screenings a day, plus a late-night showing, while Tues hosts art-house films under the banner of Cine Ambigù (Ⓦ www.retinas.org).

**FilmoTeca** Avgda. de Sarrià 33, Esquerra de l'Eixample ℡ 934 107 590, Ⓦ www.gencat.cat /cultura/icic/filmoteca; Ⓜ Hospital Clínic. Run by the Generalitat, the FilmoTeca shows three or four different films (often foreign-language, and usually in V.O.) every day – themed programming and retrospectives are its stock-in-trade. Tickets are just €2.70 per film, or there's an €18 pass allowing entry to ten films. A new cinema building is being constructed in the Raval for the FilmoTeca, but for the time being it will still be based at Avgda de Sarrià.

**Méliès** c/Villaroel 102, Esquerra de l'Eixample ℡ 934 510 051, Ⓦ www.cinesmelies.net; Ⓜ Urgell. A repertory cinema specializing in V.O. showings, with three to five different films daily in its two *salas*. Discount night Mon.

**Verdi** c/Verdi 32, and **Verdi Park**, c/Torrijos 49, Gràcia ℡ 932 387 990, Ⓦ www.cines-verdi .com; Ⓜ Fontana. Gràcia's popular sister cinemas are in adjacent streets, showing independent, art-house and V.O. movies from around the world. Late-night films at Verdi on Fri & Sat; discount night Mon.

**Yelmo-Icaria** c/de Salvador Espriu 61, Centre de la Vila, Port Olímpic ℡ 932 217 585, Ⓦ www .yelmocineplex.es; Ⓜ Ciutadella-Vila Olímpica. Fifteen screens showing mainstream Hollywood V.O. movies at a shopping centre multiplex, a few minutes' walk from the Port Olímpic. Late-night screenings Fri & Sat; discount night Mon.

## Open-air cinema

**Sala Montjuïc** Castell de Montjuïc Ⓦ www .salamontjuic.com. Every July there's a giant-screen open-air cinema established at Montjuïc castle (Mon, Wed & Fri night; tickets €4) – you're encouraged to bring a picnic. Screenings are in the original language, with Spanish subtitles, and range from current art-house hits to film club stalwarts like *Annie Hall*. The films usually start at 10.15pm, with live music first from 9pm, but with space limited to 2500 it's best to get there at opening time, 8.30pm, or buy in advance through ServiCaixa.

# Live music

Major **rock, pop and indie** bands include Barcelona on their tours, playing either at sports stadium venues (at the Palau Sant Jordi on Montjuïc and the Velòdrom d'Horta) or at the city's bigger clubs, like *Razzmatazz*, *Sala Apolo* and *Bikini* (all listed under "Clubs" in the previous chapter). Tickets for these run from €20 to €50, depending on the act though there are cheaper gigs (€5–20) almost every night of the year at a variety of smaller clubs and bars. The city's pretty hot on **jazz**, **Latin** and **blues**, while **folk**, **roots** and **world music** aficionados need to scour the club gig lists for home-grown and touring talent alike. All sorts of city venues, museums, galleries and institutions have **live music programmes** too – Caixa Forum is particularly well regarded, while the books-and-music chain **FNAC** (Ⓦwww.clubcultura.com) sponsors gigs and events at the concert halls at its stores at Plaça de Catalunya, L'Illa Diagonal and L'Illa Diagonal Mar. The **websites** Ⓦwww.atiza.com, Ⓦwww.barcelonarocks.com and Ⓦwww.gigmagazine.es provide a rundown of the Barcelona music scene, with gig calendars, band profiles and more.

Tickets for major gigs are available from the main **ticket agencies** (see chapter introduction); in addition, there's a concert ticket desk in the Plaça Catalunya FNAC store (ⓂCatalunya), while the music shops along c/dels Tallers (just off the Ramblas; ⓂCatalunya) also sell gig tickets.

The big annual **music festivals** start with the Generalitat's summer-long Festival de Barcelona Grec, while techno, rock and indie heads focus on Primavera Sound (May) and Sónar (June). Singer-songwriters are showcased every year at Barnasants (Jan–March), while for jazz fans the main event is the Festival de Jazz (Nov–Dec), as well as the jazz, blues and Latin-tinged Festival de Guitarra (April–May). There's also Gràcia's experimental and electronic music festival, known as LEM (Oct).

**Centre Artesà Tradicionàrius (CAT)** Trav. de Sant Antoni 6–8, Gràcia ☎932 184 485 Ⓦwww.tradicionarius.cat; ⓂFontana. The best place in town for folk and world gigs and recitals by Catalan and visiting performers, usually at weekends around 10pm. There are regular music and instrument workshops, while CAT also sponsors an annual international folk and traditional dance festival between Jan & April.

**Espacio Movistar** c/Pascual i Vila s/n, Les Corts Ⓦwww.espacio.movistar.es; ⓂPalau Reial/Collblanc. A huge multi-entertainment space in the university campus zone that puts on a big roster of major gigs, DJ sessions, film shows and festivals. There's also a bar and Internet lounge and plenty of student action, from Playstation booths to chill-out zones. The range is surprising, from drum lessons and song master-classes to gigs by the likes of Fatboy Slim or Craig David, and there's plenty for free.

**Harlem Jazz Club** c/Comtessa de Sobradiel 8, Barri Gòtic ☎933 100 755; ⓂJaume I. For many years, *the* hot place for jazz, though don't let the name mislead you

– every jazz style gets an airing here, from African and gypsy to flamenco and fusion. Live music nightly at 11pm & 12.30am (Sat & Sun 11.30pm & 1am); it's best to get advance tickets for the second spot. Usually free midweek, otherwise cover charge up to €10. Closed Aug.

**Jamboree** Pl. Reial 17, Barri Gòtic ☎933 191 789, Ⓦwww.masimas.com; ⓂLiceu. There's a really good range of jazz gigs here, from traditional to modern, with sessions at 9pm & 11pm (from €10), with an additional Mon night jazz, funk and hip-hop jam session (€4). Best of all, every night you can stay on for the club, playing funk, swing, hip-hop and R&B from around midnight until 5am.

**Jazzroom** c/Vallmajor 33, Sant Gervasi ☎933 191 789, Ⓦwww.masimas.com; FGC Muntaner. One of Barcelona's best jazz clubs serves up live music Tues–Sat from 9pm – some of the bigger names play here. Cover charge €10–20 depending on the act. Closed Aug.

**Jazz Sí Club** c/Requesens 2, El Raval ☎933 290 020, Ⓦwww.tallerdemusics.com; ⓂSant Antoni. Good, inexpensive

It may not have the global influence of 1980s Manchester or 1990s Seattle, but the *mestiza* sound of twenty-first-century Barcelona is causing quite a stir – a cross-cultural fusion of rock, reggae, rap, hip-hop, rai, son, flamenco, rumba and electronica. Its heartland is the immigrant melting-pot of the Raval district, whose postcode – **08001** – lends a name to the sound's hippest flagbearers. Also typically "Raval" is the collective called **Cheb Balowski**, an Algerian-Catalan fusion band, while **Macaco** draw on their South American heritage with their characteristic mix of rumba, ragga and hip-hop. The biggest star on the scene is the Parisian-born, Barcelona-resident **Manu Chao**, whose infectious, multi-million-selling album *Clandestino* (1998) kick-started the whole genre. He's widely known abroad now, and has influenced many Barcelona bands, including the world music festival favourites **Ojos de Brujo** (Eyes of the Wizard), who present a fusion reinvention of flamenco and Catalan rumba. Other hot sounds are being hatched by the ska-tinged acoustic roots outfit **Dusminguet**, the Latin American dub and reggae band **GoLem System**, the Latin fusion merchants **Radio Malanga** and the rock-and-rumba duo, **Estopa**. Street and hip-hop freestyle bands also have a loyal local following, with **Payo Malo** and **LA Kinky Beat** the names to check. There's more information on the useful *mestiza* portal ⓦwww.radiochango.com, while you can hear all the above – and more – on three great samplers, *Barcelona Raval Sessions*, *Barcelona Raval Sessions 2* and *Barcelona Zona Bastarda*. For new-wave Catalan rumba, get hold of the *Rambla Rumble Rumba* compilation.

gigs in a small club and bar associated with the music school. Every night from around 8 or 9pm there's something different, from rock, blues, jazz and jam sessions to the popular weekly Cuban (Thurs) and flamenco (Fri) nights.
**Luz de Gas** c/Muntaner 246, Esquerra de l'Eixample ⓣ932 097 711, ⓦwww.luzdegas .com; ⓜDiagonal. Live music (rock, blues, soul, jazz and covers) every night around midnight. Foreign acts appear regularly, too, mainly jazz-blues types but also old soul acts and up-and-coming rockers.
**Sala BeCool** Pl. Joan Llongueras 5, Sant Gervasi ⓣ933 620 413, ⓦwww.salabecool.com; ⓜHospital Clinic/FGC Muntaner. Thumping

uptown club venue for local and national rock, indie and electro/techno bands and DJs. Gigs currently Thurs–Sat nights, followed by DJ sessions, with cover for either running from €10 to €20, depending on who's appearing.
🏃 **Sidecar** Pl. Reial 7, Barri Gòtic ⓣ933 021 586, ⓦwww.sidecarfactoryclub.com; ⓜLiceu. The hippest concert space in the old town – pronounced "See-day-car" – has nightly gigs and DJs that champion rock, indie, roots and fusion acts. Admission for most gigs around €7–10, though some gigs up to €20. Tues–Sun 8pm–4.30am, gigs usually at 10.30pm.

# Theatre and cabaret

The **Teatre Nacional de Catalunya** (Catalan National Theatre) was specifically conceived as a venue to promote Catalan productions, and features a repertory programme of translated classics (such as Shakespeare in Catalan), original works and productions by guest companies from Europe. The other big local theatrical project is the **Ciutat del Teatre** (Theatre City) on Montjuïc, which incorporates the fringe-style Mercat de les Flors, the progressive Teatre Lliure and the Institut del Teatre theatre and dance school. The centre for commercial theatre is on and off the Ramblas and along Avinguda Paral.lel and the nearby streets. Some theatres draw on the city's strong **cabaret** tradition – more music-hall entertainment than stand-up comedy, and thus a little more accessible to non-Catalan or Spanish speakers. For **children's theatre**, see p.253.

A free monthly magazine **Teatre BCN** (Ⓦwww.teatrebcn.com) carries listings and reviews (in Catalan). **Tickets** are available from the box offices at the Palau de la Virreina (Ramblas 99), or the usual agency outlets. Same-day **half-price tickets** (Tiquet-3) for some shows can be bought at the Caixa de Catalunya desk (Mon–Sat 10am–10pm, Sun 3–7pm) in the Plaça de Catalunya tourist office.

The summer Festival de Barcelona always has a strong theatre and dance programme – many performances are at the open-air **Teatre Grec** on Montjuïc.

## Theatre venues

**L'Antic Teatre** c/Verdaguer i Callis 12, Sant Pere ☎933 152 354, Ⓦwww.lanticteatre.com; ⓂUrquinaona. A small, independent theatre with a wildly original programme of events, many free, from video shows and art exhibitions to offbeat cabaret performances, modern dance and left-field music. In the end though, the best bit may just be the bar (open daily 4–11pm) and the summer garden *terrassa*.

🏃 **Café Teatre Llantiol** c/Riereta 7, El Raval ☎933 299 009, Ⓦwww.llantiol.com; ⓂParal.lel/Sant Antoni. Idiosyncratic café-theatre whose varied shows feature a mix of mime, song, poetry, clowns, magic and dance; performances usually at 9pm & 11pm, with an additional late-night Saturday special. It is also the venue of the once-a-month Giggling Guiri (Ⓦwww.comedyinspain.com) comedy night (in English), which attracts some well-known stand-up acts. Closed Mon.

**Institut del Teatre** Pl. Margarida Xirgu s/n, Montjuïc ☎932 273 900, Ⓦwww.institutdelteatre.org; ⓂPoble Sec. Regular performances of all kinds at the school for dramatic arts and dance.

**Teatre Lliure** Pl. Margarida Xirgu, Montjuïc ☎932 289 747, Ⓦwww.teatrelliure.cat; ⓂPoble Sec. The "Free Theatre" performs the work of contemporary Catalan and Spanish playwrights, as well as reworkings of the classics, from Shakespeare to David Mamet; it also hosts visiting dance companies, concerts and recitals. Some productions have English subtitles.

**Teatre Nacional de Catalunya (TNC)** Pl. de les Arts 1, Glòries ☎933 065 700, Ⓦwww.tnc.cat; ⓂGlòries. Intended to foster Catalan works, the national theatre – built as a modern emulation of an ancient Greek temple – features major productions by Catalan, Spanish and European companies, as well as smaller-scale plays, experimental works and dance productions.

▲ Teatre Nacional de Catalunya

**Teatre Poliorama** Ramblas 115, El Raval ☎933 177 599, Ⓦwww.teatrepoliorama.com; ⓂCatalunya. Specializes in modern drama (Catalan and translation) and musicals, often utilizing the talents of offbeat companies like Tricicle and Dagoll Dagom (see box opposite).

**Teatre Romea** c/Hospital 51, El Raval ☎933 181 431, Ⓦwww.fundacioromea.org; ⓂLiceu. Has an emphasis on contemporary Catalan and Spanish playwrights, and pan-European productions, and gives space to new theatre groups and radical directors.

# Visual arts

Barcelona has dozens of private art galleries and exhibition halls in addition to the temporary displays on show in its art centres, museums and galleries. Major venues with regularly changing art exhibitions include Caixa Forum,

## Catalan theatre companies

**Els Comediants** (ⓦ www.comediants.com) – a travelling collective of actors, musicians and artists, established in 1971, who use any open space as a stage to celebrate "the festive spirit of human existence".

**La Cubana** (ⓦ www.lacubana.es) is a highly original company that started life as a street theatre group, though has since moved into television and theatre proper. It still hits the streets occasionally, taking on the role of market traders in the Boqueria or cleaning cars in the street in full evening dress.

**Dagoll Dagom** (ⓦ www.dagolldagom.com) specializes in hugely theatrical, over-the-top musicals.

**La Fura del Baus** (Vermin of the Sewer; ⓦ www.lafura.com) are performance artists who aim to shock and lend a new meaning to audience participation. They've subsequently taken on opera, cabaret, film and installations, lending each a wild, challenging perspective.

**Els Joglars** (ⓦ www.elsjoglars.com) present political theatre, and are particularly critical of the Church and government, who come in for regular satirical attacks.

**Teatre Nu** (Naked Theatre; ⓦ www.teatrenu.com) was founded in 1991 by young Catalan actors who wanted to bring theatre back to its essence and "provoke social, moral and ideological dialectic between the audience and public".

**Tricicle** (ⓦ www.tricicle.com) – a very successful three-man mime, circus and theatre group – has branched off into film and television, but always places its humour "somewhere between reality and the absurd".

CCCB, MACBA and Fundació Antoni Tàpies for contemporary art; Espai 13 at Fundacío Joan Miró for young experimental artists; MNAC and La Pedrera for blockbuster international art shows; FAD for industrial and graphic art, design, craft and architecture; and the Centre d'Art Santa Mònica for contemporary Catalan art and photography. A few more specialist places are listed below.

**Commercial galleries** cluster together in the **Barri Gòtic** on c/Palla and c/Petritxol near the cathedral; in La Ribera on c/de Montcada and Passeig del Born; in **El Raval** on c/Àngels and c/Doctor Dou near the MACBA; and in the **Eixample** on Passeig de Gràcia, c/Consell de Cent and Rambla Catalunya. Note that most commercial galleries are closed on Sundays, Mondays and in August. The weekly *Guía del Ocio* and the *Associació Art Barcelona* (ⓦ www.artbarcelona .es) have gallery listings and exhibition news. In spring **photography** fans should look out for the Primavera Fotogràfica, when photography exhibitions are held at various venues around the city.

### Art and cultural centres

**Capella de l'Antic Hospital de la Santa Creu** c/de l'Hospital 56, El Raval ☎ 934 427 171, ⓦ www.bcn.es/virreinaexposicions; Ⓜ Liceu. Contemporary art of all kinds, though often a platform for work by young Barcelona artists.

**Fundació Foto Colectania** c/Julian Romea 6, Gràcia ☎ 932 171 626, ⓦ www.colectania.es; Ⓜ Fontana. Spanish and Portuguese photography shows, with works from the 1950s onwards.

**Palau Robert** Pg. de Gràcia 107, Dreta de l'Eixample ☎ 932 388 091, ⓦ www.gencat.cat /palaurobert; Ⓜ Diagonal. Puts on a wide range of shows, all with a Catalan connection.

**Palau de la Virreina** Ramblas 99, Barri Gòtic ☎ 933 161 000, ⓦ www.bcn.cat/virreina centredelaimatge; Ⓜ Liceu. Contemporary art and photography shows in two galleries.

**Sala d'Art Jove de la Generalitat** c/Calabria 147, Esquerra de l'Eixample ☎ 934 838 361; Ⓜ Rocafort. The Generalitat's youth art space. Closed Aug.

## Commercial galleries

**Galleria Joan Prats** **Rambla de Catalunya 54, Esquerra de l'Eixample** ☎ 932 160 290, Ⓦ www .galeriajoanprats.com; Ⓜ **Passeig de Gràcia.** A well-regarded space for contemporary Catalan artists and photographers.

**H2O** **c/Verdi 152, Gràcia** ☎ 934 151 801, Ⓦ www.h2o.es; Ⓜ **Fontana/Lesseps.** Design, photography, contemporary art.

**Iguapop Gallery** **c/del Comerç 15, Sant Pere** ☎ 933 100 735, Ⓦ www.iguapop.net; Ⓜ **Jaume I.** Unique Born gallery showcasing street and pop art, graffiti and contemporary photography – and now with a funky clothes and accessories shop too.

**Kowasa** **c/de Mallorca 235, Esquerra de l'Eixample** ☎ 934 876 137, Ⓦ www.kowasa.com;

Ⓜ **Provença.** Traditional and contemporary photography and photographic art, featuring Spanish and international photographers; it's above the photography bookshop of the same name.

**Sala Parés** **c/Petritxol 5–8, Barri Gòtic** ☎ 933 187 020, Ⓦ www.salapares.com; Ⓜ **Liceu.** Possibly the most famous gallery in the city, established in the mid-nineteenth century, Sala Parés hosted Picasso's first show. It still deals exclusively in nineteenth- and twentieth-century Catalan art, putting on around twenty exhibitions a year, including a biannual "Famous Paintings" exhibition of works by some of the best-known Spanish and Catalan names.

# Gay and lesbian Barcelona

There's a vibrant gay and lesbian scene in Barcelona (or "Gaycelona", as some would have it), backed up by an established organizational infrastructure and a generally supportive city council. Information about the scene is pretty easy to come by, while locals and tourists alike are well aware of the lure of Sitges, mainland Spain's biggest gay resort, just forty minutes south by train.

The expression for the gay scene in Spanish is *"el ambiente"*, which simply means "the atmosphere" – it's the name of the useful section in the weekly listings magazine *Guía del Ocio*, which lists gay and lesbian bars, clubs, restaurants and other services.

We've picked out the best of bars, clubs, restaurants and hotels aimed specifically at a gay and lesbian clientele. They're scattered across the city, though there's a particular concentration in the so-called **Gaixample**, the "Gay Eixample", an area of a few square blocks just northwest of the main university in the Esquerra de l'Eixample. Bear in mind that you'll also be welcome at plenty of other nominally straight Barcelona dance bars and clubs.

For up-to-date **information** and other advice on the scene, you can contact any of the organizations listed below, or call the **lesbian and gay city telephone hotline** on ☎900 601 601 (toll free, daily 6–10pm only). Aside from the weekly bar and club listings in *Guía del Ocio* and *Time Out Barcelona*, there's also a good free **magazine** called *Nois* (ⓦwww.revistanois .com), which carries an up-to-date review of the scene. BarcelonaGay (ⓦwww.barcelonagay.com) has a useful map highlighting the main gay and lesbian attractions in the city, ⓦwww.gayxi.com has more gay-friendly reviews, while ⓦwww.gays-abroad.com is a forum and chat site for gay men living in or visiting Barcelona.

The biggest event of the year is **Carnival** in Sitges (see p.153), while there's the Barcelona International Gay and Lesbian **Film Festival** every October (ⓦwww.cinemalambda.com). Barcelona's annual lesbian and gay **pride march** is on the nearest Saturday to June 28, starting at Plaça Universitat. Barcelona is also often the venue of choice for other international gay and lesbian gatherings – in 2008, for example, the city hosted both the Eurogames (the European Gay and Lesbian Sports Championships) and the Girlie Circuit Festival (international lesbian rally and festival).

## Useful contacts

**Ca la Dona** c/de Casp 38, Dreta de l'Eixample ℡934 127 161, ⓦwww.caladona.org; Ⓜ Urquinaona. A women's centre with library and bar, used for meetings by various feminist and lesbian organizations; information available to callers.

**Casal Lambda** c/Verdaguer i Callis 10, Sant Pere ℡933 195 550, ⓦwww.lambdaweb.org; Ⓜ Urquinaona. A gay and lesbian centre with a wide range of social, cultural and educational events. The website is also in English.

**Coordinadora Gai-Lesbiana de Catalunya (CGL)** c/Violant d'Hongria 156, Sants ℡932 980 029, ⓦwww.cogailes.org; Ⓜ Plaça del Centre. The CGL issues the Targeta LGTB (Gay Card), which, for €10 per month gives discounts, free admission and other advantages at a wide variety of businesses and venues across the city.

**Front d'Alliberament Gai de Catalunya (FAGC)** c/Verdi 88, Gràcia ℡932 172 669, ⓦwww.fagc .org; Ⓜ Fontana. Association for gay men, with a library, meetings and events.

## Bookshops

**Antinous** c/Josep Anselm Clavé 6, Barri Gòtic ℡933 019 070, ⓦwww.antinouslibros.com; Ⓜ Drassanes. Gay bookshop with useful contacts and information board – there's a café at the back. Closed Sun.

**Cómplices** c/Cervantes 2, Barri Gòtic ℡934 127 283, ⓦwww.libreriacomplices.com; Ⓜ Liceu. Exclusively gay and lesbian bookshop; also magazines and DVDs. Closed Sun.

## Accommodation

**Outlet4Spain** ℡938 102 711, ⓦwww.outlet4spain .com. Gay-run accommodation agency, which specializes in gay-friendly hotels, villas, apartments and flat-shares in Barcelona and Sitges; the website's in English.

**Hotel Axel** c/d'Aribau 33, Esquerra de l'Eixample ℡933 239 393, ⓦwww.axelhotels.com; Ⓜ Universitat. A snazzy "heterofriendly" boutique hotel set in the Gaixample, with stylishly appointed rooms in which designer fabrics, complimentary beauty products, flat-screen TVs and Internet access come as standard. Relaxation is taken care of in the restaurant and bar, library corner, chill-out area, terrace pool and sauna, and there's a fitness centre and massage treatments available. From €170.

**Hotel California** c/Rauric 14, Barri Gòtic ℡933 177 766, ⓦwww.hotelcaliforniabcn.com; Ⓜ Liceu. Tucked down a side street that crosses c/de Ferran, this friendly old-town hotel has nicely colour-coordinated rooms with TV, a/c and full bathrooms, breakfast included in the price. There are some internal rooms, and all are double-glazed, but even so, you never quite escape the weekend noise in this part of town. From €90.

**Hostal Que Tal** c/Mallorca 290, Dreta de l'Eixample ℡934 592 366, ⓦwww.quetal barcelona.com; Ⓜ Passeig de Gràcia/Verdaguer. Pretty rooms, with and without private bath, in a good uptown location. It's a nice, if modest, choice, with an attractive courtyard patio. No credit cards. From €65, en suite from €85.

## Cafés and bars

**Aire** c/Valencia 236, Esquerra de l'Eixample ℡934 515 812, ⓦwww.arenadisco.com; Ⓜ Passeig de Gràcia. The hottest, most stylish lesbian bar in town is a surprisingly relaxed place for a drink and a dance to pop, house and retro sounds. Gay men welcome too. Thurs–Sat 11pm–3am, July & Aug also Tues & Wed.

**Átame** c/Consell de Cent 257, Esquerra de l'Eixample ℡934 549 273; Ⓜ Universitat. Contemporary music bar with a change of pace, from early evening drinks and gentility to late-night hot sounds. Daily 6pm–2am.

**Dietrich** c/Consell de Cent 255, Esquerra de l'Eixample ℡934 517 707; Ⓜ Universitat. Cornerstone of the Gaixample scene is this well-known music bar and "teatro-café" – *tranquilo* during the week, but ever more hedonistic as the weekend wears on, with drag shows, acrobats and dancers punctuating the DJ sets. Daily 6pm–2.30am.

**People Lounge** c/Villarroel 71, Esquerra de l'Eixample ℡935 327 743, ⓦwww.peoplebcn .com; Ⓜ Urgell. Stylish cafe-bar where you shouldn't feel out of place if you're over forty. Daily 8pm–2am.

**Punto BCN** c/Muntaner 63–65, Esquerra de l'Eixample ℡934 536 123, ⓦwww.arenadisco .com; Ⓜ Universitat. A Gaixample classic that attracts an uptown crowd for drinks, chat and music – it's a popular trysting place. Wed happy hour is a blast, while Fri night is party night. Daily 6pm–2.30am.

**Zeltas** c/Casanova 75, Esquerra de l'Eixample ℡934 541 902, ⓦwww.zeltas.net; Ⓜ Urgell.

## Restaurants

Barcelona has several gay- and lesbian-friendly or gay- and lesbian-run restaurants, where you'll be assured of a warm welcome and sympathetic atmosphere. **dDivine** (c/Balmes 24, Esquerra de l'Eixample ℗933 172 248, Ⓦwww.ddivine.com; Ⓜ Universitat; closed Sun, and Mon & Tues dinner) probably has the highest profile, offering weekday lunches and coffee, plus dinner with a live drag show. More relaxed, moderately priced gay-friendly eateries include the New York-style **Castro** (c/Casanova 85, Esquerra de l'Eixample ℗933 236 784, Ⓦwww.castrorestaurant .com; Ⓜ Universitat; closed Sat lunch & Sun) and fusion-Italian **Iurantia** (c/Casanova 42, Esquerra de l'Eixample ℗934 547 887, Ⓦwww.iurantia.com; Ⓜ Universitat; closed Sat lunch & Sun).

Pumped-up house-music bar for the pre-club crowd. Wed–Sun 11pm–3am.

### Clubs

As well as the gay and lesbian clubs reviewed below, the biggest club night in the city is Gay Day (Sun, at *Space Barcelona*).

**Arena Madre c/Balmes 32, Esquerra de l'Eixample** ℗934 878 342, Ⓦwww.arenadisco .com; Ⓜ **Passeig de Gràcia.** The "mother" club sits at the helm of the Arena empire, all within a city block (pay for one, get in to all) – frenetic house and chart at *Arena Madre* (Mon–Sat 12.30–5am, Sun 7pm–5am), high disco antics at *Arena Classic* (c/de la Diputació 233; Fri & Sat 12.30–6am), more of the same plus dance, R&B, pop and rock at the more mixed *Arena VIP* (Gran Via de les Corts Catalanes 593; Fri & Sat 1–6am), and the best in house at *Arena Dandy*

(Grand Via de les Corts Catalanes 593; Fri & Sat 1–6am).

**Dboy Ronda de Sant Pere 19–21, Dreta de l'Eixample** ℗933 180 686, Ⓦwww .matineegroup.com; Ⓜ **Urquinaona.** The old Salvation, reborn, is bigger and better than ever, offering a nonstop fusion of beats. Fri & Sat 12.30–5am.

**Kiut c/Consell de Cent 280, Esquerra de l'Eixample, no phone,** Ⓦwww.kiutdisco.com; Ⓜ **Universitat/Passeig de Gràcia.** A new "cute" lesbian dance space, from the owners of *Zeltas*. Thurs–Sun 11.30pm–5am.

**Metro c/Sepúlveda 158, Esquerra de l'Eixample** ℗933 235 227, Ⓦwww.metrodiscobcn.com; Ⓜ **Universitat/Urgell.** A gay institution in Barcelona, with cabaret nights and other events midweek. Extremely crowded at weekends in its two rooms playing either current dance and house or retro disco. Daily midnight–5am.

# Festivals and holidays

A lmost any month you choose to visit Barcelona you'll coincide with a saint's day, festival or holiday, and it's hard to beat the experience of arriving to discover the streets decked out with flags and streamers, bands playing and the entire population out celebrating. Traditionally, each neighbourhood celebrates with its own *festa*, though the major ones – like Gràcia's Festa Major and the Mercè – have become city institutions. Each is different, but there is always music, dancing, traditional costume, fireworks and an immense spirit of enjoyment – for more, see the colour section.

The religious calendar has its annual highlights too, with Carnaval, Easter and Christmas a big time for parades, events and festivities across the city. Meanwhile, biggest and best of the annual arts and music events are the Generalitat's (city council's) summer Festival de Barcelona Grec, the ever-expanding Sónar extravaganza of electronic music and multimedia art, and the rock and indie fest Primavera Sound.

There's a **month–by–month calendar** below of the best annual festivals, holidays, trade fairs and events, though it's not an exhaustive list. For more information about what's going on at any given time, call into the cultural information office at the **Palau de la Virreina**, Ramblas 99, or check out the Ajuntament's useful **website** (ⓦ www.bcn.cat/cultura).

Incidentally, not all **public holidays** coincide with a festival, but many do – there's a complete list on p.39. In addition, saints' day festivals – indeed all Catalan celebrations – can vary in date, often being observed over the weekend closest to the dates given.

## January

**Cap d'Any New Year's Eve** Street and club parties, and mass gatherings in Pl. de Catalunya and other main squares. You're supposed to eat twelve grapes in the last twelve seconds of the year for twelve months of good luck. The next day, Jan 1, is a public holiday.

**Cavalcada dels Reis Afternoon of Jan 5** This is when the Three Kings (who distribute Christmas gifts to Spanish children) arrive by sea at the port and ride into town, throwing sweets as they go. The parade begins at about 5pm on Jan 5; the next day is a public holiday.

**Barnasants Dates vary, Jan–March,** ⓦ www .barnasants.com A singer-songwriter festival

(Catalan/Spanish, plus Brazilian and Latin American artists), with around 50 gigs held over three months in city clubs and concert venues.

**Festa dels Tres Tombs Jan 17** Costumed horseback parade through the Sant Antoni neighbourhood with local saint's day festivities to follow. *Tomb* is the Catalan word for a circuit, or tour, so the riders make three processional turns of the neighbourhood.

## February

**Festes de Santa Eulàlia Feb 12** ⓦ www.bcn .cat/santaeulalia. The signal for a week's worth of music, *sardanes*, children's processions, *castellers* and fireworks in honour of one of Barcelona's two patron saints, the thirteen-year-old girl martyred by the Romans. See colour section for more.

**Carnaval/Carnestoltes Week before Lent, sometimes in March** ⓦwww.bcn.cat/carnaval Costumed parades, dances, concerts, open-air barbecues and other traditional carnival events in every city neighbourhood. However, it's Sitges, down the coast, which has the best Catalan celebrations.

## March/April

**Festes de Sant Medir de Gràcia First week in March** ⓦwww.santmedir.org Horse-and-carriage parade around Gràcia, before heading to the Sant Medir hermitage in the Collserola hills. Later, the procession returns to Gràcia, where thousands of sweets are thrown to children along the route, and there's plenty of traditional dancing and feasting.

**Setmana Santa Easter, Holy Week** Religious celebrations and services at churches throughout the city. Special services are on Thurs and Fri in Holy Week at 7–8pm, Sat at 10pm; there's a procession from the church of Sant Agustí on c/de l'Hospital (El Raval) to La Seu, starting at around 4pm on Good Friday; and Palm Sunday sees the blessing of the palms at La Seu. Public holidays on Good Friday and Easter Monday.

**Dia de Sant Jordi St George's Day, April 23** ⓦwww.bcn.cat/stjordi Celebrating Catalunya's patron saint and coinciding with the International Day of the Book, with book and flower stalls throughout the city. Men are traditionally presented with a book while women are given a rose. See colour section for more.

**Feria de Abril de Catalunya Last week in April** ⓦwww.fecac.com The region's biggest Andalucian festival, with ten days of food, drink and flamenco. All the action goes down at the big marquees erected at the Fòrum plaza (Diagonal Mar).

**Festival de Guitarra April & May** ⓦwww.theproject.cat A spring-season perennial, the annual guitar festival showcases all sorts of musical styles, jazz and Latin, blues and fusion, with some big names playing every year. Gigs are at concert halls across the city.

**Saló Internacional del Còmic Dates vary, April or May** ⓦwww.ficomic.com The International Comic Fair takes place over three days, with stalls, drawing workshops and children's activities at one of the city's exhibition halls.

## May

**Dia del Treball May 1** May Day/Labour Day is a public holiday, with union parades along main city thoroughfares.

**Dia de San Ponç May 11** A traditional saint's day, celebrated by a market running along c/de l'Hospital in the Raval, with fresh herbs, flowers, cakes, aromatic oils and sweets.

**Festival de Música Antiga Usually first two weeks** ⓦwww.auditori.org The Early Music Festival attracts medieval and Baroque groups from around the world, with concerts based at L'Auditori concert hall, but there are free fringe shows outdoors in old-town squares.

**Barcelona Poesia Second or third week** ⓦwww.bcn.cat/barcelonapoesia Week-long poetry festival with readings and recitals in venues across the city. It incorporates the Jocs Floral (Floral Games), a revived medieval Catalan poetry competition, while Spanish and foreign poets converge for the International Poetry Festival at the Palau de la Música Catalana.

**Dia Internacional dels Museus May 18** On International Museum Day, there's free entrance to all city-run museums – local press have details of participating museums, opening hours and special events.

**Primavera Sound Usually last week** ⓦwww.primaverasound.com The city's hottest music festival heralds a three-day bash down at the Parc del Fòrum (Diagonal Mar), attracting top international names in the rock, indie and electronica world. It's extended into the city too, with club gigs and free street gigs now part of the scene.

**Festival de Flamenco de Ciutat Vella Usually last week** ⓦwww.flamencociutatvella.com, ⓦwww.tallersdemusics.com Annual old-town flamenco bash, organized by the Taller de Músics (music workshop) and centred on the CCCB. Five days of guitar recitals, singing and dancing, plus DJ sessions and chill-out zone, and lectures and conferences on all matters flamenco.

## June

**Sónar Usually 2nd or 3rd week** ⓦwww.sonar.es The three-day International Festival of Advanced Music and Multimedia Art is

Europe's biggest and most cutting-edge electronic music, multimedia and urban art festival, attracting up to 100,000 visitors. Sónar by day centres on events at MACBA/ CCCB (Museu d'Art Contemporani de Barcelona); by night the action shifts to out-of-town L'Hospitalet, with all-night buses running from the city to the Sónar bars and clubs. Separate day, night and general tickets available – buy well in advance, online, by phone or from the Palau de la Virreina.

**Festa de la Música June 21 ⓦwww.bcn.cat /festadelamusica** Every year on this day, scores of free concerts are held in squares, parks, civic centres and museums in every neighbourhood across the city – buskers to orchestras, folk to techno. There are concerts in the 2 or 3 preceding days too, so you're bound to catch something you like.

**Verbena/Dia de Sant Joan June 23–24** The "eve" and "day" of St John herald probably the wildest celebrations in the city, with a "night of fire" of bonfires and fireworks (particularly on Montjuïc), drinking and dancing. *Coca de Sant Joan*, a sweet flatbread, and *cava* are the traditional accompaniments to the merriment – see colour section for more. The day itself (June 24) is a public holiday.

**De Cajón June & 1st week July ⓦwww .theproject.cat** Busy festival promoters The Project have inaugurated another flamenco fest, as big-name flamenco stars perform a series of one-off concerts in major city concert halls.

**Festival de Barcelona Grec June–Aug ⓦwww .barcelonafestival.com** Starting in the last week of June (and running throughout July and into Aug), this is the city's main performing arts festival, with a strong programme of theatre, music and dance productions, many staged at Montjuïc's Teatre Grec. See *Festive Barcelona* colour section for more.

## July

**Dies de Dansa 1st week ⓦwww.marato.com** Part of the summer Grec festival, this four-day contemporary dance extravaganza sees free daytime performances in buildings, parks, streets, squares, museums and galleries across the city, plus evening events and video projections at the CCCB.

**Summercase Barcelona Two days in July, dates vary ⓦwww.summercase.com** The sound of summer is the huge annual rock and indie concert at the Parc del Fòrum

(with a simultaneous sister gig in Madrid), held over a weekend in July. It's the summer version of November's big-name indie festival.

## August

**Festa Major de Gràcia Mid-Aug ⓦwww .festamajordegracia.cat** A fine example of what was once a local festival in the erstwhile village of Gràcia, with music, dancing, decorated floats and streets transformed into magical scenes, plus noisy fireworks, parades of giants and devils, and human castle-building in main squares. The festivities last a week – don't miss them if you're in town.

**Festa Major de Sants Last week of Aug** Another week's worth of traditional festivities in an untouristed neighbourhood, in the streets behind Barcelona Sants station.

## September

**Diada Nacional Sept 11** Catalan national day, commemorating the eighteenth-century defeat at the hands of the Bourbons. It's a public holiday in Barcelona, and special events include the city's more radical Catalan nationalists throwing bricks through burger-bar windows, fighting with the police and showing their patriotism by spraying graffiti on every available space.

**Festes de la Mercè Sept 24** Huge annual festival dedicated to another of Barcelona's

▲ Festes de la Mercè

If you look beyond the big-name acts and the major annual celebrations, there's a whole world of off-the-radar festive fun in Barcelona, with some events just putting a toe in the water and others growing more elaborate with each year. February's **Minifestival** (Ⓦwww.minifestival.net), for example, provides a neat suburban counterpoint to the bigger city music fests, highlighting international indie acts that you've definitely never heard of. In May, **Loop** (Ⓦwww.loop-videoart.com), the international fair and festival for video-art, attracts hundreds of artists from dozens of countries. September sees the ever-improving **Asia Festival** (Ⓦwww.casaasia.es/festival), with dance, theatre, music, DJs, children's activities, performance art and workshops showcasing the culture of Asia and the Pacific Region. By October, digi-heads and Second Lifers are ready for **Artfutura** (Ⓦwww.artfutura.org), the digital culture and creativity festival, while alternative Christmas shopping is best done at **Drap-Art** (Ⓦwww.drapart.org), the Festival of Creative Recycling, which puts on its annual bash and market at the CCCB (Ⓦwww.cccb.org) and FAD (Ⓦwww.fadweb.org).

⑮

**FESTIVALS AND HOLIDAYS**

patron saints, the Virgin of Mercè, and celebrated for a week around this date (Sept 24 is a public holiday). Highlights include costumed giants, breathtaking firework displays, and competing teams of *castellers* – see colour section for more. During the week, the concurrent alternative music festival, known as BAM (Ⓦwww.bcn.cat/bam), puts on free rock, world and fusion gigs at emblematic old-town locations and at Parc del Fòrum.

**Festa Major de Sant Miquel/Barceloneta Last week** Traditional festivities on the waterfront as Barceloneta celebrates its saint's day with fireworks, parades, *castellers*, music and dancing.

### October

**LEM Throughout Oct** Ⓦwww.gracia-territori.com Experimental and electronic music and art festival organized by the Gràcia Territori Sonor collective, with free or cheap concerts, events and happenings held in Gràcia's bars, cafés and galleries.

**Festival de Tardor Ribermúsica Third week** Ⓦwww.ribermusica.org Wide-ranging four-day music festival held in the Born, with free concerts in historic and picturesque locations.

**Festival Internacional de Jazz Last week in Oct and through Nov** Ⓦwww.theproject.cat The biggest annual jazz festival in town has been going for four decades and attracts superstar solo artists and bands to the clubs and concert halls, as well as putting on smaller-scale street concerts.

**Festival Opera Butxaca Last week in Oct and through Nov** Ⓦwww.festivaloperabutxaca.org

The "Pocket Opera Festival" showcases new Catalan and European operas in chamber and medium format, with performances in the smaller theatres and spaces at the Liceu, TNC, L'Auditori and other venues.

### November

**Tots Sants All Saints' Day, Nov 1** When the Spanish remember their dead with cemetery visits and special meals, it's traditional to eat roast chestnuts (*castanyes*), sold by street vendors, sweet potatoes and *panellets* (almond-based sweets). It's also a public holiday.

**Wintercase Barcelona End of Nov** Ⓦwww.wintercase.com Gloom-mongers, mullets and guitar-merchants celebrate at this one-night indie music showcase, with similar one-night gigs also held in Madrid, Valencia and Bilbao.

### December

**Fira de Santa Llúcia Dec 1–22** For more than 200 years the Christmas season has seen a special market and crafts fair outside the cathedral. Browse for gifts or watch the locals snapping up Christmas trees, Nativity figures and traditional decorations.

**Nadal/Sant Esteve Dec 25–26** Ⓦwww.bcn.cat/nadal Christmas Day and St Stephen's Day are both public holidays, which Catalans tend to spend at home – the traditional gift-giving is on Twelfth Night (Jan 6). Each year, there's a Christmas Nativity scene erected in Plaça de Sant Jaume, Barri Gòtic, which stays there for the whole of Dec and 1st week in Jan.

# 16

# Sports and outdoor activities

Barcelona is well placed for access to the sea and mountains, which is one of the reasons it was picked for the 1992 Olympics. A spin-off from the games was an increased provision of top-quality sports and leisure facilities throughout Catalunya, which have attracted an increasing number of major games and events – the city is now gearing up for the European Athletics Championships (Ⓦ www.bcn2010.org), to be held here in 2010. However, while there are scores of sports centres and swimming pools in the city, there aren't actually that many that will appeal to tourists or casual visitors. Most people are content to hit the city beaches or take off for a hike or jog in the surrounding hills of the Parc de la Collserola.

Attending the big match, whatever that might be, is a different matter. **Tickets** for all major sporting events can be bought from the agencies, **ServiCaixa** (Ⓣ 902 332 211, Ⓦ www.servicaixa.com) or **TelEntrada** (Ⓣ 902 101 212, Ⓦ www.telentrada.com). The main source of information about municipal sports facilities is the Ajuntament's **Servei d'informació Esportiva** (Ⓣ 010, Ⓦ www.bcn.cat, look under "Esports"), which has a drop-in office (Direcció d'Esports) on Montjuïc at Avgda. de l'Estadi 30–40 (Ⓜ Espanya), at the side of the Picornell swimming pool.

## Basketball

Second only to football in popularity, basketball has been played in Barcelona since the 1920s. Games are usually played September to June at weekends, with most interest in the city's two main teams. **Club Joventat de Badalona**, founded in 1930, were European champions in 1994, while **FC Barcelona** (an offshoot of the football club as early as 1926) finished runners-up five times before finally becoming European champions in 2003. Tickets to games are fairly inexpensive (€11–60, depending on the seat and game), and it's easiest to go and watch FC Barcelona, as Badalona is out in the sticks. The team plays at the Palau Blaugrana, adjacent to the Camp Nou, and you can either buy tickets online (Ⓦ www.fcbarcelona.com) or go to the stadium (the day before the game) – see "Football" below for main stadium contact details.

# Cycling

Cycling is being heavily promoted by the city authorities as a means of transport. There's a successful bike-sharing scheme (known as Bicing), while around 160km of cycle paths traverse the city, with plans to double the network in the future. All locals have yet to embrace the bike, and some cycle paths are still ignored by cars or are clogged with pedestrians, indignantly reluctant to give way to two-wheelers. But, on the whole, cycling around Barcelona is not the completely hairy experience it was just a few years ago.

The best way to see the city by bike – certainly as a first-time visitor – is to take a **bike tour** (see Basics, p.29); bikes and equipment will be provided. Or you can simply **rent a bike** from one of the outlets also listed on p.29, in which case you might want to pick up the map detailing current **cycle paths**. It's available from the tourist office, or on the city council's website Ⓦ www.bcn .cat/bicicleta. The nicest place to get off the road is the **Parc de la Collserola**, where there are bike trails for varying abilities through the woods and hills. Montjuïc is another popular place for mountain-biking – there's a weekend rental outfit up behind the castle. Bikes are allowed on the metro, on FGC trains, and on the Montjuïc and Vallvidrera funiculars.

The city hosts a variety of annual cycling events, including the main regional race, the **Volta a Catalunya** (Ⓦ www.voltacatalunya.cat) every May. June sees the Ajuntament's annual **Festa de la Bici** (Bicycle Fiesta), while September is another big month, with races during the Mercè festival and a day during the city's "Mobility Week" dedicated to cycling. In October, there's the **Escalada a Montjuïc**, an annual international hill-climb race on Montjuïc.

## Useful contacts

**Amics de la Bici c/Demóstenes 19, Sants** ☎ 933 394 060, Ⓦ www.amicsdelabici.org; Ⓜ Plaça de Sants. The "Friends of the Bike" organize a full range of events and activities, from rides to bike mechanic courses.

**Esport Ciclista Barcelona** Ⓦ www.ecbarcelona .com. Founded in 1929, the cycle sports club organizes the Escalada a Montjuïc – details available on their website.

# Football

To be honest, there's only one sport in Barcelona and that's football, as played by local heroes **FC** (Futbol Club) **Barcelona**. The team is worshipped at the

## Bye bye bulls

Although bullfights are an integral part of many southern Spanish festivals, there has never been great interest in Catalunya. It's tourism on the Costa Brava that continues to support much of the region's organized bullfighting, while small-scale bullfights are still seen as part of some local villages' annual *festa*. However, a few provincial towns have already imposed outright bans on the activity, while the city of Barcelona declared itself an anti-bullfight city in 2004. There's only one surviving bull ring in Barcelona, the **Plaza de Toros Monumental**, Gran Via de les Corts Catalanes 749 (Ⓜ Monumental), and this has been the scene of protests at the start of each bullfight season for some years now. In fact, campaigners in the city hope to make Barcelona bullfight-free in the near future, and the city council is now talking openly about the possibility of other uses for the bull ring, perhaps as a site for the Encants flea market.

splendid Camp Nou stadium in the north of the city and, even if you don't coincide with a game, the stadium's football museum and tour alone is worth the trip. All the details are on p.139. The other local team – though not to be compared – is **RCD** (Reial Club Deportiu) **Espanyol**, whose games are currently played at the Olympic stadium on Montjuïc, though by the 2009/2010 season they are due to move to a new 40,000-seater stadium being built at Cornellà, west of the city centre.

The season runs from late August until May, with games usually played on Sundays (though sometimes on other days). You'll have little problem getting a **ticket** to see an Espanyol game: either just turn up on the day, or buy them up to three days in advance from the stadium ticket office. It's also fairly straightforward to get tickets for FC Barcelona. The Camp Nou seats 98,000, which means it's only really full for big games against rivals like Real Madrid, or for major European ties. For all other games, some tickets are put on general sale a week before each match (and may be available at ticket booths on the day), or try ServiCaixa. Touts and season-ticket holders at the ground also offer spare tickets for most matches. The cheapest seats at both grounds start at €20, though for a typical league game at Barcelona you're more likely to end up paying €30–50 (and be seated *very* high up).

### Team contacts

FC Barcelona Camp Nou, Avgda. Arístides Maillol, Les Corts ⊕934 963 600, ⓦwww .fcbarcelona.com; Ⓜ Collblanc/Maria Cristina.

RCD Espanyol Estadi Olímpic, Pg. Olímpic 17–19, Montjuïc ⊕932 927 700, ⓦwww .rcdespanyol.com; Ⓜ Espanya, then free shuttle bus from Pl. d'Espanya on match days.

## Horse riding

The municipal riding school on Montjuïc offers lessons and courses for adults (beginners especially welcome), children and disabled people, or you can just have a taster with an hour-long riding session from around €15.

### Riding school

Escola Municipal d'Hípica La Foixarda Avgda. Montanyans 1, Montjuïc ⊕934 261 066;

Ⓜ Espanya, then bus #50. Office open Mon–Fri 5.30–8pm, Sat & Sun 9am–1.30pm & 5–9pm.

## Ice-skating

There are a couple of ice rinks in the city, including one at FC Barcelona's Camp Nou stadium, and a seasonal rink at the Parc del Fòrum at Diagonal Mar. At the Roger de Flor rink there's a bar from where you can watch the action. It's a good idea to check hours and restrictions before you go, as weekends and holidays especially can see the rinks inundated with children.

### Ice rinks

Pavelló Pista Gel Camp Nou, c/Arístides Maillol 12, Les Corts ⊕934 963 630, ⓦwww.fcbarcelona.com; Ⓜ Collblanc/Maria Cristina. Morning and afternoon skating sessions daily throughout the year, times vary. Admission €11, including

skate rental. Also a skating school, for classes of all ages and levels.

Skating Pista de Gel c/Roger de Flor 168, Dreta de l'Eixample ⊕932 452 800, ⓦwww.skatingclub.cat; Ⓜ Tetuan. Morning and afternoon skating sessions daily throughout the year, times vary. Admission €14, including skate rental.

# Roller blading/skating/skateboarding

The Passeig Marítim and Port Olímpic area (Ⓜ Ciutadella-Vila Olímpica) see heavy **skate and blade** traffic, while other popular runs include Arc de Triomf (Ⓜ Arc de Triomf), Parc Joan Miró (Ⓜ Tarragona) and Barceloneta, next to the Palau del Mar (Ⓜ Barceloneta). The Fòrum site down at Diagonal Mar (Ⓜ El Marseme Forum) has acres of wide open space. You're supposed to keep off all marked cycle paths. Meanwhile, *the* place for **skateboarders** is the piazza outside MACBA, the contemporary art gallery in the Raval.

# Running and jogging

The **Passeig Marítim** (Ⓜ Ciutadella-Vila Olímpica) is the best place for a seafront run – there's a five-kilometre promenade from Barceloneta all the way to the River Besòs, with a fitness circuit on the way at Mar Bella beach. To get off the beaten track, you'll need to head for the heights of Montjuïc or the Parc de la Collserola.

There's a half-marathon (Mitja Marató de Barcelona) held in the city every February or March, while the full **Barcelona Marathon** (Marató Barcelona; application forms and details on Ⓦ www.barcelonamarato.es) takes place in March. There are more road races during the September Mercè festival, while **La Cursa** (Ⓦ www.cursaelcorteingles.com; May), the annual twelve-kilometre run organized by El Corte Inglés department store, attracts up to 50,000 fun-runners onto the streets. It's one of the longest established city runs, held since 1979, and the 1994 edition, attracting 110,000 runners, stills hold the Guinness world record for number of participants.

# Sports centres

Every city neighbourhood has a sports centre, most with swimming pools but also offering a variety of other sports, games and activities. Schedules and prices vary, so it's best to contact the centres directly for any sport you might be interested in. Most have a general daily admission fee (around €15) if all you want is a swim and use of the gym. A couple of the more useful centres are listed below, but for a full rundown call ☏ 010 or consult the sports section database on Ⓦ www.bcn.cat.

**Poliesportiu Marítim** Pg. Marítim 33, Vila Olímpica ☏ 932 240 440, Ⓦ www.claror.org; Ⓜ Ciutadella-Vila Olímpica. Large complex by the Port Olímpic with a pool, gym and sauna, plus a wide range of organized activities, games and treatments, from aerobics,

---

## Follow that car

Catalunya's motor racing circuit, the **Circuit de Catalunya** (Ⓦ www.circuitcat.com), hosts the annual Formula 1 Spanish Grand Prix at the end of April, as well as a whole series of other Spanish and Catalan bike and motor races throughout the year, from truck-racing to endurance rallies. The track is out near Granollers, north of the city (trains from Sants/Pg. de Gràcia), a 20-minute walk from Montmeló station, but during the Grand Prix there are also shuttle-bus services and direct buses from Barcelona. For Formula 1, you need to sort out tickets well in advance (they go on sale the previous August), but all the current information is on the website, while sports travel companies can offer special race packages.

dance and yoga to indoor biking, beach tennis and hydrotherapy. Mon–Fri 7am–midnight, Sat 8am–9pm, Sun 8am–4pm. **Poliesportiu Municpal Frontó Colom Ramblas 18, Barri Gòtic** ☎ **933 023 295,** ⓦ **www .frontocolom.com;** Ⓜ **Drassanes.** Centrally situated sports centre with pool and gym, where you can see traditional Spanish *frontón* (handball) or Basque *jai alai*, reputedly the fastest sport in the world. Mon–Fri 7.30am–10.30pm, Sat 9am–8pm, Sun 9am–2.30pm.

## Swimming

The city **beaches** are fine for a stroll across the sand and an ice cream, but the water's none too welcoming and you'd do best to save your swimming for the region's coastal beaches (Sitges is the best) or one of Barcelona's many municipal **pools**. There are scores of them, but we've picked out three of the best below. You may be required to show your passport before being allowed in, and you'll need to wear a swimming cap. If you're hardy enough, the annual Christmas swimming cup involves diving into the port on December 25 and racing other like-minded fools.

▲ Piscina Municipal de Montjuïc

## Swimming pools

**Club Natació Atlètic Barceloneta** Pl. del Mar, Barceloneta ☎ 932 210 010, ⓦ www.cnab.org; Ⓜ Ciutadella-Vila Olímpica. One indoor pool, two outdoor, plus bar, restaurant and gym facilities. Mon–Fri 6.30am–11pm, Sat 7am–11pm, Sun 8am–5pm (until 8pm mid-May to Sept). Daily admission for non-members is around €10.

**Piscina Municipal de Montjuïc** Avgda. Miramar 31, Montjuïc ☎ 934 430 046; Funicular de Montjuïc. The city's most beautiful outdoor pool, high on Montjuïc. Mid-June to early Sept, daily 11am–6.30pm. Admission €4.90.

**Piscines Picornell** Avgda. de l'Estadi 30–40, Montjuïc ☎ 934 234 041, ⓦ www.picornell.cat; Ⓜ Espanya, then bus #50. Remodelled and expanded for the Olympics, the fifty-metre indoor pool is open all year, while the outdoor pool is open to the public from June–Sept. Nudist sessions all year on Sat night, plus Sun pm Oct–May. Indoor pool and other facilities Mon–Fri 7am–midnight, Sat 7am–9pm, Sun 7.30am–4pm; outdoor pool usually 9am–9pm. Outdoor €5.10, indoor €9.20, includes gym and sauna.

# Tennis

The main municipal tennis centre at Vall d'Hebron is the best place to play. Unlike many clubs in the city, you can rent courts by the hour without being a member. There are asphalt and clay courts, costing around €15 an hour, plus a pool, gym and café. Rackets are available for rent. Other municipal tennis courts are listed on ⓦ www.bcn.cat, while for private clubs consult the website of the Federació Catalana de Tennis (ⓦ www.fctennis.org). One of these, the Reial Club de Tennis Barcelona-1899 (ⓦ www.rctb1899.es), hosts the **Barcelona Open** every April.

## Tennis courts

**Centre Municipal de Tenis** Pg. Vall d'Hebron 178–196, Vall d'Hebron ☎ 934 276 500; Ⓜ Montbau.

Public hours Mon–Fri 8am–11pm, Sat & Sun 8am–9pm.

# Watersports

Courses and instruction in catamaran and laser sailing, kayaking and windsurfing, from two hours to two days, are available from the Port Olímpic's sailing club, Centre Municipal de Vela. At Base Nàutica, by Mar Bella beach, you can rent catamarans and windsurfers, and there's a popular bar here as well. Prices at either vary considerably, but you can expect to pay around €35 for a couple of hours' windsurfing or €200 for a two-day elementary sailing course.

## Watersports centres

**Base Nàutica Municipal** Avgda. Litoral, Platja Mar Bella ☎ 932 210 432, ⓦ www.basenautica .org; Ⓜ Ciutadella-Vila Olímpica, then bus #41. Daily 9.30am–9pm.

**Centre Municipal de Vela** Moll de Gregal, Port Olímpic ☎ 932 257 940, ⓦ www.velabarcelona .com; Ⓜ Ciutadella-Vila Olímpica. Mon–Fri 9am–9pm, Sat & Sun 9am–8pm.

⑯

**SPORTS AND OUTDOOR ACTIVITIES** | Tennis • Watersports

# Shopping

W hile for sheer size and scope Barcelona cannot compete with Paris or other fashion capitals, it is one of the world's most stylish cities – architecture, fashion and decoration are thoroughly permeated by Catalan *disseny* (design). All of this makes for great shopping, from designer clothes and accessories to crafts and household goods. Many visitors will find the city to be relatively cheap for a lot of items, and even more so if you coincide with the **annual sales** (*rebaixes*, *rebajas*) that follow the main fashion seasons – mid-January until the end of February, and throughout July and August. Non-EU residents can get an IVA (ie VAT) refund on each purchase over the value of €90; if there's a **"Tax-Free Shopping"** sticker displayed at the store (Ⓦ www.spainrefund.com), ask for the voucher and claim the refund at the airport before leaving.

Shop **opening hours** are typically Monday to Saturday 10am to 1.30/2pm and 4.30 to 7.30/8pm. though all the bigger shops stay open over lunchtime, while smaller shops close on Saturday afternoons or may vary their hours in other ways. **Major department stores and shopping malls** open Monday

## Where to shop

The best **general shopping area** for clothes, souvenirs, arts and crafts is the Barri Gòtic, particularly between the upper part of the Ramblas and Avinguda Portal de l'Àngel. Established designer and **high-street fashion** is at home in the Eixample, along Passeig de Gràcia, Rambla de Catalunya and c/de Pelai, as well as along Avinguda Diagonal in Les Corts. Hot **new designers and boutiques** – including shoe, street- and skatewear specialists – can be found in La Ribera, around Passeig del Born (c/Flassaders, c/Rec, c/Calders, c/Espartería, c/Vidrería, c/Bonaire), but also down c/d'Avinyó in the Barri Gòtic, between c/del Carme and MACBA in El Raval, and along c/Verdi in Gràcia. For **secondhand and vintage clothing**, stores line the whole of c/de la Riera Baixa (El Raval), with others nearby on c/del Carme and c/de l'Hospital, and on Saturdays there's a street market here. More bargains are in the **remainder stores, wholesalers and discount outlets** found along c/Girona in the Eixample, between the Gran Via and Ronda Sant Pere.

For **antiques** – books, furniture, paintings and artefacts – you need to trawl c/de la Palla, c/Banys Nous and surrounding streets in the Barri Gòtic, best combined with the antique market on Thursdays in front of the cathedral. **Delis and specialist food shops** tend to be concentrated around the Passeig del Born in La Ribera. Independent **music and CD stores** are concentrated on and around c/dels Tallers (El Raval), just off the top of the Ramblas. And don't forget the city's **museums and galleries**, where you'll find reasonably priced items ranging from postcards to wall-hangings.

to Saturday 10am–10pm, though the cafés, restaurants and leisure outlets in malls are usually open on Sunday too. All the stores below are open in August unless otherwise stated. Barcelona's daily food **markets**, all in covered halls, are generally open from Monday to Saturday, 8am–3pm and 5–8pm (local variations apply), though the most famous, La Boqueria on the Ramblas, opens throughout the day.

## Antiques

**L'Arca del Avia c/Banys Nous 20, Barri Gòtic** ☎933 021 598, Ⓦwww .larcadelavia.com; Ⓜ Liceu. Catalan brides used to fill up their nuptial trunk (*arca*) with embroidered bed linen and lace, and this shop is a treasure-trove of vintage and antique textiles. Period (eighteenth to early-twentieth century) costumes can be hired or purchased as well – one of Kate Winslet's *Titanic* costumes came from here. Closed Aug.

**Bulevard dels Antiquarius Pg. de Gràcia 55–57, Dreta de l'Eixample** ☎932 154 499, Ⓦwww .bulevarddelsantiquaris.com; Ⓜ Passeig de Gràcia. An arcade with over seventy shops full of antiques of all kinds, from toys and dolls to Spanish ceramics or African art. Closed Sat in Aug.

**Mercantic c/Rius i Taulet 120, Sant Cugat del Vallès** ☎936 744 950, Ⓦwww.mercantic.com; FGC Sant Cugat. This permanent antiques and collectables market is out in the suburbs but makes a great trip for casual browsers and serious collectors alike. Everything from furniture to farm machinery, old radios to vintage jewellery, postcards to erotic drawings, plus an outdoor Sun flea market (until 3pm), weekly lot auctions (Sat) and trade markets (1st Sun of each month). Closed Sun afternoon, all Mon & Aug.

## Arts, crafts and gifts

**Art Escudellers c/Escudellers 23–25, Barri Gòtic** ☎934 126 801, Ⓦwww.escudellers-art .com; Ⓜ Liceu. Enormous shop selling a wide range of ceramics, glass, jewellery and decorated tiles from different regions of Spain. Shipping can be arranged, and there's also a gourmet wine and food section.

**Artesania Catalunya c/Banys Nous 11, Barri Gòtic** ☎934 674 660, Ⓦwww .artesania-catalunya.com; Ⓜ Liceu. The local government's arts and crafts promotion board has an old-town showroom, where it's always worth looking in on the current exhibitions. Most of the work is contemporary in style, from basketwork to glassware, though traditional methods are still very much encouraged.

**La Carboneria c/Groch 1, Barri Gòtic** ☎932 684 889, Ⓦwww.drapart.org; Ⓜ Jaume I/Barceloneta. The Drap-Art creative recycling organization offers a shop and exhibition space for artists to show their wildly inventive wares, from trash-bangles to tin bags.

**Cereria Subirà Bxda. Llibreteria 7, Barri Gòtic** ☎933 152 606; Ⓜ Jaume I. Barcelona's oldest shop (founded 1760) has a beautiful interior, selling unique hand-crafted candles.

**Fantastik c/de la Mercè 31, Barri Gòtic** ☎932 954 877, Ⓦwww.fantastik.es; Ⓜ Drassanes/Barceloneta. At the "bizarre bazaar" (the shop with the bicycle outside) there are beguiling gifts, crafts and objects from four continents, from Chinese robots and African baskets to Russian domino sets and Vietnamese kitchen scales. Much of it is unclassifiable kitsch, and there's usually more in show in the upstairs "Kitchen Gallery".

**Papirum Bxda. Llibreteria 2, Barri Gòtic** ☎933 105 242; Ⓜ Jaume I. For all your writing needs – hand-painted paper, draughtsman's pens, leather-bound notebooks and more.

**Taller Textil Teranyina c/Notariat 10, El Raval** ☎933 179 436, Ⓦwww.teresarosa.com; Ⓜ Catalunya. Teresa Rosa Aguayo opened her Raval textile workshop in 1987, and still weaves striking contemporary carpets, rugs and wall-hangings and makes textile jewellery and other objects. You can call in any time to see the design work being carried out, or sign up for one of the courses. Closed Sat & Sun.

## Books

### General

**Casa del Llibre Pg. de Gràcia 62, Dreta de l'Eixample** ☎932 723 840, Ⓦwww.casadellibro .com; Ⓜ Passeig de Gràcia. Barcelona's biggest book emporium, strong on literature, humanities and travel, with lots of English-language titles and Catalan literature in translation.

⑰

Crafts have always been central to Barcelona's industry, with a history dating back to the Middle Ages. Many of the street names in the Born (Ⓜ Jaume I/Barceloneta), particularly, refer to the crafts once practised there; eg c/de la Argentería, silversmith's street, c/Mirallers, the street where they used to make mirrors, c/Vidriería, glassmakers' street, or c/Sombrerers, where hats (*sombreros*) were made. Over the last decade or so, neighbourhoods like the Born, El Raval and Poble Nou have once again become craft centres as empty buildings and warehouses have been opened up as workshops. Some artists work behind closed doors, while others have a space at the front where they sell their limited series or unique pieces.

A good way to see the Ciutat Vella (old town) workshops is to coincide with the **Tallers Oberts**, or open workshops (Ⓦ www.tallersoberts.org), usually held over the last two weekends of May, when there are studio visits, exhibitions, children's workshops, guided tours and lots of other events. Or contact My Favourite Things (see p.30 for details), who can organize a workshop tour on request, introducing you directly to selected artists.

**Elephant Books** c/Creu dels Molers 12, Poble Sec ☎ 934 430 594, Ⓦ www.lfantbooks.4t.com; Ⓜ Poble Sec. Only stocks English-language books, with cheap prices for current novels, classics, children's books and secondhand.

**Laie** c/Pau Claris 85, Dreta de l'Eixample ☎ 933 181 739, Ⓦ www.laie.es; Ⓜ Passeig de Gràcia. This has been Barcelona's favourite bookshop for years, though probably just as much for its café-restaurant, which is a good place to unwind. There are lots of English-language titles.

### Art, design and photography

**Kowasa** c/de Mallorca 235, Esquerra de l'Eixample ☎ 932 158 058, Ⓦ www.kowasa.com; Ⓜ Provença. The city's best bookstore for photography and photographic art.

**Museu Nacional d'Art de Catalunya** Palau Nacional, Montjuïc ☎ 936 220 376, Ⓦ www.mnac.es; Ⓜ Espanya. Doubled in size since the museum refurbishment, the MNAC bookshop has the city's widest selection of books on Catalan art, architecture, design and style. Closed Mon.

**Ras** c/Doctor Joaquim Dou 10, El Raval ☎ 934 127 199, Ⓦ www.rasbcn.com; Ⓜ Liceu. Specializes in books and magazines on graphic design, architecture, photography and contemporary art. The exhibitions here are always worth a look. Closed Mon.

### Comics and graphic books

**Norma Comics** Pg. de Sant Joan 9, Dreta de l'Eixample ☎ 932 448 423, Ⓦ www.normacomics.com; Ⓜ Arc de Triomf. Spain's best comic and graphic-novel shop, for everything from manga to the caped crusader, plus DVDs and all kinds of related items.

### Cuisine

**Buffet & Ambigù** Ptge. 1800 s/n, El Raval ☎ 932 430 178, Ⓦ www.catalogobuffet.com; Ⓜ Liceu. To keep on top of Spain's charge to the summit of modish European cuisine, pay a visit to the "gastronomic library", hidden up a covered passageway behind *Bar Ra*. Thousands of cookbooks, many in English, chart the recipes, exploits and philosophies of the latest chef and restaurants, including several Barcelona hotspots.

### Secondhand

**Hibernian Books** c/Montseny 17, Gràcia ☎ 932 174 796, Ⓦ www.hibernian-books.com; Ⓜ Fontana. Barcelona's best secondhand English bookstore has around 40,000 titles in stock – you can part-exchange, and there are always plenty of giveaway bargains available.

### Travel, guides and maps

**Altaïr** Gran Via de les Corts Catalanes 616, Esquerra de l'Eixample ☎ 933 427 171, Ⓦ www.altair.es; Ⓜ Universitat. Europe's biggest travel superstore has a massive selection of travel books, guides, maps and world music, plus a programme of travel-related talks and exhibitions.

**Llibreria Quera** c/Petritxol 2, Barri Gòtic ☎ 933 180 743, Ⓦ www.llibreriaquera.com; Ⓜ Liceu. The most knowledgeable place in town for

Catalan and Pyrenean maps and trekking guides. Closed Sat in Aug.

## Clothes, shoes and accessories

### Designer fashion

**Antonio Miró** c/Consell de Cent 349, Dreta de l'Eixample ☎934 870 670, ⓦwww.antoniomiro .es; ⓜPasseig de Gràcia. The showcase for Barcelona's most innovative designer, Antonio Miró, especially good for classy suits, though now also branding jeans, accessories, fragrances and household design.

**Armand Basi** Pg. de Gràcia 49, Dreta de l'Eixample ☎932 151 421, ⓦwww.armandbasi .com; ⓜPasseig de Gràcia. Outlets also at L'Illa and El Corte Inglés. Colourful men's and women's jackets and jeans from the hot Spanish designer. There's also a full range of accessories – watches to fragrances – though the must-have items are the designer table- and kitchenware created with superchef Ferran Adrià.

**Camisería Pons** c/Gran de Gràcia 49, Gràcia ☎932 177 292, ⓦwww.camiseriapons.com; FGC Gràcia. Originally a *modernista* shirt shop, this has been transformed into a showcase for contemporary Spanish fashion designers.

**Cuca Fera** c/Cremat Gran 9, La Ribera ☎932 683 710; ⓜJaume I. Original children's clothing, from T-shirts to matching outfits – it's down the alleyway behind the Picasso Museum.

**Custo Barcelona** Pl. de les Olles 7, La Ribera ☎932 687 893, ⓦwww.custo-barcelona.com; ⓜBarceloneta; plus others. Where the stars get their T-shirts. Hugely colourful and highly priced designer Ts, tops and sweaters for men and women.

▲ Shopping for shoes on Passeig del Born

**Giménez & Zuazo** c/Elisabets 20, El Raval ☎934 123 381, ⓦwww.boba.es; ⓜCatalunya. Two collections a year of cutting-edge women's fashion that's funky and informal.

**Jean-Pierre Bua** Avgda. Diagonal 469, Esquerra de l'Eixample ☎934 397 100, ⓦwww .jeanpierrebua.com; ⓜHospital Clinic. The city's high temple for fashion victims: a postmodern shrine for Yamamoto, Gaultier, Miyake, Galliano, McQueen, Westwood, Miró and other international stars.

**Naifa** c/Doctor Joaquim Dou 11, El Raval ☎933 024 005; ⓜLiceu. Original, colourful, informal, very reasonably priced men's and women's clothing.

**Natalie Capell, Atelier de Moda** c/Banys Vells 4, entrance at c/Carassa 2, La Ribera ☎933 199 219; ⓜJaume I. Her own very elegant designs, in 1920s- and 1930s-style.

**Purificacion Garcia** Pg. de Gràcia 21, Dreta de l'Eixample ☎934 877 292, ⓦwww .purificaciongarcia.es; ⓜPg. de Gràcia. A designer with real flair and an eye for fabrics – Garcia's first job was in a textile factory. She's also designed clothes for films, theatre and TV, and her costumes were seen at the opening ceremony of the Barcelona Olympics. The eponymous shop's a beauty, with the more casual items and accessories not particularly stratospherically priced.

### High-street fashion

**Mango** Pg. de Gràcia 8–10, Dreta de l'Eixample ☎934 121 599, ⓜPasseig de Gràcia; Pg. de Gràcia 65, Dreta de l'Eixample ☎932 157 530, ⓜPasseig de Gràcia; plus others, ⓦwww.mango.com. Now available worldwide, Barcelona is where Mango began and prices here are cheaper than in North America and other European countries. See also Mango Outlet on p.246.

**Zara** Pg. de Gràcia 16, Dreta de l'Eixample ☎933 187 675, ⓦwww.zara.com; ⓜPasseig de Gràcia; plus others. Trendy but cheap seasonal fashion for men, women and children from the Spanish chain. The Pg. de Gràcia branch is the flagship store.

### Jewellery, textiles and accessories

**Almacenes del Pilar** c/Boqueria 43, Barri Gòtic ☎933 177 984, ⓦwww .almacenesdelpilar.com; ⓜLiceu. A world of frills, lace, cloth and materials used in the making of Spain's traditional regional costumes. You can pick up a decorated fan for just a few euros, though quality items go for a whole lot more.

**Atalanta Manufactura Pg. del Born 10, La Ribera** ☎932 683 702; Ⓜ**Jaume I.** Boutique-*atelier* making naturally dyed and painted silk and linen, including lovely scarves and wall-hangings.

**Joaquín Berao Rambla de Catalunya 74, Esquerra de l'Eixample** ☎932 150 091, ⓦwww .joaquinberao.com; Ⓜ**Passeig de Gràcia.** Avant-garde jewellery by a Madrid designer in a beautifully presented shop.

**Mandarina Duck Pg. de Gràcia 44, Dreta de l'Eixample** ☎932 720 364; Ⓜ**Passeig de Gràcia.** Funky, colourful travel bags, backpacks, handbags and other carriers.

**Obach Sombrería c/del Call 2, Barri Gòtic** ☎933 184 094; Ⓜ**Liceu.** An excellent selection of traditional hats and caps of all types, from berets to stetsons.

## Secondhand, vintage and discount outlets

**Contritem c/Riera de Sant Miquel 30, Gràcia** ☎932 187 140; Ⓜ**Diagonal.** Discount outlet for Spanish and Italian designer labels. Closed two weeks Aug.

🏃 **Lailo c/Riera Baixa 20, El Raval** ☎934 413 749; Ⓜ**Liceu.** Secondhand and vintage clothes shop with a massively wide-ranging stock – if you're serious about the vintage scene, this is your first stop, though there are loads of other places down the street as well. Fancy dress costumes, tuxes and gowns also available for hire.

**Mango Outlet c/Girona 37, Dreta de l'Eixample** ☎934 122 935; Ⓜ**Girona.** Last season's Mango gear at unbeatable prices, with items starting at just a few euros.

**La Roca Village La Roca del Vallès** ☎938 423 900, ⓦ**www.larocavillage.com.** The out-of-town outlet mall is one for serious designer discount-hounds, with 100 stores selling designer gear at up to sixty percent off normal prices. It's half an hour from the city centre and you can get there by bus or train – there are full public transport details on the website.

**Stockland c/Comtal 22, Barri Gòtic** ☎933 180 331; Ⓜ**Urquinaona.** A bargain-hunter's dream. Top-name haute couture from Spanish designers at thirty- to sixty-percent discounts.

### Shoes

**Camper c/Pelai 13-37, El Triangle, Dreta de l'Eixample** ☎902 364 598, ⓦ**www.camper.com;** Ⓜ**Catalunya; plus others.** Spain's favourite shoe store opened its first shop in Barcelona in 1981. Providing hip, well-made, casual city footwear at a good price has been the cornerstone of its success.

**Czar Pg. del Born 20, La Ribera** ☎933 107 222; Ⓜ**Jaume I.** A galaxy of running shoes, pumps, sneakers, bowling shoes and baseball boots – if your Starsky and Hutch Adidas SL76s have worn out, they can sell you another pair.

🏃 **La Manual Alpargatera c/d'Avinyó 7, Barri Gòtic** ☎933 010 172, ⓦwww .lamanualalpargatera.com; Ⓜ**Liceu.** This traditional workshop makes and sells *alpargatas* (espadrilles) to order, as well as producing other straw, rope and basket work.

**Muxart c/Rosselló 230, Esquerra de l'Eixample** ☎934 881 064, Ⓜ**Diagonal; Rambla de Catalunya 47, Esquerra de l'Eixample** ☎934 677 423, ⓦ**www.muxart.com;** Ⓜ**Catalunya.** Barcelona's top-class shoe designer, selling gorgeous footwear and handbags for men and women.

**U-Casas c/Espaseria 4, La Ribera** ☎933 100 046, ⓦ**www.casasclub.com;** Ⓜ**Jaume I; plus others.** Casas has four lines of shoe stores across Spain, with the U-Casas brand at the young and funky end of the market. Never mind the shoes, the stores are pretty spectacular, especially at the branch in the Born where an enormous shoe-shaped bench-cum-sofa takes centre-stage.

## Department stores and shopping malls

**Bulevard Rosa Pg. de Gràcia 55, entrances on Rambla de Catalunya, c/de Valencia and c/d'Aragó, Dreta de l'Eixample** ☎933 090 650, ⓦ**www.bulevardrosa.com;** Ⓜ**Passeig de Gràcia.** Barcelona's first shopping arcade features over one hundred shops, specializing in chic designer gear, shoes and accessories.

**Centre Comercial Barcelona Glòries Avgda. Diagonal 208 at Pl. de les Glòries Catalanes, Glòries** ☎934 860 404, ⓦ**www.lesglories.com;** Ⓜ**Glòries.** Huge 230-store mall with all the national high-street fashion names (H&M, Zara, Bershka, Mango) as well as children's wear, toys and games, ice-cream parlours, a dozen bars, cafés and restaurants, and a cinema complex.

**El Corte Inglés Pl. de Catalunya 14, Dreta de l'Eixample** ☎933 063 800, Ⓜ**Catalunya; Avgda.**

del Portal de l'Angel 19–21, Barri Gòtic ℡933 063 800, ⓜCatalunya; plus uptown branches at Avgda. Diagonal 471, 545 & 617, Les Corts, ⓜMaría Cristina; ⓦwww.elcorteingles.es. The city's biggest department store – visit the flagship Pl. de Catalunya branch for nine floors of clothes, accessories, cosmetics, household goods, toys and top-floor café; while for music, books, computers and sports gear, head for the Portal de l'Angel branch.

**Diagonal Mar** Avgda. Diagonal 3, Diagonal Mar ℡902 530 300, ⓦwww.diagonalmarcentre.es; ⓜMaresme Forum or T4 tram. The city's newest major mall (the largest in Catalunya) anchors the Diagonal Mar zone, and features the usual high-street suspects (El Corte Inglés, H&M, Zara, Mango, Sephora and FNAC) plus designer clothes and accessories, cafés, restaurants and a cinema.

**L'Illa** Avgda. Diagonal 545–559, Les Corts ℡934 440 000, ⓦwww.lilla.com; ⓜMaría Cristina. The landmark uptown shopping mall is stuffed full of designer fashion (including the local Custo), plus Camper (shoes), FNAC (music and books), Sfera (cosmetics), Decathlon (sports), El Corte Inglés (a department store), Caprabo (a supermarket) and much more.

**El Mercadillo** c/Portaferrissa 17, Barri Gòtic ℡933 018 913; ⓜLiceu. Double-decker complex of shops selling skate-, club- and beachwear and shoes – look out for the camel marking the entrance. There's a bar upstairs with a nice patio garden.

**El Triangle** Pl. de Catalunya 4, Dreta de l'Eixample ℡933 180 108; ⓜCatalunya. Shopping centre at the top of the Ramblas, dominated by the flagship FNAC store, which specializes in books (good English-language selection), music CDs and computer software. Also has a Habitat, Sephora for cosmetics, various clothes shops, plus a café on the ground floor next to the extensive newspaper and magazine section.

### Design, decorative art and household goods

**Ganivetería Roca** Pl. del Pi 3, Barri Gòtic ℡933 021 241; ⓜLiceu. Handsome old shop, dating from 1911, selling a big range of knives, cutlery, corkscrews and other household goods – including a fine array of gentlemen's shaving gear.

**Germanes Garcia** c/Banys Nous 15, Barri Gòtic ℡933 186 646; ⓜLiceu. Enormous warehouse-showroom devoted to the art of basket-, raffia- and wickerware – cradles to tables, plantholders to wardrobes.

**Gotham** c/Cervantes 7, Barri Gòtic ℡934 124 647, ⓦwww.gotham-bcn.com; ⓜJaume 1. The place to come for retro (1930s to 1970s) furniture, lighting, homeware and accessories, plus original designs. Closed Sat in Aug.

**Indio** c/del Carme 24, El Raval ℡933 175 442; ⓜCatalunya. The most traditional place in town to buy linen, pillows, blankets, sheets and tablecloths – the *modernista* facade, long cutting counters, wood panels and marble floor survive from its nineteenth-century glory days.

**Vinçon** Pg. de Gràcia 96, Eixample ℡932 156 050, ⓦwww.vincom.com; ⓜPasseig de Gràcia. The grandaddy of household style, pioneered by Fernando Amat – known as the Spanish Terence Conran. It's a fantastic building, never mind what's on sale, with various separate street entrances and separate sections for bedroom (Tinc Çon; c/Rosselló 246) and kitchen (Kitchen Çon; c/Pau Claris 179) stuff, plus temporary art and design exhibitions in La Sala Vinçon.

**Vitra** Pl. Comercial 5, La Ribera ℡932 687 219, ⓦwww.vitra.com; ⓜJaume I. Home and workplace furniture specialist with stunning chairs by the likes of Frank O. Gehry, Philippe Starck, Charles and Ray Eames, and Ron Arad.

### Tomb Bus

The Tomb Bus shopping line service connects Pl. de Catalunya with the Diagonal (Pl. Pius XII), an easy way to reach the uptown L'Illa and El Corte Inglès shopping centres. There are over 20 stops on the circular route, which passes many of the city's other big-name stores and boutiques. Departures are every 7 minutes or so (Mon–Fri 7am–9.38pm, Sat 9.10am–9.20pm); tickets (available on the bus) are €1.65 one way, €6.25 for one day's unlimited travel.

### Food and drink

There's a full list of city markets at ⓦwww .bcn.es/mercatsmunicipals. The ones picked out below are all covered more fully in the guide. The main local **supermarket** chain is Caprabo (ⓦwww.caprabo.es), which has a useful branch in the Mercat de la Barceloneta, though most other branches are located in residential neighbourhoods, away from the tourist sights. The most convenient downtown supermarket is that in the basement of El Corte Inglés (Pl. de Catalunya), and there's also the fairly basic Carrefour Express at Ramblas 113.

### Daily food markets

**Mercat de la Barceloneta** Pl. de la Font, Barceloneta; ⓂBarceloneta.
**Mercat de la Concepció** c/de Valencia, Dreta de l'Eixample; ⓂPasseig de Gràcia.
**Mercat de la Llibertat** Pl. de la Llibertat, Gràcia; ⓂFontana.
**Mercat Sant Antoni** Ronda de Sant Pau/Ronda de Sant Antoni, El Raval; ⓂSant Antoni.
**Mercat Sant Josep/La Boqueria** Ramblas; ⓂLiceu.
**Mercat Santa Caterina** Avgda. Francesc Cambó 16, Sant Pere; ⓂJaume I.

### Specialist food stores

🏃 **La Botifarreria de Santa Maria** c/Santa Maria 4, La Ribera ☎933 199 123; ⓂJaume I. If you ever doubted the power of the humble Catalan pork sausage, drop by this designer temple-deli where otherwise beautifully behaved locals jostle at the counter for the day's home-made *botifarra*, plus rigorously sourced hams, cheeses, pâtés and salamis. There are even branded T-shirts for true disciples.
**Bubó** c/Caputxes 10, La Ribera ☎932 687 224, ⓦwww.bubo.ws; ⓂJaume I. There are chocolates and then there are Bubó chocolates – extraordinary creations by pastry and chocolate maestro Carles Mampel. The very classy shop (with tastings and drinks de rigueur) is complemented by *Bubó's* minimalist new-wave tapas place, *Bubobar*, next door at no. 6.
**Casa Gispert** c/Sombrerers 23, La Ribera ☎933 197 535, ⓦwww.casagispert.com; ⓂJaume I. Roasters of nuts, coffee and spices for over 160 years – it's a truly delectable store with some tantalizing smells, and there are gourmet deli items available too.
🏃 **A Casa Portuguesa** c/Verdi 58, Gràcia ☎933 68 525, ⓦwww.acasaportuguesa.com; ⓂFontana. A sleek deli-café-cum-gallery

on Gràcia's buzziest street showcases the food, wine and culture of Portugal. It's a great place to pop in for a coffee after trawling the designer and streetwear stores of Carrer Verdi – they make Portuguese specialities daily (including the famous *pasteis de Belém*, little custard tarts), and have a full programme of wine tastings, food festivals and other events. Closed Mon.
**Colmado Quilez** Rambla de Catalunya 63, Esquerra de l'Eixample ☎932 152 356; ⓂPasseig de Gràcia. A dying breed now, this classic Catalan grocery has windows and shelves piled high with tins, preserves, bottles, jars and packets, plus a groaning *xarcuteria* counter.
🏃 **Formatgeria La Seu** c/Daguería 16, Barri Gòtic ☎934 126 548, ⓦwww.formatgerialaseu.com; ⓂJaume I. The best farmhouse cheeses from independent producers all over Spain. The owner, who's Scottish, will introduce you into the world of cheese at one of the regular cheese-and-wine tastings, or you can simply try before you buy. Closed Mon & Aug.
**Jamonísimo** c/Provença 85, Esquerra de l'Eixample ☎934 390 847, ⓦwww.jamonisimo.com; ⓂHospital Clinic. When Ferran Adrià, Heston Blumenthal and other kitchen maestros are in town, this is where they come to taste and buy the world's finest, artisan-made cured hams.
**Papabubble** c/Ample 28, Barri Gòtic ☎932 688 625, ⓦwww.papabubble.com; ⓂDrassanes. Groovy young things rolling out home-made candy to a chill-out soundtrack. Come and watch them at work, sample a sweetie, and take home a gorgeously wrapped gift. Closed Mon & Aug.

### Wine

**Vila Viniteca** c/Agullers 7 & 9, La Ribera ☎937 777 017, ⓦwww.vilaviniteca.es; ⓂBarceloneta. Very knowledgeable specialist in Catalan and Spanish wines. Pick your vintage and then nip over the road for the gourmet deli part of the operation.

## Markets

**Antiques** Avgda. de la Catedral, Barri Gòtic; ⓂJaume I. Every Thurs from 9am; closed Aug. The tourist location outside the cathedral attracts high prices. Better for bargains is the market on the Port Vell harbourside (ⓂBarceloneta) at weekends from 11am. See also *Mercantic* listed under "Antiques".

**Art Pl. Sant Josep Oriol, Barri Gòtic; Ⓜ Liceu.** The square is filled with stalls and easels every weekend from 10am, with local artists banging out still lives to harbour views.

**Christmas Avgda. de la Catedral, and surrounding streets, Barri Gòtic; Ⓜ Jaume I.** Traditional decorations, gifts, Christmas trees and more at the annual Fira de Santa Llúcia; daily Dec 1–22, 10am–9pm.

**Coins, books and postcards Mercat Sant Antoni, Ronda de Sant Pau/Ronda de Sant Antoni, El Raval; Ⓜ Sant Antoni.** Every Sun 9am–2pm. This will move location during renovation works (until 2012) but will remain in the market vicinity.

**Coins and stamps Pl. Reial, Barri Gòtic; Ⓜ Liceu.** Specialist dealers and collectors do battle every Sun 10am–2pm.

**Farmers' market Pl. del Pi, Barri Gòtic; Ⓜ Liceu.** First and third Fri, Sat & Sun of the month – honey, cheese, cakes and other produce; also during the Festa de la Mercè in Sept, and the Festa de Sant Ponç in c/de l'Hospital on May 11.

**Flea market Els Encants, c/Dos de Maig, northwest side of Pl. de les Glòries Catalanes, Glòries; Ⓜ Glòries/Encants.** Every Mon, Wed, Fri & Sat 9am–6pm, plus Dec 1–Jan 5 Sun 9am–3pm, for clothes, jewellery, antiques, junk and furniture. It's still open for now, but the city's oldest flea market is due a move because of the remodelling of the Glòries district. It will either have a new location at Glòries or possibly a new home at the Monumental bull ring.

**Flowers and birds Ramblas; Ⓜ Liceu.** Stalls present daily; flowers also in abundance at Mercat de la Concepció, c/de Valencia, Eixample.

## Museums, galleries and attractions

**L'Aquàrium Moll d'Espanya, Port Vell; Ⓜ Drassanes or Barceloneta.** A fish-related extravaganza, from the mundane (T-shirts, stationery, posters, games, toiletries) to cult must-haves (Mariscal-designed bathroom transfers).

**Botiga Palau de la Música c/Sant Pere Més Alt 1, Sant Pere; Ⓜ Urquinaona.** Shop associated with the Palau de la Música Catalana, just across the square – *modernista*-styled porcelain, jewellery and crystal plus art supplies, artistic reproductions and choral music CDs.

**CosmoCaixa c/Teodor Roviralta 47–51, Tibidabo; FGC Avgda. del Tibidabo.** The science museum shop is the place to buy space jigsaws, planet mobiles, model lunar-rovers, dinosaur kits, star charts and natural history books.

**Museu d'Art Contemporani de Barcelona Pl. dels Àngels, El Raval; Ⓜ Universitat.** Designer aprons, espresso cups, T-shirts, posters, gifts and toys, plus art and design books.

**Museu Barbier-Mueller c/de Montcada 14, La Ribera; Ⓜ Jaume I.** The pre-Columbian art museum shop has a wide range of ethnic artefacts, from wall-hangings and jewellery to terracotta pots and figurines. Definitely the place to pick up your panama hat.

## Music

**Casa Beethoven Ramblas 97 ☎ 933 014 826, Ⓦ www.casabeethoven.com; Ⓜ Liceu.** Wonderful old shop selling sheet music, CDs and music reference books – not just classical, but also rock, jazz and flamenco. Closed Aug.

**Discos Castelló c/Tallers 3, El Raval ☎ 933 182 041, plus Tallers 7 ☎ 933 025 946, Tallers 9 (Overstocks) ☎ 934 127 285 and Tallers 79 ☎ 933 013 575, Ⓦ www.discoscastello.es; Ⓜ Catalunya.** You could spend half a day flitting from shop to shop, each with its own speciality and vibe: classical recordings at no. 3; a bit of everything at no. 7; hip-hop, alternative rock, *mestiza*, hardcore and electronia at no. 9; and jazz and 70s pop/rock no. 79.

**Espai Licei Gran Teatre del Liceu, Ramblas 51 ☎ 934 859 913; Ⓜ Liceu.** The shop in the opera house extension has the widest range of opera CDs and DVDs in the city, plus Liceu-branded T-shirts, ceramics, coffee mugs and other souvenirs.

**Etnomusic c/del Bonsuccés 6, El Raval ☎ 933 011 884, Ⓦ www.etnomusic.com; Ⓜ Catalunya.** World-music specialist, especially good for reggae, Latin and all types of South American music.

**Wah Wah Discos c/Riera Baixa 14, El Raval ☎ 934 423 703, Ⓦ www .wah-wahsupersonic.com; Ⓜ Liceu.** Vinyl heaven for record collectors – rock, indie, garage, 70s punk, electronica, blues, folk, prog, jazz, soul and rarities of all kinds.

## Sports

**Botiga del Barça FC Barcelona, Camp Nou, Les Corts ☎ 934 923 111, Ⓦ www.shop.fcbarcelona .com; Ⓜ María Cristina.** You can buy Barça

## Made in Barcelona

The world owes Barcelona, big time. For a start, in the fashion world there are the global brands **Mango** (women's clothes), **Camper** (shoes) and **Custo** (designer T-shirts), each of which started out in the city. Suitably togged up, you don't just drink a beer here, it's an **Estrella Damm** (tagline, the "beer of Barcelona"), a brew that sponsors everything from the Primavera Sound rock festival to Americas Cup yacht racing – in a neat bit of local synergy, they got Custo to knock up a typically colourful limited-edition design bottle to celebrate their 130th birthday in 2006. And then there are **Chupa Chups** (from the Spanish *chupar*, to lick), the lolly on a stick invented by one Enric Bernat in 1958 – Salvador Dalí, no less, designed the company logo; Kojak in the 1970s TV series wouldn't be without one; and Chupa Chups even made it aboard the *Mir* space station. Meanwhile, radical poet, publisher and inventor Alejandro Finisterre (admittedly, born in Galicia) was convalescing outside Barcelona after a bomb injury suffered during the Civil War, when he first came up with the idea for the game of **table football** (*bar football, foosball*). He took out a patent in Barcelona in 1937 and, though there are competing claims, he's often regarded as the man subsequently responsible for endless hours wasted in bars worldwide.

shirts anywhere on the Ramblas, but for official merchandise the stadium megastore has it all – including that all-important lettering service for the back of the shirt that elevates you to the squad.

**Decathlon c/de la Canuda 20, at Pl. Vila de Madrid, Barri Gòtic** ☎933 426 161, ⓦwww .decathlon.es; Ⓜ Catalunya; plus others. They've got clothes and equipment for 63 sports in the old-town megastore, so you're bound to find what you want. Also bike rental and repair.

### Toys, magic, costume and party wear

🏃 **Almacen Marabi c/Flassaders 30, La Ribera, no phone;** Ⓜ Jaume I. Mariela Marabi, originally from Argentina, makes handmade felt finger dolls, mobiles, puppets and animals of extraordinary invention. Her eye-popping workshop also has limited-edition pieces by other selected artists and designers.

**Drap c/del Pi 14, Barri Gòtic** ☎933 181 417, ⓦwww.ample24.com/drap; Ⓜ Liceu. Everything

is in miniature in this extraordinary dolls' house outfitters. Really, everything – asking for a set of bedroom furniture hardly stretches the talents of a place that can fit out a minuscule dentist's surgery or a complete art gallery.

🏃 **El Ingenio c/Rauric 6–8, Barri Gòtic** ☎933 177 138, ⓦwww.el-ingenio.com; Ⓜ Liceu. Juggling, magic and street-performer shop with a *modernista* storefront. It's also the place to come for carnival costumes and masks, made in the workshop on the premises.

**El Rey de la Màgia c/Princesa 11, Sant Pere** ☎933 193 920, ⓦwww.elreydelamagia.com; Ⓜ Jaume I. Spain's oldest magic shop contains all the tricks of the trade, from rubber chickens to Dracula capes. They also do weekend magic shows (Sat at 6pm, Sun at noon).

**Xalar Bxda. Llibreteria 4, Barri Gòtic** ☎933 150 458; Ⓜ Jaume I. Designer and hand-crafted toys – traditional games, dolls' houses, toy theatres and puppets.

# Children's Barcelona

T aking your children to Barcelona doesn't pose insurmountable travel problems, but it's as well to be aware of the potential difficulties before you go. Below we've pointed out some of the things you might find tricky, as well as providing a few pointers for a smooth stay. Once you're happily ensconced, and have cracked the transport system, you'll find that not only will your children be given a warm welcome almost everywhere you go, but in many ways the city appears as one huge playground, whether it's a day at the beach or a daredevil cable-car ride. There's plenty to do for children of all ages, much of it free or inexpensive, while if you coincide with one of Barcelona's festivals, you'll be able to join in with the local celebrations, from sweet-tossing and puppet shows to fireworks and human castles. "Children's attractions" rounds up the best of the options for keeping everybody happy; for sporting suggestions and outdoor activities, see Chapter 16. Finally, for plenty more ideas, check out the English-language resource and support site ⓦwww .kidsinbarcelona.com, which is packed with information on everything from safe play areas to babysitting services.

## Public transport

With very young children, the main problem is using **public transport**, especially the metro, which seems almost expressly designed to thwart access to pushchairs and buggies. Most stations are accessed by stairs or escalators, and there are steps and stairs within the system itself, making it difficult for single travellers with young children to get around easily. Even with two adults, you often face a stiff climb out of stations with the pushchair. However, the stations on lines 1 and 2 – including Universitat, Catalunya, Passeig de Gràcia and Sagrada Família – are accessible by lift from street level, and many FGC stations have lifts to the platforms, too, including Espanya (for Montserrat trains) and Aringuda. del Tibidabo (for Tibidabo). All city buses have been adapted for wheelchair access and so have room to handle a buggy. Children under 4 **travel free** on public transport, while there are reduced prices for tickets on the sight-seeing Bus Turístic and the cable cars.

## Products, clothes and services

Disposable **nappies** (diapers), **baby food**, **formula milk** and other standard items are widely available in pharmacies and supermarkets, though not necessarily with the same range or brands that you will be used to at home. Organic baby food, for example, is hard to come by – you can sometimes find the odd jar in a health-food store – and most Spanish non-organic baby foods contain small amounts of sugar or salt. If you require anything specific for your baby or child, it's best to bring it with you or check with the manufacturer about equivalent brands.

For relatively cheap, well-made babies' and children's **clothing**, Prénatal (Ⓦwww.prenatal.es) has an excellent range, and there are branches all over the city. Chicco (branches at Ronda de Sant Pere 5 and in Diagonal Mar shopping centre; Ⓦwww.chicco.es) is the place for baby and toddler clothes and gear. Or go to Galeries Maldà (c/Portaferrissa 22, Barri Gòtic) or El Corte Inglés (Pl. de Catalunya 14, Eixample) for more children's and babies' clothes and designer labels.

Most establishments are baby-friendly in the sense that you'll be made very welcome if you turn up with a child in tow. Many museum cloakrooms, for example, will be happy to look after your pushchair as you carry your child around the building, while restaurants will make a fuss of your little one. However, specific facilities are not as widespread as they are in the UK or USA. **Baby-changing areas** are relatively rare, except in department stores and shopping centres, and even where they do exist they are not always up to scratch. By far the best is at El Corte Inglés, while El Triangle and Maremàgnum have pull-down changing tables in their public toilets.

## Restaurants, accommodation and babysitting

Local restaurants tend not to offer **children's menus** (though they will try to accommodate specific requests), highchairs are rarely provided, and restaurants open relatively late for lunch and dinner. Despite best intentions, you might find yourself eating in one of the international franchise restaurants, which tend to be geared more towards families and open throughout the day.

Suitable **accommodation** is easy to find, and most hotels and pensions will be welcoming. However, bear in mind that much of the city's budget accommodation is located in buildings without lifts; while, if you're travelling out of season, it's worth noting that some older-style pensions don't have heating systems – and it can get cold. If you want a cot provided, or baby-listening and -sitting services, you'll have to pay the price of staying in one of the larger hotels – and, even then, never assume that these facilities are provided, so always check in advance. Renting an **apartment** is often a good idea, even for just a weekend or short stay, as you'll get a kitchen and a bit more space for the kids to play in.

You'll pay from around €10–12 per hour for **babysitting** if arranged through your hotel, or contact Tender Loving Canguros (from €7 per hour plus fee; Mon–Sat 9am–9pm; ☏647 605 989, Ⓦwww.tlcanguros.com), whose nannies and babysitters all speak English.

## Children's attractions

If you've spent too much time already in the showpiece museums, galleries and churches, any of the suggestions below should head off a children's revolt. Most have been covered in the text, so you can get more information by turning to the relevant page. Admission charges are almost always reduced for children, though the cut-off age varies from attraction to attraction.

## Cinema, shows and theatre

**Cinema** Children's film sessions are held at the **FilmoTeca** (see p.223), Sun 5pm.

**Font Màgica** The sound-and-light show in front of the Palau Nacional on Montjuïc (p.96) is always a hit, though it starts quite late.

**Imax Port Vell** Three different screens showing giant-screen and 3D documentaries on nature, space and the human body. See p.88.

**Magic shows** The magic shop, **El Rey de la Màgia** (c/Princesa 11, Sant Pere, ☎933 193 920, ⓦ www.elreydelamagia.com; Ⓜ Jaume I), has weekend magic shows (Sat 6pm, Sun noon; €8), with an hour of magic plus a visit to the shop's magic museum.

**Statues and street theatre** The Ramblas is one big outdoor show for children, with human statues a speciality, not to mention buskers, pavement artists, magicians, and food, bird and flower markets.

**Theatre** There are children's puppet shows, music, mime and clowns at the **Fundació Joan Miró** (Avgda. Miramar 71–75, Montjuïc ☎934 439 470, ⓦ www.fundaciomiro-bcn .org; Ⓜ Espanya & bus #50), with performances Sat 5.30pm & Sun 11.30am & 1pm. **Jove Teatre Regina** (c/Sèneca 22, Gràcia ☎932 181 512, ⓦ www.jtregina.com; Ⓜ Diagonal) puts on music and comedy productions for children (Sat & Sun 6pm).

## Museums, galleries and attractions

**L'Aquàrium** Adults might find the Aquarium a bit of a disappointment, but there's no denying its popularity with children. Under-4s get in free, and there are discounts for 4- to 12-year-olds.

**Hands-on** Most of the major museums and galleries run children's activity programmes, especially in school holidays. The "Niños" section in the weekly *Guía del Ocio* magazine lists the possibilities, from art and craft workshops at the Fundació Joan Miró and MACBA to chocolate-making at the Museu de la Xocolata.

**Museums** Museums with a special interest for children include **Cosmocaixa** (Science Museum the **Museu del Football Club Barcelona** (FC Barcelona Museum; **Museu d'Història de la Ciutat** (City History Museum); **Museu de Cera** (Wax Museum; **Museu de Zoología** (Zoology Museum and **Museu Marítim** (Maritime Museum).

**Parc Zoològic** All the usual suspects, plus children's zoo and dolphin shows; free for under-3s, discounts for under-12s.

**Poble Espanyol** Open-air "museum" of Spanish buildings, craft demonstrations, gift shops, bars and restaurants. Family-ticket available.

## Parks and gardens

**Gardens** Top choice is the **Parc del Laberint** in Horta, where the hillside gardens, maze and playground provide a great day out. For a city-centre surprise, seek out the **Jardins de la Torre de les Aigües** (c/Roger de Llúria 56, Dreta de l'Eixample), which from the end of June to the end of Aug, transform from an urban garden into a beach, complete with sand and paddling pool.

**Parks** In the city, the **Parc de la Ciutadella** has the best range of attractions, with a boating lake and a zoo. Older children will love the bizarre gardens and buildings of Gaudí's **Parc Güell**, while the **Parc de Collserola** is a good target for a walk in the hills and a picnic. At **Parc del Castell de l'Oreneta** (daily 10am–dusk), behind Pedralbes monastery,

▲ Playground at Plaça de Vicenç Martorell

there are miniature train rides and pony rides on Sun and public holidays (not Aug); it's at the end of c/Montevideo (take bus #66 from Pl. Catalunya or #64 from Pl. Universitat to the end of the line and walk up Avgda. d'Espasa).

**Playgrounds** Most city kids use the squares as playgrounds, under parental supervision. In **Gràcia**, Plaça de la Virreina and Plaça de Rius i Taulet are handsome traffic-free spaces with good bars with attached *terrassas*. Wherever your children play, however, you need to keep an eagle eye out for dog dirt. In the old town, the nicest dog- and traffic-free playground is in **Plaça de Vicenç Martorell**, in El Raval, where there are some fenced-off swings in front of a great café, *Kasparo*. **Parc del Fòrum**, at Diagonal Mar, also has a good children's playground and lots of other child-oriented attractions.

## Rides and views

**Bike tours** Join a group bike tour for a safe way to see the sights on two wheels. See p.29.

**Cable cars** The two best rides in the city are the cross-harbour cable car from Barceloneta to Montjuïc (p.90), and the Telefèric de Montjuïc (p.97), which then takes you up to the castle at the top of Montjuïc. Neither is for the faint-hearted child or sickly infant.

**Las Golondrinas** Sightseeing boat rides around the port and local coast. See p.30.

**Mirador de Colón** See the city from the top of the Columbus statue at the bottom of the Ramblas. See p.86.

**Torre de Collserola** Stunning views from the telecommunications tower near Tibidabo. Under-3s go free. See p.147.

## Theme parks

**Catalunya en Miniatura Torrelles de Llobregat, 17km southwest of Barcelona (A2 highway, exit 5)**

℡936 890 960, ⓦwww.catalunyaenminiatura .com. A theme park with 170 Catalan monuments in miniature, plus mini-train rides, children's shows and playground. Daily 10am–6pm, later opening April–Sept; closed Mon Nov–Feb.

**Illa Fantasia Vilassar de Dalt, 25km north of Barcelona, just short of Mataró (exit 92 on the main highway)** ℡937 514 553, ⓦwww .illafantasia.com. Supposedly the largest water park in Europe, with slides, splash pools, swimming pools, water games and picnic areas. Buy a combined ticket (*billete combinado*) at Barcelona Sants station and you can travel free on the train to Premià de Mar, and then take the free connecting bus to the park. Mid-May to mid-Sept daily 10am–7pm.

**Port Aventura 1hr south of Barcelona, near Salou and La Pineda (exit 35 on A7)** ℡977 779 090, ⓦwww.portaventura.es. Universal Studios' massive theme park based on five different cultures – Mexico, the Wild West, Polynesia, China and the Mediterranean – plus the Costa Caribe water adventure park. There are also four on-site hotels, a beach club, shops, restaurants and shows, as well as fairground rides (including the biggest roller coaster in Europe). Two-day and two-park combina- tion tickets offer the best value. Trains from Passeig de Gràcia/Barcelona Sants run directly to Port Aventura's own station (1hr 15min; info from RENFE ℡902 240 202). Daily: March–Oct 10am–8pm; July & Aug 10am–midnight; Christmas & New Year; Nov–Dec Sat & Sun only.

**Tibidabo** Dubbed "La Muntanya Magica", the rides and shows in the mountain-top amusement park (see p.145) are unbeatable as far as location goes, though tame compared to those at Port Aventura.

# Contexts

# Contexts

# A history of Barcelona and Catalunya

Catalan cultural identity can be traced back as far as the ninth century. From the quilt of independent counties of the eastern Pyrenees, a powerful dynastic entity, dominated by Barcelona, and commonly known as the Crown of Aragón, developed over the next six hundred years. Its merger with Castile-León in the late 1400s led to eventual inclusion in the new Spanish Empire of the sixteenth century – and marked the decline of Catalan independence and its eventual subjugation to Madrid. It has rarely been a willing subject, which goes some way to explaining how ingrained are the Catalan notions of social and cultural divorce from the rest of the country.

## Early civilizations and invasions

In the very earliest times, the area which is now Catalunya saw much the same population movements and invasions as the rest of the Iberian peninsula. During the **Upper Paleolithic** period (35,000–10,000 BC) cave-dwelling hunter-gatherers lived in parts of the Pyrenees, and **dolmens**, or stone burial chambers, from around 5000 BC still survive. No habitations from this period have been discovered but it can be conjectured that huts of some sort were erected, and farming had certainly begun. By the start of the **Bronze Age** (around 2000 BC), the Pyrenean people had begun to move into fortified villages in the coastal lowlands.

The first of a succession of **invasions** of the region began sometime after 1000 BC, when the Celtic "urnfield people" crossed the Pyrenees into the region, settling in the river valleys. These people lived side by side with indigenous Iberians, and the two groups are commonly, if erroneously, referred to as **Celtiberians**.

Meanwhile, on the coast, the **Greeks** had established trading posts at Roses and Empúries by around 550 BC. Two centuries later, though, the coast (and the rest of the peninsula) had been conquered by the North African **Carthaginians**, who founded Barcino (later Barcelona) in around 230 BC, on a low hill where the cathedral now stands. The Carthaginians' famous commander, Hannibal, went on to cross the Pyrenees in 214 BC and attempted to invade Italy. But the result of the Second Punic War (218–201 BC) – much of which was fought in Catalunya – was to expel the Carthaginians from the Iberian peninsula in favour of the Romans, who made their new base at the former Carthaginian stronghold of Tarragona.

## Roman Catalunya

The **Roman colonization** of the Iberian peninsula was far more intense than anything previously experienced and met with great resistance from the Celtic and Iberian tribes. It was almost two centuries before the conquest was complete, by which time Spain had become the most important centre of the Roman Empire after Italy. Tarragona (known as Tarraco) was made a provincial capital; fine monuments were built, the remains of which can still be seen in and around the city, and an infrastructure of roads, bridges and aqueducts came into being – much of which was used well into recent times. Barcelona was of less importance, although in 15 BC the emperor Augustus granted it the lengthy name of Colonia Julia Augusta Faventia Pia.

In the first two centuries AD, the Spanish mines and the granaries of Andalucia brought unprecedented wealth, and **Roman Spain** enjoyed a period of stable prosperity in which the region of Catalunya played an influential part. In Tarraco and the other Roman towns, the inhabitants were granted full Roman citizenship; the former Greek settlements on the Costa Brava had accepted Roman rule without difficulty and consequently experienced little interference in their day-to-day life.

Towards the third century AD, however, the Roman political framework began to show signs of decadence and corruption. Although at a municipal level the structure did not disappear completely until the Muslim invasions of the eighth century, it became increasingly vulnerable to **barbarian invasions** from northern Europe. The Franks and the Suevi swept across the Pyrenees, sacking Tarraco in 262 and destroying Barcelona. It was subsequently retaken by the Romans and rather belatedly defended by a circuit of walls and towers, part of which can still be seen. Within two centuries, however, Roman rule had ended, forced on the defensive by new waves of Suevi, Alans and Vandals and finally superseded by the **Visigoths** from Gaul, former allies of Rome and already Romanized to some degree.

The Visigoths established their first Spanish capital at Barcelona in 415 (before eventually basing themselves further south at Toledo), and built a kingdom encompassing most of modern Spain and the southwest of modern France. Their triumph, however, was relatively short-lived. Ruling initially as a caste apart from the local people, with a distinct status and laws, the Visigoths lived largely as a warrior elite, and were further separated from the local people by their adherence to Arian Christianity, which was considered heretical by the Catholic Church. Under their domination, the economy and the quality of life in the Roman towns declined, while within their ranks a series of plots and rivalries – exacerbated by their system of elective monarchy – pitted members of the ruling elite against each other. In 589 King Reccared converted to Catholicism, but religious strife only multiplied – resistance on the part of Arian Christians lead to reaction, one of the casualties of which was the sizeable Jewish population of the peninsula, who were enslaved en masse in the seventh century.

## The Moors and the Spanish Marches

Divisions within the Visigothic kingdom coincided with the Islamic expansion in North Africa, which reached the shores of the Atlantic in the late seventh century. In 711 (or 714, no one is sure) Tariq ibn Ziyad, governor of Tangier, led a force of several thousand largely Berber troops across the Straits of Gibraltar (the name of which is a corruption of the Arabic, *jebl at-Tariq*, "Tariq's mountain") and routed the Visigothic nobility near Jerez de la Frontera. With no one to resist, the stage for the **Moorish conquest of Spain** was set. Within ten years, the Muslim Moors had advanced to control most of modern Catalunya – they destroyed Tarragona and forced Barcelona to surrender although the more inaccessible parts of the Pyrenees retained their independence. It was not simply a military conquest. The Moors had little manpower, and so granted a limited autonomy to the local population in exchange for payment of tribute. They did not force the indigenous people to convert to Islam, and Jews and Christians lived securely as second-class citizens. In areas of the peninsula that remained under Muslim power through the ninth century, a new ethnic group emerged: the "Mozarabs", Christians who lived under Muslim rule, and adopted Arabic language, dress and social customs.

In the power vacuum of southern France, Moorish raiding parties continued beyond the Pyrenees and reached as far north as Poitiers in 732, where Charles Martel, the de facto ruler of Merovingian France, dealt them a minor defeat, which convinced them to withdraw. Martel's son Pepin, and his famous grandson **Charlemagne** (768–814), both strove to restore order in the south and push back the invaders, with Charlemagne's empire including the southern slopes of the Pyrenees and much of Catalunya. After being ambushed and defeated by the Basques at Roncesvalles in 778, Charlemagne switched his attention to the Mediterranean side of the Pyrenees, attempting to defend his empire against the Muslims. He took Girona in 785 and his son Louis directed the successful siege of Barcelona in 801. Continued Frankish military success meant that Muslim influence in Catalunya had waned long before the Battle of Las Navas de Tolosa in 1212 (see p.260) – the turning point for the reconquest of the peninsula as a whole.

With the capture of Barcelona, the **Frankish counties** of Catalunya became a sort of buffer zone, known as the **Spanish Marches**. Separate territories, each ruled by a count and theoretically owing allegiance to the Frankish king (or emperor), were primitive proto-feudal entities, almost exclusively agrarian, and ruled by a small hereditary military elite.

## From Wilfred the Hairy to Ramon Berenguer IV

As the Frankish empire of Charlemagne disintegrated in the decades following his death, the counties of the Marches began to enjoy greater independence, which was formalized in 878 by Guifré el Pelós – known in English as **Wilfred the Hairy**. Wilfred was count of Urgell and the Cerdagne and, after adding Barcelona to his holdings, named himself its first count, founding a dynastic line that was to rule until the 1400s. He also made important territorial gains, inheriting Girona and Besalú, and regaining control of Montserrat. In the wake of the Muslim withdrawal from the area, **Christian outposts** had been established throughout Catalunya, and Wilfred continued the process, founding Benedictine monasteries at Ripoll (about 880) and Sant Joan de les Abadesses (888), where his daughter was the first abbess.

Wilfred died in 898 on an expedition against Muslim enemies and was followed by a succession of rulers who attempted to consolidate his gains. Early counts, like **Ramon Berenguer I** (1035–76), concentrated on establishing their superiority over the other local counts, which was bitterly resisted. **Ramon Berenguer III** (1144–66) added considerable territory to his realms with his marriage in 1113 to a Provençal heiress, and made alliances and commercial treaties with Muslim and Christian powers around the western Mediterranean.

The most important stage in Catalunya's development as a significant power, however, came in 1137 with the marriage of **Ramon Berenguer IV** to Petronella, the two-year-old daughter of King Ramiro II of Aragón. This led to the **dynastic union of Catalunya and Aragón**. Although this remained a loose and tenuous federation – the regions retained their own parliaments and customs – it provided the platform for rapid expansion over the next three centuries. As importantly, Ramon managed to tame almost all of the other counts, forcing them to recognize his superior status and in the course of this he promulgated the **Usatges de Barcelona**, a code of laws and customs defining feudal duties, rights and authorities – sneakily putting Ramon I's name on them to make them appear older than they were. He also captured Muslim Tortosa and Lleida in 1148–49, which mark the limits of the modern region of Catalunya, but now the region began to look east for its future, across the Mediterranean.

# The Kingdom of Catalunya and Aragón

Ramon Berenguer IV was no more than a count, but his son **Alfons I** (who succeeded to the throne in 1162) also inherited the title of King of Aragón (where he was Alfonso II), and became the first count-king of what historians later came to call the **Crown of Aragón**. To his territories he added Roussillon and much of southern France, becoming known as "Emperor of the Pyrenees"; he also made some small gains against the Berber Almohads who now dominated Muslim Iberia, and allied with and intrigued against neighbouring Christian kingdoms of Navarre and Castile.

Under the rule of Alfons's son, Pere (Peter) the Catholic, the kingdom suffered both successes and reverses. Pere gained glory as one of the military leaders in the decisive defeat of Muslim forces at the **Battle of Las Navas de Tolosa** in 1212, but, swept up into the Albigensian Wars through his ties of lordship to the Counts of Toulouse, he was killed by Catholic forces at Muret a year later. In the years of uncertainty that followed the succession of his five-year-old son, **Jaume I** (1213–76), later known as "the Conqueror", his rivals took advantage of the power vacuum and stripped the count-kings of Provence. Although they would retain Roussillon and acquire Montpellier, for all intents and purposes this signalled the **end of Catalan aspirations north of the Pyrenees**.

## The golden age

In spite of these setbacks, Catalunya's age of glory was about to begin in earnest, with the 63-year reign of the extraordinary Jaume. Shrugging off the tutelage of his Templar masters at the age of thirteen, he then personally took to the field to tame his rebellious nobility. This accomplished, he embarked on a series of campaigns of conquest, which brought him Muslim Mallorca in 1229, Menorca in 1231 and Ibiza in 1235 (which explains why the Balearics share a common language with the region). Next he turned south and conquered the city of Valencia in 1238, establishing a new kingdom of which he was also ruler. Valencia, however, was no easy territory to govern, and the region's Muslim inhabitants rose up in a series of revolts that outlasted the king's reign.

Recognizing that **Mediterranean expansion** was where Catalunya's future lay, Jaume signed the **Treaty of Corbeil** in 1258, renouncing his rights in France (except for Montpellier, the Cerdagne and Roussillon), in return for the French

King Louis's renunciation of claims in Catalunya. In this period Catalunya's **economic development** was rapid, fuelled by the exploits of Barcelona's mercantile class, who were quick to see the possibilities of Mediterranean commerce. Maritime customs were codified in the so-called *Llibre del Consolat de Mar*, trade relations were established with North Africa and the Middle East, and consulates opened in foreign ports to protect Catalan interests.

Equally important during Jaume's reign was the establishment of the **Corts**, Catalunya's first parliament – one of the earliest such bodies in Europe, and demonstrative of the confidence developing within the region. In 1249, the first governors of Barcelona were elected, nominating councillors to help them who became known as the Consell de Cent.

On Jaume's death, his kingdom was divided between his sons, one of whom, **Pere II** ("the Great"), took Catalunya, Aragón and Valencia. Connected through marriage to the Sicilian Crown, Pere used the 1282 "Sicilian Vespers" rising against Charles of Anjou to press his claim to the island. In August that year, Pere was crowned at Palermo, and Sicily became the base for Catalan exploits throughout the Mediterranean. Athens and Neopatras were taken between 1302 and 11 by Catalan mercenaries, the *almogávares*, and famous sea-leaders-cum-pirates such as Roger de Flor and Roger de Llúria fought in the name of the Catalan-Aragonese crown. Malta (1283), Corsica (1323), Sardinia (1324) and Naples (1423) all fell under the influence of successive count-kings.

With the territorial gains came new developments with a wider significance. Catalan became used as a trading language throughout the Mediterranean, and 1289 saw the first recorded meeting of a body that became known as the **Generalitat**, a sort of committee of the Corts. Within it were represented each of the three traditional estates – commons, nobility and clergy – and it gradually became responsible for administering public order and justice, and maintaining an arsenal and fleet for the defence of the kingdom.

## Social and economic developments

By the mid-fourteenth century Catalunya was at its economic peak. Barcelona had become an important city with impressive new buildings, both religious and secular, to match its status as a regional superpower – the cathedral, church of Santa María del Mar, the Generalitat building, the Ajuntament (with its Consell de Cent meeting room) and the Drassanes shipyards all testify to Barcelona's wealth in this period. Catalan became established as a **literary language**, and Catalan works are recognized as the precursor of much of the great medieval European literature: the Mallorcan Ramon Llull's *Book of Contemplation* appeared in 1272, and his romance *Blanquerna* was written a century before Chaucer's *Canterbury Tales*. **Architecture** progressed from Romanesque to Gothic styles, with churches displaying features that have become known as Catalan-Gothic – such as spacious naves, hexagonal belfries and a lack of flying buttresses.

Even while this great maritime wealth and power were being celebrated in such fashion, the seeds of decline were being sown. The **Black Death** made its first appearance in the Balearics in 1348 and visited Catalunya several times over the next forty years, and by the end of the century half the population had succumbed to the disease. As a result, there was increasing pressure on the peasantry by the landowners, who were determined not to let their profits fall.

# The rise of Castile

The last of Wilfred the Hairy's dynasty of Catalan count-kings, Martin the Humane (Martí el Humà), died in 1410 without an heir. After nearly five

The Catholic monarchs, Ferdinand and Isabel, shared in the religious bigotry of their contemporaries, although Isabel, under the influence of her personal confessor, Tomás de Torquemada, was the more reactionary of the two. In Catalunya, the Inquisition was established in 1487, and aimed to purify the Catholic faith by rooting out heresy. It was directed mainly at the secret **Jews**, most of whom had been converted by force (after the pogrom of 1391) to Christianity. It was suspected that their descendants, known as **New Christians**, continued to practise their old faith in secrecy, and in 1492, an edict forced some seventy thousand Jews to flee the country. The Jewish population in Barcelona was completely eradicated in this way, while communities elsewhere – principally in Girona, Tarragona and Lleida – were massively reduced, and those who remained were forced to convert to Christianity.

hundred years of continuity, there were six claimants to the throne, and in 1412 nine specially appointed counsellors elevated Ferdinand (Ferran) de Antequera, son of a Catalan princess, to the vacant throne.

Ferdinand ruled for only four years, but his reign and that of his son, Alfons, and grandson, John (Joan) II, spelled the end for Catalunya's influence in the Mediterranean. The Castilian rulers were soon in dispute with the Consell de Cent; illegal taxes were imposed, funds belonging to the Generalitat were appropriated, and most damagingly non-Catalans started to be appointed to key positions in the Church, state offices and the armed forces. In 1469 John's son, Prince Ferdinand (Ferran), who was born in Aragón, married Isabel of Castile, a union that would eventually finish off Catalan independence.

Both came into their inheritances quickly, Isabel taking Castile in 1474 and the Catalan-Aragónese crown coming to Ferdinand in 1479. The two largest kingdoms in Spain were thus united, the ruling pair becoming known as "**Los Reyes Católicos**" ("Els Reis Catòlics" in Catalan), the Catholic monarchs. Their energies were devoted to the reconquest and unification of Spain: they finally took back Granada from the Moors in 1492, and initiated a wave of Christian fervour at whose heart was the **Inquisition**.

Also in 1492, the final shift in Catalunya's outlook occurred with the triumphal return of **Christopher Columbus** from the New World, to be received in Barcelona by Ferdinand and Isabel. As trade routes shifted away from the Mediterranean, this was no longer such a profitable market. Castile, like Portugal, looked to the Americas for trade and conquest, and the exploration and exploitation of the New World was spearheaded by the Andalucían city of Seville. Meanwhile, Ferdinand gave the Supreme Council of Aragón control over Catalan affairs in 1494. The Aragónese nobility, who had always resented the success of the Catalan maritime adventures, now saw the chance to complete their control of Catalunya by taking over its ecclesiastical institutions – with Catalan monks being thrown out of the great monasteries of Poblet and Montserrat.

## Habsburg and Bourbon rule

Charles I a **Habsburg**, came to the throne in 1516 as a beneficiary of the marriage alliances made by the Catholic monarchs. Five years later he was elected emperor of the **Holy Roman Empire** (as Charles V), inheriting not only Castile, Aragón and Catalunya, but also Flanders, the Netherlands, Artois, the Franche-Comté and all the American colonies. With such responsibilities, it became inevitable that attention would be diverted from Spain, whose chief function became to sustain the Holy Roman Empire with gold and silver from the Americas. It was in this era that Madrid was established as capital city of the Spanish Empire, and the long rivalry began between Madrid and Barcelona.

Throughout the **sixteenth century**, Catalunya continued to suffer under the Inquisition, and – deprived of trading opportunities in the Americas – became an impoverished region. Habsburg wars wasted the lives of Catalan soldiers, banditry in the region increased as the economic situation worsened, and emigration from certain areas followed. By the middle of the **seventeenth century**, Spain's rulers were losing credibility as the disparity between the wealth surrounding Crown and Court and the poverty of the mass of the population produced a source of perpetual tension.

With Spain and France at war in 1635, the Catalans took advantage of the situation and revolted, declaring themselves an **independent republic** under the protection of the French King Louis XIII. This, the "War of the Reapers" – after the marching song *Els Segadors* (The Reapers), later the Catalan national anthem – ended in 1652 with the surrender of Barcelona to the Spanish army. The **Treaty of the Pyrenees** in 1659 finally split the historical lands of Catalunya as the Spanish lost control of Roussillon and part of the Cerdagne to France.

In 1700, when the Habsburg king Charles II died heirless, France's Louis XIV saw an opportunity to fulfil his longtime ambition of putting a Bourbon on the Spanish throne. He managed to secure the succession of his grandson, Philippe d'Anjou, under condition that the latter renounced his rights to the throne of France. This deal put a Bourbon on the throne of Spain, but led to war with the other claimant, Archduke Charles of Austria: the resulting **War of the Spanish Succession** lasted thirteen years from 1701, with Catalunya (along with England) lining up on the Austrian side in an attempt to regain its ancient rights and in the hope that victory would give it a share of the American trade dominated by the Castilians since the late fifteenth century.

However, the **Treaty of Utrecht** in 1714 gave the throne to the **Bourbon** (*Borbón* in Castilian, *Borbó* in Catalan) Philippe, now Philip V of Spain, and initiated a fresh period of repression from which the Catalans took a century to recover. Barcelona lay under siege for over a year, and with its eventual capitulation a fortress was built at Ciutadella to subdue the city's inhabitants – the final defeat, on September 11, is still commemorated every year as a Catalan holiday, La Diada. The universities at Barcelona and Lleida were closed, the Catalan language was banned, the Consell de Cent and Generalitat were abolished – in short, Catalunya was finished as even a partially autonomous region.

Throughout the **eighteenth century**, Catalunya's interests were subsumed within those of Bourbon Spain, and successive monarchs were determined to Castilianize the region. When neighbouring France became aggressively expansionist following the Revolution of 1789, Spain was a natural target, first for the Revolutionary armies and later for the machinations of Napoleon. In 1805, during the **Napoleonic Wars**, the French fleet (along with the Spanish who had been forced into an alliance) was defeated at Trafalgar. Shortly after, Charles IV was forced to abdicate; Napoleon installed his brother Joseph on the throne three years later. Attempting to broaden his appeal among Spain's subjects, the French emperor proclaimed a separate government of Catalunya – independent of Joseph's rule – with Catalan as its official language. The region's response was an indication of how far Catalunya had become integrated into Spain during the Bourbon period – despite their history the Catalans supported the Bourbon cause solidly during the ensuing **Peninsular War** (1808–14), ignoring Napoleon's blandishments. Girona was defended heroically from the French in a seven-month siege, while Napoleon did his cause no good at all by attacking and sacking the holy shrine and monastery at Montserrat. Fierce local resistance was eventually backed by the muscle of a British army, and the French were at last driven out.

## The slow Catalan revival

Despite the political emasculation of Catalunya, there were signs of **economic revival** from the end of the seventeenth century onwards. During the 1700s there was a gradual growth in agricultural output, partly caused by a doubling of the population: more land was put under cultivation, and productivity improved with the introduction of easy-to-cultivate maize from the Indies. Barcelona also saw a steady increase in trade, since from 1778 Catalunya was allowed to trade with the Americas for the first time; in this way, the shipping industry received a boost and Catalunya was able to export its textiles to a wider market. The other great export was wine, whose widespread production in the region also dates from this period. A chamber of commerce was founded in Barcelona in 1758, and other economic societies followed as commercial interests increased.

After the Napoleonic Wars, industry in Catalunya developed apace – it was an **industrialization** that appeared nowhere else in Spain. In the mid-nineteenth century, the country's first **railway** was built from Barcelona to Mataró, and later extended south to Tarragona, and north to Girona and the French border. **Manufacturing** industries appeared as the financial surpluses from the land were invested, encouraging a shift in population from the land to the towns; olive oil production in Lleida and Tarragona helped supply the whole country; and previously local industries flourished on a wider scale – in the wine-growing districts, for example, *cava* (champagne-like wine) production was introduced in the late nineteenth century, supported closely by the age-old cork industry of the Catalan forests. From 1890, hydroelectric power was harnessed from the Pyrenees, and by the end of the century **Barcelona** was the fastest-growing city in Spain – it was one of only six with more than 100,000 inhabitants.

Equally important was the first stirring of what became known as the **Renaixença** (Renaissance), in the mid-nineteenth century. Despite being banned in official use and public life, the Catalan **language** had never died out. Books began to appear again in Catalan – a dictionary in 1803 and a grammar in 1814 – and the language was revived among the bourgeoisie and intellectuals in the cities as a means of making subtle nationalist and political points. Catalan **poetry** became popular, and the late medieval **Jocs Florals** (Floral Games), a sort of literary competition, were revived in 1859 in Barcelona: one winner was the great Catalan poet, Jacint Verdaguer (1845–1902). Catalan **drama** developed (although even in the late nineteenth century there were still restrictions on performing wholly Catalan plays), led mainly by the dramatist Pitarra. The only discipline that didn't show any great advance was prose literature – partly because the Catalan language had been so debased with Castilian over the centuries that writers found it difficult to express themselves in a way that would appeal to the population.

Prosperity led to the rapid **expansion of Barcelona**, particularly the mid-nineteenth century addition to the city of the planned Eixample district. Encouraged by wealthy patrons and merchants, architects such as Josep Puig i Cadafalch, Lluís Domènech i Montaner and Antoni Gaudí I Cornet were in the vanguard of the **modernista** movement which changed the face of the city. Culture and business came together with the **Universal Exhibition** of

1888, based around the *modernista* buildings of the Parc de la Ciutadella, and the **International Exhibition** on Montjuïc in 1929, which boasted creations in the style of *modernisme's* successor, *noucentisme*.

## The seeds of civil war

In 1814, the repressive Ferdinand VII had been restored to the Spanish throne, and, despite the Catalan contribution to the defeat of the French, he stamped out the least hint of liberalism in the region, abolishing virtually all Catalunya's remaining privileges. On his death, the Crown was claimed both by his daughter Isabel II (with liberal support) and by his brother Charles (backed by the Church and the conservatives). The ensuing **First Carlist War** (1833–39) ended in victory for Isabel, who came of age in 1843. Her reign was a long record of scandal, political crisis and constitutional compromise, until liberal army generals under the leadership of General Prim eventually effected a coup in 1868, forcing Isabel to abdicate. However, the experimental **First Republic** (1873–75) failed, and following the **Second Carlist War** the throne went to Isabel's son, Alfonso XII.

Against this unstable background, local dissatisfaction increased and the years preceding World War I saw a growth in working-class **political movements**. Barcelona's textile workers organized a branch affiliated to the communist First International, founded by Karl Marx, and the region's wine growers also banded together to seek greater security. Tension was further heightened by the **loss of Cuba** in 1898, which only added to local economic problems, with the return of soldiers seeking employment in the cities where there was none.

A call-up for army reserves to fight in Morocco in 1909 provoked a general strike and the so-called **Tragic Week** (Setmana Trágica) of rioting in Barcelona, and then throughout Catalunya, in which over one hundred people died. Catalans objected violently to the suggestion that they should go to fight abroad for a state that did little for them at home, and the city's streets saw burning churches, barricades and popular committees, though there was little direction to the protest. What the Tragic Week did prove to Catalan workers was the need to be better organized for the future. A direct result was the establishment of the Confederación Nacional del Trabajo – the **CNT** – in 1911, which included many of the Catalan working-class organizations.

During **World War I** Spain was neutral, though inwardly turbulent since soaring inflation and the cessation of exports following the German blockade of the North Atlantic hit the country hard. As rumblings grew among the workers and political organizations, the army moved decisively, crushing a general strike of 1917. The Russian Revolution had scared the conservative businessmen of the region, who offered cooperation with the army in return for political representation in the country's government. However, the situation did not improve. Violent strikes and assassinations plagued Barcelona, while the CNT and the union of the socialists, the CGT, both saw huge increases in their membership. In 1923, **General Primo de Rivera**, the captain-general of Catalunya, overthrew the national government in a military coup that had the full backing of the Catalan middle class, establishing a dictatorship that enjoyed initial economic success. There was no real stability in the dictatorship, however, and new political factions were taking shape throughout the country. The general resigned in 1930, dying a few months later, but the hopes of some for the restoration of the monarchy's political powers were short-lived. The success of the anti-monarchist parties in the municipal elections of 1931 led to the abdication of the king and the foundation of the **Second Republic**.

# The Second Republic

In 1931, Catalunya, under Francesc Macià, leader of the Republican Left, declared itself to be an **independent republic**, and the Republican flag was raised over the Ajuntament in Barcelona. Madrid refused to accept the declaration, though a statute of limited autonomy was granted in 1932. Despite the initial hope that things would improve, the government was soon failing to satisfy even the least of expectations that it had raised. In addition, all the various strands of political ideology that had been fermenting in Spain over the previous century were ready to explode. **Anarchism** in particular was gaining strength among the frustrated middle classes as well as among workers and peasantry. The **Communist Party** and the left-wing **socialists**, driven into alliance by their mutual distrust of the "moderate" socialists in government, were also forming a growing bloc. There was little real unity of purpose on either Left or Right, but their fear of each other and their own exaggerated boasts made each seem an imminent threat. On the Right, the **Falangists** (founded in 1923 by José Antonio Primo de Rivera, son of the dictator) made uneasy bedfellows with conservative traditionalists and dissident elements in the army upset by modernizing reforms.

In an atmosphere of growing confusion, the left-wing **Popular Front** alliance, including the Catalan Republican Left, won the general election of January 1936 by a narrow margin, and an all-Republican government was formed. In Catalunya, Lluís Companys became president of the Generalitat. Normal life, though, became increasingly impossible: the economy was crippled by strikes, peasants took agrarian reform into their own hands, and the government singularly failed to exert its authority over anyone. Finally, on July 17, 1936, the military garrison in Morocco rebelled under **General Francisco Franco**'s leadership, to be followed by uprisings at military garrisons throughout the country. It was the culmination of years of scheming in the army, but the event was far from the overnight success its leaders almost certainly expected. Much of the south and west quickly fell into the hands of the Nationalists, but Madrid and the industrialized northeast remained loyal to the Republican government. In Barcelona, although the military garrison supported Franco, it was soon subdued by local Civil Guards and the workers, while local leaders set up militias in preparation for the coming fight.

In October 1936, Franco was declared military commander and head of state; fascist Germany and Italy recognized his regime as the legitimate government of Spain in November. The Civil War was on.

# Civil War

The **Spanish Civil War** (1936–39) was one of the most bitter and bloody the world has seen. Violent reprisals were visited on their enemies by both sides – the Republicans shooting priests and local landowners wholesale, and burning churches and cathedrals; the Nationalists carrying out mass slaughter of the population of almost every town they took. It was also to be the first modern war – Franco's German allies demonstrated their ability to inflict terror on civilian populations with their bombing raids on Gernika and Durango, while radio became an important propaganda weapon, with Nationalists offering starving Republicans the "white bread of Franco".

Catalunya was devoutly Republican from the outset with many of the rural areas particularly attracted by anarchism, an ideology that embodied their traditional values of equality and personal liberty. However, despite sporadic help from Russia and the 35,000 volunteers of the **International Brigades**, the Republic could never compete with the professional armies and the massive assistance from fascist Italy and Nazi Germany that the Nationalists enjoyed. Foreign volunteers arriving in Barcelona were sent to the front with companies that were ill-equipped, lines of communication were poor, and, furthermore, the Left was torn by international divisions that at times led almost to civil war within its own ranks. George Orwell's account of this period in his *Homage to Catalonia* is instructive: fighting in an anarchist militia, he was eventually forced to flee the country when the infighting became intolerable, though many others like him were not so fortunate and ended up in prison or executed.

Eventually, the nonintervention of the other European governments effectively handed victory to the Nationalists. The Republican government fled Madrid first for Valencia, and then moved on to base itself at Barcelona in 1937. The **Battle of the Ebro** around Tortosa saw massive casualties on both sides; Nationalist troops advanced on Valencia in 1938, and from the west were also approaching Catalunya from their bases in Navarre. When Bilbao was taken by the Nationalists, the Republicans' fight on the **Aragón front** was lost. The final Republican hope – that war in Europe over Czechoslovakia would draw the Allies into a war against fascism and deprive Franco of his foreign aid – evaporated in September 1938, with the British Prime Minister Chamberlain's capitulation to Hitler at Munich, and Franco was able to call on new arms and other supplies from Germany for a final offensive against Catalunya. The **fall of Barcelona** came on January 25, 1939 – the Republican parliament held its last meeting at Figueres a few days later. Republican soldiers, cut off in the valleys of the Pyrenees, made their way across the high passes into France, joined by women and children fearful of a fascist victory. Among the refugees and escapees was **Lluís Companys**, president of the Generalitat, who was later captured in France by the Germans, returned to Spain and, under orders from Franco, was shot at the castle prison on Montjuïc in 1940.

## Catalunya in Franco's Spain

Although the Civil War left more than half a million dead, destroyed a quarter of a million homes and sent a third of a million people (including 100,000 Catalans) into exile, Franco was in no mood for reconciliation. With his government recognized by Allied powers, including Britain and France, he set up **war tribunals** that ordered executions and provided concentration camps in which upwards of two million people were held until "order" had been established by authoritarian means. Until as late as the mid-1960s, isolated partisans in Catalunya (and elsewhere in Spain) continued to resist fascist rule.

The **Catalan language** was banned again, in schools, churches, the press and in public life; only one party was permitted, and censorship was rigorously enforced. The economy was in ruins, and Franco did everything possible to further the cause of Madrid against Catalunya, starving the region of investment and new industry. Pyrenean villagers began to drift down into the towns and cities in a fruitless search for work, accelerating the depopulation of the mountains.

After **World War II** (during which the country was too weak to be anything but neutral), Spain was economically and politically isolated. There were serious strikes in 1951 in Barcelona and in 1956 across the whole of Catalunya.

What saved Franco was the acceptance of **American aid**, offered by General Eisenhower in 1953 on the condition that Franco provide land for US air bases – a condition he was more than willing to accept. Prosperity did increase after this, fuelled in the 1960s and 1970s by a growing tourist industry, but Catalunya (along with the Basque Country, another thorn in Franco's side) was still economically backward, with investment per head lower than anywhere else in the country. Absentee landlords took much of the local revenue, a situation exacerbated by Franco's policy of encouraging emigration to Catalunya from other parts of Spain (and granting the immigrants land) in an attempt to dilute regional differences.

Despite the **cultural and political repression**, the distinct Catalan identity was never really obliterated: the Catalan Church retained a feisty independence, while Barcelona emerged as the most important publishing centre in Spain. Clandestine language and history classes were conducted, and artists and writers continued to produce work in defiance of the authorities. Nationalism in Catalunya, however, did not take the same course as the Basque **separatist movement**, which engendered the terrorist organization ETA (Euzkadi ta Azkatasuna; "Basque Homeland and Freedom"). There was little violence against the state in Catalunya and no serious counterpart to ETA. The Catalan approach was subtler: an audience at the Palau de la Música sang the unofficial Catalan anthem when Franco visited in 1960; a massive petition against language restrictions was raised in 1963; and a sit-in by Catalan intellectuals at Montserrat was organized in protest against repression in the Basque Country.

As Spain became comparatively more wealthy, so the political bankruptcy of Franco's regime and its inability to cope with popular demands became clearer. Higher incomes, the need for better education and a creeping invasion of Western culture made the anachronism of Franco ever more apparent. His only reaction was to attempt to withdraw what few signs of increased liberalism had crept through, and his last years mirrored the repression of the postwar period.

## Franco's death and the new democracy

When Franco died in 1975, **King Juan Carlos** was officially designated to succeed as head of state – groomed for the succession by Franco himself. The king's initial moves were cautious in the extreme, appointing a government dominated by loyal Franquistas, who had little sympathy for the growing opposition demands for "democracy without adjectives". In the summer of 1976, demonstrations, particularly in Madrid, ended in violence, with the police upholding the old authoritarian ways.

To his credit, Juan Carlos recognized that some real break with the past was urgent and inevitable, and, accepting the resignation of his prime minister, set in motion the process of **democratization**. His newly appointed prime minister, Adolfo Suárez, steered through a Political Reform Act, which allowed for a two-chamber parliament and a referendum in favour of democracy; he also legitimized the Socialist Party (the PSOE) and the Communists, and called elections for the following year, the first since 1936.

In the elections of 1977, the **Pacte Democratico per Catalunya** – an alliance of pro-Catalan parties – gained ten seats in the lower house of the Spanish parliament (Basque nationalists won a similar number) dominated by Suárez's own centre-right UCD party but also with a strong Socialist presence. In a spirit of consensus and amnesty, it was announced that Catalunya was to be granted a degree of autonomy, and a million people turned out on the streets of Barcelona to witness the re-establishment of the Generalitat and to welcome home its president-in-exile, **Josep Tarradellas**. A new Spanish constitution of 1978 allowed for a sort of devolution within a unitary state, and the **Statute of Autonomy** for Catalunya was approved on December 18, 1979, with the first regional elections taking place in March 1980. Although the Socialists had won the mayoral election of 1978, it was the conservative **Jordi Pujol i Soley** and his coalition party **Convergència i Unió** (CiU) who gained regional power – and who proceeded to dominate the Catalan parliament for the next quarter of a century. In a way, the pro-conservative vote made it easy for the central government to deal with Catalunya, since the demands for autonomy here did not have the extreme political dimension they had in the Basque Country.

After the failure of an attempted **military coup** in February 1981, led by Civil Guard Colonel Tejero, the **elections of 1982** saw Felipe González's PSOE elected with a massive swing to the Left in a country that had been firmly in the hands of the Right for forty-three years. The **1986 general election** gave González a renewed mandate, during which time Spain entered the **European Community**, decided by referendum to stay in NATO, and boasted one of the fastest-growing economies in Western Europe. However, high unemployment, wage controls and a lack of social-security measures led to diminishing support and the PSOE began losing much of its credibility. Narrow victories in two more elections kept the Socialists in power, but after the 1993 results were counted it was clear that they had failed to win an overall majority and were forced to rely on the support of the Catalan nationalist coalition, CiU, to retain power. This state of affairs well suited Jordi Pujol, who was now in a position to pursue some of the Catalan nationalists' more long-cherished aims, in particular the right to retain part of the region's own income-tax revenue.

## Contemporary politics

Following allegations of sleaze and the disclosure of the existence of a secret "dirty war" against the Basque terrorists, the calling of a **general election in 1996** came as no surprise and neither did the overall result. In power for almost fourteen years, the PSOE finally succumbed to the greater appeal of the conservative Partido Popular (PP), under **José María Aznar** – the first conservative government in Spain since the return of democracy. However, the PP came in well short of an outright majority, and Aznar was left with the same problem as González before him – relying on the Catalan nationalists and other smaller regionalist parties to maintain his party in power.

In the **general election of 2000**, the PP won a resounding victory in the national parliament, whilst Catalunya was left under CiU control. For the first time, the PP was no longer dependent on other parties to pass legislation and was high on confidence, though within two years Aznar's government had begun to lose its way. In particular, Aznar's fervent support of US and British **military action in Iraq** in 2003 led to huge discontent. Polls showed that ninety percent of Spaniards opposed the conflict – manifested in Barcelona by a cacophonous nightly anti-war banging of pots and pans from the city's balconies.

However, in the local elections of 2003, Aznar and the PP defied the polls, holding off the PSOE in many major cities (Barcelona excepted). With the PSOE beset by corruption scandals and affected by the strong separatist showing in regional elections, it seemed that the best the PSOE could hope for was to deny the PP an absolute majority in the **2004 general election**. That was before the dramatic events of March 11, 2004, when terrorists struck at the heart of **Madrid**, killing 200 people in coordinated train bombings. Spain went to the polls in shock a few days later, and voted in the PSOE against all expectations. With millions on the streets in the days after the attacks, it seemed the PP had been punished both for supporting the war in Iraq, and – prematurely to many – for blaming the bombings on the Basque separatists, ETA.

The Socialists took power in a minority administration led by PSOE prime minister **José Luis Rodriguez Zapatero**, forced to rely on parliamentary support from Catalan separatists and other regional parties. A leftish coalition in Catalunya itself soon raised the whole question of Catalunya's status within the Spanish nation, since Zapatero had previously promised to accept whatever demands for greater autonomy emanated from the new Catalan parliament. The consequent **statute of autonomy bill**, approved by the Catalan government in September 2005 and sent to Madrid, opened up all sorts of national fault-lines, as the bill sought to go well beyond Spanish constitutional limits, defining Catalunya as a "nation" within Spain and claiming full tax-raising powers and a parallel judicial system. Zapatero was immediately put under pressure from his own PSOE party – many of whose members have no truck with Catalan separatism – while there was predictable opposition from the PP and from much of the Madrid-based media. More worrying was the rumble from a Spanish general that the army might be forced to intercede if the Spanish constitution and national unity were threatened – he was quickly sacked, but it's a reminder that military intervention in democratic Spain (as recently as 1981) is still considered an option by some of the more extreme conservative forces in the country.

A watered-down version of the statue was **approved by referendum** in 2006, increasing Catalunya's tax-raising powers and redefining in general (though not legal) terms the region as a "nation". But it satisfied few, and the arguments are not likely to go away, since the statute was subsequently contested in the courts by other autonomous Spanish regions and by the PP. In 2008, it was still before the Constitutional Court of Spain, pending a final judgement. Meanwhile, the calling in early 2006 of a cease-fire by armed Basque separatist organization ETA further put regionalism high on the Spanish national agenda.

In the end, Zapatero managed to fight the **2008 general election** largely on his handling of the economy, and he and the PSOE were re-elected to office, though with just short of an absolute majority. But regionalism in all its forms won't disappear, as underscored by a supposed ETA assassination of a Basque politician during the election campaign. Zapatero, meanwhile, can point to measures such as the withdrawal of troops from Iraq, an increase in the minimum wage and maternity leave, and even the legalization of gay marriage as evidence of a new direction for Spain. He just has to hope that the economy – after a decade of high growth – doesn't disintegrate beneath him while he pursues the long-term structural reform that most analysts agree Spain requires.

# Barcelona snapshot

It only takes a few minutes in Barcelona to realize that wherever you might be, you're emphatically not in Spain. Or, rather you are – just not in the clichéd Spain of paella, sangria, bullfights and flamenco. Instead, Barcelona is a dynamic modern city that considers itself almost a place apart, with a deeply felt Catalan identity rooted in a rich, and at times, glorious past. The language is an easy identifier, with Catalan street and business signs taking precedence over Castilian Spanish by law. Or just take note of the burgeoning number of .cat domain names to know that the least Spanish city in Spain always does things its own way.

## City and state

Barcelona is the capital of the province of Catalunya, whose official title is the **Comunitat Autonoma de Catalunya**. It's one of seventeen "autonomous communities" recognized by the new Spanish constitution of 1978, with Catalunya defined as a "nationality" (rather than, crucially, a "nation") by the original 1979 Statute of Autonomy.

The Catalan government – the **Generalitat** – based in Barcelona, enjoys a high profile, employing eighty thousand people in sixteen departments or ministries, controlling social services, urban planning, culture, regional transport, industry, trade, tourism, fisheries and agriculture. However, as long as the budget is based on **tax** collected by central government and then returned proportionately, the scope for real independence is limited, as the Generalitat has no tangible resources of its own and is forced to **share jurisdiction** on strategic matters such as health, education and justice with the Spanish state. In addition, although an autonomous part of Spain, Catalunya is not officially recognized at international level.

However, over the years steps have been taken to create at least the illusion of independence. Catalan (as opposed to Spanish) tourism, trade and industry are increasingly promoted abroad, while two of the most visible symbols of the Spanish state, the Guardia Civil and the Policía Nacional, are gradually being scaled down, with urban **policing** and rural and highway duties being taken over by the Mossos d'Esquadra, Catalunya's autonomous police force. Culturally, emphasis has been on the promotion of the **Catalan language** – currently one of the fastest-growing languages in the world. All Catalunya's children are taught in Catalan, while the entire machinery of regional government and business is conducted in Catalan.

In the end, further independence for Catalunya might well be trumped by the onward march of **European integration**. Spain's regional governments already have representatives at the European Union, working on committees alongside the Spanish delegates. In addition, the Spanish government is committed to consulting the regions on any European issues that affect them directly, and there are ongoing discussions about making Catalan an official EU language.

## Parliament and local politics

The **Parlament de Catalunya** (Parliament of Catalunya) comprises a single chamber of 135 members, with elections held every four years. It sits in the old Ciutadella arsenal building in Parc de la Ciutadella, in parliamentary sessions that run from September to December and February to June, though extraordinary sessions can be called outside these months. As well as legislating for Catalunya within the strictures of the Statute of Autonomy, parliament also appoints the senators who represent the Generalitat in the Spanish Senate and has the right to initiate legislation in the Spanish Congress.

Barcelona itself is divided into ten **administrative districts**, including the Ciutat Vella, Eixample, Gràcia, Sants-Montjuïc and Sarrià-Sant Gervasi. The city is run by a mayor and 41 city councillors who are elected by each municipal area. The seat of the city council, the **Ajuntament**, is in Plaça de Sant Jaume, opposite the Generalitat building.

From 1980 (the first elections after autonomy) until 2003, **Catalunya** consistently elected right-wing governments, led by the conservative Convergència i Unió (CiU) president of the Generalitat, **Jordi Pujol i Soley**. The Catalan predilection for the Right may come as a surprise in view of the past, but Catalunya is nothing if not pragmatic, and such administrations are seen as better able to protect Catalan business interests. The main opposition was provided by the **Partit Socialista de Catalunya** (PSC), sister party of the national PSOE, while other Catalan parties, such as the pro-independence **Esquerra Republicana de Catalana** (ERC) and the **Catalunya Verds** (ICV; Greens), have usually attracted minority support.

However, by way of contrast to conservative Catalunya, **Barcelona** itself remains by and large a PSC socialist stronghold. Part of this is due to the city's industrial heritage, but it's also in good measure the result of the large immigrant population from elsewhere in Spain, who are little attracted to the CiU's brand of Catalan nationalism. Between 1982 and 1997, the Ajuntament was led by an incredibly popular and charismatic socialist mayor, **Pasqual Maragall i Mira**, who took much of the credit for the hosting of the 1992 Olympic Games and consequent reshaping of the city. However, much to the consternation of locals, he stepped down from his post as mayor in 1997, leaving his deputy, the little-known **Joan Clos**, to fill his shoes. Clos proved himself able and won two more terms in 1999 and 2003, before being succeeded in 2006 by current mayor **Jordi Hereu**, who was re-elected in May 2007.

Maragall, meanwhile, moved on to take charge of the PSC in Catalunya, and became president after the **2003 parliamentary elections**, at the head of a coalition that provided the first left-wing Catalan government since 1980. The big surprise was the performance of the pro-independence ERC, under the leadership of **Josep-Lluís Carod-Rovira**, which effectively doubled its vote from 1999 to hold the balance of power. It was not the easy alliance that it appeared on paper, since the separatist ERC favours full Catalan independence, not something the PSC (or the national PSOE) supports.

Prompted by the manoeuvrings of the ERC, Catalan autonomy moved to centre stage with the overwhelming approval by parliament in September 2005 of the **Estatut** – the proposed reform of the 1979 Catalan Statute of Autonomy. While political strands within Catalunya are convinced of the merits of some kind of **devolution**, the reformed statute meant different things to different parties: to the PP and conservatives, granting more regional autonomy puts at risk the Spanish nation; to the Socialists, declaring Catalunya a "nation" is a welcome step towards a strong federal state; while for the separatists, it's nothing less than a call to independence.

Not surprisingly, the stature reform caused political mayhem. A **referendum** in June 2006 approved the statue, with a 75 percent yes-vote – but turnout was remarkably low (under fifty percent), throwing some doubt on the validity of its mandate. Tension within the coalition government led to Maragall stepping down and calling an early **parliamentary election in November 2006**, which the CiU actually won, though not with a workable majority. The upshot was the same left-leaning coalition as before, with **José Montilla** of the PSC as the new president – interestingly, a native of Córdoba province in the deep south, Montilla is the first president of the Generalitat to have been born outside Catalunya. Meanwhile, a pointer to future Catalan politics is the emergence of the new **Ciutadans** (Citizens) party, a left-leaning, non-nationalistic grouping that takes exception to the official exclusive promotion of all things Catalan (especially language). It won three seats in the 2006 parliamentary election, offering a less partisan, social democratic view of how Catalunya might develop.

## Economic development

Along with the Basque Country and Madrid, Catalunya is one of the most prosperous regions in the country. The number of firms in Barcelona accounts for fifteen percent of all the companies in Spain, while around a fifth of all new firms starting business in Spain do so in Catalunya. Barcelona is Europe's most popular convention site and the continent's number-one port for cruise ships, while the airport is in Europe's top ten for passenger numbers. Catalunya boasts the highest GDP of all Spain's autonomous communities, attracts almost a quarter of Spain's total inwards investment, and has Europe's largest savings bank, La Caixa.

**Tourism** is an important factor, accounting for sixteen percent of Catalunya's GDP, with over twelve million visitors a year now coming to the region. Other major employers are telecommunications, metal products, and chemical and pharmaceutical industries, though it's as a self-proclaimed "**city of knowledge**" that Barcelona is now positioning itself, attracting an increasing amount of information and communications technology business, as well as big-budget biotechnology and aerospace companies. MareNostrum, Spain's most powerful supercomputer, for example, is located in Barcelona, not Madrid, while the Catalan city also hosts the annual Mobile World Congress (3GSM), the world's biggest wireless communications trade fair.

The **1992 Olympics** are still regarded as a turning point in the city's recent history. They were an important boost, involving radical restoration of the old-town and port areas and prompting massive new developments – at a pace that the city has endeavoured to maintain ever since. In recent years, among countless other ambitious projects, this has meant the complete renovation of the **Port Vell** neighbourhood, a cleanup of **El Raval**, the development of **Diagonal Mar** and the **Fòrum** convention and leisure site, and the ongoing regeneration of **Poble Nou** as part of the so-called **Project 22@**. This last project alone has already attracted more than a thousand companies and created over 30,000 jobs, with new social-housing schemes to follow.

Other **current development schemes** include the complete remodelling of the Glòries district, the further expansion of the city's airport and metro system, the completion of a high-velocity train (AVE) link with Madrid and France, and concomitant building of a new transport interchange at Sant Andreu-Sagrera, and the transformation of the Arenes bull ring into a city gateway and leisure centre. Over the next decade, massive new city **business and residential areas** are also being planned near the port and by the river Besòs – all evidence that Barcelona's economic development is far from finished.

## Immigration

While immigrants from elsewhere in Spain have long settled in Barcelona (indeed, were encouraged to do so by Franco to dilute Catalan nationalism), those bearing the brunt of **racism** are the newcomers from North Africa, the

Indian subcontinent and South America. While the large Pakistani community in El Raval is generally respected for the life and business it's injected into the neighbourhood, popular local wisdom has come to equate North Africans with petty crime, whereas Romanies are treated largely as pariahs. It's dangerous nonsense, with at least some of its roots in a Catalan nationalism that prides itself on a certain cultural superiority, but such bigoted views aren't simply confined to the Right – senior figures on the Left, too, have warned of the "dangers" of allowing too many "foreigners" into Catalunya.

The facts, of course, tell a different story. Just eleven percent of the Catalan population at large has its origin outside Spain, though as most of these people live or work in the capital it's easy to construct a prejudice from their higher profile in the city. In contrast, almost a third of the Catalan population comes from other parts of Spain, while the fastest-growing immigrant population is actually that of other Europeans, free to settle in Catalunya with the relaxation of EU residency rules. All told, 160 different nationalities are represented in Barcelona, with foreign residents amounting to almost fifteen percent of the population (broadly similar to other major European cities).

## Social life and community

Economic success has led to familiar urban social problems. Almost two-thirds of Catalunya's seven million inhabitants now live in the city and its metropolitan region, with many complaining that the high-profile regeneration projects do little for their needs. **Hotel building** has reached epidemic proportions and rents and property prices in general have boomed, depriving the young, the old and the poor of affordable **housing** and other amenities. That said, both the Olympic and Project 22@ schemes have incorporated social housing, leisure facilities and green spaces, while the **public transport** system in particular is something of a European model of excellence.

Nonetheless, there are tensions in an increasingly crowded, developed city. Noise in residential areas is a perennial problem, and the Ajuntament has been getting tough in enforcing **noise restrictions** and closing down transgressing bars and clubs. The city council has also been getting more serious about dealing with squatters, known as **okupas**, whose banner- and graffiti-clad buildings have long been a familiar sight, especially in and around Gràcia. In the past, Barcelona has been tolerant of the *okupas* but concern from some residents about drugs and noise has persuaded the city council to close down many squats in recent years. In the same vein, the police have come down hard on **botellóns** – the mass, impromptu outdoor drinking parties that sprout up in Barcelona and other Spanish cities from time to time.

**Tourism**, too, has brought its own problems, as Barcelona has acquired a not-always-welcome reputation as a party town. The roaming stag parties and unsociable late-night behaviour by visitors causes much hand-wringing at City Hall (and much street-hosing early each morning), while certain old-town areas such as the Ramblas or the Born are now virtual tourist-only zones for much of the year. Locals in the Barri Gòtic have also had to contend with the noise and other problems caused by an explosion in the number of tourist apartments, many of them unregulated – the Ajuntament closed over 500 of them in 2008 and has said it won't approve any new apartment licences in the old town.

## Green Barcelona

From the huge, high-profile photovoltaic plant at the Fòrum site to the city buses powered by compressed natural gas, Barcelona likes to see itself as a future "sustainable" city. Its hosting of the 2004 **Universal Forum of Cultures** expo might have been politically controversial, but at its heart was a vision of **sustainable development** that the city authorities embraced with vigour. Subsequent urban-renewal projects have all incorporated innovative "green" methodology, while the city has pioneered several successful green schemes, from neighbourhood recycling of rubbish and rain-water to the Bicing **bike-sharing** project and charge-points for electric vehicles. However, in 2008, the worst **drought** in Spain since the 1940s brought Barcelona's green image into sharp relief. With Catalan reservoirs at only a fifth of capacity, drinking and ornamental fountains were closed (including the famous tourist ones at Montjuïc and outside the Sagrada Família), beach showers turned off and severe water restrictions put in place. In the end, water had to be imported to Barcelona by ship (the first time a major European city had had to be relieved in this way), and it's a solution that will be probably be repeated in future years until new desalination plants come on stream.

# Catalan cookery

M any people judge the food of Catalunya to be the best in Spain. The region certainly has one of the oldest culinary traditions: its inns were celebrated by travellers in medieval times, while the first Spanish cookery book was published in Barcelona in 1477. Histori-cally, Catalunya shares some of its dishes and methods with the region of Valencia to the south and parts of France (such as Roussillon) to the north, but nonetheless it's possible to identify within its borders a distinct cuisine. Fish and rice have always played a major part in Catalan cookery, but there's also an emphasis on mixed flavours, which you won't find anywhere else in Spain – some common traditional examples are rabbit cooked with snails, chicken with shellfish, meat or poultry with fruit, and vegetables with raisins and nuts. Meanwhile, contemporary Catalan chefs (see p.204) have rewritten the rulebook regarding taste and texture, and their deconstructivist menus – featuring intensely flavoured foams, reductions and concentrates – are currently at the forefront of cutting-edge European cuisine.

We've stuck to traditional **recipes** below, the sort of dishes you're likely to eat on a day-to-day basis in Barcelona and Catalunya. You don't need much in the way of special **equipment**, though a *paella* (the dish is named after the wide, flat metal pan it's cooked in) and a *cassola* (earthenware casserole dish) are both useful. They're widely available these days from specialist cookery stores. Other than that, you only need to be insistent on the best and freshest **ingredients** – the finest tomatoes you can buy, proper salted anchovies, authentic rice and, above all, good olive oil. All the recipes below are for four people, unless otherwise stated.

## Pa amb tomàquet

The "bread with tomato" combination is a classic taste of Catalunya, eaten for breakfast, or as a snack or appetizer. In traditional grill-restaurants and taverns, you'll often be brought the wherewithal to do-it-yourself before your meal arrives – a basket of toasted bread, a handful of garlic cloves and an over-ripe tomato or two. The basic method is given below, but, for more of a meal, pile on shavings of ham or cheese, grilled vegetables or anchovy fillets.

### Ingredients
Good continental bread
Vine-ripened tomatoes
Peeled garlic cloves
Olive oil
Salt

### Method
Cut large slices from a loaf of good continental bread, preferably the dense, heavy variety, and grill them (a ribbed cast-iron grill-pan is ideal for this). Cut the garlic cloves in two and drag the cut sides over the toast. Cut the tomatoes in two and squeeze and rub well over the garlic-impregnated toast. Dribble generous amounts of olive oil over the slices and add salt to taste.

## Amanida Catalana

Salad (*amanida*) is usually served as a first course in Catalunya and can be very filling.

## Ingredients

3 large tomatoes, thickly sliced
2 hard-boiled eggs, quartered
24 green olives
1 large Spanish onion, very thinly sliced
1 large roasted red pepper (see Escalivada, below), cut into strips
Crunchy lettuce, as much as you require
200g tinned tuna
8 plump anchovy fillets

## Method

This is one of the most common of restaurant salads, and with it you can improvise to your heart's content, but don't toss the ingredients all together – it's a composed salad, laid out on a plate, rather than a bowl of mixed salad. For a more elaborate dish, you can add shredded carrot or pickled vegetables, sliced cheese or thinly cut dry-cured ham or pork, salami or spiced sausage. Dress the salad with salt and olive oil.

## Escalivada

This fantastic mix of grilled peppers, onions and aubergine is a restaurant and domestic staple. It's usually available as a starter or an accompaniment to grills and roasts, or you can buy it ready-made on deli counters in Catalan markets. It's also very easy to make.

## Ingredients

2 large aubergines
4 red peppers
4 small onions
Olive oil
1 garlic clove, chopped very finely (optional)
Salt

## Method

Grill the vegetables whole on a barbecue, or under a grill, turning them until the skins are blackened all over. Or simply place them on separate trays and roast them in the oven on a high heat for the same effect – you'll still need to turn them periodically. When they are done, put the blackened vegetables in a shallow casserole dish or on a tray and cover them with a cloth or lid for ten minutes (some people place them in a paper bag). This process allows them to steam while they cool down, making it easier to remove the blackened skins. When they are cool enough to handle, peel the skins. Slice the soft internal pulp of the aubergine into strips; seed the peppers and cut into thin strips; remove the tough outer skin of the onions and separate out the soft inner leaves. Spread out the vegetables on a serving dish, dribble with oil, scatter with minced garlic if you like, and season with salt.

## Espinacs a la Catalana

"Catalan spinach" can either be served as a starter or as an accompaniment to a main dish. You can use greens instead of fresh spinach, but you should remove the hard stems before cooking.

## Ingredients

500g fresh spinach
3 tbsp raisins, soaked in hot water, then drained
3 tbsp pine nuts
2 tbsp olive oil
2 cloves garlic, finely chopped
1 small onion, finely chopped

## Method

Put the spinach in boiling water, cook for three minutes until tender and then drain, squeezing out excess water. Put to one side. Heat the oil in the pan, add the garlic and onion and cook gently until soft, taking care not to burn the garlic. Add the spinach, drained raisins and pine nuts, and toss together while heating through. Add salt and pepper to taste.

## Sarsuela

This wonderful fish casserole is served in most coastal towns, using whatever fish and shellfish is available. You'll have to buy what you can, though you should be aiming for large prawns in their shells, different kinds of white fish (such as cod or hake), squid, mussels or clams. In Catalunya, crayfish or lobster are often added, too. The point is to go for a variety of fish: the word *sarsuela* refers to a comic musical variety show.

## Ingredients

3–4 tbsp olive oil
2 garlic cloves, finely chopped
2 large tomatoes, skinned, seeded and finely chopped
2 onions, sliced
1 tbsp Spanish brandy
1 tsp paprika
1 bay leaf
1 cup/quarter-pint dry white wine
2 tbsp chopped parsley
2 lemons, cut into wedges
Assorted white fish, enough for a couple of fair-sized chunks each
8 large prawns in their shells
4 small squid
16 mussels/32 clams
Ground black pepper
Salt

## Method

Clean the fish and cut into chunks; slice the squid into rings; leave the large prawns as they are. Scrub and clean the mussels or clams. Boil the fishy leftovers (skin and heads; if you've bought fillets, use a couple of chunks and a few small prawns) in a pot of water, adding salt and pepper, some fresh herbs and a sliced onion, to give a fish stock – which, when reduced a little, should be strained and put aside.

Heat the oil in a large pot or casserole, add the garlic, onion and chopped tomatoes and cook slowly for ten minutes – this is the *sofregit* (see box opposite). Turn up the heat, add the brandy and flame, then turn it back down and add the paprika, fish stock, white wine and bay leaf. Stir the mixture, put in the chunks of white fish and simmer for five minutes. Stir, add the squid and

The sauce is the source of good food, as a Catalan might say. Everything starts with a **sofregit**, basically sliced onion, chopped tomato and garlic that has been sautéed down to a soft, almost jam-like consistency. This underpins the construction of countless classic Catalan dishes, which might then be thickened before serving with the addition of a **picada** – a smooth paste (made in a mortar and pestle) of garlic, almonds, hazelnuts, fried bread, saffron, olive oil and parsley. The southern Catalan **romesco** sauce, made with chilli peppers, is a spicier version of *picada*, used as a dip (for grilled spring onions or fish) rather than as an ingredient. **All i oli** (garlic and oil) is a fiery Catalan mayonnaise, made without eggs, served with grilled meat (traditionally rabbit), fish and shellfish or stirred into *fideuà*. And there's also **samfaina**, a ratatouille-like stew of garlic, onion, tomato, aubergine and pepper. Again, this can be served as an accompaniment (perhaps for roast chicken or salt cod), but it's also made into a sauce by cooking a lot longer until sticky and then puréeing.

prawns and simmer for another five minutes; then add the mussels or clams, cover and cook for a further five minutes or so, until the fish is ready and the mussels or clams have opened. Take care not to break up the fish by stirring too often. Add salt and pepper to taste, and garnish with fresh parsley and lemon wedges before serving.

## Grilled fish with romesco sauce

There are many different varieties of *romesco* sauce, which originates from the Tarragona province, and you can experiment with the quantities of the ingredients below until you find the taste that suits you. Made with small chilli peppers, fresh or dried, it can be a very hot sauce, though you can substitute cayenne pepper or even paprika for these, if you want to control the heat.

### Ingredients
4 fish steaks, marinaded in olive oil, chopped garlic and lemon juice
2 lemons, quartered
2 tbsp olive oil
1 small onion, finely chopped
3 tomatoes, skinned, seeded and chopped
3 garlic cloves, finely chopped
10–15 almonds (toasted under the grill)
2 tbsp dry white wine
Chilli peppers/cayenne pepper/ paprika to taste
1 tbsp red wine vinegar
Salt

### Method
Fry the onion and the garlic in the olive oil until soft. Add the tomatoes, white wine and chilli peppers, and cook over a low heat for twenty minutes. Crush or grind the almonds and add to the mixture, adding enough extra olive oil to achieve the consistency of a purée. Add the vinegar and a pinch of salt. Either put the whole lot through a blender or food processor, or pass through a sieve – you're aiming for a smooth, rather thick sauce. Leave to cool at room temperature. Take the fish out of the marinade, grill, and serve with lemon wedges. Serve the sauce separately, to be dipped in or spooned over.

# Pollastre amb gambes

The combination of chicken (*pollastre*) and prawns (*gambes*) is typically Catalan, otherwise known as *mar i muntanya* (sea and mountain).

## Ingredients
8 chicken pieces
12–16 medium prawns in their shells, washed
3 tbsp olive oil
1 onion, finely chopped
2 garlic cloves, finely chopped
2 tomatoes, skinned, seeded and chopped
1 carrot, peeled and finely chopped
Quarter-cup Spanish brandy
Half-cup dry white wine
Quarter-cup beef stock (you can use a stock cube)
2 tbsp chopped parsley
Ground pepper
Salt

## Method
Salt and pepper the chicken pieces, heat the oil in a large pan, and then add the chicken pieces and prawns. Take the prawns out after a minute or so, put to one side, and cook the chicken until golden-brown on all sides. Add the onion, garlic, tomatoes and carrot, and cook until soft (about 15min). Turn up the heat, add the brandy and flame (stand well back), then – when the flames have died down – turn the heat back down and add the wine, stock, half the parsley, salt and pepper. Cover and cook for another twenty minutes, then add the prawns and cook for another ten minutes. Take out the chicken and prawns, put them on a warm serving dish and strain the sauce over them, sprinkling with the rest of the parsley.

# Crema Catalana

The one dessert you'll be offered everywhere in Catalunya is *Crema Catalana*. It rounds off a meal impressively if you make it at home; the only tricky part is caramelizing the sugar topping.

## Ingredients
2 cups milk
Peel of half a lemon
1 cinnamon stick
4 egg yolks
7 tbsp sugar
1 tbsp cornflour

## Method
Simmer the milk with the lemon peel and cinnamon stick for a few minutes, then take out the lemon and cinnamon from the pan. Beat the egg yolks and half of the sugar together, beat in the cornflour, too, then add the beaten egg mixture slowly into the milk and continue to simmer. Stir constantly until thick and smooth, taking care not to let the mixture boil, and then pour into a wide, shallow serving dish. Let the mixture cool and then put in the fridge.

When you want to serve it, sprinkle the rest of the sugar evenly over the custard so that it forms a thick layer on the top. To caramelize the sugar topping, you can use a kitchen blowtorch – or simply heat a wide knife or metal spatula and press down on the sugar until it goes brown and crunchy. Repeat this over the whole top of the dessert, wiping the knife or spatula clean and reheating it every time.

# Books

The selection of books reviewed below provides useful background on the city's history, people and institutions. Despite a long pedigree, Catalan literature is hard to find in translation, though novels set in Barcelona by (mostly foreign) authors provide a feel of the city past and present. In Barcelona, most of the major **bookshops** (see p.243) carry English-language guides and titles about the city, or look in the **museum bookshops** (particularly in MNAC, MACBA, Caixa Forum, Museu Picasso and Fundació Joan Miró) for books on art, design and architecture. The online literary magazine Ⓦ**www.barcelonareview.com** has plenty in the archive on Spanish and Catalan writers, art, culture and life, and there's also the very useful Lletra (Ⓦ**www.lletra.net**), an excellent online resource (in English) for Catalan literature.

## History

### Barcelona

🏃 **Jimmy Burns** *Barça: A People's Passion*. On one level, it's simply an informative history of the city's famous football team, alma mater of Cruyff, Lineker, Maradona, Ronaldinho et al. However, like the club itself, the book is so much more than that, as Burns examines Catalan pride and nationalism through the prism of sport.

**Felipe Fernandez-Armesto** *Barcelona: A Thousand Years of the City's Past*. An expertly written appraisal of what the author sees as the formative years of the city's history, from the tenth to the early twentieth century.

🏃 **Robert Hughes** *Barcelona*. The renowned art critic casts his accomplished eye over two thousand years of Barcelona's history and culture, with special emphasis on the nineteenth and early twentieth centuries – explaining, in his own words, "the zeitgeist of the place and the connective tissue between the cultural icons".

🏃 **Matthew Stewart** *Monturiol's Dream*. Witty and engaging account of the life and work of Narcís Monturiol, the nineteenth-century Catalan utopian visionary, revolutionary and inventor of the world's first true submarine. Stewart places Monturiol firmly at the centre of Barcelona's contemporary social and political turmoil – printing seditious magazines, manning the barricades in the 1850s, fleeing into exile and returning to pursue his pioneering invention.

**Colm Tóibín** *Homage to Barcelona*. Echoing Orwell, the Irish writer pays his own homage to the city, tracing Barcelona's history through its artists, architects, personalities, organizations and rulers.

### Spain

**John Hooper** *The New Spaniards*. Excellent portrait of post-Franco Spain and the new generation, now in a second revised edition of 2006 that brings the twenty-first-century country into focus.

**Hugh Thomas** *Rivers of Gold: The Rise of the Spanish Empire*. Thomas' scholarly but eminently accessible history provides a fascinating snapshot of Spain's most glorious period – the meteoric imperial rise in the late fifteenth and early sixteenth centuries, when characters such as Ferdinand and Isabel, and Columbus and Magellan, shaped the country's outlook for the next three hundred years.

🏃 **Giles Tremlett** *Ghosts of Spain*. The Guardian's Madrid correspondent takes a warts-and-all look at contemporary Spain, and finds the dark days of the Civil War never very far from the surface, even now. It's a terrific read – if you buy just one book for general background on how modern Spain works and what its people think, this should be it.

## The Civil War

**Gerald Brenan** *The Spanish Labyrinth*. First published in 1943, Brenan's record of the background to the Civil War is tinged by personal experience, yet still impressively rounded.

🏃 **George Orwell** *Homage to Catalonia*. Stirring account of the Civil War fight on the Aragón front and Orwell's participation in the early exhilaration of revolution in Barcelona. A forthright, honest and entertaining tale, covering Orwell's injury and subsequent flight from the factional infighting in Republican Spain.

**Paul Preston** *A Concise History of the Spanish Civil War* and *Franco*. The leading historian of twentieth-century Spain offers *Civil War*, an easily accessible introduction to the subject, and *Franco*, a penetrating and monumental biography of Franco and his regime.

**Hugh Thomas** *The Spanish Civil War*. Exhaustive political study of the period that is still the best single telling of the convoluted story of the Civil War.

# Art, architecture and style

🏃 **Gijs van Hensbergen** *Gaudí: The Biography*. A worthy biography of "arguably the world's most famous architect". Van Hensbergen puts substantial flesh on the man while placing his work firmly in context, as Spain lost its empire and Catalunya slowly flexed her nationalist muscles.

**John Richardson** *A Life of Picasso*. The definitive multi-volume biography - Volume 1, covering the period 1881–1906, is an extremely readable account of the artist's early years, covering the whole of his time in Barcelona.

**Phyllis Richardson** *Style City: Barcelona*. Part guide, part celebration of everything that's considered cool about contemporary Barcelona. The book covers the sharpest restaurant interiors to the latest galleries, artisans' studios to Art Nouveau bars, accompanied by 350 colour photographs that show Barcelona in its most flattering light.

**Philippe Thiébaut** *Gaudí: Builder of Visions*. Read van Hensbergen for the life, but pick up this pocket-sized volume for its excellent photographic coverage – not just Gaudí buildings and interiors, but sketches, historical photographs and architectural insights that add up to a useful gateway to his work in the city and surroundings.

# Food and wine

**Colman Andrews** *Catalan Cuisine*. The best available – possibly the *only* available – English-language book dealing with Spain's most adventurous regional cuisine. Full of historical and anecdotal detail, it's a pleasure to read, let alone cook from (no pictures, though).

**Penelope Casas** *The Foods and Wines of Spain*. Casas roams across every region of Spain in this classic Spanish cookery book, including the best dishes that Catalunya has to offer. Her *Paella* and *Tapas: The Little Dishes of Spain* cover the rest of the bases.

**Jan Read** *Wines of Spain*. All you need to know to sort out your Penedès from your Priorat – an explanation of regions and producers, plus tasting notes and tips for wine tourists.

# Novels set in Barcelona

**Bernado Atxaga** *The Lone Man*. The noted Basque writer set his well-received psychological thriller during the 1982 World Cup, when two ETA gunmen hole up in a Barcelona hotel.

**John Bryson** *To the Death, Amic*. Barcelona, under siege during the Civil War, is the backdrop for a coming-of-age novel recounting the adventures of ten-year-old twins Enric and Josep.

**Miguel Cervantes** *Don Quixote*. Barcelona is the only city that Cervantes gives its real name in his

## Catalan literature and writers

Catalan was established as a literary language as early as the thirteenth century, and a **golden age** of medieval Catalan literature followed, lasting until the mid-sixteenth century, with another cultural and literary flowering in the nineteenth century known as the **Renaixença** (Renaissance). However, this long pedigree has suffered two major interruptions: first, the rise of Castile and later Bourbon rule, which saw the Catalan language eclipsed and then suppressed; and a similar suppression under Franco, when there was a ban on Catalan books and publications. In the post-Civil War period, there was some relaxation of the ban, but it's only been since the return of democracy to Spain that Catalan literature has once again been allowed to flourish.

Catalan and Spanish speakers and readers are best served by the literature, since there's little still in translation – Amazon (ⓦ www.amazon.com) is a good first stop for the translated authors mentioned below. The vernacular works of mystic and philosopher **Ramon Llull** (1233–1316) mark the onset of a true Catalan literature – his *Blanquerna* was one of the first books to be written in any Romance language, while the later chivalric epic *Tirant lo Blanc* (*The White Tyrant*) by **Joanot Martorell** (1413–68) represents a high point of the golden age. None of the works of the leading lights of the nineteenth-century *Renaixença* are readily available in translation, and it's to *Solitud* (*Solitude*) by **Victor Català** (1869–1966) that you have to look for the most important pre-Civil War Catalan novel. This tragic tale of a woman's life and sexual passions in a Catalan mountain village was first published in 1905, pseudonymously by Caterina Albert i Paradís, who lived most of her life in rural northern Catalunya.

During and after the Civil War, many authors found themselves under forcible or self-imposed exile, including perhaps Spain's most important modern novelist, **Juan Goytisolo** (born Barcelona, 1931), a bitter enemy of the Franco regime (which banned his books). Goytisolo has spent most of his life abroad – in Paris picaresque classic – in the Barcelona chapters, Don Quixote and Sancho Panza see the ocean for the first time, while Quixote fights a duel on Barceloneta beach against the Knight of the White Moon.

**Ildefonso Falcones** *Cathedral of the Sea*. Falcones, a lawyer living in Barcelona, sets his first novel in the expansionist years of the fourteenth century, where work is underway on the building of the city's most magnificent church, Santa María del Mar. It's a highly realistic, excitingly plotted tale that lifts the skirts of medieval Barcelona to show an authentic picture of a city on the make. It was a Spanish award-winner on publication and has become something of a publishing sensation, in the manner of *The Shadow of the Wind* – you'll see it piled high in bookshops across the city.

**Juan Marse** *Lizard Tails* and *Shanghai Nights*. Marse spent his formative years in a Barcelona scarred by Civil War, and ruptured childhood and family hardship are themes that emerge in much of his work. Only a couple of works have thus far been translated into English: *Lizard Tails* is an evocation of post-Civil War childhood, while *Shanghai Nights* – again, Barcelona and war to the fore – is billed as "a tale of the human spirit".

🏃 **Eduardo Mendoza** *City of Marvels, The Truth About the Savolta Case* and *The Year of the Flood*. Mendoza's first and best novel, *City of Marvels*, is set in the expanding Barcelona of 1880–1920, full of rich underworld characters and riddled with anarchic and comic turns. The milieu is reused with flair in *The Truth About the Savolta Case*, while *The Year of the Flood* adds a light

**C**

CONTEXTS | Books

and Marrakesh – with his great trilogy (*Marks of Identity*, *Count Julian* and *Juan the Landless*) confronting the whole ambivalent idea of Spain and Spanishness. Other notable exiles included **Pere Calders i Rossinyol** (1912–94), best known for his short stories, and **Mercè Rodoreda i Gurgui** (1909–83), whose *Plaça del Diamant* (*The Time of Doves*), *El Carrer de les Camèlies* (*Camellia Street*) and *La Meva Cristina i Altres Contes* (*My Cristina and Other Tales*) are relatively easily found in translation. For something lighter, there are the works of **Maria Antònia Oliver i Cabrer** (born 1946), novelist, children's author and short-story writer born in Mallorca, whose early novels were influenced by her birthplace, but whose *Estudi en Lila* (*Study in Lilac*) and *Antipodes* introduce fictional Barcelona private eye Lonia Guiu.

Not all Catalan writers write in Catalan, but rather in Spanish, including perhaps the best-known of all – **Manuel Vasquez Montalban** (1939–2003), crime writer *par excellence*, and novelist, poet, journalist, political commentator and committed communist to boot. His Pepe Carvalho books do nothing less than expose the shortcomings of the new Spanish democracy in fast-changing Barcelona. Montalban's contemporary **Juan Marse** (born 1933) uses the post-Civil War dictatorship as the background for many of his Barcelona-set novels, and it's the same period that spawned the Barcelona blockbuster *The Shadow of the Wind* by **Carlos Ruiz Záfon** (born Barcelona, 1964), and its prequel *The Angel's Game*. For other new Catalan writers, such as **Albert Sánchez Piñol** (born Barcelona, 1965), nationality seems incidental at best – his well-regarded first novel, *Cold Skin*, is a creepy psychological sci-fi, tale of solitude on an Antarctic island where something stirs as soon as the sun goes down. His latest novel, *Pandora in the Congo*, is a highly original literary adventure story that starts in the dark heart of the African jungle.

touch to an unusual amorous entanglement in 1950s Barcelona.

🏃 **Manuel Vasquez Montalban** *Murder in the Central Committee, Southern Seas, The Angst-Ridden Executive, An Olympic Death, Offside, The Man of My Life* and *Tatoo*. Montalban's greatest creation, the fast-living gourmand-detective Pepe Carvalho, ex-communist and CIA agent, first appeared in print in 1972, investigating foul deeds in the city in a series of wry and racy Chandleresque thrillers. *Murder in the Central Committee* is a good place to start, as Carvalho confronts his communist past. *Southern Seas* won the Planeta, Spain's biggest literary prize, while the city's businesses, institutions and events come under typical scrutiny in *The Angst-Ridden Executive, An Olympic Death* and *Offside*. Twenty-first-century Catalan politics and business comes under the spotlight in the last Carvalho novel, *The Man of My Life*, while the early *Tatoo*, published for the first time in English (2008), plunges you right back into "sex, death and food in 1970s Barcelona".

**Raul Nuñez** *The Lonely Hearts Club*. A parade of grotesque and hard-bitten characters haunt the city in this oddball but likeable romantic comedy.

**Colm Tóibín** *The South*. Barcelona provides the background for Tóibín's first novel about an Irish woman looking for a new life.

**Barbara Ellen Wilson** *Gaudí Afternoon*. Pacy feminist thriller making good use of Gaudí's architecture as a backdrop for deception and skulduggery.

🏃 **Carlos Ruiz Záfon** *The Shadow of the Wind*. Top holiday read is the international bestseller by the Barcelona-born, one-time LA screenwriter Záfon. It's a Gothic literary thriller set in the aftermath of the Civil War, full of atmospheric Barcelona locations, and it generated rave reviews, not to mention selling over ten million copies worldwide. Its follow-up, a prequel called *The Angel's Game*, is due in translation in 2009.

# Language

# Language

# Language

I n Barcelona, **Catalan** (Català) has more or less taken over from Castilian (Castellano) **Spanish** as the language on street signs, maps, official buildings and notices, and so on. On paper, it looks like a cross between French and Spanish and is generally easy to read if you know those two. Spoken Catalan is harder to come to grips with, as the language itself is not phonetic, and accents vary from region to region. Few visitors realize how important Catalan is to those who speak it: never commit the error of calling it a dialect. However, despite the preponderance of the Catalan language, you'll get by perfectly well in Spanish, as long as you're aware of the use of Catalan in timetables, on menus, and the like. You'll find some basic pronunciation rules below, for both Spanish and Catalan, and a selection of words and phrases in both languages. Spanish is certainly easier to pronounce, but don't be afraid to try Catalan, especially in the more out-of-the-way places – you'll generally get a good reception if you at least try communicating in the local language.

Numerous **Spanish phrasebooks** are available, not least the *Spanish Rough Guide Phrasebook*, laid out dictionary-style for instant access. In Barcelona, *Parla Català* (Pia) is the only readily available English–Catalan phrasebook, though there are more extensive (and expensive) Catalan–English dictionaries and teach-yourself Catalan guides available online. The University of Barcelona has an excellent **online English–Catalan phrasebook**, with an audio option, Ⓦ www.intercat.gencat.es/guia.

## Pronunciation

### Castilian (Spanish)

Unless there's an accent, words ending in "D", "L", "R" or "Z" are **stressed** on the last syllable, all others on the second last. All **vowels** are pure and short; combinations have predictable results.

**A** somewhere between the "A" sound of "back" and that of "father".

**E** as in "get".

**I** as in "police".

**O** as in "hot".

**U** as in "rule".

**C** is lisped before "E" and "I", hard otherwise: "cerca" is pronounced "thairka".

**G** works the same way, a guttural "H" sound (like the "ch" in "loch") before "E" or "I", a

hard "G" elsewhere – "gigante" becomes "higante".

**H** is always silent.

**J** the same sound as a guttural "G": "jamón" is pronounced "hamon".

**LL** sounds like an English "Y": "tortilla" is pronounced "torteeya".

**N** is as in English unless it has a tilde (accent) over it, when it becomes "NY": "mañana" sounds like "man-yarna".

**QU** is pronounced like an English "K".

**R** is rolled, "RR" doubly so.

**V** sounds more like "B", "vino" becoming "beano".

**X** has an "S" sound before consonants, normal "X" before vowels.

**Z** is the same as a soft "C", so "cerveza" becomes "thairbaitha".

## Catalan

With Catalan, don't be tempted to use the few rules of Spanish pronunciation you may know – in particular the soft Spanish "Z" and "C" don't apply, so unlike in the rest of Spain the city is not "Barthelona" but "Barcelona", as in English.

**A** as in "hat" if stressed, as in alone when unstressed.

**E** varies, but usually as in "get".

**I** as in "police".

**IG** sounds like the "tch" in the English scratch; "lleig" (ugly) is pronounced "yeah-tch".

**O** a round full sound, when stressed, otherwise like a soft "U" sound.

**U** somewhere between the "U" of "put" and "rule".

**Ç** sounds like an English "S"; "plaça" is pronounced "plassa".

**C** followed by an "E" or "I" is soft; otherwise hard.

**G** followed by "E" or "I" is like the "zh" in "Zhivago"; otherwise hard.

**H** is always silent.

**J** as in the French "Jean".

**L.L** is best pronounced (for foreigners) as a single "L" sound; but for Catalan speakers it has two distinct "L" sounds.

**LL** sounds like an English "Y" or "LY", like the "yuh" sound in "million".

**N** as in English, though before "F" or "V" it sometimes sounds like an "M".

**NY** corresponds to the Castilian "Ñ".

**QU** before "E" or "I" sounds like "K", unless the "U" has an umlaut (Ü), in which case, and before "A" or "O", as in "quit".

**R** is rolled, but only at the start of a word; at the end, it's often silent.

**T** is pronounced as in English, though sometimes it sounds like a "D"; as in "viatge" or "dotze".

**V** at the start of a word sounds like "B"; in all other positions it's a soft "F" sound.

**W** is pronounced like a "B/V".

**X** is like "SH" or "CH" in most words, though in some, like "exit", it sounds like an "X".

**Z** is like the English "Z" in "zoo".

# Useful words and phrases

Words and phrases below are given in the following order: **English** - Spanish - *Catalan*.

## Basics

| | | |
|---|---|---|
| **Yes, No, OK** | Sí, No, Vale | *Sí, No, Val* |
| **Please, Thank you** | Por favor, Gracias | *Si us plau, Gràcies* |
| **Where? When?** | Dónde? Cuando? | *On? Quan?* |
| **What? How much?** | Qué? Cuánto? | *Què? Quant?* |
| **Here, There** | Aquí, Allí/Allá | *Aquí, Allí/Allá* |
| **This, That** | Esto, Eso | *Això, Allò* |
| **Now, Later** | Ahora, Más tarde | *Ara, Mès tard* |
| **Open, Closed** | Abierto/a, Cerrado/a | *Obert, Tancat* |
| **With, Without** | Con, Sin | *Amb, Sense* |

| Good, Bad | Bueno/a, Malo/a | *Bo(na), Dolent(a)* |
| Big, Small | Gran(de), Pequeño/a | *Gran, Petit(a)* |
| Cheap, Expensive | Barato, Caro | *Barat(a), Car(a)* |
| Hot, Cold | Caliente, Frío | *Calent(a), Fred(a)* |
| More, Less | Más, Menos | *Mes, Menys* |
| I want | Quiero | *Vull (pronounced "vwee")* |
| I'd like | Quisiera | *Voldria* |
| Do you know? | ¿Sabe? | *Vostès saben?* |
| I don't know | No sé | *No sé* |
| There is (is there?) | (¿)Hay(?) | *Hi ha(?)* |
| What's that? | ¿Qué es eso? | *Què és això?* |
| Give me (one like that) | Deme (uno así) | *Doneu-me (a bit brusque)* |
| Do you have? | ¿Tiene? | *Té ...?* |
| The time | La hora | *L'hora* |
| Today, Tomorrow | Hoy, Mañana | *Avui, Demà* |
| Yesterday | Ayer | *Ahir* |
| Day before yesterday | Ante ayer | *Abans-d'ahir* |
| Next week | La semana que viene | *La setmana que ve* |
| Next month | El mes que viene | *El mes que ve* |

## Greetings and responses

| Hello, Goodbye | Hola, Adiós | *Hola, Adéu* |
| Good morning | Buenos días | *Bon dia* |
| Good afternoon/night | Buenas tardes/noches | *Bona tarde/nit* |
| See you later | Hasta luego | *Fins després* |
| Sorry | Lo siento/Disculpéme | *Ho sento* |
| Excuse me | Con permiso/Perdón | *Perdoni* |
| How are you? | ¿Cómo está (usted)? | *Com va?* |
| I (don't) understand | (No) Entiendo | *(No) Ho entenc* |
| Not at all/You're welcome | De nada | *De res* |
| Do you speak English? | ¿Habla (usted) inglés? | *Parleu anglès?* |
| I (don't) speak Spanish/Catalan | (No) Hablo español | *(No) Parlo Català* |
| My name is ... | Me llamo ... | *Em dic ...* |
| What's your name? | ¿Como se llama usted? | *Com es diu?* |
| I am English/ | Soy inglés(a)/ | *Sóc anglès(a)/* |
| Scottish/ | escocés(a)/ | *escocès(a)/* |
| Australian/ | australiano(a)/ | *australian(a)/* |
| Canadian/ | canadiense(a)/ | *canadenc(a)/* |
| American/ | americano(a)/ | *americà (a)/* |
| Irish | irlandes(a) | *irlandès (a)* |

## Finding accommodation

| Do you have a room? | ¿Tiene una habitación? | *Té alguna habitació?* |
| ... with two beds/double bed | ... con dos camas/cama matrimonial | *... amb dos llits/llit per dues persones* |
| ... with shower/bath | ... con ducha/baño | *... amb dutxa/bany* |

| It's for one person | Es para una persona | *Per a una persona* |
| (two people) | (dos personas) | *(dues persones)* |
| For one night (one week) | Para una noche (una semana) | *Per una nit (una setmana)* |
| It's fine, how much is it? | ¿Está bien, cuánto es? | *Esta bé, quant és?* |
| It's too expensive | Es demasiado caro | *És massa car* |
| Don't you have anything cheaper? | ¿No tiene algo más barato? | *En té de mé sbon preu?* |

## Directions and transport

| How do I get to ...? | ¿Por donde se va a ...? | *Per anar a ...?* |
| Left, Right, Straight on | Izquierda, Derecha, Todo recto | *A la dreta, A l'esquerra, Tot recte* |
| Where is ...? | ¿Dónde está ...? | *On és ...?* |
| ... the bus station | ... la estación de autobuses | *... l'estació de autobuses* |
| ... the train station | ... la estación de ferrocarril | *... l'estació* |
| ... the nearest bank | ... el banco más cercano | *... el banc més a prop* |
| ... the post office | ... el correos/la oficina de correos | *... l'oficina de correus* |
| ... the toilet | ... el baño/aseo/servicio | *... la toaleta* |
| It's not very far | No es muy lejos | *No és gaire lluny* |
| Where does the bus to ... leave from? | ¿De dónde sale el autobús para ...? | *De on surt el autobús a ...?* |
| Is this the train for Barcelona? | ¿Es este el tren para Barcelona? | *Aquest tren va a Barcelona?* |
| I'd like a (return) ticket to ... | Quisiera un billete (de ida y vuelta) para ... | *Voldria un bitlet (d'anar i tornar) a ...* |
| What time does it leave (arrive in)? | ¿A qué hora sale (llega a)? | *A quina hora surt (arriba a)?* |

## Numbers

| 1 | un/uno/una | *un(a)* |
| 2 | dos | *dos (dues)* |
| 3 | tres | *tres* |
| 4 | cuatro | *quatre* |
| 5 | cinco | *cinc* |
| 6 | seis | *sis* |
| 7 | siete | *set* |
| 8 | ocho | *vuit* |
| 9 | nueve | *nou* |
| 10 | diez | *deu* |
| 11 | once | *onze* |
| 12 | doce | *dotze* |
| 13 | trece | *tretze* |
| 14 | catorce | *catorze* |

| | | |
|---|---|---|
| 15 | quince | *quinze* |
| 16 | dieciseis | *setze* |
| 17 | diecisiete | *disset* |
| 18 | dieciocho | *divuit* |
| 19 | diecinueve | *dinou* |
| 20 | veinte | *vint* |
| 21 | veintiuno | *vint-i-un* |
| 30 | treinta | *trenta* |
| 40 | cuarenta | *quaranta* |
| 50 | cincuenta | *cinquanta* |
| 60 | sesenta | *seixanta* |
| 70 | setenta | *setanta* |
| 80 | ochenta | *vuitanta* |
| 90 | noventa | *novanta* |
| 100 | cien(to) | *cent* |
| 101 | ciento uno | *cent un* |
| 102 | ciento dos | *cent dos (dues)* |
| 200 | doscientos | *dos-cents (dues-centes)* |
| 500 | quinientos | *cinc-cents* |
| 1000 | mil | *mil* |
| 2000 | dos mil | *dos mil* |

## Days and months

| | | |
|---|---|---|
| Monday | lunes | *dilluns* |
| Tuesday | martes | *dimarts* |
| Wednesday | miércoles | *dimecres* |
| Thursday | jueves | *dijous* |
| Friday | viernes | *divendres* |
| Saturday | sábado | *dissabte* |
| Sunday | domingo | *diumenge* |
| January | enero | *gener* |
| February | febrero | *febrer* |
| March | marzo | *març* |
| April | abril | *abril* |
| May | mayo | *maig* |
| June | junio | *juny* |
| July | julio | *juliol* |
| August | agosto | *agost* |
| September | septiembre | *setembre* |
| October | octubre | *octobre* |
| November | noviembre | *novembre* |
| December | diciembre | *desembre* |

# Food and drink

Words and phrases below are given in the following order: **English** - Spanish - *Catalan*.

## Some basic words

| | | |
|---|---|---|
| To have breakfast | Desayunar | *Esmorzar* |
| To have lunch | Comer | *Dinar* |
| To have dinner | Cenar | *Sopar* |
| Knife | Cuchillo | *Ganivet* |
| Fork | Tenedor | *Forquilla* |
| Spoon | Cuchara | *Cullera* |
| Table | Mesa | *Taula* |
| Bottle | Botella | *Ampolla* |
| Glass | Vaso | *Got* |
| Menu | Carta | *Carta* |
| Soup | Sopa | *Sopa* |
| Salad | Ensalada | *Amanida* |
| Hors d'oeuvres | Entremeses | *Entremesos* |
| Omelette | Tortilla | *Truita* |
| Sandwich | Bocadillo | *Entrepà* |
| Toast | Tostadas | *Torrades* |
| Tapas | Tapes | *Tapes* |
| Butter | Mantequilla | *Mantega* |
| Eggs | Huevos | *Ous* |
| Bread | Pan | *Pa* |
| Olives | Aceitunas | *Olives* |
| Oil | Aceite | *Oli* |
| Vinegar | Vinagre | *Vinagre* |
| Salt | Sal | *Sal* |
| Pepper | Pimienta | *Pebre* |
| Sugar | Azucar | *Sucre* |
| The bill | La cuenta | *El compte* |
| I'm a vegetarian | Soy vegetariano/a | *Sóc vegetarià/vegetariana* |

## Cooking terms

| | | |
|---|---|---|
| Assorted | surtido/variado | *assortit* |
| Baked | al horno | *al forn* |
| Char-grilled | a la brasa | *a la brasa* |
| Fresh | fresco | *fresc* |
| Fried | frito | *fregit* |
| Fried in batter | a la romana | *a la romana* |
| Garlic mayonnaise | alioli | *all i oli* |
| Grilled | a la plancha | *a la plantxa* |
| Pickled | en escabeche | *en escabetx* |

| Roast | asado | *rostit* |
|---|---|---|
| Sauce | salsa | *salsa* |
| Sautéed | salteado | *saltat* |
| Scrambled | revuelto | *remenat* |
| Seasonal | del tiempo | *del temps* |
| Smoked | ahumado | *fumat* |
| Spit-roasted | al ast | *a l'ast* |
| Stewed | guisado | *guisat* |
| Steamed | al vapor | *al vapor* |
| Stuffed | relleno | *farcit* |

## Fish and seafood/Pescado y mariscos/peix i marisc

| Anchovies | Anchoas/Boquerones | *Anxoves/Seitons* |
|---|---|---|
| Baby squid | Chipirones | *Calamarsets* |
| Bream | Dorada | *Orada* |
| Clams | Almejas | *Cloïses* |
| Crab | Cangrejo | *Cranc* |
| Cuttlefish | Sepia | *Sipia* |
| Eels | Anguilas | *Anguiles* |
| Hake | Merluza | *Lluç* |
| Langoustines | Langostinos | *Llagostins* |
| Lobster | Langosta | *Llagosta* |
| Monkfish | Rape | *Rap* |
| Mussels | Mejillones | *Musclos* |
| Octopus | Pulpo | *Pop* |
| Oysters | Ostras | *Ostres* |
| Perch | Mero | *Mero* |
| Prawns | Gambas | *Gambes* |
| Razor clams | Navajas | *Navalles* |
| Red mullet | Salmonete | *Moll* |
| Salmon | Salmón | *Salmó* |
| Salt cod | Bacalao | *Bacallà* |
| Sardines | Sardinas | *Sardines* |
| Scallops | Vieiras | *Vieires* |
| Sea bass | Lubina | *Llobarro* |
| Sole | Lenguado | *Llenguado* |
| Squid | Calamares | *Calamars* |
| Swordfish | Pez espada | *Peix espasa* |
| Trout | Trucha | *Truita (de riu)* |
| Tuna | Atún | *Tonyina* |
| Whitebait | Chanquete | *Xanguet* |

# Meat and poultry/Carne y aves/Carn i aviram

| Beef | Buey | *Bou* |
|------|------|-------|
| Boar | Jabalí | *Senglar* |
| Charcuterie | Embutidos | *Embotits* |
| Chicken | Pollo | *Pollastre* |
| Chorizo sausage | Chorizo | *Xoriço* |
| Cured ham | Jamón serrano | *Pernil serrà* |
| Cured pork sausage | Longaniza | *Llonganissa* |
| Cutlets/Chops | Chuletas | *Costelles* |
| Duck | Pato | *Ànec* |
| Ham | Jamón York | *Pernil dolç* |
| Hare | Liebre | *Llebre* |
| Kid/goat | Cabrito | *Cabrit* |
| Kidneys | Riñones | *Ronyons* |
| Lamb | Cordero | *Xai/Be* |
| Liver | Hígado | *Fetge* |
| Loin of pork | Lomo | *Llom* |
| Meatballs | Albóndigas | *Mandonguilles* |
| Partridge | Perdiz | *Perdiu* |
| Pigs' trotters | Pies de cerdo | *Peus de porc* |
| Pork | Cerdo | *Porc* |
| Rabbit | Conejo | *Conill* |
| Sausages | Salchichas | *Salsitxes* |
| Snails | Caracoles | *Cargols* |
| Steak | Bistec | *Bistec* |
| Tongue | Lengua | *Llengua* |
| Veal | Ternera | *Vedella* |

# Vegetables/Verduras y legumbres/Verdures i llegums

| Artichokes | Alcachofas | *Carxofes* |
|------------|------------|-----------|
| Asparagus | Esparragos | *Esparrecs* |
| Aubergine | Berenjena | *Albergínia* |
| Avocado | Aguacate | *Alvocat* |
| Broad/lima beans | Habes | *Faves* |
| Cabbage | Col | *Col* |
| Carrots | Zanahorias | *Pastanagues* |
| Cauliflower | Coliflor | *Col-i-flor* |
| Chickpeas | Garbanzos | *Cigrons* |
| Courgette | Calabacín | *Carbassó* |
| Cucumber | Pepino | *Concombre* |
| Garlic | Ajo | *All* |
| Haricot beans | Judías blancas | *Mongetes* |
| Herbs | Hierbas | *Herbes* |
| Lentils | Lentejas | *Llenties* |

| Leeks | Puerros | *Porros* |
| Mushrooms | Champiñones | *Xampinyons* |
| Onion | Cebolla | *Ceba* |
| Peas | Guisantes | *Pèsols* |
| Peppers | Pimientos | *Pebrots* |
| Potatoes | Patatas | *Patates* |
| Spinach | Espinacas | *Espinacs* |
| Tomatoes | Tomates | *Tomàquets* |
| Turnips | Nabos | *Naps* |
| Wild mushrooms | Setas | *Bolets* |

## Fruit/Fruta/Fruita

| Apple | Manzana | *Poma* |
| Apricot | Albaricoque | *Albercoc* |
| Banana | Plátano | *Plàtan* |
| Cherries | Cerezas | *Cireres* |
| Figs | Higos | *Figues* |
| Grapes | Uvas | *Raïm* |
| Melon | Melón | *Meló* |
| Orange | Naranja | *Taronja* |
| Peach | Melocotón | *Pressec* |
| Pear | Pera | *Pera* |
| Pineapple | Piña | *Pinya* |
| Strawberries | Fresas | *Maduixes* |

## Desserts/Postres/Postres

| Cake | Pastel | *Pastís* |
| Cheese | Queso | *Formatge* |
| Fruit salad | Macedonia | *Macedonia* |
| Crème caramel | Flan | *Flam* |
| Ice cream | Helado | *Gelat* |
| Rice pudding | Arroz con leche | *Arròs amb llet* |
| Tart | Tarta | *Tarta* |
| Yoghurt | Yogur | *Yogur* |

## Catalan specialities

**Amanida Catalana** Salad served with sliced meats (sometimes cheese)

**Ànec amb peres** Duck with pears

**Arròs a banda** Rice with seafood, the rice served separately

**Arròs a la Cubana** Rice with fried egg and home-made tomato sauce

**Arròs a la marinera** Paella: rice with seafood and saffron

**Arròs negre** "Black rice", cooked in squid ink

**Bacallà a la llauna** Salt cod baked with garlic, tomato and paprika

**Bacallà amb mongetes** Salt cod with stewed haricot beans

**Botifarra (amb mongetes)** Grilled Catalan pork sausage (with stewed haricot beans)

**Bunyols** Fritters, which can be sweet (like little doughnuts, with sugar) or savoury (salt cod or wild mushroom)

**Calçots** Large char-grilled spring onions, eaten with *romesco* sauce (available Feb–March)

**Canelons** Cannelloni

**Conill all i oli** Rabbit with garlic mayonnaise

**Conill amb cargols** Rabbit with snails

**Crema Catalana** Crème caramel, with caramelized sugar topping

**Entremesos** Hors d'oeuvres of mixed meat and cheese

**Escalivada** Grilled aubergine, pepper and onion

**Escudella i carn d'olla** A winter dish of stewed mixed meat and vegetables, served broth first, meat and veg second

**Espinacs a la Catalana** Spinach cooked with raisins and pine nuts

**Esqueixada** Salad of salt cod with peppers, tomatoes, onions and olives – a summer dish

**Estofat de vedella** Veal stew

**Faves a la Catalana** Stewed broad beans, with bacon and botifarra – a regional classic

**Fideuà** Short, thin noodles (the width of vermicelli) served with seafood, accompanied by all i olli

**Fideus a la cassola** Short, thin noodles baked with meat

**Fricandó (amb bolets)** Braised veal (with wild mushrooms)

**Fuet** Catalan salami

**Llagosta amb pollastre** Lobster with chicken in a rich sauce

**Llenties guisades** Stewed lentils

**Mel i mató** Curd cheese and honey – a typical dessert

**Oca amb naps** Goose with turnips

**Pa amb tomàquet** Bread (often grilled), rubbed with tomato, garlic and olive oil

**Panellets** Marzipan cakes – served for All Saints' Day

**Perdiu a la vinagreta** Partridge in vinegar gravy

**Perdiu amb col** Partridge with cabbage dumplings

**Pollastre al cava** Chicken with *cava* (champagne) sauce

**Pollastre amb gambes** Chicken with prawns

**Postres de música** Cake of dried fruit and nuts

**Rap amb all cremat** Monkfish with creamed garlic sauce

**Salsa romesco** Spicy sauce (with chillis, ground almonds, hazelnuts, garlic, tomato and wine), often served with grilled fish

**Samfaina** Ratatouille-like stew (onions, peppers, aubergine, tomato), served with salt cod or chicken

**Sarsuela** Fish and shellfish stew

**Sípia amb mandonguilles** Cuttlefish with meatballs

**Sopa d'all** Garlic soup, often with egg and bread

**Suquet de peix** Fish and potato casserole

**Xató** Mixed salad of olives, salt cod, preserved tuna, anchovies and onions

## Drinks

| | | |
|---|---|---|
| Beer | Cerveza | *Cervesa* |
| Wine | Vino | *Vi* |
| Champagne | Champan | *Xampan/Cava* |
| Sherry | Jerez | *Xerès* |
| Coffee | Café | *Cafè* |
| Espresso | Café solo | *Cafè sol* |
| Large black coffee | Café Americano | *Cafè Americà* |
| Large white coffee | Café con leche | *Cafè amb llet* |
| Small white coffee | Café cortado | *Cafè tallat* |
| Decaff | Descafeinado | *Descafeinat* |
| Tea | Té | *Te* |
| Drinking chocolate | Chocolate | *Xocolata* |
| Juice | Zumo | *Suc* |
| Crushed ice drink | Granizado | *Granissat* |
| Milk | Leche | *Llet* |

| Tiger nut drink | Horchata | *Orxata* |
| Water | Agua | *Aigua* |
| Mineral water | Agua mineral | *Aigua mineral* |
| ... (sparkling) | ... (con gas) | *... (amb gas)* |
| ... (still) | ... (sin gas) | *... (sense gas)* |

# A glossary of Catalan words

**Ajuntament** Town hall (city council)
**Avinguda** Avenue
**Barcino** Roman name for Barcelona
**Barri** Suburb or quarter
**Bodega** Cellar, wine bar or warehouse
**Caixa** Savings bank
**Call** Jewish quarter
**Camí** Path
**Capella** Chapel
**Carrer** Street
**Casa** House
**Castell** Castle
**Cava** Catalan "champagne"
**Comarca** County
**Correus** Post office
**Església** Church
**Estació** Station
**Estany** Lake
**Festa** Festival
**Font** Waterfall
**Forn** Bakery
**Generalitat** Catalan government
**Gòtic** Gothic (eg Barri Gòtic, Gothic Quarter)
**Granja** Milk bar/café

**Guiri** Foreigner
**Llotja** Stock exchange building
**Mercat** Market
**Modernisme** Catalan Art Nouveau
**Monestir** Monastery or convent
**Museu** Museum
**Palau** Aristocratic mansion/palace
**Passatge** Passage
**Passeig** Promenade/boulevard; also the evening stroll thereon
**Pastisseria** Cake/pastry shop
**Pati** Inner courtyard
**Plaça** Square
**Platja** Beach
**Pont** Bridge
**Porta** Gateway
**Rambla** Boulevard
**Renaixença** Renaissance
**Ríu** River
**Sant/a** Saint
**Sardana** Catalunya's national folk dance
**Serra** Mountain range
**Seu** Cathedral
**Terrassa** Outdoor terrace

**L**

**LANGUAGE** | A glossary of Catalan words

# Travel store

# Visit us online

# www.roughguides.com

Information on over 25,000 destinations around the world

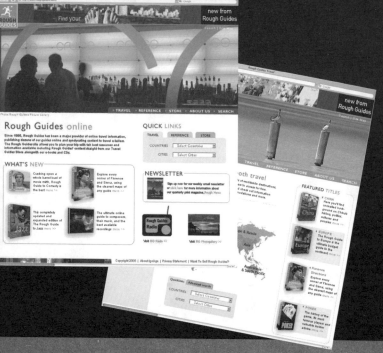

- **Read** Rough Guides' trusted travel info
- **Access** exclusive articles from Rough Guides authors
- **Update** yourself on new books, maps, CDs and other products
- **Enter** our competitions and win travel prizes
- **Share** ideas, journals, photos & travel advice with other users
- **Earn** points every time you contribute to the Rough Guide
  community and get rewards

## BROADEN YOUR HORIZONS

# Small print and

# Index

# A Rough Guide to Rough Guides

Published in 1982, the first Rough Guide – to Greece – was a student scheme that became a publishing phenomenon. Mark Ellingham, a recent graduate in English from Bristol University, had been travelling in Greece the previous summer and couldn't find the right guidebook. With a small group of friends he wrote his own guide, combining a highly contemporary, journalistic style with a thoroughly practical approach to travellers' needs.

The immediate success of the book spawned a series that rapidly covered dozens of destinations. And, in addition to impecunious backpackers, Rough Guides soon acquired a much broader and older readership that relished the guides' wit and inquisitiveness as much as their enthusiastic, critical approach and value-for-money ethos.

These days, Rough Guides include recommendations from shoestring to luxury and cover more than 200 destinations around the globe, including almost every country in the Americas and Europe, more than half of Africa and most of Asia and Australasia. Our ever-growing team of authors and photographers is spread all over the world, particularly in Europe, the USA and Australia.

In the early 1990s, Rough Guides branched out of travel, with the publication of Rough Guides to World Music, Classical Music and the Internet. All three have become benchmark titles in their fields, spearheading the publication of a wide range of books under the Rough Guide name.

Including the travel series, Rough Guides now number more than 350 titles, covering: phrasebooks, waterproof maps, music guides from Opera to Heavy Metal, reference works as diverse as Conspiracy Theories and Shakespeare, and popular culture books from iPods to Poker. Rough Guides also produce a series of more than 120 World Music CDs in partnership with World Music Network.

Visit www.roughguides.com to see our latest publications.

Rough Guide travel images are available for commercial licensing at www.roughguidespictures.com

## Rough Guide credits

**Text editor**: Christina Valhouli
**Layout**: Sachin Tanwar
**Cartography**: Karobi Gogoi
**Picture editor**: Mark Thomas
**Production**: Rebecca Short
**Proofreader**: Karen Parker
**Cover design**: Chloë Roberts
**Photographer**: Chris Christoforou
**Editorial**: **London** Ruth Blackmore, Andy Turner, Keith Drew, Edward Aves, Alice Park, Lucy White, Jo Kirby, James Smart, Natasha Foges, Róisín Cameron, Emma Traynor, James Rice, Emma Gibbs, Kathryn Lane, Monica Woods, Mani Ramaswamy, Joe Staines, Peter Buckley, Matthew Milton, Tracy Hopkins, Ruth Tidball; **New York** Andrew Rosenberg, Steven Horak, AnneLise Sorensen, Ella Steim, Anna Owens, Sean Mahoney, Paula Neudorf; **Delhi** Madhavi Singh, Karen D'Souza
**Design & Pictures**: **London** Scott Stickland, Dan May, Diana Jarvis, Nicole Newman, Sarah Cummins, Emily Taylor; **Delhi** Umesh Aggarwal, Ajay Verma, Jessica Subramanian, Ankur Guha, Pradeep Thapliyal, Anita Singh, Nikhil Agarwal
**Production**: Vicky Baldwin

**Cartography**: **London** Maxine Repath, Ed Wright, Katie Lloyd-Jones; **Delhi** Jai Prakash Mishra, Rajesh Chhibber, Ashutosh Bharti, Rajesh Mishra, Animesh Pathak, Jasbir Sandhu, Alakananda Bhattacharya, Swati Handoo, Deshpal Dabas
**Online**: **London** George Atwell, Faye Hellon, Jeanette Angell, Fergus Day, Justine Bright, Clare Bryson, Áine Fearon, Adrian Low, Ezgi Celebi, Amber Bloomfield; **Delhi** Amit Verma, Rahul Kumar, Narender Kumar, Ravi Yadav, Debojit Borah, Rakesh Kumar, Ganesh Sharma
**Marketing & Publicity**: **London** Liz Statham, Niki Hanmer, Louise Maher, Jess Carter, Vanessa Godden, Vivienne Watton, Anna Paynton, Rachel Sprackett, Libby Jellie, Holly Dudley; **New York** Geoff Colquitt, Nancy Lambert, Katy Ball; **Delhi** Ragini Govind
**Manager India**: Punita Singh
**Reference Director**: Andrew Lockett
**Operations Manager**: Helen Phillips
**PA to Publishing Director**: Nicola Henderson
**Publishing Director**: Martin Dunford
**Commercial Manager**: Gino Magnotta
**Managing Director**: John Duhigg

## Publishing information

This 8th edition published February 2009 by
**Rough Guides Ltd**,
80 Strand, London WC2R 0RL
345 Hudson St, 4th Floor,
New York, NY 10014, USA
14 Local Shopping Centre, Panchsheel Park,
New Delhi 110017, India
**Distributed by the Penguin Group**
Penguin Books Ltd,
80 Strand, London WC2R 0RL
Penguin Group (USA)
375 Hudson Street, NY 10014, USA
Penguin Group (Australia)
250 Camberwell Road, Camberwell,
Victoria 3124, Australia
Penguin Group (Canada)
195 Harry Walker Parkway N, Newmarket, ON,
L3Y 7B3 Canada
Penguin Group (NZ)
67 Apollo Drive, Mairangi Bay, Auckland 1310,
New Zealand

Cover concept by Peter Dyer.
Typeset in Bembo and Helvetica to an original design by Henry Iles.
Printed in China
© Jules Brown

320pp includes index

A catalogue record for this book is available from the British Library.
ISBN: 978-1-84836-020-4

The publishers and authors have done their best to ensure the accuracy and currency of all the information in **The Rough Guide to Barcelona**, however, they can accept no responsibility for any loss, injury, or inconvenience sustained by any traveller as a result of information or advice contained in the guide.

1   3   5   7   9   8   6   4   2

## Help us update

We've gone to a lot of effort to ensure that the 8th edition of **The Rough Guide to Barcelona** is accurate and up to date. However, things change – places get "discovered", opening hours are notoriously fickle, restaurants and rooms raise prices or lower standards. If you feel we've got it wrong or left something out, we'd like to know, and if you can remember the address, the price, the hours, the phone number, so much the better.

Please send your comments with the subject line "**Rough Guide Barcelona Update**" to ✉ mail@roughguides.com. We'll credit all contributions and send a copy of the next edition (or any other Rough Guide if you prefer) for the very best emails.
Have your questions answered and tell others about your trip at
🌐 community.roughguides.com

## Acknowledgements

Jules would like to thank Lluis Bosch, Thomas Lorenzo and Katrien Claus in Barcelona, and Dominique Ruiz in Reus for their valuable help.

Thanks also to Christina for making things run smoothly at Rough Guides.

## Readers' letters

Thanks to all the readers who have taken the time to write in with comments and suggestions (and apologies if we've inadvertently omitted or misspelt anyone's name):

Anouk de Wit, Carmen Turiera, Nuria Maruny, Tiphanie Chauvin, Artemis Georgiou, Wim Haghenbeek, Julia Speht, Liz Kingdom, Rory Worthington, James Booth, Jonas Ludvigsson, Tarjei T. Jensen, Jane E. Bednar, John Buckman, Albert Padrol, Colin Armstrong, Pepi Giménez, Marta Anfruns, Per Blohm, Chloe Hiddleston and Peter Henshaw, Jane Laird, Joel Fram, Jonathan Fisk, Norman A. Small, David Chillingworth.

SMALL PRINT

## Photo credits

All photos © Rough Guides except the following:

### Cover
Front picture: Miró Museum © Pavan Aldo
/4cornersimages
Back picture: Plaça Reial © Charles Bowman
/photolibrary.com
Inside back picture: Arc de Triomf, Parc de la
Ciutadella © Chris Christoforou/Rough Guides

### Full page
Casa Batlló at dusk © Ian Cumming/Axiom

### Introduction
Detail of tiles © Heidi Grassley/Axiom
Paseo de Colon Beach © Imagestate/Alamy
Cathedral exterior © Peter Higgins/Getty

### Things not to miss
**03** Montserrat © Terry Williams/Getty Images
**06** Shopping © Philipp Hympendahl/Alamy
**07** *Portrait of Jacqueline*, 1957 (oil on canvas) by
Pablo Picasso (1881-1973) © The Bridgeman
Art Library
**08** Gran Teatre del Lideu © Kevin Foy/Alamy
**14** Tapas bar © Heidi Grassley/Axiom

**15** Sagrada Família © Steve Benbow/axiom
**18** Camp Nou stadium © Khaled Kassem/Alamy
**19** Parc Guell © Ian Cumming/Axiom

### Antoni Gaudí and modernisme colour insert
The spires of Sagrada Família © Julian Martin
/Corbis
The roof of La Pedrera © Chris Bradley/Axiom

### Festive Barcelona colour insert
Sardana Monument © Jon Arnold Images/Alamy
Giant parade © LOOK Die Bildagentur
Fotografen/Alamy
Catalan Festival and fireworks © Con A/Alamy
Sagrada Família and fireworks © Alamy
Castellers forming human pyramid © Paul
Kingsley/Alamy

### Black and whites
**p.234** Human pyramid © LOOK Die Bildagentur
Fotografen/Alamy

SMALL PRINT

Selected images from our guidebooks are available for licensing from:

ROUGH**GUIDES**PICTURES**.COM**

# Index

Map entries are in colour.

**INDEX**

INDEX

# Map symbols

maps are listed in the full index using coloured text

| | | | | |
|---|---|---|---|---|
| ----- | International boundary | ⊠ | Post office |
| --- | Chapter boundary | ⊞ | Hospital |
| ▓▓▓ | Motorway | ✈ | Airport |
| ═══ | Major road | ★ | Bus stop |
| ══ | Minor road | ◉ | RENFE |
| ▬▬▬ | Pedestrianised road | ◆ | Metro station |
| ⅏ | Steps | ⌀ | FGC station |
| }·····{ | Tunnel | ⌂ | Abbey |
| ═•═ | Railway | ♠ | Monastery |
| ······ | Funicular railway | ♦ | Church (regional) |
| •---• | Cable Car | ✡ | Synagogue |
| ----- | Footpath | ▓ | Building |
| ━━ | Wall | ⊞ | Church |
| ── | Waterway | ▢ | Market |
| ♦ | Place of interest | ⬭ | Stadium |
| ⅏ | Viewpoint | ▨ | Park/ forest |
| ⊙ | Statue | ▨ | Beach |
| ⓘ | Tourist office | ⊞ | Cemetery |

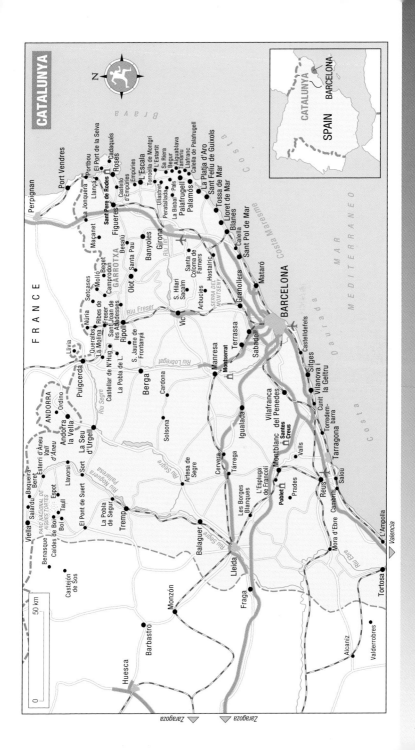

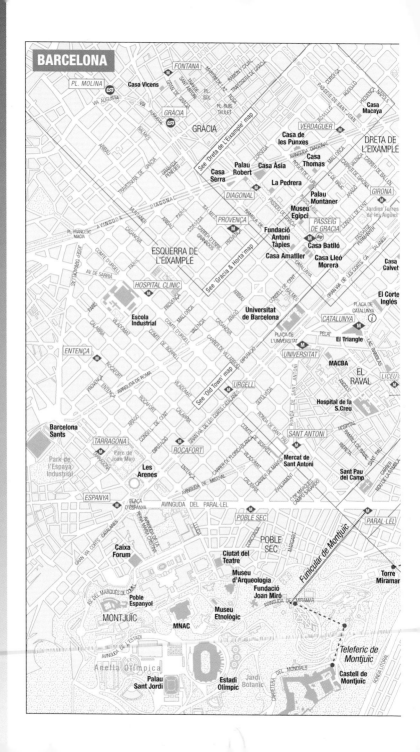

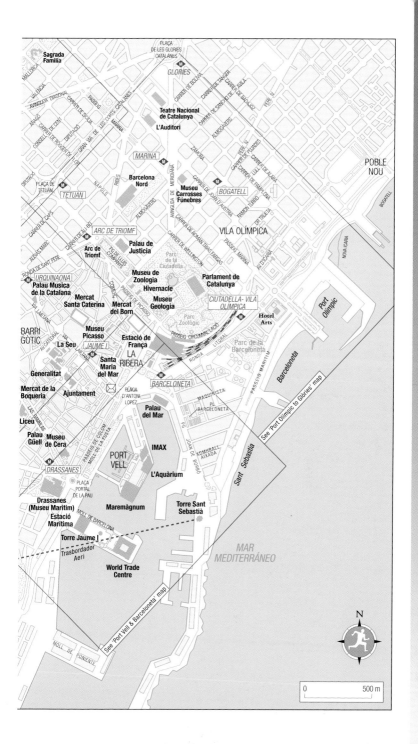

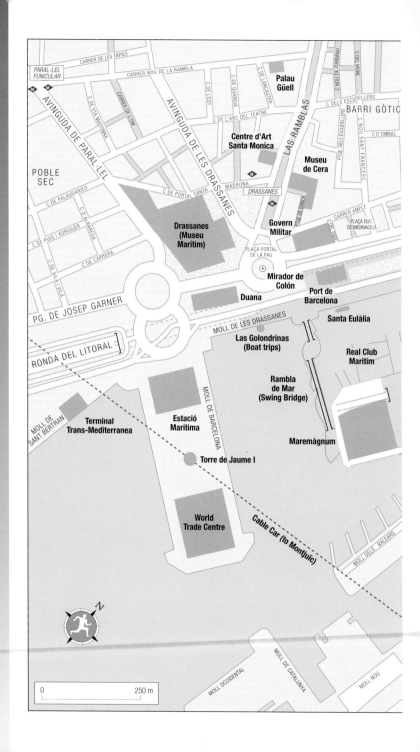

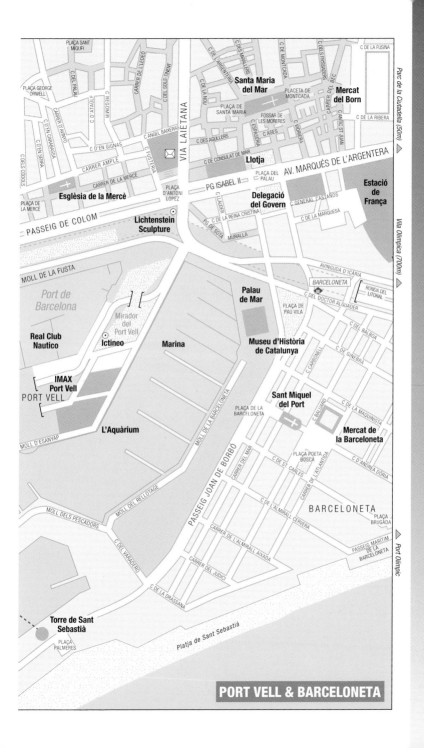

PLAÇA SANT
MIQUEL

PLAÇA GEORGE
ORWELL

C DEL PALAU

C DEL SOS-TINENT

CARRER DE LLEDÓ

C DE L'ARGENTERA

C DE MORALLES

C DE LA NOU

C DE MONTCADA

C DES FRESQUERS

C DELS FRESQUERS

C DE LA FUSINA

Parc de la Ciutadella (50m)

CARRER D'ARINYÓ

C D'EN CARABASSA

C D'EN SERRA

C REGOMIR

C D'ATAÚLF

VIA LAIETANA

Santa Maria
del Mar

PLAÇA DE
SANTA MARIA

C DE BEC

CANTIC ST JUAN

PLACETA DE
MONTCADA

Mercat
del Born

C DE MIRALLERS

C DE LA NOU

C ANGEL BAIXERAS

C DES AGULLERS

FOSSAR DE
LES MORERES

C SASES

C DE LA RIBERA

Vila Olímpica (700m)

C DELS CÒDOLS

CARRER AMPLE

C FUSTERIA

C DES AGULLERS

C DE CONSULAT DE MAR

Llotja

CARRER DE LA MERCÉ

PLAÇA
D'ANTONI
LOPEZ

PG ISABEL II

PLAÇA DEL
PALAU

AV. MARQUÉS DE L'ARGENTERA

Estació
de
França

PLAÇA DE
LA MERCÉ

Església de la Mercè

C LAUDER

PG DE SOTA

Delegació
del Govern

C DE LA REINA CRISTINA

MURALLA

C GENERAL CASTAÑOS

C DE LA MARQUESA

PASSEIG DE COLOM

Lichtenstein
Sculpture

MOLL DE LA FUSTA

AVINGUDA D'ICÀRIA

BARCELONETA

RONDA DEL
LITORAL

Port de
Barcelona

Mirador
del
Port Vell

Palau
de Mar

C DEL DOCTOR ALGUADER

PLAÇA DE
PAU VILA

C DE BALBOA

Real Club
Nautico

Ictineo

Marina

Museu d'Història
de Catalunya

C CARBONELL

C DE GINEBRA

IMAX
Port Vell

PORT VELL

L'Aquàrium

MOLL D'ESANYAP

MOLL DE LA BARCELONETA

PLAÇA DE LA
BARCELONETA

Sant Miquel
del Port

C GALIANO

C DE LA MAQUINISTA

Mercat de
la Barceloneta

C D'ANDREA DÒRIA

MOLL DEL RELLOTGE

PASSEIG JOAN DE BORBÓ

CARRER DEL MAR

PLAÇA POETA
BOSCÁ

C DE ST CARLES

CARRER DE L'ATLÀNTIDA

BARCELONETA

PLAÇA
BRUGADA

MOLL DELS PESCADORS

C DEL VARADERO

CARRER DE L'ALMIRALL AIXADA

C DE L'ALMIRALL CERVERA

PASSEIG MARÍTIM
DE LA
BARCELONETA

Port Olímpic

CARRER DEL JUDICI

Torre de Sant
Sebastià

PLAÇA
PALMERES

C DE LA DRASSANA

Platja de Sant Sebastià

**PORT VELL & BARCELONETA**

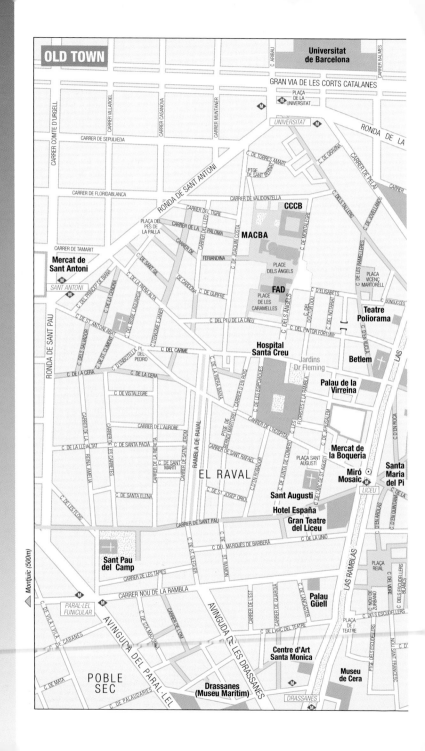

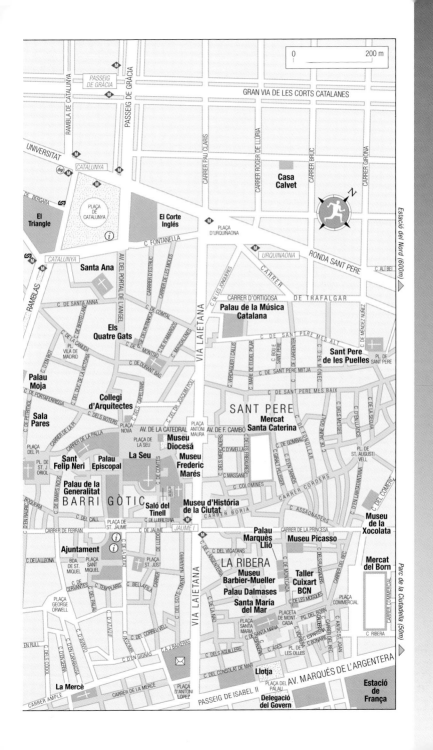

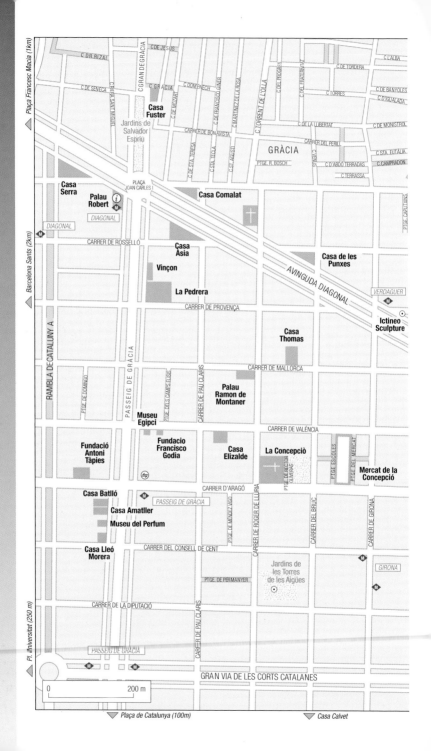

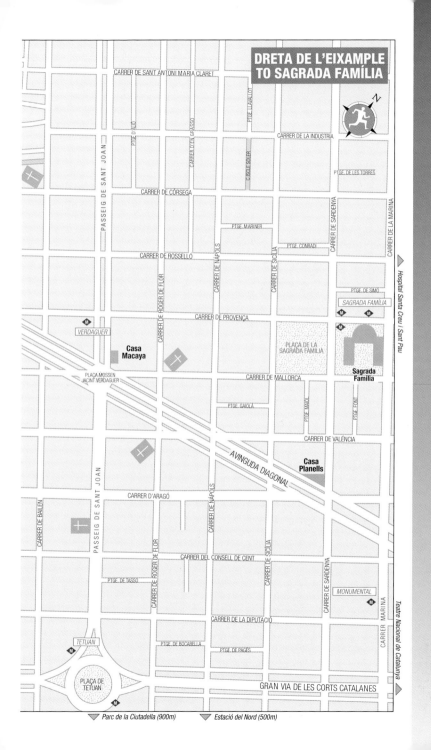

# DRETA DE L'EIXAMPLE TO SAGRADA FAMÍLIA

CARRER DE SANT ANTONI MARIA CLARET

PASSEIG DE SANT JOAN

PTGE D'ILIO

CARRER D'EN GRASSO

PTGE LLIVALLOL

CARRER DE LA INDUSTRIA

C ISCLE SOLER

PTGE. DE LES TORRES

CARRER DE CÓRSEGA

CARRER DE SARDENYA

CARRER DE LA MARINA

PTGE. MARINER

PTGE. CONRADI

CARRER DE ROSSELLÓ

CARRER DE NAPOLS

CARRER DE SICILIA

PTGE. DE SIMÓ

SAGRADA FAMÍLIA

CARRER DE ROGER DE FLOR

CARRER DE PROVENÇA

VERDAGUER

Casa Macaya

PLAÇA DE LA SAGRADA FAMÍLIA

Sagrada Família

PLAÇA MOSSÈN JACINT VERDAGUER

CARRER DE MALLORCA

PTGE. GAIOLÀ

PTGE MAIOL

PTGE CONI

CARRER DE VALÈNCIA

AVINGUDA DIAGONAL

Casa Planells

PASSEIG DE SANT JOAN

CARRER DE BAILEN

CARRER D'ARAGÓ

CARRER DE NAPOLS

CARRER DE ROGER DE FLOR

CARRER DEL CONSELL DE CENT

CARRER DE SICILIA

CARRER DE SARDENYA

MONUMENTAL

PTGE. DE TASSO

CARRER DE LA DIPUTACIÓ

CARRER MARINA

TETUAN

PTGE. DE BOCABELLA

PTGE. DE PAGÈS

PLAÇA DE TETUAN

GRAN VIA DE LES CORTS CATALANES

▽ Parc de la Ciutadella (900m)     ▽ Estació del Nord (500m)

Hospital Santa Creu i Sant Pau ▷

Teatre Nacional de Catalunya ▷

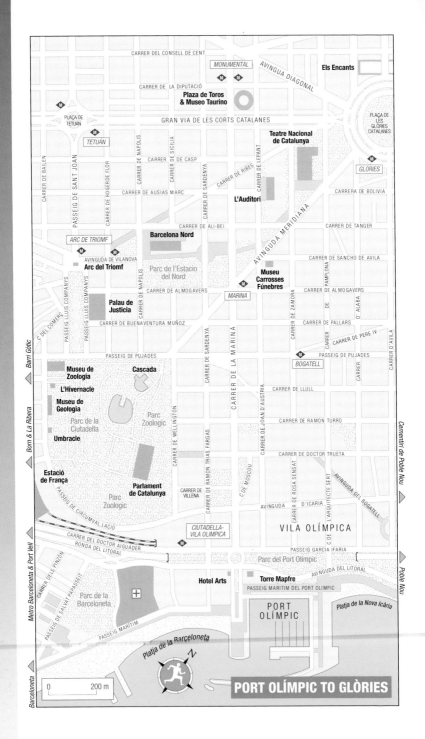

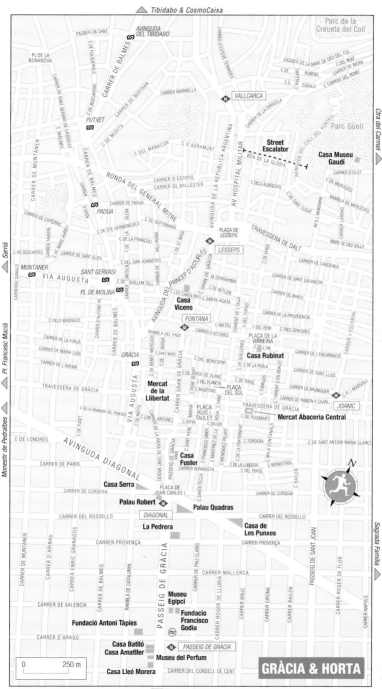

△ Tibidabo & CosmoCaixa

Parc de la Creueta del Coll

PASSEIG DE SANT

AVINGUDA DEL TIBIDABO

PL DE LA BONANOVA

CARRER DE BALMES

CARRER DE BERTRAN

CARRER MARMELLA

Ⓜ VALLCARCA

PASSEIG DE LA MARE DE DÉU DEL COLL

C DE BALEARS

C DE RUBENS

C DEL BEAT

CARRER DE MORA

C DE BISCAIOUNS

C DE L'EUDALD

C S.

CARRER DE MUNTANER

C DE ST GERVASI DE CASSOLES

C DE BERLINS

C DE TORRENT DEL REMEI

PUTXET Ⓢ

Cira del Carmel

CARRER DE BALMES

C MUSIU

C DEL MANACOR

C D'AGRAMUNT

AVINGUDA DE LA REPÚBLICA ARGENTINA

CARRER DE LA FARIGOLA

CARRER DEL COLL DEL PORTELL

Parc Güell

Street Escalator

BDA DE LA GLÒRIA

AVINGUDA DEL COLL DEL PORTELL

Casa Museu Gaudí

RONDA DEL GENERAL MITRE

CARRER D'ESCIPIO

CARRER DE BALLESTER

AV HOSPITAL MILITAR

C DELS ALBIGESOS

C DE SANT CUGAT

CARRER D'OLOT

C DE MERCEDES

RAMBLA DE MERCEDES

CARRER D'AREN

CARRER DE PADUA

PADUA

C DE SEPTIMANIA

PLAÇA DE LESSEPS

CARRER LARRIAD

AV S.J. MUNTANYA

CARRER DE COPÈRNIC

CARRER TAVERN

C DE STE HERMENGILD

C DE LA FRANCOLI

VALLIRANA

C DE ST MAGI

TRAVESSERA DE DALT

MARE DE DÉU SALUT

C DE MARC AURELI

C DELS DESCARTES

CARRER DE SANT ELIES

C DEL SAN JOANISTES

Ⓜ LESSEPS

CARRER DE FERRO

CARRER DE CARDENER

MUNTANER Ⓢ

SANT GERVASI

VIA AUGUSTA Ⓢ

CARRER SANÒLO

C DE ALFONS XII

C DE GUILLEM TELL

C DE INCOLDES

AVINGUDA DEL PRÍNCEP D'ASTÚRIES

C GRAN DE GRÀCIA

M SERRAHIMA

CARRER DE SANT SALVADOR

CARRER DE SANT SALVADOR

CARRER DE MARTI

Sarrià

PL DE MOLINA Ⓢ

LES CAROLINES C SANTA AGATA

C DE BETLEM

Casa Vicens

C DELS MADRAZO

C DE LA OLLA

CARRER DE LA PROVIDENCIA

Pl. Francesc Macià

CARRER DE BALMES

RAMBLA DEL PRAT

FONTANA

CARRER D'ASTURIES

TORRENT DE L'OLLA

C DEL TOPAZI

C DEL ROBI

PLAÇA DE LA VIRREINA

TRES SENYORES

CARRER DE LA FORJA

C SANT MARC

C DE BENET MERCADÉ

C DEL MONTSENY

C MATEU

C DE L'OR

Casa Rubinat

CARRER DE L'ENCARNACIÓ

CARRER DE L'ESCORIAL

CARRER DE MARIA CUBI

BERGA

C DE GUILLERIES

C DE LA PERLA

CARRER DE L'AVENIR

GRÀCIA Ⓢ

C DE ROS DE OLANO

C DE TEROL

C DEL PLANETA

TORRIJOS

CARRER DE SANT LLUIS

TRAVESSERA DE GRÀCIA

VIA AUGUSTA

Mercat de la Llibertat

C GRAN DE GRÀCIA

C DE PERE SERAFÍ

C DEL PROGRÉS

C MASPONS

PLAÇA DEL SOL

C D'EN DEN DÉRIA

CARRER DE BRUNIQUER

C FI I MARGALL Ⓜ

C DE LA GRANADA DEL PENEDÈS

C LLUIS ANTÚNEZ

C DE NEPTU

C DE RIERA DE SANT MIGUEL

MARTÍ

PLAÇA RUIS I TAULET

C GOYA

RIOJA

C DILUVI

CARRER DE RAMON Y CAJAL

Mercat Abaceria Central

JOANIC Ⓜ

TRAVESSERA DE GRÀCIA

C DE PUIGMARTÍ

C DE SANT ANTONI MARIA CLARET

C DE LA GRANADA

C DE TUSET

TRAVESSERA DE GRÀCIA

C DE L'AVENIR

Casa Fuster

FRANCISCO GINER

C MARTÍNEZ DE LA ROSA

C MENÉNDEZ PELAYO

PASSEIG DE GRÀCIA

C DE LA FRATERNITAT

C MÍLA FON IANALS

C TORDERA

Monestir de Pedralbes

C DE LONDRES

AVINGUDA DIAGONAL

CARRER DE PARIS

Casa Serra

PLAÇA DE JOAN CARLES I

Palau Robert Ⓜ

DIAGONAL

Palau Quadras

C SANTA TECLA

C DE LA LLIBERTAT

C DEL PEROL

C MONISTROL

C BAILÈN

CARRER DE CORSEGA

CARRER DEL ROSSELLÓ

Casa de Les Punxes

CARRER DEL ROSSELLÓ

CARRER DE CORSEGA

N

La Pedrera

CARRER PROVENÇA

CARRER PROVENÇA

PASSEIG DE SANT JOAN

CARRER DE MUNTANER

CARRER D'ARIBAU

CARRER ENRIC GRANADOS

CARRER DE BALMES

RAMBLA DE CATALUNYA

PASSEIG DE GRÀCIA

CARRER DE PAU CLARIS

CARRER DE LLÚRIA

CARRER BRUC

CARRER GIRONA

CARRER BAILÈN

CARRER ROGER DE FLOR

CARRER NÀPOLS

Sagrada Família

CARRER MALLORCA

Museu Egipci

Fundació Antoni Tàpies

CARRER DE VALENCIA

Fundacio Francisco Godia

CARRER D'ARAGO

Casa Batlló

Casa Amatller

Ⓜ PASSEIG DE GRÀCIA

Museu del Perfum

Casa Lleó Morera

CARRER DEL CONSELL DE CENT

0        250 m

**GRÀCIA & HORTA**

▽ Plaça de Catalunya

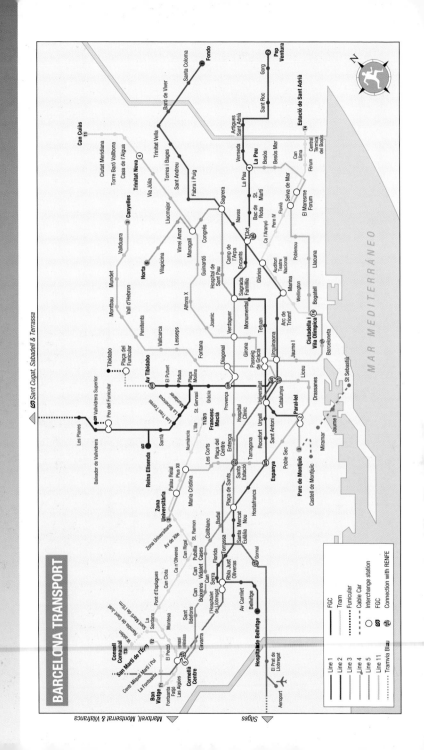